CW00544756

The Grammar of Multiple Head-Movement

OXFORD STUDIES IN COMPARATIVE SYNTAX

RICHARD KAYNE, GENERAL EDITOR

Parameters of Predicate Fronting
Edited by Vera Lee-Schoenfeld and Dennis Ott

A Unified Theory of Polarity Sensitivity: Comparative Syntax of Arabic
Ahmad Alqassas

Smuggling in Syntax
Edited by Adriana Belletti and Chris Collins

Anti-contiguity: A Theory of Wh-Prosody
Jason Kandybowicz

Nominal Arguments and Language Variation
Li Julie Jiang

Variation in P: Comparative Approaches to Adpositional Phrases
Edited by Jacopo Garzonio and Silvia Rossi

Locality and Logophoricity: A Theory of Exempt Anaphora
Isabelle Charnavel

The Syntactic Variation of Spanish Dialects
Edited by Angel J. Gallego

The Linker in Khosian Languages
Chris Collins

Questions of Syntax
Richard S. Kayne

Exploring Nanosyntax
Edited by Lena Baunaz, Liliane Haegeman, Karen De Clercq, and Eric Lander

Dravidian Syntax and Universal Grammar
K.A. Jayaseelan and R. Amritavalli

The Morphosyntax of Portuguese and Spanish in Latin America
Edited by Mary A. Kato and Francisco Ordóñez

Deconstructing Ergativity: Two Types of Ergative Languages and Their Features
Maria Polinsky

Rethinking Parameters
Edited by Luis Eguren, Olga Fernandez-Soriano, and Amaya Mendikoetxea

Argument Licensing and Agreement
Clair Halpert

The Cartography of Chinese Syntax
Edited by Wei-Tien Dylan Tsai

Beyond Functional Sequence
Edited by Ur Shlonsky

The Architecture of Determiners
Thomas Leu

A Comparative Grammar of Borgomanerese
Christina Tortora

Chinese Syntax in a Cross-Linguistic Perspective
Edited by Audrey Li, Andrew Simpson, and Wei-Tien Dylan Tsai

Functional Structure from Top to Toe
Edited by Peter Svenonius

The Grammar of Multiple Head-Movement

A Comparative Study

Phil Branigan

Memorial University of Newfoundland

OXFORD
UNIVERSITY PRESS

Oxford University Press is a department of the University of Oxford.
It furthers the University's objective of excellence in research, scholarship,
and education by publishing worldwide. Oxford is a registered trade mark of
Oxford University Press in the UK and certain other countries.

Published in the United States of America by Oxford University Press
198 Madison Avenue, New York, NY 10016, United States of America.

Cataloging-in-Publication data is on file at Library of Congress

ISBN: 978-0-19-7-677032

DOI: 10.1093/oso/9780197677032.001.0001

Integrated Books International, United States of America

ABSTRACT

The concept of head-movement plays a central role in transformational analysis and comparative syntax. But finding a satisfactory theoretical formulation of this concept has proven challenging, particularly given recent arguments that only phrasal movement can belong to the core syntactic derivation.

The research reported here resolves the problem of head-movement with a model which integrates the phenomenon of multiple head-movement. It is shown that head-movement involves two distinct components: a [uSTEM] feature valuation operation which takes place within the core syntax at the phase level, and a substitution transformation which operates as a part of the externalization process, forming complex words from atomic roots and affixes. Languages may differ in the timing of the valuation operation—sometimes it follows labeling; sometimes it precedes it. When valuation precedes labeling, multiple head-movement is possible.

Evidence which supports this new theoretical model is provided with case studies in a number of languages, including detailed examinations of the verb prefix system in Russian and the tripartite morphological structures in Innu-aimûn. The resulting analyses resolve a host of problems in Slavic and Algonquian grammatical studies. Slavic grammars exploit multiple head-movement in structures where T and participial suffixes attract prefixes before they attract verb stems. This approach eliminates bracketing paradoxes and clarifies the relationship between verb raising, ellipsis, and adverb placement. Algonquian grammars employ multiple head-movement throughout the grammar, so that all affixal functional heads can attract multiple heads to them. This analytic result offers a simpler, more comprehensive overall picture of how complex words in such polysynthetic languages can be derived from familiar underlying syntactic structures. Finally, the implications of these results for the theory of parameters and language learnability are considered.

CONTENTS

ABBREVIATIONS

n	unspecified n
v	unspecified v
1⟩2	1st person subject with 2nd person object
2⟩1	2nd person subject with 1st person object
3⟩1	3rd person subject with 1st person object
3	3rd person
ACC	accusative
APPL	applicative
ASP	aspect
ATTEN	attenuative
CJ	conjunct
CNTN	continuative
COMPL	completive
COND	conditional
CUMUL	cumulative
DAT	dative
DEF	definite
DELIM	delimitative
DEM	demonstrative
DIM	diminutive
DIR	direct
DIST	distal
DISTR	distributive
DSTL	distal
DUB	dubitative
DUR	durative
EXCESS	excessive
FNL	final
FUT	future
GEN	genitive
IC	internal change
IMP	imperative
IMPF	imperfective

INCEP inceptive
INDIR indirect
INF infinitive
INV independent inverse
IRR irrealis
LOC locative
NEG negative
NOM nominative
OBV obviative
PASS passive
PERD perdurative
PL plural
POSS possessive
PRET preterite
PRF perfect
PROX proximal
PRS present
PST past
REFL reflexive
REL relative
REPET repetitive
SG singular
SML semelfactive
SUBJ subjunctive
TERM terminative

PREFACE

This work represents the result of a ten-year process where a number of threads in several different areas eventually spun into one. Along the way, I've had the benefit of advice, insights, critiques, and encouragement from many colleagues, acquaintances, and friends, who I would like to recognize here.

My largest debt in the work presented here is to my colleague, friend, and erstwhile research partner Marguerite MacKenzie. Much of what I understand about Algonquian languages, and about Innu-aimûn, in particular, comes from her patient guidance and from her walking me through the intricacies of an endless stream of examples. Originally, this work was to be a joint endeavor, but then the internal logic of the analysis pushed it away from a study of Innu-aimûn alone and towards a more theoretically focused, comparative, generative study, so it ended up in my hands. But Marguerite still deserves a mountain of credit for anything that is sensible in the presentation of the Innu-aimûn data here, and all my gratitude for her mentorship and practical help over a lengthy span of years in which we worked together on these sorts of things.

For some of the primary data provided here, I am indebted to my Innu expert informants, who have been generous with their knowledge and patient with my tedious, repetitive questions. This group of people includes: Kanani Penashue, Caroline Jack, and the late Bernadette Jack.

Many of the original, half-formed concepts which developed into something further here come from conversations and joint research with Julie Brittain. I started learning about Algonquian grammar from Julie when she was a student, and the process hasn't stopped since. I could not have undertaken this project without Julie's influence and presence in my intellectual life.

Sara MacKenzie's and Carrie Dyck's expertise was also invaluable to me when I occasionally found that I needed to say something about phonology, and particularly in working out some of the kinks in the discussion of the Slavic *yers* and the bracketing paradoxes in which they feature. Just for the fun of it, Carrie found me a new solution to the problem of how Russian secondary imperfective suffixes are realized, and I am still in awe.

In the process of working through these ideas and writing it up to the present form, I've drawn on support and encouragement from my other colleagues and friends at Memorial: Sandra Clarke, Vit Bubenik, Doug Wharram, Maureen Scheidnes, and Nick Welch.

The analysis of verb forms in Innu-aimûn where an object-oriented predicate serves as the initial component in the verb is at the heart of the overall approach taken here, at least in how this work developed over time. I first started to look at these structures in response to some questions that Paul Hirschbühler asked me about how *spray-load* constructions are expressed in this language. I am grateful to Paul for setting me on a path which turned out to be much more involved than I would have ever imagined.

Yvan Rose's skepticism about parameter theory has influenced my thinking about how to characterize the typological variation which this work is largely concerned with. His generous sharing of his wide knowledge of current acquisition theory helped me to see more clearly what sorts of factors should be brought into the discussion of any learnability question. Both have informed the content of Chapter 5 quite a lot. Subsequent conversations with Marit Westergaard and Ian Roberts helped sharpen the result to where it is.

Debate, discussion, disputation, and some friendly chats with a spirited collection of Algonquian linguists has also been integral in my process. Of this group, I am particularly indebted for comments and data-rich observations to Yves Goddard, Jeff Muehlbauer, Clare Cook, Rose-Marie Déchaine, Betsy Ritter, Rich Rhodes, Rand Valentine, Chris Wolfarth, Marie-Odile Junker, Charlotte Reinholz, Éric Matthieu, Brandon Fry, Will Oxford, Jessica Coon, and Heather Bliss. Phil Lesourd's pointed critique of some of these ideas at a particular juncture was instrumental in encouraging me to be less cautious in exploring their consequences, which is usually a good thing. His response persuaded me (against my natural inclinations) that in order to develop these notions properly, it was necessary to go big, or go home.

A handful of non-Algonquianists have also provided patient council on the more theoretical issues addressed here. I am grateful to Fritz Newmeyer, Ian Roberts, Anders Holmberg, Heidi Harley, Theresa Biberauer, and Pino Longobardi. It was actually an encouraging series of email exchanges with Ian which started me on the path from the original analysis of Innu-aimûn grammar to this much broader result. A good chat with Elan Dresher helped me to better understand with the learnability questions discussed in Chapter 5. Todd Wareham loaned me his time and expertise to help wrestle with the formal side of the resulting algorithm, as well as the memory implications. Charles Yang helped me to understand the potential role of the Tolerance Principle in processing syntactic exceptions in the resulting grammatical spaces.

On the Slavic side, I could not have developed the material in Chapter 3 without generous advice in conversations—online and in person—with David Pesetsky, Željko Bošković, and Vera Gribanova. When I first started to think about the apparent similarities in Slavic and Algonquian grammars, I contacted David, and he gave me a quick education in some critical issues that I needed to know about, as well as pointers to some of the literature that I would need to know in this area. Later feedback from Željko and Vera helped me sharpen my analysis and to situate it in the current context with more confidence.

A part of the work reported here actually results from my trying to respond to comments made by reviewers on a paper submitted to *Natural Language and Linguistic Theory*. My response ended up being too long for a paper, so I folded it into this work instead. But I nevertheless am indebted to three anonymous reviewers for that journal, as well as to Masha Polinsky, who provided me with still more helpful advice in her capacity as *NLLT* editor.

As this material developed, I had the opportunity to present selected portions of it to audiences at the 41st Algonquian conference, WSCLA 19, CamCos3, ICHL 22, and the International Workshop on Syntactic Analyticity and Grammatical Parameters. The ensuing discussions at these venues helped me to refine my thinking still more. In particular, Ian Roberts, Heidi Harley, Anders Holmberg, Hagit Borer, and Jenneke van der Wals each provided useful critiques and suggestions for other material and analyses that might be worth considering.

Two anonymous reviewers provided careful notes on the initial version submitted to Oxford University Press. These included suggestions on the organization of Chapters 2–4 which materially improved the presentation of this material.

Finally, I could not have brought this book to fruition without the patience and support of my wife Noreen, to whom it is dedicated, with love.

CHAPTER 1

Introduction

In grammatical theory, as in other branches of science, progress typically comes from examining what occurs at the margins of experience, where phenomena can be found which do not conform to the usual rules. For linguists, the "margins" are sometimes those carefully formulated test sentences which virtually never occur in natural speech but which we construct to test a hypothesis. But the margins can also be simply areas of grammar which have not yet informed generative grammatical theory, because this is a relatively young branch of science and the linguistic universe is pretty big. And sometimes, for good reasons, linguists even choose to marginalize known phenomena which resist fruitful analysis, given current tools and levels of understanding.

In the work reported in this monograph, I have attempted to develop a better understanding of *head-movement*, a very common morpho-syntactic phenomenon, by close strutiny of a cluster of cases in which head-movement violates familiar expectations. It is widely accepted that the main grammatical constraint controlling head-movement is the Head Movement Constraint (HMC) of Travis (1984), but this constraint is flouted in many of the linguistic structures examined here. More specifically, the strictures of the HMC turn out to be sometimes inactive for specific grammars and this then allows *multiple head-movement* to take place in some syntactic contexts.

This "marginal" morphosyntactic phenomenon turns out be not so uncommon, although it is found only in specific, limited grammatical contexts in many of the languages where it can be found. It is shown here that multiple head-movement forms a part of the grammar in Finnish, in English, in Peranakan Javanese, in northern Norwegian and Swedish dialects, and generally in the Slavic and Algonquian language families. What is more, careful attention to the contexts in which multiple head-movement takes place allows new generalizations to be identified. And these, in turn, allow a new model to

The Grammar of Multiple Head-Movement: A Comparative Study. Phil Branigan, Oxford University Press.
 DOI: 10.1093/oso/9780197677032.003.0001

be formulated of how head-movement fits into the overall architecture of grammatical computation.

In one form or another, the HMC is central to most models of head-movement. In fact, it is probably widely supposed that one criterion for a successful model of head-movement must be that it should derive the HMC from deeper axiomatic principles. But if the work reported here is correct, then models of head-movement which do so must actually be wrong, because the HMC must not be part of the axiomatic foundation for a theory of head-movement, because it does not always hold. Instead, the existence of grammars which enable multiple head-movement means that we require a model of head-movement which can derive the HMC for some languages and which can ignore it for others.

The immediate, most significant empirical results of this study are a better understanding of the morphosyntax of two unrelated language families: Slavic and Algonquian. Grammars in both of these language families include morpho-syntactic structures which pose immediate and thorny challenges for any theory of how complex words are built up. Within these two quite large groups of languages, I devote the most attention to the particular analysis of Russian (Slavic) and Innu-aimûn (Algonquian), largely as a matter of convenience, although occasionally data from related languages will be brought into the exposition.

The results of these case studies also have implications for larger questions concerning the architecture of the grammatical system. Some of these involve how head-movement should be modeled. I show that a grammatical system which includes multiple head-movement operations employs a different specification of the locality conditions in identifying moving heads and their X^0 target than languages which do not. The difference turns on a timing parameter which regulates the order of certain phase-level operations.

The examination of how multiple head-movement operates in different languages also has consequences for the theory of linguistic parameters. The case studies presented here will show that multiple head-movement is a pervasive phenomenon in some languages (Algonquian) and a marginal one in others (Finnish, English), while its role is somewhere in between in others (Slavic). A parameter theory must then include the resources to express these different degrees of generality. Moreover, since actual languages must be actually acquired by children, there must be learning paths which allow children to deduce how much or how little multiple head-movement their target languages must allow. How well existing parametric models satisfy these *desiderata* is considered in Chapter 5.

1.1 WHAT IS MULTIPLE HEAD-MOVEMENT?

The operation of *multiple head-movement* is first proposed by Collins (2002). Cole, Hara & Yap (2008) exploit this idea in the analysis of word order in Perenakan Javanese. (To my knowledge, that exhausts the existing scholarly literature on the topic.)

According to Collins, multiple head-movement displaces multiple heads to a single word-sized landing position by adjoining them to an attracting higher head. The process is illustrated schematically in (1), in which α, β, and γ are raised to a higher head F.

(1)

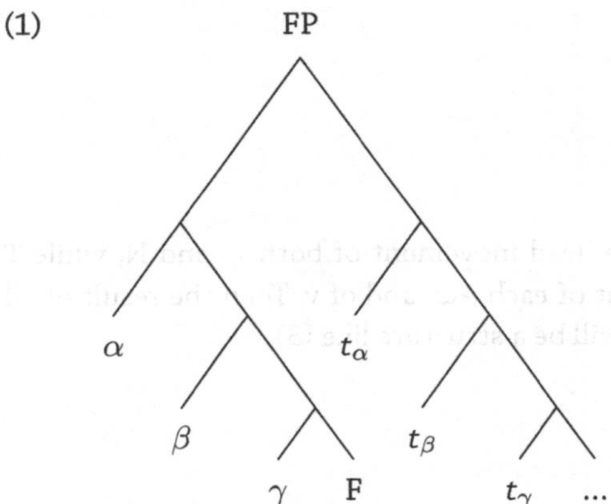

In this position, a syntactically unified subset cluster of these heads is then identified morpho-phonologically as a single word. As Collins notes, the ordering of heads in the derived X^0 unit resembles the ordering of wh-phrases in multiple wh-questions, and may be assimilated to the idea of "tucking in" proposed by Richards (1997).

A large part of what is presented in this monograph is put forward to show that multiple head-movement is real, and a phenomenon which plays a substantial role in the grammars of a range of unrelated languages, in a variety of syntactic contexts. As will be shown in the following chapters, depending on the language and syntactic context, this process can take place with C, T, D, *v*, *p*, and *n* as the attracting upper heads, depending on the context. In a sizable clause, therefore, we may see the interactions of multiple head movements. Consider the structure (2).

(2)

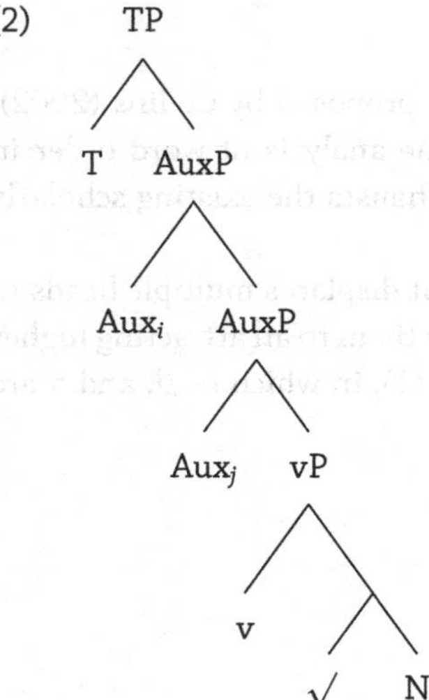

Suppose that v triggers multiple head-movement of both √ and N, while T triggers multiple head-movement of each Aux and of v. Then the result of all the movements triggered in (2) will be a structure like (3).

(3)

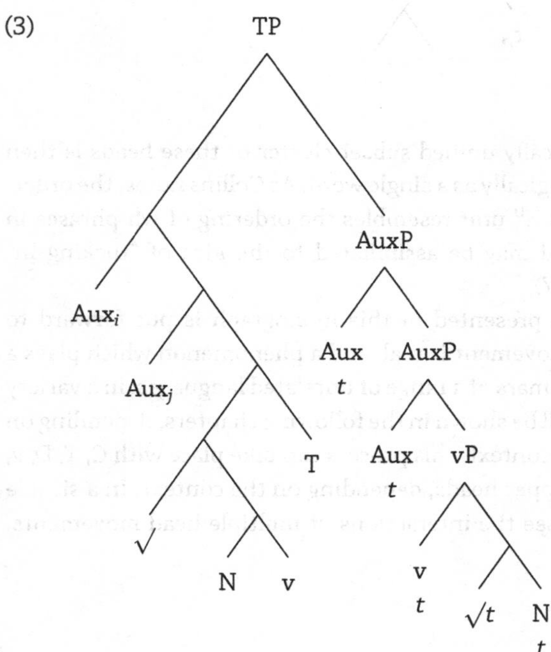

Collins's original proposal has not shown tremendous traction as a theoretical construct to date. In part, this is because the theoretical premises on which his analysis is based have been challenged on independent grounds. Multiple wh-movement to specifier positions of the same head, for example, is a controversial operation, given the alternative analysis of Slavic questions advanced by Krapova & Cinque (2008). Another issue is certainly the tendentious status of head-movement as a syntactic operation in recent models, particularly given Chomsky's (2001) hypothesis that core syntax does not include head-movement. Chomsky's (2000) suggestion that head-movement should be understood as a post-syntactic, non-core phenomenon is also compelling, as is the corollary that core syntactic transformations should be reduced to a single Merge operation.[1] Since Merge is subject to the Extension Condition, and can only apply at the root of a phrase marker, the implication is that head-movement cannot be a part of core syntax.

But if head-movement is excluded from the core syntax, then there is no reason why it should be subject to the same constraints—such as "tucking in"—which control phrasal movement. In fact, if head-movement is excluded from the core syntactic derivation, then the only constraints we should expect it to observe are those that reflect the process of "externalization," which turns syntactic representations into phonetic ones.

Finding a way to reconcile the possibility of multiple head-movement with such considerations is the task undertaken in Chapter 2, where a model of multiple head-movement is crafted which does not depend on any parallelism with multiple wh-movement operations. In order to do so, the nature and architectural place of familiar head-movement operations is reconsidered as well, and a general model of head-movement is developed as a necessary part of the characterization of multiple head-movement. But even if the model which I offer turns out ultimately to be flawed, the general finding that multiple head-movement occurs at all has important and immediate theoretical significance. In particular, if multiple head-movement is real, then head-movement is real, and should not be reconceptualized as an artifact of other syntactic relationships. Thus, for example, Brody's (2000) "Mirror theory" will be difficult to maintain if multiple head-movement is real. The same will be true of Svenonious's (2012) "spanning" model, which develops out of Mirror theory. More generally, models of morphosyntax in which complex morphology reflects the head-complement relationship in any less transformational way than the Emonds/Pollock/Bakerian account provides may face difficulty accommodating the patterns documented here.

1. The lengthy rationale offered in Berwick & Chomsky (2015), for example, is difficult to ignore.

1.2 THE MORPHOSYNTACTIC CHALLENGE FROM SLAVIC ASPECT

A vast literature has identified a host of very specific analytic challenges presented by complex verbs in Slavic languages. These have to do with how the grammar generates verbs—and some participial and nominalized forms derived from them—in which nuanced aspectual distinctions are expressed morphologically. The general problem is evident in even relatively simple verbs, where the significant distinction between *perfective* and *imperfective* forms must be treated. (Why and how this distinction is significant for the syntactic derivation will be discussed in detail in Chapter 3.) For example, while most Russian simplex verbs are automatically imperfective, a small class of verbs are inherently perfective, including *rešit'* 'to decide' and *dat'* 'to give', among others. Inherently perfective verbs can be made imperfective by the addition of a *secondary imperfective* suffix, which provides the verb pairs in the table (4).[2]

(4)

Perfective	Imperfective	
dat'	davat'	'give'
rešit'	rešat'	'decide'
brosit'	brosat'	'throw'

Used as the sole verb in a finite clause, both imperfective and perfective forms of the verb must also bear a tense/agreement suffix.

(5) a. Ivan da-l mne knigu.
Ivan give-PST.ms me book
'Ivan gave me a book.'

b. Druz'ja da-va-li mne knigi.
friends give-IMPF-PST.p me books
'Friends were giving me books.'

The finite imperfective forms thus include two suffixes, the secondary imperfective suffix and the tense/agreement suffix. The immediate morphosyntactic question then becomes how the grammar generates such forms. The answer provided by a rich Slavic aspectological tradition is that the morphology alone

2. The *a* vowel represented as part of the secondary imperfective suffix may actually be a thematic vowel, which might reasonably be introduced into the morphology in some other position, or post-syntactically. I assume that this degree of attention to surface details will not affect the substance of my arguments, so I will eschew it for the most part. In addition, the intricacies of the morphophonological rules which produce the secondary imperfective forms are not important to the general discussion here, so they will not be discussed. Matushansky (2009) provides a nice summary of the details (and an attractive proposal for how to model them).

is responsible, where affixation produces lexical items, prior to the syntactic derivation (Jakobson 1957, Isacenko 1960). The obvious alternative which fits with much contemporary morpho-syntactic analysis is that successive cyclic head-movement is responsible for adding both affixes to the verb stem, starting from a structure like (6) for (5b).

(6)

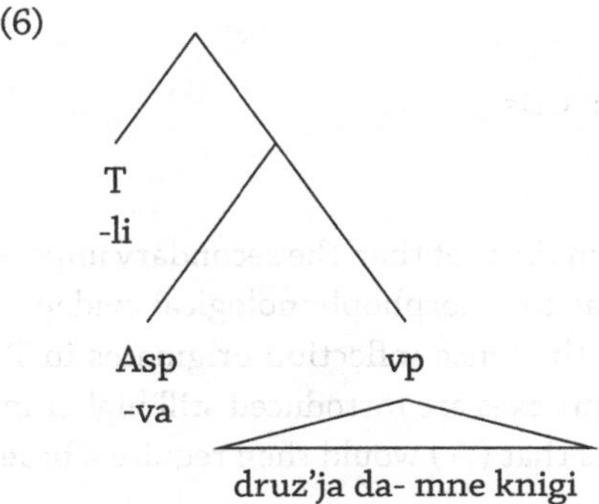

Movement of the verb stem *da-* to Asp in this structure would then be followed by movement of *da-va* to T.

A purely morphological approach to these data cannot be easily reconciled with what has been learned about the interactions between tense/agreement morphology and the syntactic derivation since the earliest generative models of Chomsky (1957).[3] But the alternative head-movement account faces a number of serious obstacles as well. For one thing, Bailyn (1995) has argued that the verb remains within the verb phrase in Russian, like in English. If so, then head-movement cannot bring the verb stem together with its affixes. Worse, if the secondary imperfective affix is a syntactic head between T and the verb phrase, even an English-like affix-hopping analysis seems unlikely to succeed for Russian, because affix-hopping cannot operate in successive cyclic fashion (as far as we know). Bailyn's argument then forces us to conclude that the secondary imperfective morphology is not introduced as a syntactic head, but is provided to the verb stem by some other, pre-syntactic, purely morphological means.

But even that conclusion is difficult to sustain when other properties of the system of morphological marking of aspect are brought to bear on the analysis of Slavic verbal morphology. A variety of prefixes attach to the verb to contribute new aspectual information. Some examples of Russian verbs with such aspectual prefixes appear in (7).

3. See also Svenonius (2005b) (and others) on the limits of the Jakobsonian model of the Slavic verb.

(7) a. Saša na-pisa-l grutstnuju pesnju.
Sasha PRF-write-PST.3m sad song
'Sasha wrote a sad song.'

b. Marina po-exa-la v Leningrad.
Marina PRF-go-PST.3f to Leningrad
'Marina went to Leningrad.'

c. On pere-za-pisa-l diski.
he re/PRF-re/PRF-write-PST.3m CDs
'He re-recorded the CDs.'

These prefixes are attached further from the root than the secondary imperfective and the inflectional suffixes are, as the morphophonological evidence discussed in Pesetsky (1979) shows.[4] If the tense inflection originates in T, it then should follow that the aspectual prefixes are introduced still higher in the syntactic structure. The implication is that (7c) would then require a base structure something like (8).

(8)

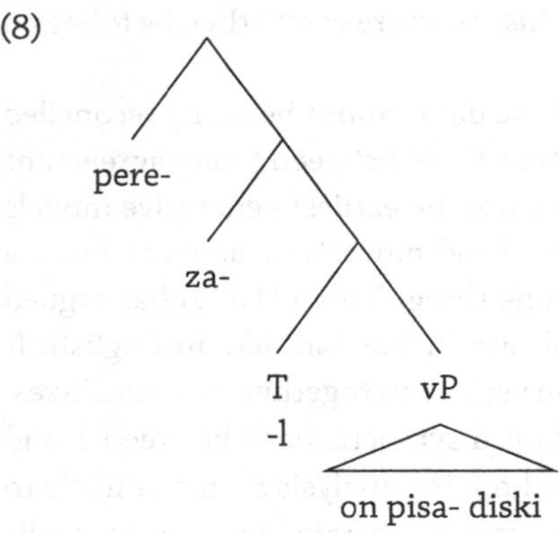

But this structure is inconsistent with the semantics of prefixal verbs in at least two respects. First, the tense scopes over the prefixes. Second, some prefixes combine with specific verbs to produce idiosyncratic lexical meanings; in (7c), the combination of *pisa-* and *za-* produces the meaning 'record', rather than any compositional interpretation. Such unpredictable meanings should be impossible with a base structure like (8) where the prefix and stem are so far from each other.

4. The details of Pesetsky's argument are presented and evaluated in Chapter 3.

So the challenge posed by Slavic aspectual morphology for any morphological theory is substantial, and it is clear that no simple head-movement analysis will be able to accommodate this type of data. (There are further complications when interactions of prefixes with the secondary imperfective suffix are examined, but these will be considered, among other things, in Chapter 3.)

1.3 THE MORPHOSYNTACTIC CHALLENGE OF TRIPARTITE STEM STRUCTURES IN ALGONQUIAN

The challenges posed for morphosyntactic theory by the morphological structure of verbs and nouns in Algonquian languages are still more daunting. Until fairly recently, the bulk of the literature on the grammars of Algonquian languages has focused on sound and word structures, rather than on sentence structure. For example, Bloomfield's (1962) description of Menomini includes 23 pages on (surface) phonology, 401 pages on morphology, including morphophonology, and 71 pages on phrase and clause structure.

Aside from the relatively greater difficulty of examining syntactic structures generally, one reason for this analytic imbalance in the literature has to do with the enormous wealth in expressive opportunities which are provided by individual words in these languages. It is common in descriptions of polysynthetic languages to read that a single word can be an entire sentence, but in many polysynthetic languages, these word-sized sentences convey fairly simple propositions. In Algonquian languages, the morphological complexity of the verb allows word-sized sentences to convey remarkably complex ideas. Thus, for example, Goddard (1988) shows that in Mesquakie (Fox), a single word may express what English would require a multi-clausal structure to convey: (9a).

(9) a. kikenow-:kišikikenowenemak.
'when I thought they were finished with the clan feast.'

b. (nekotahi) iniyeka ototeweniwačimapi.
'It is said of them that (they) have a town (somewhere).'

In the tradition initiated by Bloomfield (1962), Algonquian languages generate verbs and nouns according to a '*tripartite*' templatic structure. Bloomfield (p. 68) states: "Stems which are not secondary derivatives are formed by *primary formation*. The immediate constituents of primary stems are *finals*, *medial suffixes* (or *medials*) and *roots*." In other sections, he uses the term "initial" in place of 'root,' particularly when the "initial" is itself bimorphemic. For an Innu-aimûn verb like *kuîshkuâpetshinam* 'straighten a cordlike object manually', for example, the tripartite structure would be as in (10).

(10)

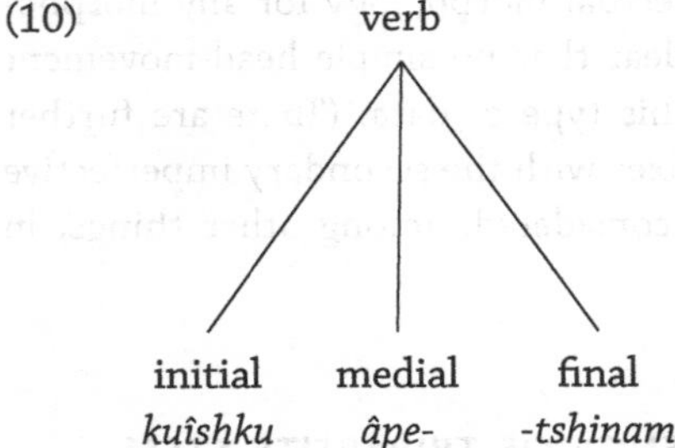

The initial *kuishku* occurs independently as a particle *kuishk*^{u} 'straight, directly'. The medial *-ape-* is found in any number of verbs which apply to cordlike objects or (unaccusative) subjects. And the final *-tshinam* appears regularly in verbs which signify an activity which one accomplishes by using one's hands.

Of the non-final components, initials are always present, and medials are often optional constituents. Finals are more complex, and behave differently in different parts of speech. Noun finals are often silent, or absent, depending on one's theoretical predisposition. (Bloomfield (1946) opted for a silent final analysis; Goddard (1988) prefers to treat nouns as categories in which the final may be absent altogether.) Verb finals are often internally complex, with a series of smaller morphemes combined into a larger morphological unit.

The bulk of the literature on Algonquian grammars follows Bloomfield or extends his basic framework in the analysis of the morphological structure of complex words. But the Bloomfieldian approach leaves many questions unanswered which are of interest both for the understanding of how individual languages work and for situating Algonquian in a broader (universal) theory of morphosyntax. For one thing, while the tripartite structures are pervasive units in any Algonquian language, a comprehensive account of the semantic roles played—and not played—by initials, medials, and finals is not available. And there is good reason for this gap in the literature; none of the three word components maps to a single semantic function, or even a family of functions. Instead, the same job can be done by initials, medials, or finals, depending on the other elements present in a given word. In (11a), for example, the verbal content is expressed by the initial component, in (11b), by the medial, and in (11c) by the final.

(11) a. *ashkutikueu.*
ashkû-tîku-e-u.
await-caribou-FNL-3
'S/he waits for caribou.'

b. *matauapatam*ᵘ.
mâtâu-âpat-am-u.
strange-see-FNL-3
'S/he sees a mirage, something strange.'

c. *kutauashkupatau.*
kutâu-âshku-pât-â-u.
disappear-sticklike-run-FNL-3
'S/he runs into the woods, disappearing.'

And in (11a), the medial serves to indicate what would appear to be the semantic object of the final *-e*. In (11b), however, the initial *matau-* indicates features of the object, while in (11c), the initial *kutâu-* refers to the end result (disappearance) of the action on the subject.

While this shifting functionality of the individual components of tripartite word structures is recognized and documented in the literature, to my knowledge there has been no explanation provided which goes much beyond cataloguing what actually occurs. (There are an impressive number of insightful studies of this sort, including Bloomfield (1962), Wolfart (1973), Goddard (1979), Valentine (2001), Drapeau (2014), among others.) But one would hope to uncover what the basis is for both the form and the meanings of complex words, and this requires that the underlying principles which generate tripartite (and smaller) word structures be identified.

The Bloomfieldian schema offers no explanation of what the functions of the parts of the tripartite structure are. What is more, lacking clarity on this matter, it is difficult to characterize any relationships which are found between the three components of a complex word. This is particularly problematic for words in which initials and finals appear to show a dependancy which excludes a medial. These are common, as exemplified in (12).

(12) a. *tshînishinu* 's/he slips accidentally', *tshîn-apiss-inu* 's/he slips accidentally on a rock', *tshîn-akun-eshin* 's/he slips accidentally on a snowy surface'.

b. *tshînieu* 's/he sharpens it', *tshînapissipuneu* 's/he sharpens it with a file', *tshinikaueu* 's/he sharpens it with an axe'.

c. *pîmapiteu* 's/he has crooked teeth', *pîmiputâu* 's/he saws it crooked'; *pîmashkuâueu* 's/he twists it, using a stick'.

d. *pimaputâu* 's/he lets it float along with the current', *pimashtan* 'it moves along with the wind'; *pimashkutâu* 's/he lays it (a sticklike thing) on the ground'

In the (12a) verbs, the combination of a *tshin* initial and the finals *-in*, *-shin*, and *-eshin* signifies a slipping action. But in (12b), the same initial combines with *-e*, *pune-*, and *-ue* to mean 'sharpen'. In both cases, the contribution of the medial to the overall meaning is determined only on the basis of the semantics of the initial-final pairing. So *apiss* 'stone' and *akun* 'snow' are the surfaces to slip on in (12a) while *apiss* and *ika* are the tools used for sharpening in (12b). Similarly, (12c) and (12d) examples differ in what initial *pim* means: with finals in (12c), it means 'crooked', but with the finals that signify a type of motion in (12d), it means 'along'. And the presence of medial *-ashku* 'sticklike' does not affect the initial-final relationship in either case.

Another indication that the tripartite template does not fully capture the necessary morphological pattern is found in many verbs where more than three components are found. Verbs with multiple finals are commonplace, as in (13). (See section A.5 in the appendix for discussion of how these might be analysed.) In (13a), for example *-ute* 'walk' and *-sh* '(diminutive)' must both count as finals. Besides the *-e* final which marks verbal direction and object agreement in (13b), there are two suffixes *-en* and *-im* which regularly appear in verbs indicating mental or emotional states, and these must also count as finals.

(13) a. *shash pimuteshu nussim.* (Drapeau 2014: p. 407)
shâsh pim-ûte-sh-u n-uss-im.
already along-walk-DIM-3 1-son-POSS
'My son is already walking.'

b. *Auass natuenimeu utinnikuema.*
auâss natu-en-im-e-u ut-innîkue-m-a.
child seek-FNL-FNL-FNL-3 3-doll-POSS-OBV
'The child asks for her doll.'

There can also be more than one medial within a verb: (14).

(14) a. *minuashkukateu.*
minu-âshku-kât-e-u.
good-sticklike-leg-FNL-3
'S/he has nice legs.'

b. *musheiashkupuameshinu mani ne ishkueu.* (Drapeau 2014: p. 438)
mûshe-âshku-puâm-eshin-u mânî ne ishkueu.
bare-sticklike-thigh-lie.down-3 regularly this woman
'This woman often lies down with her thighs exposed.'

More generally, an approach to verbal morphology which assumes that word structure can be adequately understood by reference to an abstract shape—the tripartite template—begs the critical question where such a shape comes from. For Bloomfield, it was reasonable to suppose that grammars can implement quite arbitrary patterns. But development of a minimalist generative analysis requires that surface generalizations must find an explanation based on deeper principles, principles which moreover have some plausible relationship to cognitive or computational imperatives. The tripartite template lacks these features.

A related issue is the question of how words which appear outside a tripartite structure are associated with it. In particular, "preverbs" and "prenouns" are found to the left of complex verbs and nouns, respectively, as in (15). In (15a), the verb is preceded by preverbs *ka* and *uî*. The noun in (15b) follows its prenoun *ussi*.

(15) a. *Tshika ui mamitunenimakanuat auassat.*
tshi-ka=uî=mâmitun-en-im-âk-ân-u-at auâss-at.
2-FUT=want=think.about-FNL-FNL-FNL-1pi-3-p child-p
'We must think about the young.'

b. *Nishtesh ashineiku ussi-utapan.*
ni-shtesh ashinei-k-u ûssi=utâpân.
1-older.brother prides.onself-FNL-3 new=car
'My older brother takes pride in his new car.'

For Bloomfield, both preverbs and prenouns are introduced into the derivation through compounding operations, which therefore form still larger word-sized units. Russell (1999: p. 207) observes that "his major justification for this is that the person prefix appears to show morphosyntactic sensitivity to the properties encoded in the suffixes, therefore the entire complex must constitute a single morphological domain." As we will see in Chapter 4, however, there is ample evidence that preverbs and prenouns often originate as independent syntactic units, often functioning as heads of phrases.

1.4 THE CLAIMS AND WHAT IS TO COME

This investigation is conducted within a general framework of contemporary minimalist syntactic theory. The overall conclusions which I draw from the material presented here bear on a range of concerns in linguistic theory, including the types of variation to include in typological studies, formal questions about the architecture of I-language, and problems in how language acquisition undertakes to set morphosyntactic parameters. The conclusions I draw are the following. First, multiple head-movement provides a viable analysis of a range of constructions in a disparate variety of languages, and actually resolves some long-standing problems which have resisted explanation. So the morphosyntactic derivation must include mechanisms which make multiple head-movement possible, and typological studies should recognize the rule played by multiple head-movement in different languages.

Secondly, the characteristics of head movement operations—including both conventional head-movement and multiple head-movement—can be accommodated in a general minimalist model in which the core syntax allows only movement which satisfies the Extension Condition. This is because head-movement reflects a response in the externalization component of the derivation to a phase-level feature valuation operation. The latter ensures that head-movement must be sensitive to syntactic locality constraints; the former accounts for the typical semantic vacuity of head-movement operations.

Thirdly, the distribution of multiple head-movement across languages cannot be fully explained in purely microparametric models of parameter space. Nor does the acquisition of the multiple head-movement option in particular languages fit well into parameter setting models which rely on "cues" or "triggers" in the data available to a child. Instead, the best fit comes from a model which includes both stochastic processes and a procedure which fractures parameter space into smaller subparts, when necessary.

Chapter 2 introduces a model of head-movement capable of accommodating both compliant and multiple head-movement, and then examines a number of cases where the latter operates in pockets of the grammar in a wide variety of languages. (Some of these cases are already a part of the literature; others are given a new treatment.) In Chapter 3, it is shown that multiple head-movement is a central part of the prefixation system in the Slavic languages. Chapter 4 demonstrates that a comparable sytem is part of the grammars of Algonquian grammars, where it is pervasive. And then Chapter 5 considers the implications of the findings of the previous chapters for the general theory of parameters, and for how learnability models might accommodate the type of parametric theory which seems to be required.

CHAPTER 2

A modular theory of head movement

2.1 SITUATING HEAD-MOVEMENT

In this work, I advocate for the proposition that syntactic theory must accommodate multiple head-movement derivations in which heads can be displaced upwards in a structure so that one or more other heads sometimes raise to the same X^0 target. An immediate issue which this proposal must confront is that such derivations clearly violate the *Head Movement Constraint* (Travis 1984). In its original form, the HMC limits movement of X^0 constituents (other than clitics) to a landing site located at next head up, in a head-complement structure Travis 1984.[1] I will refer to movement which does not satisfy this constraint as *cavalier* head-movement; the empirical necessity for *cavalier* head-movement will be amply demonstrated in what follows. More familiar head-movement operations which do satisfy the HMC will be dubbed *compliant* head-movement. Since a considerable body of work has shown the importance of the HMC in a tremendous range of syntactic contexts, it makes sense to start by considering how one might accommodate cavalier head-movement in a minimalist model at all. In other words, a necessary step in my argument is to demonstrate that cavalier head-movement and compliant head-movement can co-exist as syntactic options within a general theory of morphosyntax.[2]

1. For Travis, head movement which does not fall under this constraint is an ECP violation, because the trace of the displaced head is not properly governed.
2. Roberts (2020) develops an alternative model of multiple head-movement in Algonquian grammar, based on a (much) earlier version of the present study. I consider Roberts's analysis in Chapter 4, and I show that the features of Innu-aimûn grammar do not support his specific premises. Nevertheless, the model developed here is influenced by Roberts's ideas.

The Grammar of Multiple Head-Movement: A Comparative Study. Phil Branigan, Oxford University Press.
 DOI: 10.1093/oso/9780197677032.003.0002

Developing such an account is complicated by the tenuous status of the HMC itself in current models. Since minimalist syntax has developed without any principles which are fully analogous to the ECP, it is not obvious what the foundation for the HMC should be, which raises the question whether the HMC is a real (derived) principle of grammar. If it is not, then obviously it cannot be the basis for skepticism about the idea of multiple head-movement. On the other hand, the HMC is a familiar, comfortable idea which occupies a central place in syntactic analysis, and so even if it lacks an axiomatic basis, it is sometimes sensible to prefer the devil you know over a stranger (who might end up being equally diabolical). More generally, the HMC does serve a valuable role by limiting the number of possible languages, and moving in the opposite direction requires solid empirical justification. I believe, however, that the case studies examined here do so.

My strategy will therefore be to de-diabolicize both the HMC and the idea of cavalier head-movement by providing both with a more solid foundation. In order to do so, the general principles which govern familiar head-movement operations must also be elucidated. This is no small task, obviously. Dekany's (2018) survey of the issues elucidates many of the difficulties which any model of head-movement must confront. Many are technical, but some are connected to foundational questions for linguistic theory as a whole.

The challenge of showing that cavalier head-movement and compliant head-movement should both count as legitimate parts of a syntactic derivation is made more daunting by the fact that many instances of the former will frequently resemble cases of the latter. Even when the HMC does not apply, other general principles of grammar will often ensure that heads raise only to the next higher head position. Principles of phase theory limit the options in many cases; "relativized minimality" effects will constrain many of the remaining cases.

The first step, then, is to establish how and why "normal" (compliant) head-movement satisfies the HMC. Finding a basis for the HMC is essential in order to begin to make progress on the larger project at hand.

Addressing the nature of the HMC requires that the nature of (compliant) head-movement be considered at the same time. If we accept Chomsky's arguments that head-movement is not a part of the core syntax, then the properties of head-movement should not mirror those of phrasal movement. But exclusion from core syntax does not imply a complete divorce from the syntactic derivation. Even if the core syntax does nothing but build binary structure, the "externalization" procedures which transform these structures into expressive language still need to be characterized. In the model of Chomsky (2008), the non-core transformations are all controlled at the phase level, where preparation for externalization is effected. The phase level would then appear to be a viable point in the syntactic derivation at which head-movement might be determined. This appears to be the only option, in fact, if we accept Chomsky's general premise that core syntax is nothing but the Merge operation.[3]

As for the process of externalization, it remains an open research question what operations and procedures are involved in deriving a physical form from syntactic representations.[4] It presumably begins with "Transfer," a phase-level operation which identifies a part of a syntactic structure as ready to be processed into a phonetic string (Chomsky 2000). Some subsequent parts of this process are self-evident; morphophonology, phonology proper, phonetic variability must all belong to this part of the grammar. It is less obvious that word order must be established post-syntactically. On the one hand, some of results of Kayne's (1995) Linear Correspondence Axiom may be reinterpreted as suggested by Chomsky (1994, 2007), as an algorithm which establishes word order for the phonetic string on the basis of antisymmetrical c-command relations. On the other hand, if the need for antisymmetry is actually a driving force within the syntactic derivation, then the syntactic representation might already provide the word order for what comes next. Happily, confronting the problems of head-movement does not require a prior resolution of such questions for the order of phrasal elements. If linear order is a property of the syntactic representation, then head-movement is a mechanism which will alter where a head is situated within an already linearized structure.[5] If linear order is determined post-syntactically, then the effect of head-movement will depend on whether it takes place before linearization takes place or after. If head-movement precedes linearization, then it simply establishes a new location for the raised head in a hierarchical structure. If it takes place later, then the effect will (again) be a new linear order, with a head preceding a new set of constituents.

Consider, for example, the architecture of linearization proposed by Idsardi & Raimy (2013). In this model, linearization has three stages: Immobilization, Vocabulary Insertion, and Serialization. The first establishes relations of adjacency within a hierachical structure provided by the core syntactic derivation. If head-movement were to take place before Immobilization, then an immobilized structure would include complex heads in their final (hierarchical)

3. The alternative would be that head-movement is entirely a matter for the morphophonology. Rather than divert the discussion with an argument that head-movement cannot be divorced entirely from the syntax, I rely on the substance of the chapters that follow to make that point.

4. Cf. Collins (2017), Idsardi & Raimy (2013), Arregi & Nevins (2012), among others.

5. On the other hand, the phenomenon of multiple head-movement appears to be incompatible with the extension of Kayne's LCA discussed in Collins (2017) and Collins & Kayne (2020). In that model, complex words are formed by Merge operations—internal and external—within the core syntactic derivation, subject to the Extension Condition. It follows that no complex morphology which mirrors a "tucking in" derivation should ever be found. In Chapter 3, this result is spelled out in more detail for the case of Russian verbal prefixes.

position, and this would then serve as the basis for later operations, such as Vocabulary Insertion. On the other hand, if Immobilization precedes head-movement, then the latter operation will alter adjacency relationships before Vocabulary Insertion takes place. Vocabulary Insertion operations, however, must clearly be ordered after head-movement, because structures established by head-movement will typically serve as the basis for selection of the correct allomorphic forms in Vocabulary Insertion.

The model of head-movement developed below appears to be compatible which each of these possibilities. However in the discussion which follows, I assume that word order is determined post-syntactically, simply in order to have a familiar theoretical language to operate with.

In some cases, it is actually quite clear that head-movement cannot take place until the phase level. Swedish placement of finite verbs offers a good example of why this conclusion can be drawn: (1).

(1) a. . . . att Ingmar inte äter kött.
that Ingmar not eats meat
'. . . that Ingmar does not eat meat.'

b. Ingmar äter inte kött.
Ingmar eats not meat
'Ingmar does not eat meat.'

c. På tisdag äter Ingmar inte kött.
on Tuesday eats Ingmar not meat
'On Tuesday Ingmar does not eat meat.'

In normal Swedish embedded clauses, the finite verb does not raise to T, and as a result, it must appear to the right of the *inte* negator, as in (1a). In root clauses, however, it does raise (Holmberg 1986) and appears in second position, as in (1b,c). The nature of the second position is controversial, particularly in clauses like (1b), where the subject occupies the "first position." But there is no disputing that the verb must raise past the negator in all verb-second clauses, so it raises at least to T. In cases like (1c), where the finite verb precedes the subject, the verb must have raised further, presumably to C (Holmberg 1986). But the final position of the Swedish finite verb cannot be determined before the CP level is reached, since the verb will raise only if C is not a clause-embedding complementizer like *att*. So head-movement of the verb to T cannot take place before the CP phase is built.

What is more, if our model includes a Feature Inheritance component (Chomsky 2008, Richards 2007), then even simpler cases of head-movement must take place no earlier than the phase level. Compare the derivations of (2a) and (2b), if tense information is transferred from the C phase head.

(2) a. Jenna will not have sold her bike.
b. Jenna had not sold her bike.

In (2a), where C transfers future tense features to T, no head movement of the *have* auxiliary occurs. In (2b), it does. Only in the latter will the trigger for head-movement be provided to T (whatever that is). But the crucial distinctions are absent from the structure until the phase level, so verb-raising cannot take place until after Feature Inheritance from C has occurred.

2.2 A DRIVER FOR HEAD-MOVEMENT

The next question is why head-movement should be connected with phase-level operations. Answering this question requires that we also consider why head-movement takes place at all. The conventional language for deriving the necessity of head-movement takes the driving force to be the affixal status of one of the two heads involved, an idea which arguably originates in Chomsky (1957). But being an affix is a morphological property of a morpheme, and not a property which is necessarily directly accessible to the syntactic derivation. What is worse, the idea that head-movement is driven by affixal status leads inexorably to the conclusion that an invisible X^0 category like English root interrogative C must be an affix. And yet the only evidence that this silent C is affixal is the observation that T raises to it. In order to avoid such evident circularity, I propose instead that at the phase level, the syntactic derivation has access to grammatical features which enable the formation of word-sized constituents, but which are not themselves morphological properties.

Given such criteria, the challenge is to find a way to characterize head-movement in which only phase-level operations operate on the structure generated by the Merge core, and to obtain a satisfactory degree of empirical coverage thereby. What then must occur at the phase level to allow head-movement to emerge with the patterns that are actually attested? Let us begin by entertaining the hypothesis that head-movement takes place to solve a problem which arises from earlier operations within the syntactic derivation, and that this problem must be solved in order to allow the Transfer operation to provide an appropriate structure for encoding through externalization. Within the strictures of minimalism, the only alternative to such a hypothesis would be that head-movement takes place to solve a problem which will arise later, which would necessarily involve significant "look-ahead" and an automatic increase in computational complexity within the derivation.

The problem which head-movement resolves must involve properties of the structure which are visible within the syntactic derivation, and this criterion presumably excludes purely phonetic properties. It should also exclude morphophonological information which is introduced into the structure as part of the process of externalization itself; allomorphy, for example, should not be a part of the calculation.[6]

Head-movement typically produces a result in which two independent X^0 units join together to form a single larger X^0 unit. The problem solved by head-movement should therefore involve the presence of two X^0 units which belong together—in some sense—but are located too far apart. The question then becomes how to make sense of the idea that two X^0 units may "belong together." This idea can be made more precise by formulating it as a relationship between elements with specific formal features. For example, one might say that two X^0 items "belong together" if there is some feature *f* which they both bear, and if all instances of *f* must be contained in the same (small) unit for successful externalization.

The *f* feature itself should be something which plays a necessary role in externalizing syntactic structure. Otherwise, postulating such a feature would again be a circular exercise. One obvious possibility is that *f* is what identifies a constituent as a "word" for Transfer. If language contains only one "generative engine" (Marantz 2000), then the same syntactic operations produce complex words and complex phrasal structure. But words and phrases are often treated differently in externalization. For example, words are associated with a wide variety of phonological rules which are distinct from those employed for phrasal structures—indeed, major branches of phonological theory are based on the distinction, including Lexical Phonology and Stratal OT.[7] The linearization of individual morphemes in complex words also may be determined on a different basis from how phrase structure is linearized. If both words and phrases are formed by Merge operations, then some extra information must be available at Transfer so that branching structures at the word level can be distinguished from phrasal structures, and the *f* feature can be where this extra information is provided.[8]

To take a concrete example, compare the complex word *intolerable* with a phrase like *on the fence*. Both will be formed by two Merge operations, which generate comparable structures: (3).

6. More generally, if one assumes some version of Distributed Morphology (Halle & Marantz 1993), then the type of morphophonological information introduced through *Vocabulary Insertion* rules should not be accessible within the syntactic derivation, and therefore should not be what drives head-movement operations.

7. See Bermúdez-Otero (2010) for a recent overview of the issues, for example.

8. In the reflections on this issue in Chomsky (1994), he concludes that X^0 phrases are identified as "word-like elements" by the Morphology component. "If some larger unit appears within an X^0, the derivation crashes." But this approach relies on some prior notion of an X^0 category, which is precisely what needs an explanation.

(3) a.

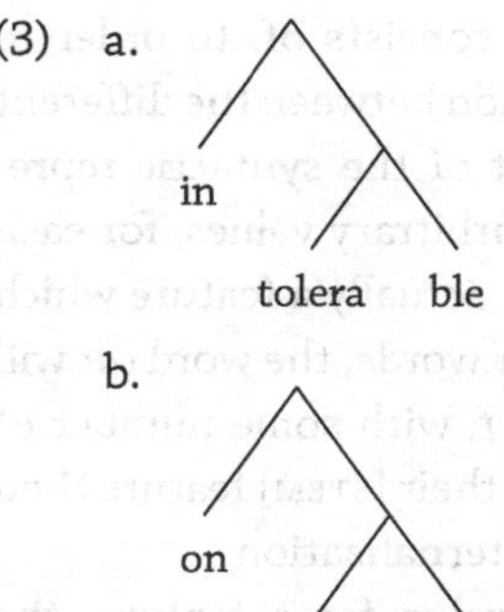

But these two structures should not be equivalent for the purposes of morphophonological interpretation. Since S-M interface clearly treats these as different, it must have a basis to distinguish them. The presence of a common f feature will enable words to be identified as such, regardless of the role it plays in driving head-movement.[9]

By this logic, any sufficiently complex syntactic structure—such as a sentence—will contain multiple words, and therefore multiple different tokens of the f feature: f, f', f'', etc. It is the presence of such features that allow a Merge-based structure like (4a) to be realized as a structure with distinct words like (4b).

(4) a.

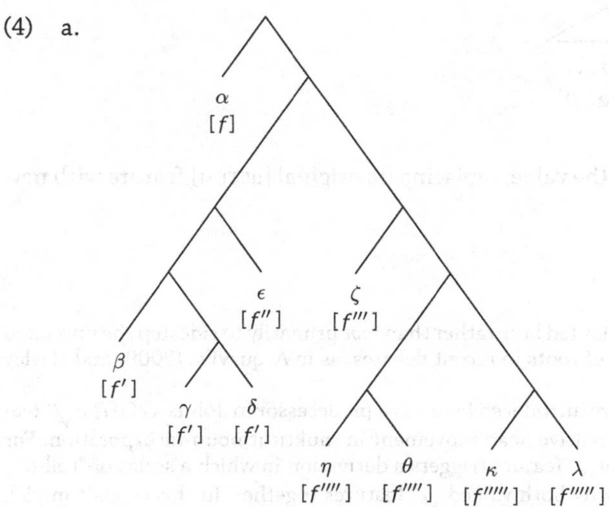

b. $\alpha\ \beta\text{-}\gamma\text{-}\delta\ \epsilon\ \zeta\ \eta\text{-}\theta\ \kappa\text{-}\lambda$

9. Nobrega (2015) also proposes that words are identified on the basis of formal features. For him, it is edge features which are valued by categorizing heads which establish a structure as a word, and this drives a limited range of head-movement. The model of head-movement developed here is more general, and therefore it requires a featural driver with broader scope.

Now let us consider what the *f* feature actually consists of. In order to avoid "reifying indices" (Chomsky 1995), the distinction between the different *f* tokens must be made on the basis of the content of the syntactic representation itself, and not by adding new features, or arbitrary values, for each additional word in a structure. This suggests that *f* is actually a feature which takes as its value the stem of a lexical item.[10] In other words, the word *cat* will bear a feature [STEM(cat)] (rather than the notation *f*, with some number of ′ primes). Two X^0 units which bear the same value for their [STEM] feature then can be said to "belong together" for the process of externalization.

But in order for two items to bear the same value for a feature, the derivation must include a mechanism which allows a feature value on one to be obtained from the other. There is no need to invent a new operation for valuation of [STEM] features, happily, since standard minimalist models already include what is needed. We need only suppose that some X^0 items enter the derivation with an unvalued [STEM] feature: [uSTEM].[11] A [uSTEM] feature will be illegitimate at the S-M interface, and the X^0 unit bearing it will therefore have to find a [STEM] value within its c-command domain. In other words, the presence of a [uSTEM] feature in a terminal node makes it a *probe* which must seek a matching *goal*.

(5)

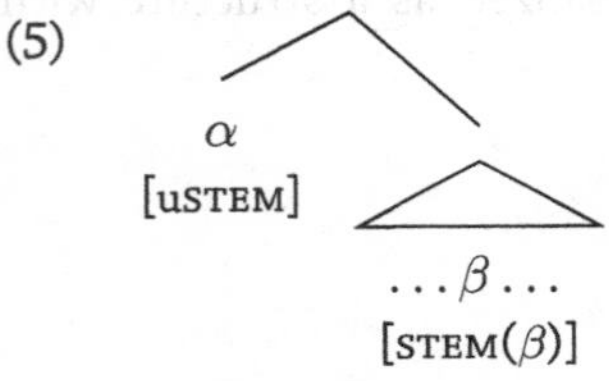

Finding one, it copies the value, replacing its original [uSTEM] feature with new value.

10. The term *stem* is adopted here rather than *root* primarily to sidestep the unrelated question of the identify of roots in recent debates, as in Acquaviva (2009) and Harley (2014), and others.

11. The [uSTEM] feature introduced here has a predecessor in Johns' (2007) $u\sqrt{}$ feature, which also serves to drive head-movement in Inuktitut noun-incorporation. For Johns, valuation of the $u\sqrt{}$ feature triggers a derivation in which a series of "roll-up" operations ultimately bring both valued $\sqrt{}$ features together. In this elegant model, surface satisfaction of the HMC actually reflects the output of phrasal movement operations in Inuktitut. I maintain, however, that roll-up derivations cannot provide the effects of head-movement in all other languages, especially head-initial ones, so the HMC must still be based on some theory of actual head-movement. In Chapter 3, the possibility of explaining multiple head-movement phenomena with roll-up derivations is considered, and shown to be untenable. But the idea that head-movement responds to something like a $u\sqrt{}$ feature will remain indispensable.

As a notational convenience, I will sometimes employ a more concise annotation convention for such stem values, with an *i*, *j*, *k*, etc. index representing the actual stem values. In other words, the stem feature of *with* might be represented simply as [STEM(*i*)], where the index *i* stands in for *with* itself. In places where the actual stem is written as the value for a [STEM] feature, I will generally be cavalier in how that stem is written, since nothing seems to turn on such details, and since there is no conventional way to refer to the identity of a root without using its phonological form, which is often dependent on the local morphological context.

Notation aside, the idea that the value for a feature may equate to the lexical identity of another head necessarily entails that such heads actually have a lexical identity within the syntactic derivation. I must assume that the syntactic structure contains this information, and that there is no "late insertion" of lexical roots. Specifically, I will be assuming the "weak" version of Distributed Morphology, where bundles of morphosyntactic features and roots are both accessible to core syntactic operations.

The concept being put forward here has analogs within other areas of grammar in the recent literature, particularly in the theory of agreement. I am proposing that head-movement is driven by a valuation process which establishes a feature value which is actually the identity of another constituent within the same phrase marker. Essentially the same mechanism is advanced to account for first- or last-conjunct agreement by Bhatt & Walkow (2013) and Marusic, Nevins & Badecker (2015). Atlamaz & Baker (2017) also employ this concept in an analysis of how agreement targets can compete for realization in some split ergative structures. In these models, agreement takes place in two steps: Agree-Link and Agree-Copy, where only the former belongs to the core syntactic derivation. Agree-Link involves a probe-goal operation where the identity of the goal is recorded as a feature of the probe, so that a later Agree-Copy operation may make use of features of the former in realizing the morphological shape of the latter. The Agree-Link operation is fully comparable to my [uSTEM] valuation operation, except for the role which is played by the value (=link) after it has been established. Even the notation proposed by Atlamaz & Baker (2017) is comparable to mine. Given a probe P and a matching goal G, they express the output of Agree-Link as: $P_{[\rightarrow G]}$. Were I to adopt that same convention, the output of feature valuation for the [uSTEM] feature might be $\alpha_{[\rightarrow \beta]}$, with the arrow interpreted as referring specifically to a [STEM] feature, rather than agreement or anything else. I will keep to the notation proposed here simply to avoid complicating the notation further.

For some cases, no stem feature at all might be present in a lexical item. This could be the case for particular X^0 units which do not participate in head-movement and syntactic word formation.

The presence of a [uSTEM] feature will often coincide with the morphological property of being an affix, since [uSTEM] features will be what drives head-movement.[12] But while being a morphological affix is probably sufficient to ensure the presence of [uSTEM] in the syntactic representation, it is not necessary. The presence of [uSTEM] in a particular lexical item can be simply a variable, contingent feature included in the lexicon of a language. On the other hand, [uSTEM] features may well be induced into the derivation on the basis of other factors, at least in some cases. There is a substantial literature which relates feature "strength" to the richness of inflectional features on the attracting head (Taraldsen 1978, Koeneman & Zeijlstra 2012). This hypothesis could be readily implemented in terms of [uSTEM] feature valuation through a mechanism which connects rich inflection to the presence of a [uSTEM] feature. More nuanced connections between the distribution of [uSTEM] features and other properties of a lexical item might also be considered. For example, Biberauer & Roberts (2008) argue that head-movement in Romance and Germanic languages are both driven by properties of T, but that it is specifically the richness of tense features which matter. If so, then this would imply a connection between tense features and [uSTEM] features.

To sum up, I propose that [uSTEM] features introduced in lexical items constitute obstacles to interpretation which are resolved through valuation of these feature using standard mechanisms. But the resulting valued [STEM] features are also interface-problematic in turn, because all X^0 units which bear the same [STEM] feature belong together for externalization. Let us codify this idea as the S-M interface interpretive principle (6), for future reference.

(6) *Stem Feature Constraint* (SFC)
Terminal items which contain the same [STEM] feature must be realized within a single X^0 category.

Making sense of this constraint requires that the notion of an X^0 category be characterized more precisely. The following recursive definition accomplishes this: (7).

(7) Node α is an X^0 category if and only if
a. α is a terminal node, or
b. α is composed of X^0 categories which contain matching [STEM] features.

12. Since morphemes which bear a [uSTEM] feature will typically be affixes, it would be superfluous to associate them with both [uSTEM] feature and affixal features. Instead, one might suppose that affixal characteristics are assigned to the appropriate units at the PF interface. Even if all [STEM] features are valued at this point, since [uSTEM] feature valuation takes place at the phase level, phasal memory should suffice to allow the original status of the appropriate atoms to be recovered.

How the definition (7) plays out in a particular case can be seen with a word like *uncontroversial*, supposing the structure (8).

(8)

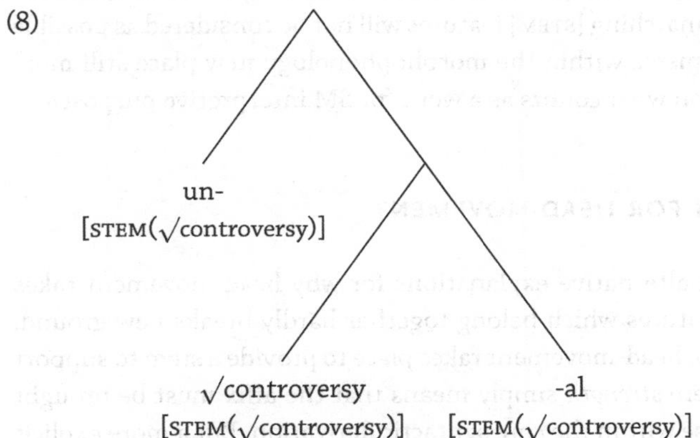

By part a. of the definition in (7), the terminal nodes *un-*, *-al*, and *√controversy* are all X^0 categories. The recursive language in part b. then identifies *controversial* as an X^0 category. The SFC is then satisfied by this structure because both the matching [STEM] features in *controversial* are found within this X^0 category, and the [STEM] feature in *un-* finds a match within its X^0 sister as well. Of course, if either *√controversy* or *-al* were to lack a [STEM] feature, then the node *controversial* would not count as an X^0 category, and the SFC would be violated at the next level of structure.

The SFC will now be the driving force which compels head-movement operations to take place. Note, however, that the SFC is an interface constraint, regulating the legitimacy of syntactic representations. It does not directly constrain the morphological realization of the X^0 units to which it applies. In other words, the SFC is a necessary condition for morphological realization of words, but not a sufficient one. The task of identifying a structure as an actual morphophonological word remains the purview of the morphology. As such, similar X^0 configurations, produced within the syntax and satisfying the SFC, may still be given quite different treatments in the morphological component.

If matching [STEM] features are (one) mechanism which distinguishes complex word structures from phrasal structures, then the [STEM] features become relevant for interpretation at the S-M interface, because it is primarily for the operation of the morphophonology that the difference matters. These features establish what will count as "words" for this interface, so they must be brought close enough to each other by the derivation so that the interface may treat them as such.

In considering how the SFC is to apply to the derivation, it is important to keep in mind that this is a constraint which specifically applies to the interface between the syntax and what comes next in the "externalization" process. This constraint does not ensure full isomorphism between syntactic X^0 units and morphophonological words. Instead, the SFC simply establishes a boundary condition for interpretation at the SM interface—units which are not associated with matching [STEM] features will not be considered as possible SM "words." Mechanisms within the morphophonology may place still more stringent demands on what counts as a word for SM interpretive purposes.

2.3 A MECHANISM FOR HEAD-MOVEMENT

In comparison with alternative explanations for why head-movement takes place, the idea of features which belong together hardly breaks new ground. For Chomsky (1995), head-movement takes place to provide a stem to support a "strong" affix, where *strength* simply means that the affix must be brought together with its base within the core syntactic derivation. But a more explicit model of how "strength" may be operationalized makes it easier to consider in more detail how this concept interacts with other aspects of the derivation. In particular, the claim that two matching [STEM] features must appear together makes it possible to consider what the minimal mechanism for accomplishing this result might look like.

Let us start from the (uncontroversial) premise that head-movement, like feature valuation, Feature Inheritance, and other phase level transformations, is not constrained by the Extension Condition. The Extension Condition is a property of core syntax, but not of the extra phase-level operations which enable externalization. On the other hand, the processes which enable head-movement must not exploit this greater freedom to completely disrupt the structures provided by Merge. So our goal should be a model in which a minimally disruptive, externalization-enabling operation is what makes head-movement possible.

Consider the familiar case of English auxiliary inversion in a wh-question. I assume this involves movement of T to C, as usual. (Cartographic nuance is not important here.) If C in (9a) bears a [uSTEM] feature and T has a valued [STEM] feature, then C will find a match in T and both will end up with a common [STEM(*i*)] feature. This means that the structure (9a) violates the SFC and it must be transformed into a structure in which both [STEM(*i*)]-bearing units appear together. The minimally different structure which satisfies the SFC will be (9b).[13]

13. I ignore here the question of the point in the derivation at which the subject raises from the vP.

(9) a. [wh-XP [C [DP [T vP]]]]
b. [wh-XP [[T C] [DP [T vp]]]]

Or equivalently, in a set-theoretic notation for phrase structure, (10a) is changed to (10b).

(10) a. $\{XP, \{C, \{DP, \{T, vP\}\}\}\}$
b. $\{XP, \{\{C, T\}, \{DP, \{T, vP\}\}\}\}$

The characterization provided in (10) appears to be the least one could say to accommodate the word order in auxiliary inversion contexts. The difference between (10a) and (10b) is that C is replaced by a set made up of C and T. This is very close to what has been often claimed about head-movement, except that the relation of "adjunction" plays no part in (10). (More on this below.) More generally, the structural change realized in head-movement is one in which a constituent α is replaced in a phrase marker by a set which consists of two members: α and another constituent β copied from within the same phrase marker.

(11) *Head-Movement*
$\{\ldots\alpha\ldots\beta\ldots\} \rightarrow \{\ldots\{\alpha, \beta\}\ldots\beta\ldots\}$

In (11), the intended meaning of the ... notation is that β need not be a member of the set which appears as an initial "sister" to α—or vice versa; it may be more deeply embedded, as a member of a member of that set, or as a member of a member of a member, etc. Linear order is, of course, not represented in (11), which refers only to hierarchical phrase structure.

In now-classical generative terminology, the head-movement operation will be a "substitution" transformation, which replaces a specific term with another. In that respect, head-movement resembles feature valuation operations, which also take place at the phase level, and which replace unvalued features with matching valued features. Only the size of what is being replaced differs; feature valuation replaces fairly small units—single features or feature clusters—while head-movement replaces X^0 constituents with something larger. Both operations must be excluded from the core syntax, and both occur only in order to enable interface legibility.[14] On the

14. This formulation is actually consistent with earlier formulations. Chomsky (1994: p. 68) characterizes adjunction as follows: "... when α is adjoined to K, the resulting structure is necessarily [K, K] ... which replaces K in a structure containing K." A different implementation of the idea that head-movement may be a substitution operation appears in Rizzi & Roberts (1989), for whom the target of head-movement is a space reserved in an attracting C position. The model developed here differs in significant respects. The triggering role of the empty space in their analysis is played,

other hand, some feature valuation operations affect semantic interpretation, and head-movement appears not to, for the most part. This implies that head-movement, as formulated in (11), must belong to the externalization process itself and not to the set of phase-level syntactic operations.

Like other operations which effect linearization (Idsardi & Raimy 2013), head-movement will operate within a tree structure subject to strict cyclicity. In other words, the transformation (11) must apply to any smaller constituent within a syntactic structure before it can apply to a larger constituent which contains it. This ensures that head-movement will observe an upwards trajectory, which is evidently empirically necessary.

A very general transformation like (11) always brings with it the potential to overgenerate, producing both the superficial result we desire and some which we do not. The question arises, therefore, whether the derivational impact of this particular head-movement operation can be constrainted on principled grounds. It appears that it can, at least for the most apparent cases. For one thing, since (11) does not specify linear order, or even refer to c-command, it can generate a head-lowering operation as freely as a head-raising one. So head-movement might produce (12) from (10a) as an alternative to (10b). The result will again be a structure in which two X^0 categories—C and T—with the same [STEM] value appear together.

(12) $\{OP, \{C, \{DP, \{\{C, T\}, vP\}\}\}\}$

But in fact, this structure will not produce a legitimate interpretation at the interface, given general principles of how two copies of a single object are processed. The higher C in (12) c-commands the lower C within $\{C, T\}$, and therefore the lower C must be deleted/ignored at the S-M interface. The result then is effectively as if head-movement had not taken place at all, since the only visible copy of C is left distant from the T which it matches [STEM] features with. And the same result will obtain generally, since the initial [uSTEM] valuation operation which produces matching [STEM] features always requires a c-command relationship between the [uSTEM] probe and its [STEM] goal. Head-raising will be possible; head-lowering will not.

When head-raising does take place, the product is a structure in which neither copy of the displaced head c-commands the other, so it cannot be a c-command relationship which controls which copy to pronounce at the S-M interface. The SFC settles the question, though, since deletion of the copy

here, by unification of a particular feature within a local X^0 domain. Rizzi & Roberts rely on the HMC to ensure that the correct head raises up; in my model, this job is done through feature valuation, and is subject to some parametric variation. But the overall impulse is similar, and my proposal is certainly informed by their prior reasoning.

in the derived position will fail to allow both [STEM] feature matches to be pronounced together. Only the original copy can be deleted.

A second potential area of overgeneration with the head-movement transformation would be cases in which any specifier might be replaced by a set containing that specifier plus some other constituent. Clausal subjects, for example, could be replaced by a constituent made up of the subject and a vP. Then (13a) could be transformed into (13b).

(13) a. The visitors may want tea.
b. The visitors want tea may.

This type of result is clearly something which must be avoided. But many of the potentially problematic cases of overgeneration can be eliminated by simply insisting that this transformation be applied only on a Last Resort basis. Such a constraint is appropriate for a mechanism which serves only to externalize phrase structure. Even if the core Merge operation applies freely, the more complex, phase-level operations should apply only because there is a need for them, in order to enable the translation from hierarchical structures to expressive language. At the very least, considerations of enonomy or computational efficiency might rule against applications of operations which cannot help in the task of externalizing a syntactic object.

In that case, the transformation in (11) will take place only in order to solve a problem which would otherwise make externalization impossible, such as a violation of the SFC. The need for externalization might require that an X^0 constituent which violates the SFC should be replaced by one which does not.

Returning to the derivation of English root wh-questions with T to C head-movement, the idea is that C will bear [uSTEM], while English auxiliary verbs (including supportive *do*) bear valued features [STEM(*have*)], [STEM(*may*)], etc. These features are visible to C at the phase level, and so the [uSTEM] feature of C must be valued before the CP phase is complete. (Strictly speaking, valuation of [uSTEM] on the phase head could be left until the next phase level, but as C must find its stem in its sister, valuation will be impossible after the CP phase level.) Like other unvalued features, [uSTEM] acts as a probe feature, and seeks a goal in its domain. In the auxiliary inversion case, the matching goal will be the auxiliary verb in T, so the [uSTEM] feature on C takes on the [STEM] value of T.

The newly valued stem feature in C must now be interpreted to enable externalization. The [STEM] feature contributes to S-M interpretation by identifying constituents as members of the same X^0 constituent, i.e. as words. Two items with the same [STEM] value must therefore be close enough to each other to be combined morphologically into a single word. This requirement is satisfied only if head-movement occurs, meaning the transformation (11) takes place. In the resulting structure, the C, T constituent contains all elements bearing the same [STEM] feature, so externalization can take place successfully.

It should be evident that what I am proposing is very similar to previous models of head-movement. It is really the details of the implementation which are different. Instead of saying that "affixal" heads or "strong" heads trigger head-movement, I claim that heads with a [uSTEM] feature do so. One might question what the difference really amounts to, and if the [uSTEM] feature is just another name for being an affix. In fact, the two terms will often be equivalent, but in a way which requires us to rethink how the grammar encapsulates the affixal status of a terminal element. Commonly and traditionally, the concept "affix" is taken to be a morphological property of morphemes and it is natural to think of affixes as something that morphological operations operate on. Particularly if one adopts some version of Distributed Morphology, it is then easy to associate the affixal character of an element with the role it plays in operations like Vocabulary Insertion. For example, since the regular plural inflection for English nouns is an *-s* suffix, a default Vocabulary Insertion rule of the following form might seem natural: (14).

(14) [PL] → /-s/

And with the affixal status of *-s* identified by the Vocabulary Insertion rule itself, it then follows that the combination of *-s* with a preceding noun into a single word would take place after Vocabulary Insertion, as a reflection of purely morphological properties.

But as discussed already, there are reasons to prefer a driver for head-movement which is visible at the phase level, within the syntactic derivation. And that means that the concept of being an affix must also be relevant to the syntax. In turn, if we are to avoid having duplication of equivalent information in two modules of the grammar, then the affixal status of (some) terminal elements must not be determined at a post-syntactic point in the derivation. In general, operations like Vocabulary Insertion should not introduce this sort of information, except perhaps for exceptional cases. Instead, post-syntactic operations should simply operate on the structures that are fed to them by the Transfer operation (Bromberger & Halle 1989), and these structures will include the [STEM] features which identify word-sized structures for appropriate morphophonological processing.

Postsyntactic operations must have a basis for distinguishing a root from an affix—in the simplest binary structures—and the question then arises how this can be ensured if only [STEM] features are provided at the interface from syntax. For example, auxiliary *had* in a sentence with a 3rd person, plural subject should presumably have a structure like (15) for externalization. (The order of the auxilary base and T is not yet fixed at this point.)

(15)

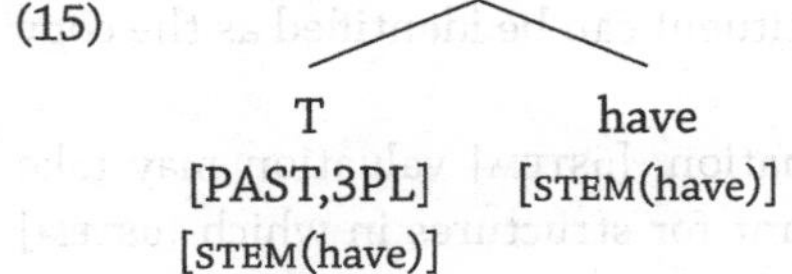

Nothing explicitly identifies T as an affix in this structure, but there is still enough information provided to distinguish T from *have* for morphophonological purposes. Since the value of the common [STEM(have)] feature is actually *have*—one of the two components of this structure—that detail can be used to establish that *have* must be the stem, and T, in turn, must be an affix.

Returning to the syntactic details, a model of head-movement driven by [STEM] features implies a specific order of operations. Consider how head-movement will be realized in English auxiliary inverting questions, for example. Since head-movement takes place only when necessary, it cannot occur before [uSTEM] valuation is completed. What is more, head-movement actually destroys the configuration which would allow [uSTEM] valuation to take place (along with other probe/goal operations), since C no longer c-commands its TP complement after it is replaced by the constituent C, T. For the same reason, head-movement can only take place after any operations which require C to c-command TP are complete. This conclusion may provide a partial explanation for the observation that head-movement has very limited semantic consequences.

Besides preventing head-movement from replacing a specifier, the [STEM] features may be exploited in the derivation to prevent other unwelcome types of overgeneration. Consider the verb phrase structure (16).

(16)

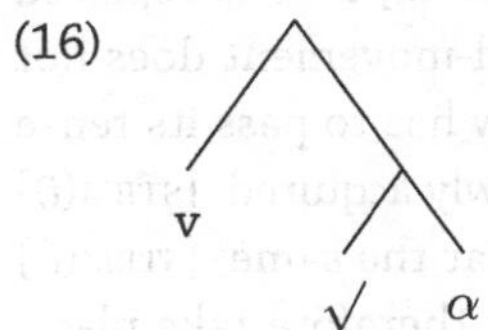

The normal role of head-movement in this structure is simply to raise the root to v. But complex X^0 units can undergo head-movement and α in (16) could be a small constituent, even monomorphemic, perhaps a pronoun or a small adjective or noun. In other words, given only the structure in (16), the sister of v is as small as many complex X^0 constituents. Nevertheless, it should normally not be possible for the entire sister of v to undergo head-movement in this configuration.

But if constituents are only identified as X^0 units (for head-movement) when they bear identical [STEM] features, then this problem cannot arise. If $\surd$ and α do not both contain [STEM(*i*)], then they cannot count together as a single "head", so only the smaller $\surd$ constituent can be identified as the copy source in the head-movement operation.

Unlike the head-movement transformation, [uSTEM] valuation may take place relatively early. And this is important for structures in which [uSTEM] valuation must interact with the Feature Inheritance operation. Consider how verb raising to T will take place in this model. If [uSTEM] valuation and head-movement takes place only at the phase level, then head-movement into T cannot occur before the CP phase is constructed. This is not a problem, happily. If C bears a [uSTEM] feature, then Feature Inheritance allows that feature to be passed along to T, just as C can pass tense and agreement features to T.[15] The same cannot be true of [uSTEM] features, which must appear only in T. So consider the derivation of French (17) in this light. (The position of the adverb *bientôt* 'soon' shows that verb raising to T actually takes place, as the adverb is found at the left edge of vP (Emonds 1978, Pollock 1989).)

(17) Marie ven-dra bientôt le camion.
Marie sell-FUT soon the truck
'Marie will sell the truck soon.'

If C bears [uSTEM], then C will probe for a matching [STEM] feature in the structure (18).

(18) [C [Marie T [bientôt Marie ven- le camion]]]

At this point in the derivation, T lacks any stem feature, as well as tense and agreement features, so C can probe past T and find the [STEM] feature in *ven-* as its goal. Feature valuation then takes place, and [uSTEM] in C is replaced with the [STEM(*i*)] value (=[STEM(*ven*)]) from *ven-*. Head-movement does not take place at this point, as already discussed. But C now has to pass its tense and agreement features to T, and this will affect the newly acquired [STEM(*i*)] feature as well. The end result is that T and *ven-* will bear the same [STEM(*i*)] feature, and the head-movement transformation must therefore take place, post-syntactically, to bring them together.[16]

The situation will be slightly more complex when both verb-raising and T-to-C movement must take place, as in (19).

15. An anonymous reviewer notes that the effect of Feature Inheritance on the [uSTEM] feature must be more absolute than is found sometimes with agreement features. In some Germanic dialects, Feature Inheritance leaves a second copy of some agreement features in C, so that agreement morphology is located in both C and T (Goeman 1980, Bennis & Haegeman 1984). This cannot be the case for the [uSTEM] case, since the verb in a simple declarative sentence in French does not raise to C from T.

16. The ordering of the [uSTEM] valuation and FI does not affect the result here.

(19) Pourquoi ven-dra-(t-)elle le camion?
why sell-FUT-she the truck
'Why will she sell the truck?'

In this case, the correct result is derived only if C bears two distinct [uSTEM] features: one for the finite T, the other because C is in a root interrogative clause. Feature valuation must apply for each [uSTEM] feature, but not at the same time. The first [uSTEM] valuation operation acts in exactly the same way as for (17), so C probes for a [STEM] feature, finds it in *be*, and Feature Inheritance passes it down to T. But then the second [uSTEM] valuation operation must apply, *after* Feature Inheritance has occurred. At this point, the structure includes a [STEM] feature on T, by virtue of the early (phase-level) operations on the first [uSTEM] feature. C therefore takes its [STEM] value from T, which is also the [STEM] value of *ven-*. And the result is a single [STEM] value on three distinct heads, all of which must now be combined to satisfy the demands of the S-M interface.

The last stage in the derivation will therefore include two separate applications of the head-movement transformation (11). The first must replace T with the constituent {*(d)ra*, *ven*}. The second must replace C with the constituent {C, {*(d)ra*, *ven*}}.

The order of these two applications of head-movement need not be stipulated, because head-movement applies cyclically. The operation which replaces T must precede the one which replaces C, because T and the verb are contained within a TP constituent which is itself contained within the larger CP where the later head-movement operation can take place.

Much the same will be true of the Swedish verb-second example (20), already discussed.

(1c) På tisdag äter Ingmar inte kött.
on Tuesday eats Ingmar not meat
'On Tuesday Ingmar does not eat meat.'

Recall that the finite verb does not raise to T in embedded clauses, but it must do so in root verb-second clauses like (1c). In this case, then C will transfer a [uSTEM] feature to T only in a non-verb-second context, and it keeps a second [uSTEM] feature for itself. The presence of two [uSTEM] features then ensures head-movement will replace T with the {verb, T} constituent, and then C with {{verb, T} , C}.[17]

17. In the multiple Feature-Inheritance model of Branigan (2020), the use of Feature Inheritance to pass [uSTEM] features downwards from C will be more systematic. Verb-second structures are derived when C transfers all its [uSTEM] features downwards, but the closest recipient of [uSTEM] will be a discourse-head like Top or Foc, to which the verb will ultimately move

In English, true V-to-T raising normally takes place only with the auxiliary verbs *have* and *be*, and their principal verb counterparts (Pollock 1989), as in (20).

(20) a. Jenna probably closed the door.
 b. Jenna has evidently completed her correspondence.
 c. Jenna is certainly in her office.

With simple past and present tenses, T must therefore bear a valued [STEM] feature. Affix hopping is purely a post-syntactic phenomenon, in this light. In all contexts in which affix-hopping does not take place, the valued [STEM] feature for non-modal T is expressed by realizing T as a form of *do*. But this raises new questions about how *have* and *be* can raise to T at all. (These questions are not unique to this model—only the shape of the answer is.)

But if head-movement is driven by the presence of [STEM] pairs, then the corollary must be that *have* and *be* raise for the same reason, despite the necessity for past and present T to bear its own [STEM] feature. But the paradox can be reconciled only if T can bear *two* distinct 'stem' features in this context. Finite T naturally bears the [STEM] feature (assigned by C), but in the context where *have* or *be* also appear in the clause, then C can evidently supply a *second, unvalued* [uSTEM] feature to T, simply as a quirk of English. (In contrast, Swedish does not arbitrarily require auxiliary verbs to raise to T.) The effect of the [uSTEM] feature in T is that the closest auxiliary verb provides a [STEM] value, and then head-movement must subsequently bring the two together. In this case, of course, the phonetic interpretation of T will be as an affix, just as it is in affix-hopping contexts.

Quotative inversion provides an additional exception to the general English pattern, since verbs other than *have* and *be* raise to T in this context (Branigan & Collins 1993, Collins & Branigan 1997).

(21) a. "What's the score?" asked the newcomers.
 b. "Don't forget the cookies!" yelled Percy.

In this case, too, the explanation for exceptional verb raising must involve a [uSTEM] feature which is not otherwise available, but which here is supplied to T through Feature Inheritance from C. In this case, it is a particular type of C which must bear responsibility for the exceptional syntactic behavior. Following Collins (1996), we may suppose that the fronted "quote" occupies the specifier position in CP, where it must serve as a co-label to a matching complementizer.[18]

18. Alternatively, as proposed in Collins & Branigan (1997), the specifier is an empty quotative operator, associated with the true quote in a larger context in which the inversion clause functions as a parenthetical phrase.

(22)

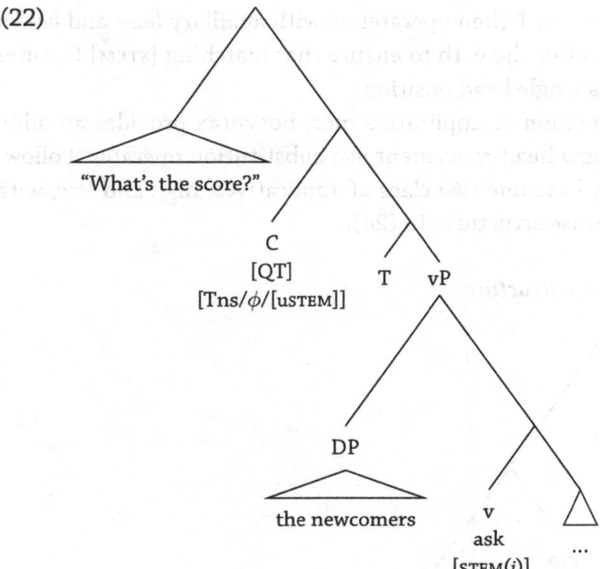

This particular *quotative* complementizer then appears to have the option of passing this novel [uSTEM] feature to T, which is then valued through Agree with the quotative verb itself. Thus, (22) becomes (23).

(23)

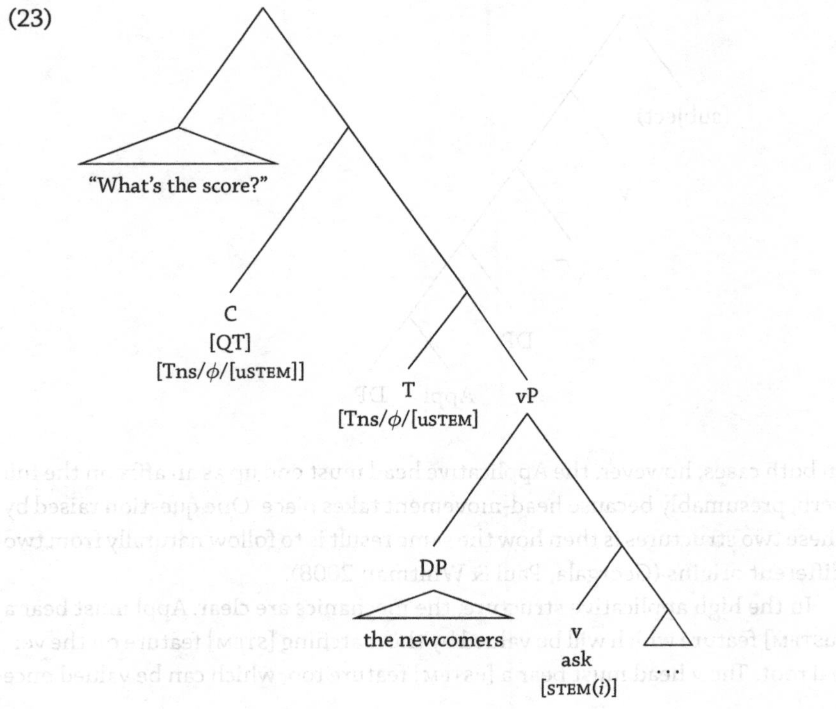

The new [uSTEM] feature on T then operates as with auxiliary *have* and *be*—it triggers head-movement of the verb to ensure that matching [STEM] features are always realized in a single head position.

The general phenomenon of applicative morphosyntax provides an additional illustration of how head-movement *qua* substitution operates. Following Pylkkänen (2002), I assume two class of applicatives: high and low, with the associated verb phrase structures in (24).

(24) a. *High applicative structure*

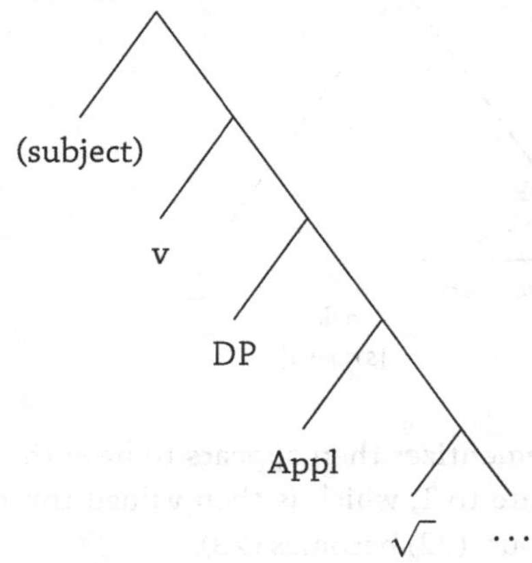

b. *Low applicative structure*

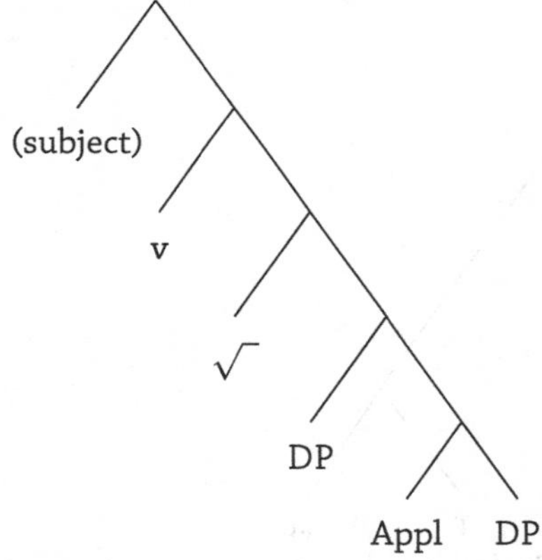

In both cases, however, the Applicative head must end up as an affix on the full verb, presumably because head-movement takes place. One question raised by these two structures is then how the same result is to follow naturally from two different origins (Georgala, Paul & Whitman 2008).

In the high applicative structure, the mechanics are clear. Appl must bear a [uSTEM] feature which will be valued by the matching [STEM] feature on the verbal root. The v head must bear a [uSTEM] feature too, which can be valued once the [STEM] feature on Appl is established. So v, Appl, and the verbal root end up with the same [STEM] feature, and head-movement must then bring them together at the phase level. The first head-movement operation will replace Appl with $\left\{\sqrt{}, \text{Appl}\right\}$; with the second, v is replaced by $\left\{v, \left\{\sqrt{}, \text{Appl}\right\}\right\}$. The end result is that all three X^0 units bearing the same [STEM] feature are combined into a single unit, to be given morphological interpretation. The structure does not specify the linear order for the three terminal units. Nor does it identify what the actual morphological root of the resulting verb will be. These details are left to the morphology to work out. Typically, of course, the morphological response is to take the verbal root as the morphological root, to which Appl is adjoined, and then v, as in the Chichewa example (25).

(25) Mavuto a-na-umb-ir-a mpeni mtsuko. (Baker 1988b)
Mavuto SP-PST-mold-APPL-Asp knife waterpot
'Mavuto molded the waterpot with a knife.'

For low applicative structures, the correct derivation will not obtain if the attracting head is always an affix, and the attracted, a root, since the opposite is actually the case in this construction. Instead, the applicative head—which is certainly a morphological affix—must be allowed to bear an inherent valued [STEM] feature. In turn, the verbal root must be able to bear either an inherent valued [STEM] feature or [uSTEM], freely. When an applicative structure is formed, the root must bear [uSTEM], or the derivation cannot converge. The [uSTEM] feature of the root will then find a match in Appl and take its value. As always, v bears [uSTEM], which can be valued by the (derived) [STEM] feature of the verbal root. Once again, two [uSTEM] valuation operations produce a structure in which all three heads bear the same [STEM] feature. Head-movement must then replace the verbal root with $\left\{\sqrt{}, Appl\right\}$, and v will be replaced with $\left\{v, \left\{\sqrt{}, Appl\right\}\right\}$. At this point, of course, the original height distinction between the verbal root and Appl will be irrelevant to how the structure is interpreted by the morphology, which sees only the complex X^0 structure. And as this structure is actually identical to the one produced for high applicatives, the morphological result can be expected to be much the same, as evidenced by the Chimwiinii example in (26).[19]

19. See McGinnis (2001) for arguments that Chimwiinii is a language with low applicatives.

(26) Ni-mw-andik-ił-il-e Nuuru xati.
SP-OP-write-APPL-ASP-FV Nuru letter
'I wrote Nuru a letter.'

(Kisseberth & Abasheikh 1974)

The process of X^0 formation through [uSTEM] valuation need not always include a step of head-movement. Consider the abstract phase structure (27), where π is a phase head and α and β are X^0 categories, possibly terminal elements.

(27)

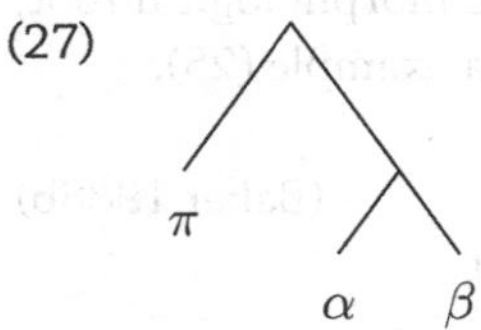

If FI transfers a [uSTEM] feature from π to α, then the S-M interface requirements will be satisfied only if β bears [STEM], so that probing α can find a goal. But once feature valuation has taken place, the constituent made of α and β will automatically be identified as a new X^0 category. The head-movement transformation cannot do anything to bring α and β closer together, and as a Last Resort operation, it is barred from applying vacuously.[20]

The existing literature on syntactic movement often employs the term "attraction" as a metaphor for the syntactic force which leads one head to raise towards another. While the mechanics proposed here are somewhat different from what other models have proposed, the term itself is quite useful as a terminological shortcut, and I will use it occasionally in the discussions which follow. But coinciding with a different set of principles which ultimately give rise to head-movement in this model, what the term "attraction" refers to must be different as well, particularly since there is no immediate, direct relationship between the [uSTEM] valuation operation and head-movement *per se*. So when I say that X *attracts* Y, the reader should understand this as referring primarily to a [uSTEM] valuation operation, which must ultimately be followed up at the point of Externalization by the head-movement operation which must bring the matching [STEM] features together. Attraction is then not an actual operation, but rather the pairing of two separate operations by the necessity that the S-M output be legitimate.

The model sketched out above is similar in many respects to what has been said previously about head-movement in minimalist syntax, and even in the Government-and-Binding theory. I replace the concept of "affixal status" (and

20. The consequence is that in the general head-movement rule (11), the $\{\ldots\beta\ldots\}$ member of the initial set/structure cannot be identical to β itself.

derivational look-ahead) with a particular syntactic feature, and I posit that head-movement is a phasal operation rather than stylistic or core syntactic. But the differences between this model and others are pretty subtle. One substantial difference, though, involves the internal structure of the constituent formed by head-movement. My claim is that two symmetrical X^0 sisters are established. In contrast, most of the previous literature has supposed that an adjunction configuration is created, where the lower head adjoins to the higher one, which continues to project.

The adjunction approach to head-movement is required in any theory based on X-bar premises. If phrase structure is always endocentric, then the head of a phrase must be inviolate. Adjunction of a raising head to an existing head is a way to preserve X-bar structure, because the target of head-movement is largely unaffected by the operation. Thus, T-to-C movement does not affect the CP status of a question, and verb raising to T leaves T as the head of the clause.

But this theory-internal desideratum becomes moot once the underlying X-bar theory is abandoned. As Chomsky (2013, 2015) emphasizes, X-bar premises introduce unwanted complications into core syntax, and the empirical effects of the X-bar premises can be derived with other mechanisms. In the labeling theory that he proposes as an alternative, many of the relevant structures are exocentric, and even endocentric structures do not obtain their categorial "label" from a head until the phase level.

In such a theory, it makes no difference to the category of a phrase if the head is altered late in the derivation, as long as the label can be identified at the right moment. And when a constituent is endocentric, and gets its label by identifying a feature matching relationship between two sisters, there is no head to worry about, so changes to one of the X^0 categories can have no effect.[21]

Again, the implications can be readily seen by verb raising to T, as in (17). Before the verb raises to T, but after feature valuation, and Feature Inheritance take place, the structure of the clause will be (28).

21. In Chomsky's (2015) account of *that*-trace effects, the subject is not permitted to raise within the CP phase because it must remain in the position where it contributes to the label of the sentence. In that sense, a part of the label must remain intact, which might suggest that T should not be altered by head-movement during the derivation of the clausal phase, contrary to what is claimed here. But head-movement does not *remove* T from the structure, and the result of head-movement is that T becomes a part of a new X^0 constituent which contains all of the content of T, so nothing is taken away from the structure by this operation, which makes head-movement different from subject displacement.

(28)

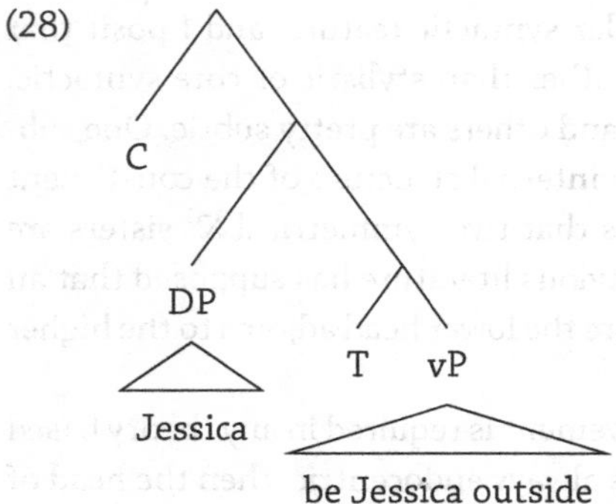

Within this structure, T and *Jessica* match in ϕ features, and T and *be* have the same [STEM] feature. The former allows a label to be assigned to the sister of C (the sentence). Once this label is assigned, head movement can replace T with {v, T} for the S-M interface.

For head-movement of the lexical root to *v*, Chomsky (2015) derives a comparable conclusion. He observes that the morphological result of root raising is not adjunction of the root to *v*, but rather adjunction of *v* to the root. Therefore, the target of head-movement cannot simply be adjoined to. What is more, he argues, the end result of root raising must be that *v* no longer c-commands its original complement, and is therefore effectively "deleted" as the head of the vP phase. The same is true in the model developed here, since replacement of *v* with $\left\{v, \sqrt{\ }\right\}$ will ensure that *v* does not c-command anything else within the vP. The effects will therefore be the same as in Chomsky's specific analysis.

While clitics are not my primary concern in this study, it is well established that some varieties of head-movement can transport a clitic along with its host to a higher head. A general model of head-movement must accommodate this phenomenon. English negative enclitic *n't* undergoes this type of movement when T raises to C, as in (29).

(29) a. Mightn't the pudding be ready yet?
b. Didn't you cash the cheque?
c. Hadn't they replied to your emails?
d. Isn't she lovely?

The ride-along step in the derivation is easily characterized. At some point before T-to-C head-movement takes place, *n't* is attached to T, presumably with adjunction, and C values its [uSTEM] feature from T. The head-movement operation then makes the substitution, replacing C with a new set consisting of C and a copy of the full T, which includes the adjoined negator.

More intricate questions arise concerning how head-movement applies at the earlier stage in the derivation when the clitic is adjoined to T, particularly when a lower head will also raise to T, as in (29c,d). If *n't* adjunction takes place before *have* or *be* raises, then the head-movement operation must replace only the *lower* "segment" of T. Otherwise, *n't* would belong to the T half of the new set: {have, -edn't}. But this structure attaches T to the clitic more closely than to the verb, and this is the opposite of what the morphology seems to expect. In fact, the suppletive form *is* in (29d) should be impossible unless *be* is attached directly to T. The implication is that only the minimal X^0 component serves as the target to be replaced in head-movement. For example, the effect of the auxiliary raising head-movement operation for (29c) is that (30a) is transformed into (30b) when *-ed* is replaced by {have, -ed}. But it is the maximal T^0 which is used to replace C in the next step, where < n't, {have, -ed} > is introduced.

(30) a. [C [she [$_T$ [$_T$ -ed] n't] have replied to your emails]
     b. [C [she [$_T$ [have [$_T$ -ed]] n't] have replied to your emails]

Similar conclusions can be drawn from French complex inversion structures like (31), where again T-to-C head-movement carries a clitic upwards (Den Besten 1983).

(31) a. Les ont=ils vendus?
     them have=they sold
     'Have they sold them?'
     b. Quand en écri-rez=vous enfin le dernier chapitre?
     when of.them write-FUT.2p=you at.last the last chapter
     'When are you finally writing the last chapter?'

In this case, movement of the clitic pronouns has long been established as a part of the core syntactic derivation. For example, movement of clitic pronouns cancels intervention effects on A-movement (Rizzi 1986). It follows that they are adjoined to T before the phase level, and hence before verb raising to T takes place.

Once again, substitution of a more complex set for the T target must replace only the minimal segment in the adjunction structure, because only then will the clitic pronouns remain outside the derived tense-inflected verb. But when T raises to C, it must be the maximal T^0 which is included in the new structure.

On the flip side, clitic adjunction to the target of head-movement also must occur, and this will typically precede head-movement. For example, French clitic pronouns raise to finite T; this must take place in the core syntactic derivation, since pronoun movement interacts with participial agreement (like wh-movement does) (Kayne 1989), and since pronoun displacement cancels out defective intervention effects in raising constructions (Rizzi 1986).

(32) a. Les 20 premières pages de son roman, Luc les a déja
the first 20 pages of his novel Luc them has already
re-écrites.
re-written/Fem.Pl

b. Luc lui semblait avoir du talent.
Luc 3s/Dat seemed to.have of.the talent
'Luc seemed to her to have talent.'

In (32a), clitic *les* must adjoin to T before head-movement replaces T with {avoir, *T*}, and in (32b), the same is true of *lui* and head-movement of *sembler* to T. Happily, this is entirely consistent with the model of head-movement developed here, as long as what is replaced is the unit to which the clitic is adjoined, and not the larger one which contains the clitic as well. Assuming "category/segment" terminology, head-movement must replace the lower segment of T, and not the entire category.

2.4 DERIVING THE HEAD MOVEMENT CONSTRAINT

With a set of mechanisms now in place as a general description of what takes place in the phenomenon of head-movement, we may return to the critical question of what concept of locality is embodied in the head-movement. The typical empirical role played by the HMC is to block derivations in which one head skips past another to appear in a third, as in the unacceptable examples in (33).

(33) a. *John was have *t* working on this problem.
b. *Be John may *t* working on this problem?

In (33a), the second auxiliary raises to T, skipping past the closer one. The polar question in (33b) is formed by movement of auxiliary *be* to C, instead of moving the modal in T.

For such cases, the HMC might be viewed as a variety of a familiar locality constraint; Rizzi (1990) argues that the HMC might be a case of Relativized Minimality.

Other superiority effects are derived in the labeling theory from the interaction of Agree and the labeling algorithm. Take A-movement from object position, for example. In a double object passive structure, it must be the higher object which raises to merge with T: (34).

(34) a. Jed was given the book.
b. *The book was given Jed.

The constrast is explained as follows. The unvalued ϕ-features on T must be valued through an Agree operation which identifies the closest nominal as the matching goal, i.e. *Jed*. While either *Jed* or *the book* may merge as sisters to TP, the result will be grammatical only if the two sisters can combine their ϕ-features to form a label for the dominating node. Since T has already agreed with *Jed*, labeling is therefore successful only if it is *Jed* which raises.[22]

The same approach can be extended to explain the superiority effect in head-movement. If head-movement takes place in order to allow two [STEM] features to appear together, then locality of head-movement may be derived from constraints on valuation of [uSTEM] features. In that case, head-movement may be left as a maximally general transformation operating at the phase level.

In the base structure (35a), T can only value its [uSTEM] feature with *have* as the matching goal category, so *-ed* will acquire [STEM(*i*)]. But then the labeling problem for the mother of T remains unresolved, because valuation alone does not make a category with [STEM] a legitimate structure at the S-M interface.

(35) a. John -ed+[uSTEM] have+ [STEM(*i*)] been working on this problem.
b. John [have+ [STEM(*i*)] -ed+ [STEM(*i*)]] have+ [STEM(*i*)] been working on this problem.

In (35b), though, the two sisters *have* and *-ed* combine as a single constituent.

The superiority effect in movement of auxiliary verbs to T now follows, but the HMC is more restrictive. Something which seems to have gone unnoticed in the literatures is that the HMC functions both as a locality constraint and as an antilocality constraint, whenever a phrase in which the head is raised also contains material outside the first projection. In particular, the general principle which ensures that X^0 movement is a head-to-head operation also ensures that modifiers adjoined to a category do not interfere with that movement.[23] Consider the (36) examples.

22. As an anomymous reviewer points out, the existence of British variants of English in which (34b) would be acceptable does not immediately follow from this approach. One might suppose that speakers who accept such sentences have a grammar in which the more distant second object can still serve as a goal for the T probe to value its ϕ features. Possibly T is able to agree twice in such grammars. Another option might be that the first object—*Jed* in (34)—may include only a defective ϕ feature complex, associated with inherent Case, so that valuation with the second object is necessary. In any case, the full working out of how these structures are to be treated appears somewhat peripheral to the issue of how head-movement can be modeled.

23. An anonymous reviewer notes that ordering constraints among modifiers can be used to argue against an adjunction analysis, as in Cinque (1999). In my opinion, the

(36) a. We may [$_{vP}$ possibly [$_{vP}$ be late]].
b. We are [$_{vP}$ probably [$_{vP}$ *t* late]].

The modifier *possibly* in (36a) is adjoined to the vP.[24] (If it were taken to be adjoined to a higher category with a silent head, the conclusion would be the same.) T need not be filled by the verb in this sentence because the modal auxiliary is not affixal, so *be* remains within vP. But in (36b), T must be filled, so *be* raises up. Notice, though, that the modifier does not intervene to block this movement, even though the adverb is certainly closer to T than *be* is. If the purpose of verb raising is to supply a base to which the affix can attach, then the adverb, which is an independent word, should be the sort of category which might intervene. But the fact that it does not do so follows from the HMC, as long as this principle ensures that only head-to-head movement is allowed for X^0 categories.

Given this Janus-like character for the HMC, it is difficult to imagine that this constraint can be formulated directly in terms of relationships between X^0 constituents in a structure. The property of being a head must also play a part, as Travis originally observed.[25]

In the labeling theory, being a head equates to serving as the label for a category. In earlier models, it is taken for granted that features of the head are visible on its "projection." Translated into labeling theoretic terminology, this implies that features of the label should be accessible for operations on the phrase. As a corollary, labeling operations must then ensure that any search operation from outside a labeled phrase will find its match on a phrase label

alternative explanation elucidated in Rice (2006) is more persuasive for many cases of such ordering constraints. In other words, these may often be attributed to semantic constraints, rather than purely syntactic ones.

24. The formal status of adjunction in a labeling-theoretic model is as yet unsettled. Chomsky (2004) suggests adjunction is a "pair-merge" operation, which creates an ordered pair rather than a binary set. If this formalism were adopted, then the antilocality effect of the HMC would ensure that one of the two members of an ordered pair is privileged as the domain from which a head can be extracted. Here I will continue to use the "category-segment" terminology of May (1977) in order to keep the discussion more accessible, but little would change in the approach being developed here if a pair-merge alternative were pursued, as far as I can tell.

25. Similar conclusions have been drawn at several points in the subsequent literature. For example, Matushansky (2006) draws similar conclusions about locality in head-movement, although her analysis of what actually occurs in head-movement is very different. Matushansky proposes that head-movement is driven by a feature-checking operation involved in satisfying the selectional features of a head by its complement. As the complement is the sister of a head, head-movement ends up as a possibility only involving heads and the heads of their complements.

Similarly, Pesetsky & Torrego (2000) propose that head-movement may take place only when movement of the phrasal projection of the moving head is impossible. For them, complements cannot raise to become specifiers of their X^0 sister, because merging the same categories twice is impossible (Chomsky 1994). Again, the effect is that only the head of a complement can undergo movement to the next head up.

before it encounters the labeling head itself. Labeling heads should thereby become inaccessible for search operations.[26]

In that light, consider how [uSTEM] valuation on T will be satisfied in (37a), with the corresponding base structure (37b). Here, and in subsequent tree representations, I use a double line to indicate categories where two segments are involved, i.e. for the host in adjunction. (This will matter more when multiple head-movement structures are examined.) This is a structure where the principal verb *be* must raise: (37).

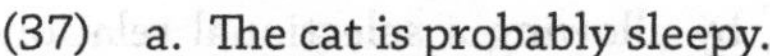

(37) a. The cat is probably sleepy.

b.

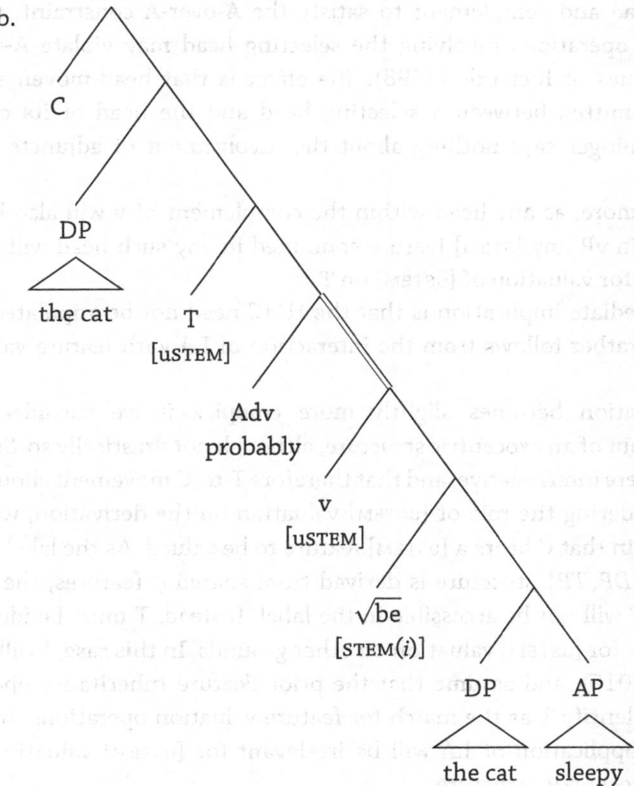

In order for the property of being a head to play a part in head-movement, the Labeling Algorithm must supply labels for the current phrase before head-movement takes place. In my terms, LA must take place before [uSTEM] valution occurs. In this case, v must be the label for the node immediately above. And since adjuncts are ignored by LA, v will also be the label for the

26. As Preminger (2018) notes, this conclusion is drawn already by Hornstein (2009) and Roberts (2010), albeit in models which do not suppose a labeling operation.

node immediately above that one.[27] Now if v has its [uSTEM] feature valued by $\sqrt{\text{be}}$, then this value should be accessible at the topmost node with the v label as well. Minimal search will ensure that the T probe finds the (topmost) label for the "vP" before it looks further inside the phrase, so the adjoined adverb can never be considered as a possible goal for [uSTEM] valuation.

Preminger (2017) draws a similar conclusion, albeit in a slightly different framework. For him, head-movement is sensitive to an A-over-A condition which ensures that head-movement will be impossible generally, since heads are always contained inside a larger category of the same type. But then he includes a loophole within his model, by allowing a selectional relation between head and complement to satisfy the A-over-A constraint, so that subsequent operations involving the selecting head may violate A-over-A, along the lines of Richards (1998). The effect is that head-movement will only be permitted between a selecting head and the head of its complement. (Preminger says nothing about the involvement of adjuncts in this model.)

What is more, as any head within the complement of v will also be contained within vP, any [STEM] feature contained in any such head will also be inaccessible for valuation of [uSTEM] on T.

The immediate implication is that the HMC need not be stipulated as an axiom, but rather follows from the interaction of LA with feature valuation operations.

The situation becomes slightly more complex if we consider head-movement out of an exocentric structure, although not drastically so. Suppose C in (37b) were interrogative, and that therefore T-to-C movement should take place. Considering the role of [uSTEM] valuation on the derivation, we must suppose again that C bears a [uSTEM] feature to be valued. As the label for the exocentric $\{DP, TP\}$ structure is derived from shared ϕ features, the [STEM] feature on T will not be accessible in the label. Instead, T must be identified as the source for [uSTEM] valuation on other grounds. In this case, I will follow Chomsky (2015), and assume that the prior Feature Inheritance operation suffices to identify T as the match for feature valuation operations. In other words, the application of LA will be irrelevant for [uSTEM] valuation from within an exocentric structure.

27. Alternatively, if labeling were implemented in a model where adjunction is a reflection of Pair-Merge, as noted in footnote 24, then this would mean that one member of an ordered pair is ignored by the labeling algorithm, so that the other member will always provide the label for the whole.

More questions arise if we consider successive cyclic head-movement derivations. In the Swedish, French, and English structures where the verb raises to T, then to C, it is C which provides the multiple [uSTEM] features driving movement. The model of multiple head-movement which will be introduced below will exploit the idea that a single head can bear multiple [uSTEM] features. But in Swedish etc., multiple [uSTEM] features can be introduced in a single phase head only if FI then distributes them among multiple heads, i.e. T and C. To understand why, consider what would happen if C retained two [uSTEM] features, in an English structure like (38).

(38)

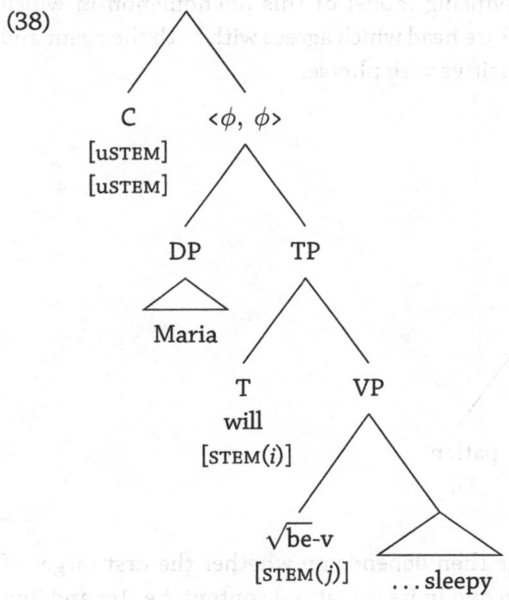

Since the features of a labeling category are accessible at the node which uses it as its label, the [STEM] features of T are accessible at TP. Therefore, when C probes for a value for one [uSTEM] feature , it finds one at TP. When C probes for a value for its second [uSTEM] feature, it will not find one before TP. In order to value the second [uSTEM] feature, it must find a new search path which leads to a more distant match, and as none is available, there can be no valuation of multiple [uSTEM] features on a single probe.

It is instructive to compare this situation with other cases of multiple feature valuation with a single probe. In some languages, a single head can value multiple sets of ϕ features, and this requires derivations which can be compared to one in which multiple [uSTEM] features might be valued.

In Innu-aimûn, "Theme" suffixes are sensitive to the features of both subjects and objects.

(39) a. *Tshi-mûpishtân.*
tshi=mûpishtu-i-n.
2-visit-2>3-PRES
'You visit him/her.'
b. *Tshi-mûpishtuk^{u}.*
tshi=mûpishtu-k^{u}.
2-visit-3>2
'S/he visits you.'

Oxford (2015) develops a convincing model of this phenomenon in which Theme morphology realizes a Voice head which agrees with both the agent and the patient arguments in a transitive verb phrase.

(40)

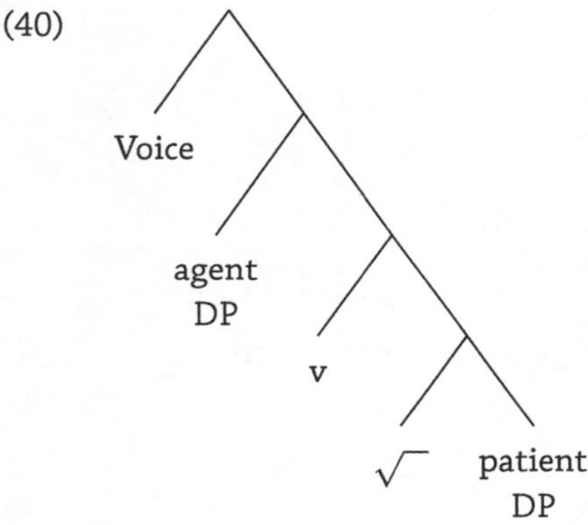

The realized form of the Theme then depends on whether the first target of agreement is richer than the second in its ϕ-featural content, i.e. 1st and 2nd persons are richer than 3rd persons.

The realization of the Voice head is never sensitive to what is found *inside* an argument of the verb. For example, while an agentive subject may contain a possessor, the features of the possessor are irrelevant to the Theme morphology.

(41) a. *Tshi-kâui mûpishtuâu.*
tshi=kâui mûpishtu-â-u.
2-mother visit-3>3-PRES
'Your mother visits him/her.'
b. **Tshi-kâui mûpishtuk^{u}.*
tshi=kâui mûpishtu-k^{u}.
2-mother visit-2>3-PRES
'Your mother visits him/her.'

c. **Tshi-kâui nâpâk*ᵘ.

tshi=kâui nâpa-kᵘ.
2=mother sleep-3>2
'Your mother sleeps.'

The ungrammaticality of (41b,c) follows if Voice cannot look inside the agentive DP to agree with the possessor, even though Voice does agree multiple times. The question then is why the features of the possessor are not accessible to a Voice probe while the features of the object are. And the obvious difference is that the possessor is contained inside a DP which is itself an agreement target for Voice. Evidently, once a probe finds a target to agree with, a search path is identified which cannot be traversed a second time for that same type of agreement. In order for the same probe to value a second set of ϕ features, it must follow a different search path. In contrast, for the grammatical examples in (39), the first match—the agent DP—is found with a path which looks at the complement of Voice, then at its DP daughter. The second agreement operation cannot make use of the identical search path to find a new match, so it must look at the other daughter of the complement of Voice, and then keep searching within that node until it finds its new match in the object DP.[28]

The same limitation should apply when a probe has multiple [uSTEM] features to value, so that a second [STEM] value should not be accessible inside a category which has already served as a valuation target.

To sum up, while HMC has certainly proven its value as a strong descriptive generalization, it must ultimately be based on premises with less arbitrary ontologies. premises. In turn, head-movement which satisfies the HMC must be driven by derivational pressures which have some independent motivation. I maintain that both desiderata can be met if we attribute the trigger for head movement to a [uSTEM] valuation operation, and if [uSTEM] valuation is constrained by Minimal Search after LA applies. Valuation of a [uSTEM] feature then creates a structure in which only head-movement will normally enable interpretation to succeed at the S-M interface.

Unlike Travis's original formulation, the model of HMC which has just been presented will not apply to all cases of movement of an X^0 constituent. Since it is not X^0 movement which falls under the HMC, but rather [uSTEM] valuation, it follows that any cases of X^0 movement which are not driven by the need to bring matching [STEM] features together will fall outside this theory. If other syntactic forces trigger movement of a category which happens to be word-sized, then we should expect that type of movement to be constrained in the same way as phrasal movement is. In particular, an approach which derives

28. In other words, reuse of the same search path would constitute an "A-over-A" violation (Chomsky 1965), if such a constraint is a part of the computational system.

HMC effects from valuation of [uSTEM] features will not apply to familiar cases of long head-movement (Borsley, Rivero & Stephens 1996, Lema & Rivero 1989, Rivero 1993). This is all to the good, since movement of the X^0 constituent in such cases is presumably not motivated by the same factors as regular, compliant head-movement.

2.5 ENABLING MULTIPLE HEAD-MOVEMENT

At this point, the foundation has been laid for a model of grammer in which multiple head-movement will be possible. Derivations which employ this type of operation must be limited, since multiple head-movement appears not to occur in all languages, so some parametric control must be involved. I propose the following. In some languages, in some contexts, as a matter of parametric variation, the syntactic context in which a [uSTEM] probe is permitted to locate its matching goal is different. In these languages, [uSTEM] valuation operations take place before the labeling algorithm applies. Up until the point when LA applies, there is no "head" for a phrasal category, and no features are accessible in a non-terminal node. The implication is that a [uSTEM] probe will not find its match in a phrasal sister, so it must look within its complement for the closest [STEM] bearing category. When this occurs, head-movement may violate the HMC, simply because a probe can look further into its complement to find a match.

I will refer to this type of parametric choice as a "valuation timing parameter." The role of such parameters is to regulate the order of phase-level operations, and as such, such a parametric choice can be regarded as a "third factor" component of the grammar, in Chomsky's (2005) terms. Assuming that some order of operations must be established, some parametric choices like this will be necessary, and need not implicate any mental mechanisms specific to human language (Obata, Baptista & Epstein 2013).[29] Chapter 5 will be concerned with how many such parameters there are and how such parametric choices fit into a general model of parametric variation, but the discussion here will be restricted to the narrower analytic question of how specific settings for valuation timing parameters can deliver the properties we find in actual languages.

My more specific claim is the following. Among the parametric choices which must be made as part of the language acquisition process are some

29. Müller (2009) develops a model of the difference beween ergative and accusative systems in which the timing of Merge and Agree operations at the vP phase constitutes the pertinent parametric choice. And Obata, Baptista & Epstein (2013) show that timing parameters appear to regulate the order of two other syntactic operations, specifically Feature Inheritance and wh-movement. This proposal allows them to account for differences in agreement in wh-questions in English and Kilega.

number of timing parameters which control the point in the derivation when feature valuation takes place. In at least some cases, a valuation timing parameter will be associated with a single feature of a functional head, or even an unvalued feature on a single token of a functional head. Given a functional category F and an unvalued feature *f*, the valuation timing parameter provides the choice (42):

(42) Valuation of feature *f* in F follows LA. (T/F)

If *f* in (42) is a [uSTEM] feature, then a positive value for the parameter ensures that any head-movement to F will satisfy the HMC, since the F probe will always find its match in the label of the closest [STEM]-bearing head. A negative value entails that the match cannot be the phrasal sister to F, although it can still be the "head" of the sister of F (eventually). In that case, the HMC will (accidentally) be satisfied in many cases by head-movement, but it can also be violated under the right circumstances.

If the setting for a given valuation timing parameter is negative for F, then the search for the match simply follows the usual pattern with other probe-goal searches, and involves only an assymetric c-command relationship. With this setting, the probe must consider any elements adjoined to a complement before it considers the head of its complement, because adjuncts will always be closer to the probe.

The elimination of HMC effects from head-movement does not mean that anything goes. The Minimal Search imperative ensures that the closest match for a [uSTEM]-bearing probe will always be selected. Phase Impenetrability still constrains the overall derivation, and the Last Resort condition on head-movement will ensure that frivolous head-movement will never occur. But a negative value for this parameter nevertheless opens up the options in one critical way—if the grammar permits multiple [uSTEM] features to appear in a single probe, the usual pattern for multiple agreement should be seen in [uSTEM] valuation, as well. When a single probe bears multiple unvalued ϕ feature sets, then it can take feature values from a series of more distant goals, as long as the closest available goal provides a value for the first unvalued ϕ set to be processed (Bobaljik & Branigan 2006, Béjar & Rezac 2009, Hiraiwa 2005: and others). Similarly, if an X^0 probe contains two or more [uSTEM] features, then it should value them in turn, matching them against ever more distant [STEM]-bearing X^0 goals.

The possibility that a probe may contain multiple [uSTEM] features is what leads to the most salient empirical effects from the negative parametric choice of (42), i.e. multiple head-movement. The role that multiple [uSTEM] features in C plays has already been demonstrated. In French, Swedish, or English, T must sometimes obtain a [uSTEM] feature from C, but in constructions where the finite verb raises past the subject, C must keep a second [uSTEM] feature for itself. The null hypothesis should be that this option is freely available, so that any lexical item which bears a [uSTEM] feature can bear multiple [uSTEM] features. For languages where the HMC is observed—i.e. languages where LA applies before [uSTEM] valuation—the number of [uSTEM] features introduced by the phase head will normally be limited to two, because C and T probes can each only value [uSTEM] once. But the general function of the [uSTEM] feature is to ensure that a particular X^0 lexical item should be combined with a stem, and constraining the number of such features to one would be an arbitrary limitation. As will be shown in the remainder of this chapter, and in subsequent ones, multiple [uSTEM] features on a single head can be found in a wide variety of languages and constructions and there can be more than two such features, where the context warrants it.

2.6 MINIMAL CASE STUDIES WITH MULTIPLE HEAD-MOVEMENT

Now on to cases. The core properties of multiple head-movement can be isolated by paying attention to how it operates in a variety of languages, a project which begins with a handful of simple case studies drawn from the existing literature.

2.6.1 Auxiliary inversion in Perenakan Javanese

Perhaps the most transparent example of multiple head-movement is found in Perenakan Javanese, as analysed by Cole, Hara & Yap (2008). The syntax of auxiliaries in this language is quite similar to that of English auxiliary verbs, at least when there is only one auxiliary in a clause. A single auxiliary appears between the subject and the principal verb in a declarative clause: (43).

(43) a. Aku isa ngomong Inggris. (Perenakan Javanese)
1s can speak English
'I can speak English.'

b. Aku pernah mangan sega.
1s PERF eat rice
'I have eaten rice before.'

In questions, the auxiliary appears before the subject, presumably because it is attracted by some sort of interrogative C (as in English).

(44) a. Isa dheen ngomong Inggris?
can 3s speak English
'Can he speak English?'

b. Pernah Tono sugeh?
PERF Tono rich
'Has Tono ever been rich?'

Multiple auxiliaries are also possible in a simple declarative clause. All auxiliaries then appear between the subject and the principal verb, in a fixed order.

(45) a. Dheen gelem isa ngomong Inggris.
3s want can speak English
'He wants to be able to speak English.'

b. *Dheen isa gelem ngomong Inggris.
3s can want speak English
'He has been able to speak English.'

c. Dheen pernah isa ngomong Inggris.
3s PERF can speak English

d. *Dheen isa pernah ngomong Inggris.
3s can PERF speak English

e. Aku pernah gelem mangan sega.
1s PERF want eat rice
'I have wanted to eat rice.'

f. *Aku gelem pernah mangan sega.
1s want PERF eat rice

In questions, however, there is some optionality in the word order when there are more than one auxiliary. One possible order involves movement of the leftmost auxiliary to the C position before the subject (as in English).

(46) a. Gelem dheen isa ngomong Inggris?
want 3s can speak English
'Does he want to speak English?'

b. Pernah dheen gelem ngomong Inggris?
PERF 3s want speak English
'Has he ever wanted to speak English?'

But it is also acceptable to situate multiple auxiliaries before the subject in questions.

(47) a. Gelem isa dheen ngomong Inggris?
want can 3s speak English
'Does he want to be able to speak English?'

b. Pernah gelem dheen ngomong Inggris?
PERF want 3s speak English
'Has he ever wanted to speak English?'

Crucially, however, the relative order of the auxiliaries themselves does not change in this case—the original leftmost auxiliary must remain to the left of the other auxiliary.

(48) a. Dheen gelem isa ngomong Inggris.
3s want can speak English
'He wants to be able to speak English.'

b. *Dheen isa gelem ngomong Inggris.
3s can want speak English

c. Gelem isa Tono ngomong Inggris.
want can Tono speak English
'Tono wants to be able to speak English.'

d. *Isa gelem Tono ngomong Inggris.
can want Tono speak English

When there are three auxiliaries, then all three may be placed before the subject in a question, and again the order of the auxiliaries mirrors the acceptable order in a statement.

(49) a. Pernah gelem isa Tono ngomong Inggris?
PERF want can Tono speak English
'Has Tono ever wanted to be able to speak English?'

The explanation which Cole, Hara & Yap develop for this pattern is persuasive. Following Collins (2002), they posit syntactic operations which optionally displace all auxiliaries up to C in questions. Formally, the displacement is accomplished by allowing C to attract **each** auxiliary in a structure like (50).

(50)

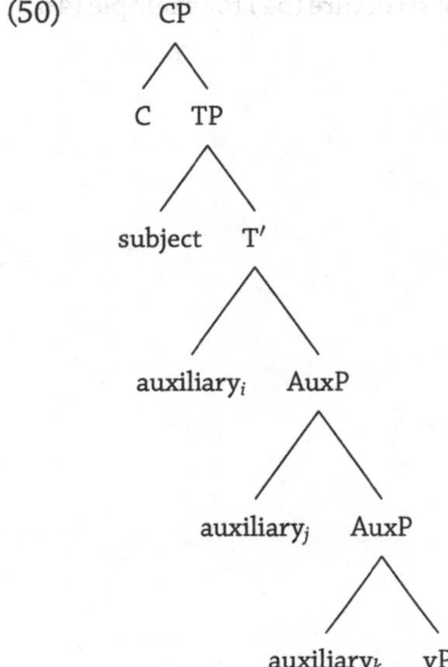

Attraction of the first auxiliary left-adjoins it to C. Attraction of subsequent auxiliaries also left-adjoins it to C, but it does so by *tucking in* between the previous one and the attracting head.[30] This produces the complex C structure: (51).

(51)

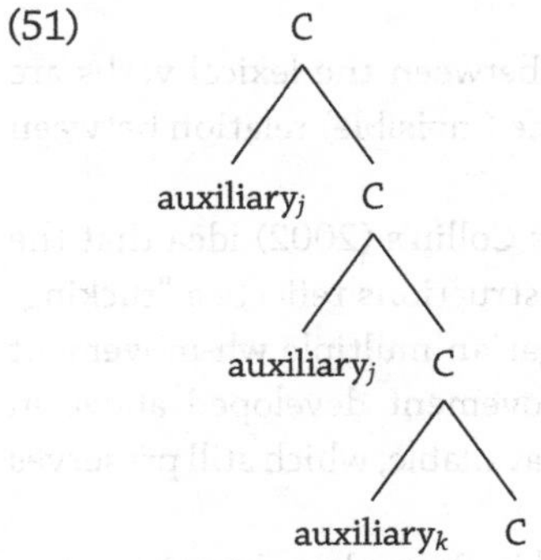

30. An anonymous reviewer questions whether tucking-in is a necessary component of this analysis; the reviewer suggests that Rizzi's (2017) version of Relativized Minimality might allow for a fully cyclic derivation without tucking-in. This elegant suggestion comes close to the alternative analysis of multiple head-movement in Innu-aimûn developed in Roberts (2020). Roberts's approach is examined in section 4.8.5. While Robert's approach differs in the technicalities of Relativized Minimality from what Rizzi proposes, the problems with Roberts's analysis that are identified would appear to apply to this reviewer's suggestion as well.

This procedure will ultimately generate the structure (52) for example (48c).

(52)

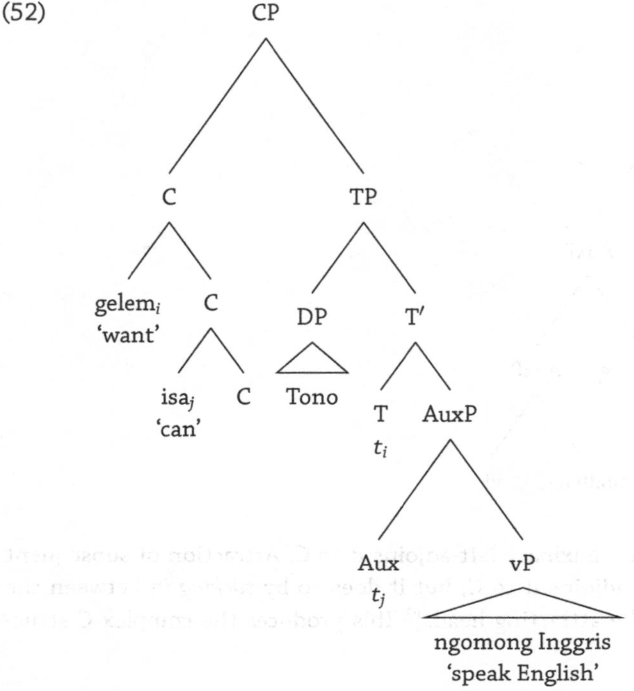

Crucially, the original precedence relations between the lexical verbs are preserved in this type of derivation, although the (invisible) relation between each auxiliary and the attracting C is altered.

The Cole, Hara & Yap (2008) analysis adopts Collin's (2002) idea that the order of heads in multiple head-movement constructions reflects a "tucking-in" procedure, similar to what is found in Bulgarian multiple wh-movement (Richards 1997). Given the model of head-movement developed above in section 2.2, a more fully grounded alternative is available, which still preserves the insight of their analysis.

We need only suppose that the C phase head in Perenakan Javanese questions values [uSTEM] features before LA applies, so the match is found under c-command, and not in the phrasal sister. In other words, the grammar of Perenakan Javanese includes a negative value for the valuation timing parameter for [uSTEM] in C. Interrogative C in this language must bear at least one [uSTEM] feature—since auxiliary inversion always occurs—but it may freely bear a larger number of [uSTEM] features instead. Extra [uSTEM] features are freely provided to interrogative C when it is drawn into the numeration for a clausal phase. (The optionality in how questions are formed must correspond to something in the grammar, after all.)

In the simplest case, C will bear only a single [uSTEM] feature. When C probes for a matching [STEM], it will find the topmost auxiliary, which must therefore undergo head-movement, forming the structure (53). The matching pair of [STEM(gelem)] features are thereby united into a single X^0 constituent.

(53)

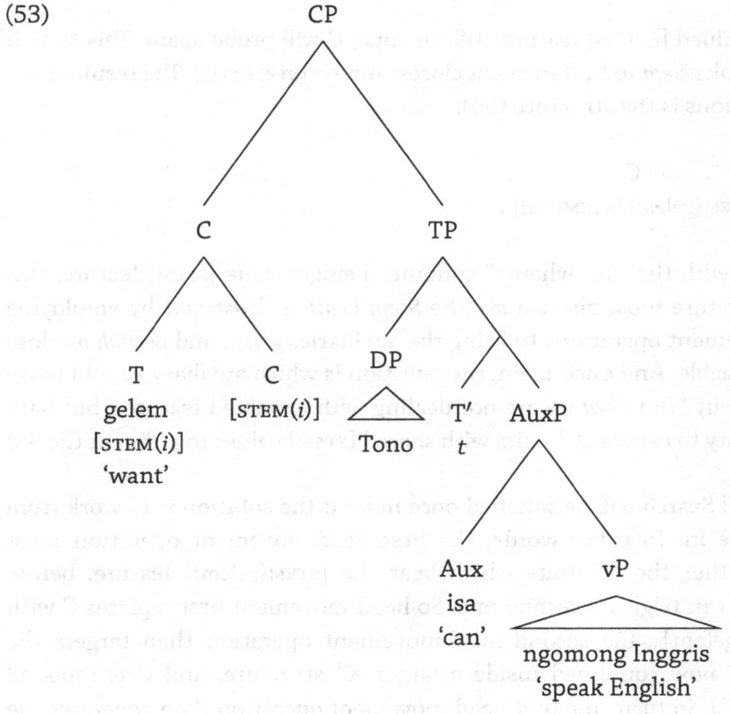

Now suppose that the same forces apply in the derivation of the (52), but that C contains a second [uSTEM] feature. The presence of two identical unvalued features in a probe poses immediate questions about how valuation of each takes place. If both are valued at the same time, with the same goal, then the presence of an extra [uSTEM] feature will be derivationally vacuous. It must be the case, then, that the two [uSTEM] features are attached *assymetrically* to C, so that one can be valued without the other. [uSTEM] features must therefore be organized hierarchically within the feature content of C, as in (54).

(54) C
[uSTEM [uSTEM]]

Even with this structure, there must be some basis for determining which [uSTEM] feature is valued first. Minimal Search considerations suggest that the outermost [uSTEM] feature should be valued before the more deeply embedded one.[31] Then the effect of the first [uSTEM] valuation operation will be (55).

(55) C
[STEM(gelem) [uSTEM]]

As an unvalued [uSTEM] feature still remains, C will probe again. This time it can overlook *gelem* to find the next closest match [STEM(isa)]. The result of the two valuations is the structure (56).

(56) C
[STEM(gelem) [STEM(isa)]]

And as with the case where C contains a single value [STEM] feature, this richer structure must also satisfy the *Stem Feature Constraint* by employing head-movement operations to bring the auxiliaries *gelem* and *pernah* as close to C as possible. And once again, the question is which auxiliary should move first, and why? But now we are not dealing with unvalued features, but with the necessity to express X^0 units with shared [STEM] values together at the SM interface.

Minimal Search will be satisfied once more if the solution is to work from the outside in. In other words, the first head-movement operation must bring together the X^0 units which bear the [STEM(gelem)] feature, before [STEM(isa)] can trigger a second one. So head-movement first replaces C with a set {C, gelem}. The second head-movement operation then targets the minimal C now contained inside a larger X^0 structure, and C is replaced with {isa, *C*}, in turn. The first head-movement operation then generates the structure (57a); the second, (57b), which is also the structure finally provided to the S-M interface.

(57) a.

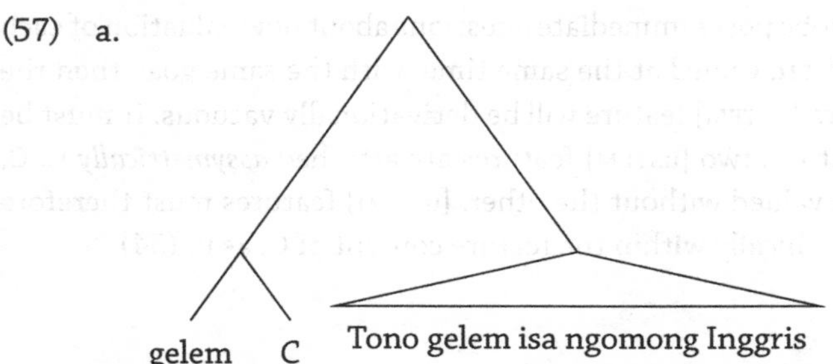

31. Bobaljik & Branigan (2006) propose a similar outside-in ordering in multiple Case assignment to ensure that ergative Case is assigned by T before absolutive Case, building on an earlier proposal by Marantz (1991).

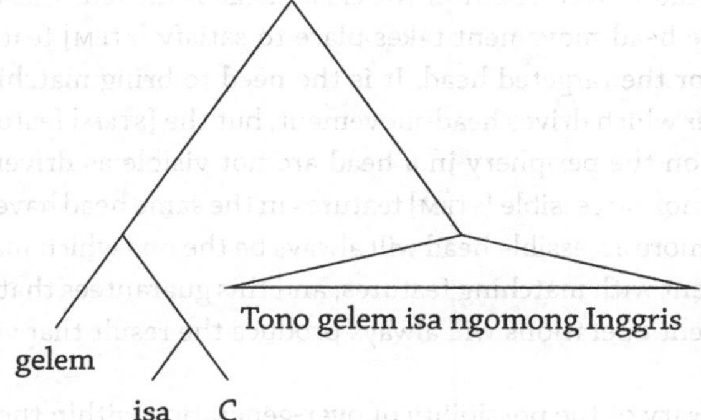

Considered more closely, the result of two head-movement operations is the structure (58), which contains two distinct pairs of matching [STEM] features.

(58)

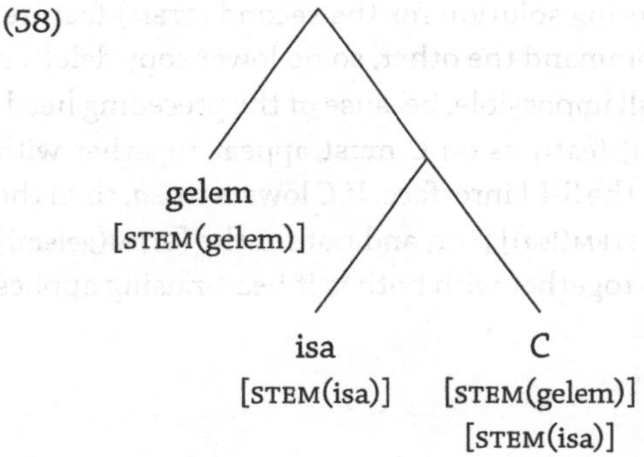

This structure nevertheless satisfies the *Stem Feature Constraint*, because $\{isa, C\}$ counts as an X^0 category, since it contains two terminal nodes with matching features. Therefore, the stem feature in *gelem* finds a matching feature within its X^0 sister, ensuring that the topmost node also counts as an X^0 category.

With compliant head-movement, the order of operations is subject to strict cyclicity. This ensures that head-movement operations lower down in a tree will occur before those involving higher heads. This result is obviously not necessary—or desirable—with multiple head-movement derivations, but strict cyclicity still obtains as a constraint on operations in the linearization phase. Two considerations ensure this result we require. The first is that no head-movement operation will take place until two heads with matching [STEM] features are found in the same domain. In a structure where a single head has obtained two [STEM] values, the cyclic domain in question will be the constituent comprised of the multivalued head and its complement. Strict cyclicity does not order operations beyond this. But the more remote head is still subject to head-movement after the closer head is moved. This is the case because multiple head-movement takes place to satisfy [STEM] features from the outside in for the targeted head. It is the need to bring matching [STEM] features together which drives head-movement, but the [STEM] features which are not located on the periphery in a head are not visible as drivers for this operation until more accessible [STEM] features in the same head have had their needs met. The more accessible head will always be the one which matches the closest constituent with matching features, and this guarantees that the order of head-movement operations will always produce the result that we actually observe.

We must be wary of the possibility of over-generation within the syntactic derivation. Head-lowering of C to *gelem* would initially bring C and *gelem* together, but then the lowered C copy would be deleted because of the higher c-commanding C. At the point at which the second head-movement operation will take place, though, the upper C no longer c-commands anything within TP, so it cannot block a head-lowering solution for the second [STEM] feature. (If C lowers, neither copy will c-command the other, so no lower copy deletion is forced.) But head-lowering is still impossible, because of the preceding head-movement operation. Both [STEM] features on C must appear together with their matches—*gelem* and *isa*—at the S-M interface. If C lowers to *isa*, then the SFC will only be satisfied for the [STEM(isa)] pair, and not for the [STEM(gelem)] pair. The only way for C to end up together with both is if head-raising applies twice, as in (57b).

2.6.2 Finnish polar answers

Multiple head-movement which shares a number of characteristics with the Perenakan Javanese case can be identified as a part of the derivation of some answers to yes-no questions in Finnish, many of the properties of which are elucidated in Holmberg (2001).[32] While there are other ways to respond to a yes-no question, example (59) (from Holmberg) exemplifies the pattern which is of interest for the present work.

(59) a. — Onko Liisa kotona?
is-Q Liisa at-home
'Is Liisa home?'

b. — On.
is
'Yes, she is.'

32. I am grateful to Anders Holmberg for pointing out the relevance of this construction.

The yes-no question which initiates this discourse fragment is derived with attraction of the finite verb by the *-ko* interrogative marker; *on* adjoins to C to form *onko*. In the simplest case, the answer to the yes-no question simply consists of the finite verb. I assume, following Holmberg, that the remainder of the answer sentence is elided, and that the verb survives ellipsis by being extracted from the elided constituent to a higher position. In other words, the fuller structure of the answer in (59) will be something like (60), with TP ellipsis producing the actual form.

(60) on [$_{TP}$ Liisa *t* kotonna]
is Liisa (is) at.home

Example (59) can be characterized simply enough by simply specifying that the functional head of a polar answer attracts the next head down. Let us suppose that the head in question is C. (Holmberg identifies it rather as Σ, within a broadly cartographic approach.) C attracts T, and TP can then be elided.

When the base structure of a polar answer contains more than simply the finite verb in the clausal zone between the left periphery and vP, then ellipsis can leave multiple elements unaffected, as in (61).

(61) a. — Onko Liisa kotona?
is-Q Liisa at-home
'Is Liisa home?'

b. — Ei ole.
not is
'No, she isn't.'

(62) a. — Onko Matti käynut Pariisissa?
has-Q Matti been/visited in-Paris
'Has Matti been to Paris?

b. — Ei ole käynut.
not has been
'No, he hasn't'.

(63) a. — Osaako Liisa puhua ranskaa?
can-Q Liisa speak French
'Can Liisa speak French?'

b. — Osaa puhua.
can speak
'Yes, she can.'

(64) a. — Onko Matti koskaan halannut käydä Roomassa?
has Matti ever wanted to.go to-Rome
'Has Matti ever wanted to go to Rome?'

b. — On halunnut käydä.
has wanted to.go
'Yes, he has.'

As can be seen, the additional material can include negators, perfective auxiliarys, modal auxiliaries, and some restructuring/pseudo-functional verbs. And crucially, the relative order of all such components in the answer remains identical to the ordering found in the base question.

The ellipsis operation itself appears to be optional. The answer in (65) is a legitimate alternative answer to the question in (62a).

(65) On käynut Matti Pariisissa.
has been Matti to-Paris
'He has.'

Assuming (again with Holmberg), that the string *Matti Pariisissa* in (65) occupies the ellipsis position, the word order in (65) confirms that both of the verbal units to its left have raised out of the category which contains this string.

The overall picture here is that C appears to attract at least the finite verb in such polar answers, but it is able to attract more than just the one head when circumstances permit. In other words, we are again looking at a multiple head-movement case, which means that Finnish C must value [uSTEM] features on the basis of c-command, not sisterhood.

Holmberg himself considers, and rejects, the possibility that extraction of more than one head from the ellipsis site is due to attraction of multiple heads by C. The reason he gives for rejecting this analytic option is that head-movement must always adjoin the moved head to the outside of the probe head, and in the case of multiple head-movement, this would ensure that the extracted heads would end up in the opposite word order to what is attested. For example, instead of (65), a derivation in which first *on* and then *käynut* were adjoined to the outside of C would produce the impossible answer sentence structure (66).

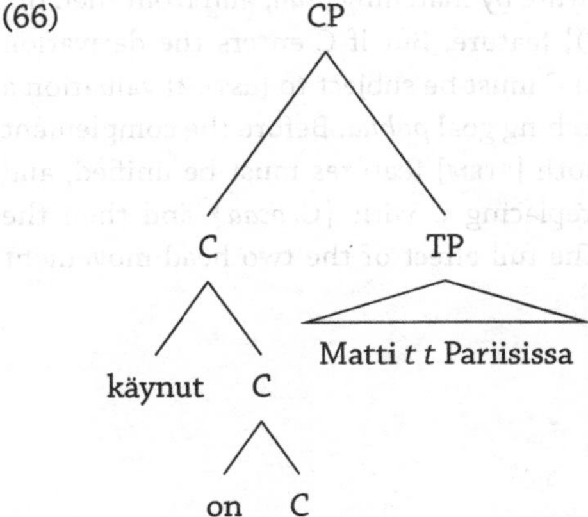

Holmberg's objection to a multiple head-movement analysis is grounded in the idea that head-movement must involve adjunction, a premise which itself is based on X-bar theory. Once X-bar theory is abandoned, this reasoning has no foundation. In the model developed here, the ultimate order for displaced heads instead simply reflects the size of the X^0 constituent which is replaced. So nothing stands in the way of a multiple head-movement treatment of these Finnish data, and Holmberg's rather more complex remnant-movement account can be put aside.

Take example (63b), for example. A multiple head-movement account can start from the (uncontroversial) premise that the base structure is (67), where C bears a single [uSTEM] feature when it provides an answer in the appropriate discourse context.

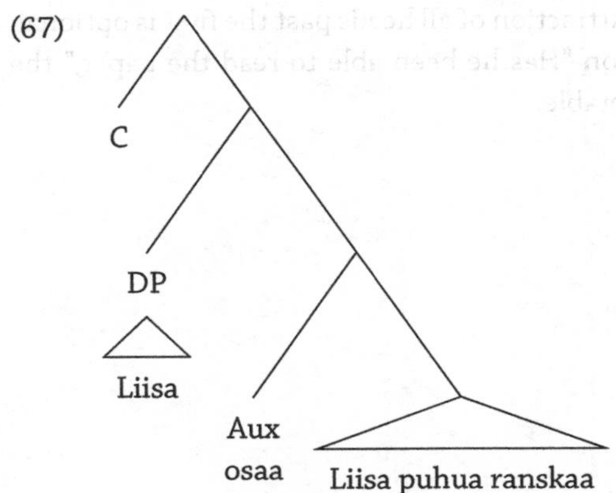

C must then value its [uSTEM] feature by matching *osaa*, and from then on, C and *osaa* bear the same [STEM(*i*)] feature. But if C enters the derivation with multiple [uSTEM] features, then C must be subject to [uSTEM] valuation a second time, this time with the matching goal *puhua*. Before the complement of C is ready for externalization, both [STEM] features must be unified, and head-movement does so by first replacing C with {C, *osaa*} and then the new minimal C, with {C, *puhua*}. The full effect of the two head-movement operations will be (68).

(68)

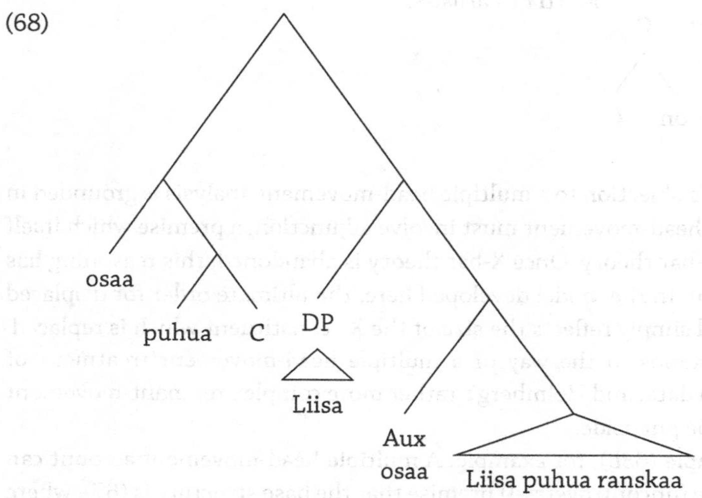

Now if TP is elided, as is optionally possible, then the phonetic output will be example (63b).

Like in Perenakan Javanese, attraction of all heads past the first is optional. Thus, in response to the question "Has he been able to read the paper," the following responses are all acceptable.

(69) a. Ei
   not

b. Ei ole
   not has

c. Ei ole voinut
   not has could

d. Ei ole voinut lukea
   not has could read

The optional extension of the verbal complex in these answer now simply reflects the optional presence of additional [uSTEM] features to C in this Finnish construction. In (69a), C values only its initial [uSTEM] feature, so only the negative auxiliary will eventually undergo head-movement, and all the remaining auxiliaries and the verb are left in the ellipsis site, and elided. In (69b), C attracts the negator and then the perfective auxiliary, leaving the modal and principal verbs in the domain of elision. In (69c), multiple head-movement applies three times, and in (69d), C attracts all the available heads upwards.

2.6.3 Scandinavian adjective "incorporation"

Another case of a structure for which multiple head-movement seems appropriate appears in Northern Swedish and Norwegian dialects which allow "adjective incorporation", as example (70d), from Holmberg & Platzack (2005). (All the data in this section are taken from this source.) The (70a–c) examples represent standard Swedish.

(70) a. en ny bil
a new car
'a new car'

b. bil-en
car-DEF
'the car'

c. den nya bil-en
the new car-DEF
'the new car'

d. ny-bil-en (Northern Swedish)
new-car-DEF
'the new car'

In the adjective incorporation construction, the doubling of definiteness marking seen in (70c)—for nominals with an adjectival modifier—is absent, as is the gender inflection otherwise found on definite adjectives—which is impossible in the standard language: (71).

(71) *nya bilen
new car-DEF
'the new car'

More than one "incorporated" adjective can be stacked within a single form: (72).

(72) Ser du star-svart-bil-en jänna?
see you big-black-car-DEF there
'Do you see that big, black, car?'

But if the phrase is not definite, no adjective incorporation is possible: (73).

(73) *en stor-svart-bil
a big-black-car

As Holmberg & Platzack (2005) note, the order found with "incorporation" of multiple stacked adjectives matches the adjective ordering found with adjectives situated outside the noun, as seen in (74).

(74) a. en stor svart bil
a big black car

b. *en svart stor bil
a black big car

(75) a. stor-svart-bil-en
big-black-car-DEF
'the big black car'

b. *svart-stor-bil-en
black-big-car-DEF

As they also observe, the adjectival ordering in (75a) is inconsistent with any remnant movement approach to analysis of this construction. Instead, they suggest the following analysis. In place of standard head-movement, they propose that adjective incorporation is actually a reflection of a phrasal movement which displaces the adjective and noun together to the left of the determiner, forming a structure like (76).

(76)

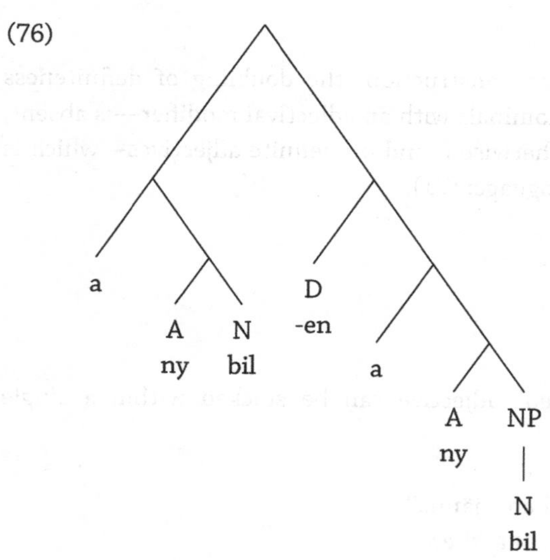

They maintain that morphophonology reacts to a structure like this by treating the entire string of constituents ending in *-en* as a word. Since the initial order of stacked adjectives will naturally be preserved in this analysis. But the cost is a derivation in which there is no particular reason why the A+N cluster should raise, and where the relationship between the syntactic structure and the morphophonological interpretation is non-isomorphic, and actually contradictory.

A more natural analysis is provided by multiple head-movement. Given the theory of head-movement developed here, the Scandinavian definite suffix must bear some number of [uSTEM] features in all varieties of Norwegian and Swedish. It need only be supposed in addition that the definite suffix in Northern Swedish and Norwegian dialects may value [uSTEM] before labeling takes place within the DP phase. This suffices to allow derivations like the one sketched in (77). In (77a), the [uSTEM] features on D will require that D serve as a probe for matching features on A, and then N. Valuation of those features in turn will generate (77b), which will later be altered by head-movement operations to (77c).

(77) a.

b.

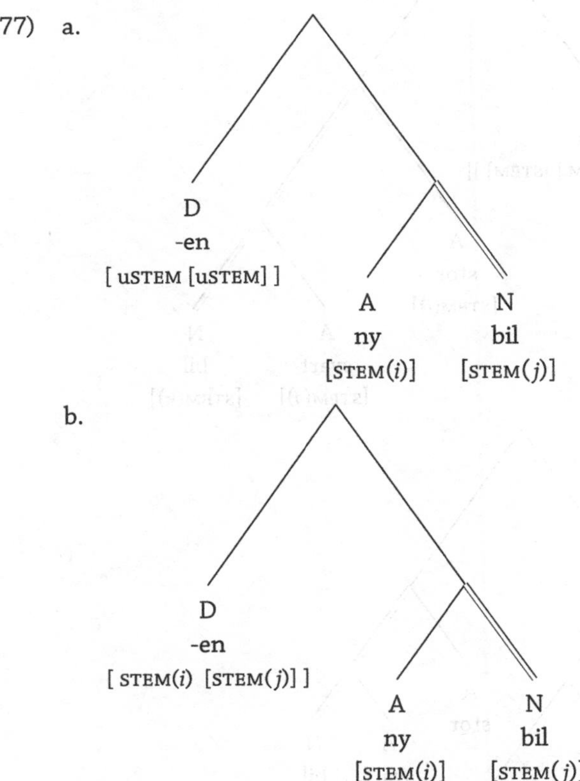

c.

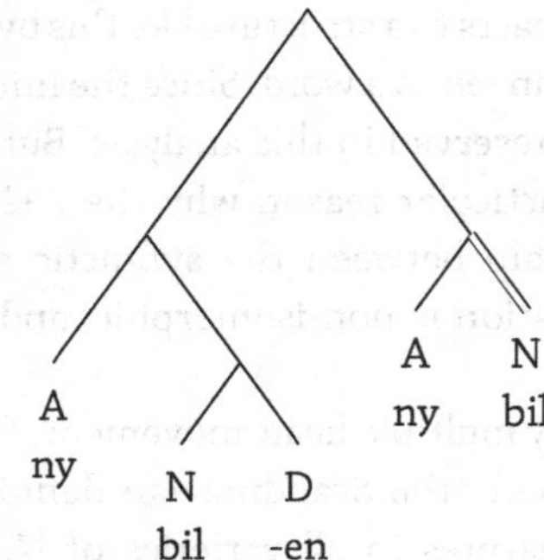

Similarly, given a structure like (78a), [uSTEM] features on D may be valued by the values on *stor*, *svart*, and *bil*, in turn. Eventual head-movement operations will then provide the structure (78b).

(78) a.

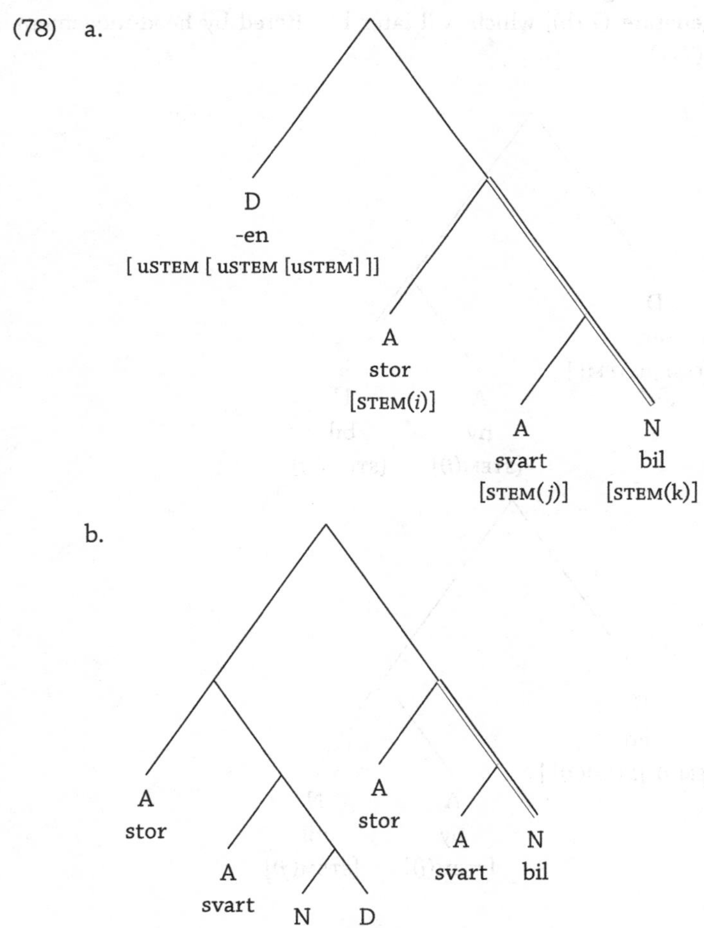

As for the morphophonological interpretation of these structures, there is little more which needs to be said. In (77c), for example, the structure of the *nybilen* constituent is identified as an X^0 unit by virtue of the shared [STEM] features, so the morphophonology can treat it simply as a word. No special morphological adjustments are necessary.

2.6.4 English brown-eyed adjectives

English provides another construction in which multiple head-movement appears to be involved. Adjectival forms like *brown-eyed* or *long-haired* are constructed from three components: an initial adjective, a subsequent nominal, and a final suffix *-ed*. The three combine to signify a property of having the second with the attributes of the first. In other words being "brown-eyed" means being a person who has brown eyes. The question is how such a form is constructed with such a meaning.

The literature on this construction (Pesetsky 1995, Heine 1997, Nevins & Myler 2014) identifies several features which distinguish it from other word-formation processes in English. Although such forms superficially resemble compounds, the semantics seem inconsistent with an analysis in which *brown* is combined with *eyed* in a compounding operation. For one thing, there is no standalone adjective *eyed* which could be combined with *brown*. For another, the contribution of *brown* is as a property of the eyes in question, and not as some sort of modifier of "eyed." The meaning demands a closer semantic association between "brown" and "eye," with *-ed* apparently scoping over the result of this prior association. For another thing, the initial component in this construction can be quantificational, as in *two-faced, three-legged, four-cornered, many-sided*. But regular compounds with initial quantifiers are rare, except in time or size expressions (*3-year-old, 3-inches-wide*).[33]

On the other hand, the prosody associated with such forms does match what is found with English compounds. The first element typically bears more stress than the second. Such a stress pattern is evidently inconsistent with a structure which directly reflects the semantics, i.e. (79).

(79)

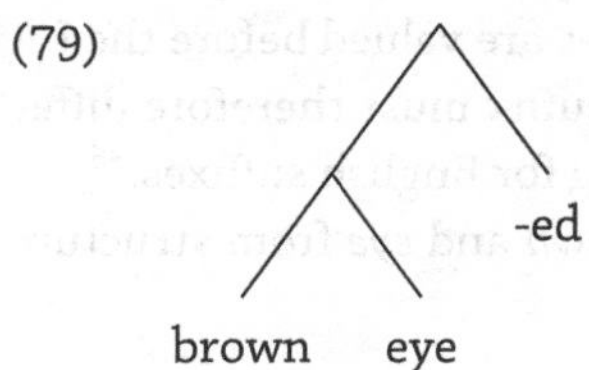

33. Possible examples of such compounds include: *twenty-one-gun salute, 100-year-egg, seven-year-itch*. Each of these examples are idiomatic, and presumably exocentric, and hence probably not pertinent to the problem considered here.

Given the (79) structure, the derivational suffix *-ed* would be expected to "close off" the word, ensuring that a single prosodic word stress would be associated with the whole.

What is more, as Takehisa (2017) observes, the form of the *-ed* suffix is sensitive to the identity of the preceding noun. In forms like *five-legged*, the suffix is pronounced as a full syllable nucleus. This does not reflect any general English constraint barring a velar stop followed by /d/, but is simply a case of contextual allomorphy, in which the form of the suffix is determined by the identity of the base to which it is attached. But the root must then be *leg* rather than *five-leg*.

It seems that the semantics and the phonology require very different structures in this construction. In Chapter 3, similar "bracketing paradoxes" will be examined in some detail. But this particular clash can be resolved quite naturally, given the possibility of multiple head-movement.

Minimally, we can posit that *-ed* is an adjective-forming head which selects a nominal complement, as in (80).

(80)
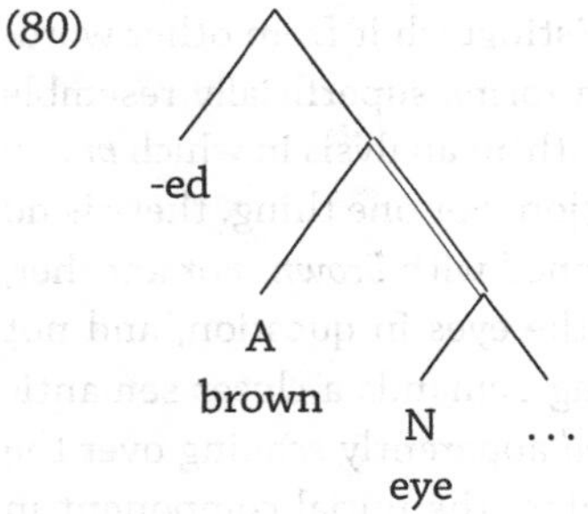

The suffix *-ed* evidently provides a meaning equivalent to inalienable 'have' (Pesetsky 1995).[34] As such, its complement must be semantically appropriate for that meaning.

Besides the selectional and semantic features of *-ed*, something must be said about what allows for a modifier, i.e. *brown*, to be included in the construction in the position where it appears. Suppose therefore that *-ed* bears two [uSTEM] features as a lexical property. In order to value these features, the valuation timing parameter must ensure that [uSTEM] features are valued before the LA applies. The parameter setting for this particular suffix must therefore differ on the microparametric level from the usual setting for English suffixes.[35]

Given these properties, *-ed* will attract both *brown* and *eye* from structure (80), forming the complex X^0 in (81).

34. Nevins & Myler (2014) argue for a more precise meaning of *-ed* as "endowed," which captures the general restriction of the nominal to inalienably possessed nouns.
35. The significance of such differences will be examined in Chapter 5.

(81)

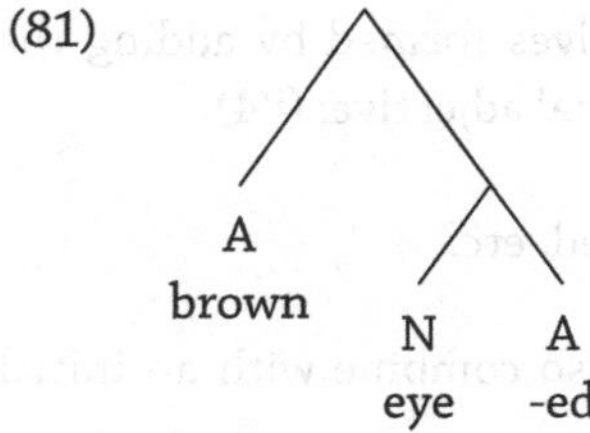

The meaning associated with this construction is thus captured by the base organization of its parts. The prosodic patterns reflect the arrangement of those parts in an X^0 structure in (81), which resembles a compound because it divides naturally into two word-sized constituents.

Similarly for *-ed* compounds for which the initial component is quantificational. For example, for *three-headed*, the base structure may be something like (82), where *three* takes *head* as its complement:

(82)

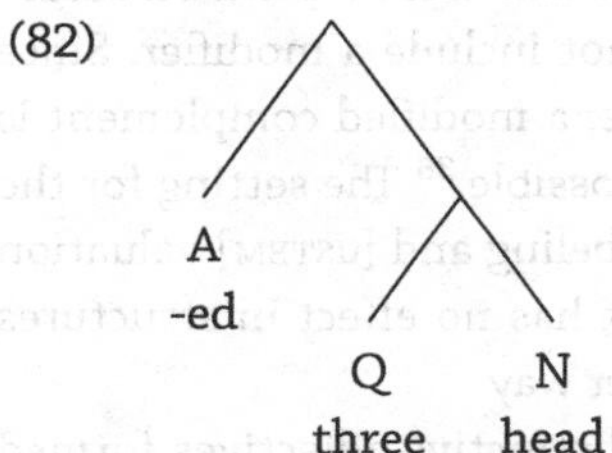

The suffix *-ed* values its [uSTEM] features in turn, first with *three* and then with *head*, and later head-movement operations will bring the two lower stems up, resulting in the actual surface form.

Given such a derivation involving multiple head-movement, the affix allomorphy found with *legged* forms also falls into place. For example, the complex adjective in *five-legged horse* will have the structure in (83) after [uSTEM] valuation and head-movement take place.

(83)

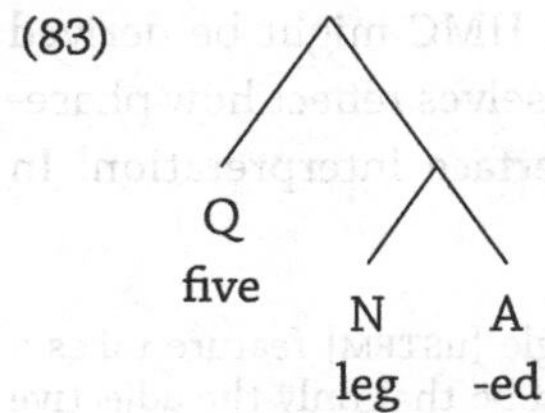

With this structure, the affix is a sister to *leg*, so the syllabic form of *-ed* in this context is no longer paradoxical, but simply run-of-the-mill contextual allomorphy.

Departing from the general rule, some adjectives formed by adding the same *-ed* suffice to a noun need not include an initial adjective: (84).

(84) talented, bearded, moneyed, storied, freckled, etc.

At least some of the adjectives in this list can also combine with an initial adjective, as illustrated in (85).

(85) a. this bearded visitor *vs.* this red-bearded visitor
b. moneyed classes *vs.* old-moneyed classes

The question then is what sets such minimal *-ed*-formed adjectives apart. Since these are lexical exceptions to a more general pattern, the obvious conclusion is that *-ed* may have slightly different properties when it selects a complement from a specific class of lexical items. In particular, *-ed* is allowed to bear a single [uSTEM] feature when it selects *beard, talent*, etc. This allows for a structure in which the nominal complement of *-ed* does not include a modifier. Since *-ed* may also freely bear a second [uSTEM] feature, a modified complement is still possible, so both of the options in (85) are possible.[36] The setting for the parameter which controls the relative order of labeling and [uSTEM] valuation can still remain the same in these cases, since it has no effect in structures where the goal for valuation is close enough either way.

Summing up, the major properties of these distinctive adjectives formed with *-ed* are readily explained under the assumption that English allows multiple head-movement in this limited pocket of the grammar.[37]

2.7 CONCLUSION

I began this chapter with the question how multiple head-movement might be reconciled with the HMC, a descriptive generalization which appears accurate over a broad range of language and constructions. The answer proposed there was to seek a better understanding of the how the HMC might be derived from deeper principles, principles which might themselves reflect how phase-level operations should serve the demands of interface interpretation. In

36. One might wonder what happens if *-ed* with a single [uSTEM] feature takes a modified complement. In that case, the expectation would be that only the adjective would raise to *-ed*, but since the un-moved nominal would lack Case, the structure would be rejected on that basis.

37. An anonymous reviewer observes that this pattern does not extend to other areas in English. English C cannot trigger multiple head-movement, for example. The implications of this type of result for the constitution of parameter space is the concern of Chapter 5.

seeking such an understanding, a model emerges which not only derives the HMC from premises with substantial empirical support—feature valuation *via* minimal search, labeling at the phase level—but also allows for parametric variation based on the need to order some grammatical operations before others. These simple conclusions can now be put to work in the analysis of the more challenging Slavic and Algonquian cases which I consider in the next two chapters.

CHAPTER 3
Multiple head-movement in Russian

The preceding chapter offered a few relatively superficial case studies of languages and constructions where multiple head-movement seems to operate. This next chapter provides a more detailed examination of how multiple head-movement operates within a more extensive range of data. I show that multiple head-movement plays a central role in the morphosyntax of verbal prefixes in the Slavic languages, where the [uSTEM] probes which trigger such head-movement are found in several distinct positions in the clausal *Mittelfeld*. Unlike the analyses already presented, the existence of a massive scholarly literature on Slavic prefixes ensures that our discussion must be more involved, and the results of the discussion more revealing.

The central proposal here is that Slavic T and a small number of aspectual and participial heads trigger multiple head-movement, employing the mechanisms already identified in the previous chapter. Most of this sketch—and the subsequent illustrative material—will be based on Russian data, simply for convenience, as the patterns in question are largely pan-Slavic. To be specific, my claim is that Russian T may bear multiple [uSTEM] features, and these are valued before labeling takes place in the C-T phase. The so-called *perfective prefixes* are goals in which T finds a value for [uSTEM] features, as is the verb that T ultimately ends up as an affix on. A sentence like (1), for example, will originate with a structure approximately as in (2), with a few structural differences which will be introduced as we proceed.

(1) Jurij pere-pisa-l pis'mo.
Yurij re-write-PST letter
'Yurij re-wrote the letter.'

The Grammar of Multiple Head-Movement: A Comparative Study. Phil Branigan, Oxford University Press.
 DOI: 10.1093/oso/9780197677032.003.0003

(2)

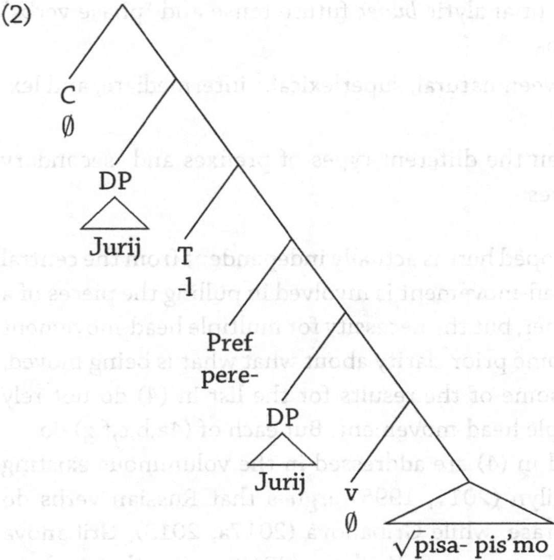

Starting from this structure, two [uSTEM] features on T find a value, first in *pere-*, then in the verb. The presence of valued [STEM] features on T, *pere* and the verb ensure that head-movement will bring the three together into a single structure for morphophological interpretation: (3), in the linearized position of T.

(3)

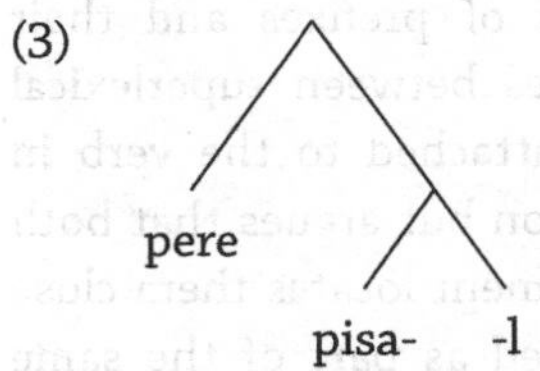

This approach will allow novel solutions to be provided to a collection of outstanding problems in Russian grammar, including the list in (4).

(4) a. contradictory evidence on whether verbs in Russian raise out of the verb phrase to a higher functional head
b. bracketing paradoxes in Russian cyclic phonology
c. bracketing paradoxes in Russian contextual allomorphy
d. future tense interpretations of perfective verbs with present tense inflection

e. the incompatibility of analytic *budet* future tense and "phase verbs" with perfective verbs
f. the differences between natural, superlexical,[1] intermediate, and lexical prefixes
g. interactions between the different types of prefixes and "secondary imperfective" suffixes

A part of the model developed here is actually independent from the central claim about what type of head-movement is involved in pulling the pieces of a complex Russian verb together, but the necessity for multiple head-movement cannot be shown without some prior clarity about what what is being moved, and from where. As such, some of the results for the list in (4) do not rely entirely on the use of multiple head-movement. But each of (4a,b,c,f,g) do.

Some of the issues listed in (4) are addressed in the voluminous existing literature. For example, Bailyn (2011, 1995) argues that Russian verbs do not raise from the verb phrase, while Gribanova (2017a, 2013), Gribanova & Harizanov (2017), and Koeneman & Zeijlstra (2012) argue that it does. Pesetsky (1985) argues that bracketing paradoxes are present in both the cyclic phonology and in allomorph selection; Halle (2007) and Halle & Nevins (2009) maintain that the cyclic phonology does not motivate any such "paradox." Jakobson (1957) derives the lack of *budet* futures with prefixed verbs from the "perfective" nature of both, but Forsyth (1970) argues that *budet* is actually imperfective, so that Jakobson's account cannot be supported. As for the different types of prefixes and their morphosyntactic status, Smith (2013) distinguishes between superlexical and lexical prefixes, but supposes that both are attached to the verb in the lexicon. Svenonius (2005b) adopts her distinction but argues that both originate as syntactic heads, and that phrasal movement locates them close enough to the verb to allow them to be interpreted as part of the same word in the morphophonology. Tatevosov (2008, 2014, 2011) accepts and extends Svenonius's conclusions about the base position of the prefixes, but supposes that regular head-movement operations can attach the different prefixes to the verb. And everyone has a different story about the secondary imperfectives.

These works, and many others, include insightful observations and compelling arguments which apply to the specific analytic questions that they address. And in isolation, some of the conclusions look persuasive. For example, Bailyn's argument from the distribution of manner adverbs that the verb does not raise to T is persuasive on its own, but it sheds no light on the lack of perfective verbs in analytic futures or on how different classes of perfectives

1. Svenonius (2005b) tentatively ascribes this terminology to Smith (2013).

interact with secondary imperfective inflections. And Tatevosov's demonstration that intermediate prefixes differ from both superlexical and lexical prefixes appears correct, but it says nothing about the distribution of manner adverbs or about the bracketing paradoxes that Pesetsky identifies. What literature overall lacks is a means to bring each of these problems into the same fold, so that the explanation of one set of facts can be applied to the others.

Consider the intricate model proposed by Harizanov & Gribanova (2019), for example. In this model, there are two types of head-movement: one syntactic, subject to the HMC, the other, post-syntactic "amalgamation," which unites two separate terminal nodes into one morphophonological word. (Amalgamation subsumes affix-hopping and postsyntactic head raising for them.) Russian verbs undergo syntactic head-movement to a position between T and v—presumably Asp—and T is added to the verb in this middle position through amalgamation. In this way, they can claim to account for the existence of verb-stranding VP ellipsis and the distribution of manner adverbs at the same time, because the verb raises out of elided VPs, but it does not raise high enough to pass the pertinent adverbs.

There are specific limitations in this model, which are discussed in section 3.3.3, as there are specific ones for each of the others in the list of works just mentioned. But the larger issue, which the multiple head-movement approach can overcome, is simply that Harizanov & Gribanova frame their analysis to answer a set of empirical questions which is smaller than one would ideally want addressed. They offer a solution for (4a), but not for (4b–g).

Since my claim is that all of these issues should be addressed together, it would be disingenuous to go through even the major works on these topics in detail, one at a time, to point out how they do not succeed in answering questions that they do not purport to answer. To that end, I begin by developing the multiple head-movement model of the Russian verbal system, introducing the crucial data and the corresponding theoretical premises bit by bit. And once the overall picture is complete, a summary comparison with the proposals found in the existing literature will be in order.

3.1 MORPHOLOGICAL COMPONENTS OF RUSSIAN TENSE/ASPECT

The demonstration that an analysis based on multiple head-movement is necessary, and preferable to the alternatives, begins with a model of how multiple head-movement interacts with other relevant grammatical features of Russian grammer. The building blocks which the syntax has access to are a good place to start.

There are two formal tenses provided in T: past and non-past (Jakobson 1957). (It will however be convenient to identify the non-past affixes as PRS in the glosses for the Russian data.)

The tense inflection is found either on the principal verb or on an auxiliary verb. The auxiliary verbs are the future auxiliary *bud'*—the non-past form of copular *byt'*—or a "phase verb":[2] *zakončit'* 'finish', *načat'* 'begin', *prodolžat'* 'continue'.

(5) a. Petja budet čitat' etu knigu zavtra.
Petja will read/PF-read this book tomorrow
'Petja will read this book tomorrow.'

b. Petja zakonči-l stroit' dom.
Petja finish-PST.m build house
'Petja finished building the house.'

c. Petja nača-l čitat' lekciju.
Petja begin-PST.m read lecture
'Petja began to give a lecture.'

d. Petja prodolža-l guljat'.
Petja continue-PST walk
'Petja continued walking.'

There is a set of verbal prefixes, most of which are homophonous with prepositions, as in (6), where the prefix *na-* is homophonous with the preposition *na* 'on'.

(6) Nataša na-pisa-la pis'mo.
Natasha PRF-write-PST.f letter
'Natasha wrote the letter.'

With a few frozen exceptions, verbal prefixes in Slavic alter the aspectual character of the simple stem to which they attach from *imperfective* to *perfective*. 'Perfective' verbs inflected with present tense endings are interpreted as future tense forms, as seen in (7), while perfective and imperfective forms inflected with past tense endings differ in more familiar ways.

(7) a. Zavtra ja po-jd-u v kino.
tomorrow I PRF-go-1s to cinema
'Tomorrow I will go to the cinema.'

b. Segodn'a ja id-u v kino.
today I go-1s to cinema
'Today I am going to the cinema.'

2. The term "phase" in this context simply reflects accepted Slavicist grammatical terminology, and does not correspond to any concept of minimalist phase theory.

c. Igor' pro-čita-et knigu.
   Igor PRF-read-3s book
   'Igor will read a book.'

d. Ty s-dela-eš eta dlja menja.
   you PRF-do-2s this for me
   'You will do this for me.'

The prefixes can be further divided into four subcategories, based on their meaning and distribution. The categories are: natural, superlexical, intermediate, and lexical prefixes. Each prefix actually falls into multiple subcategories, but expresses a different meaning in each.

Prefixes serving as *natural perfective* prefixes (Janda 2007) signify the *perfective* aspect, which is the marked basic aspect. (Imperfective aspectual is the unmarked case.) Different verbs are associated with different natural perfective prefixes, as a lexical property. Each of the verbs in (7) employ the prefixes shown to mark the verb as perfective.

For example, *na-* is the natural perfective prefix for *pisat'* 'write', *melit'* 'target', *točit'* 'sharpen', while *s-* is the natural perfective prefix for *est'* 'eat', *delat'* 'do', and *gnut'* 'bend'.

In place of the natural perfectives prefixes, verbs may combine with superlexical prefixes (Babko-Malaya 1999, Svenonius 2005b), which add a variety of semantic nuances to the verbal event, aspectual or *aktionsart*-related in nature, but not specifically perfective.

(8)

Prefix	Superlexical meaning
na-	Cumulative
po-	Delimitative
za-	Inceptive
pere-	Distributive
pro-	Perdurative
ot-	Terminative

The presence of a superlexical prefix also ensures that the verb is interpreted as perfective.

Tatevosov (2014) identifies the members of the intermediate prefix category as (9).

(9)

Prefix	Intermediate meaning
do-	Completive
pere-	Repetitive
pod-	Attenuative

Intermediate prefixes also appear to signify perfectivity and to add specific new aspectual meanings , but they differ from superlexical prefixes in where they may appear and how many there can be in a single complex verb (Tatevosov 2008). Tatevosov illustrates some of the possibilities with (10).

(10) a. Vasja pere-do-pisa-l stat'ju.
Vasja REPET-COMPL-write-PST.m paper
'Again, Vasja performed a final stage of writing a paper.'

b. Vasja do-pere-pisa-l stat'ju.
Vasja COMPL-REPET-write-PST.m paper
'Vasja completed re-writing a paper.'

c. Vasja do-do-pisa-l knigu.
Vasja COMPL-COMPL-write-PST.m paper
'Vasja completed finishing writing a book.'

d. Vasja pere-pere-pisa-l stat'ju.
Vasja REPET-REPET-write-PST.m paper
'Vasja re-wrote his paper again.'

The final subcategory of prefixes are the lexical prefixes (Svenonius 2005b). The semantic effects of members of this last class are less predictable (Babko-Malaya 1999). These will be examined in more detail below.

Besides the different types of prefixes, Russian verbs can combine with two aspectual suffixes: semelfactive *-nu*, and the "secondary imperfective" suffix *-yva*. Semelfactive forms refer to brief, momentary actions, as in *prygnut'* 'jump', *doxnut'* 'sigh', *kriknut'* 'cry out', or *gljanut'* 'glance'. They are grammatically perfective, even without a perfective prefix added on.

Secondary imperfective forms are harder to characterize. The *-yva* suffix is usually described as a means to make a perfective verb into an imperfective one, and this is certainly the effect in some cases, like (11a). But secondary imperfectives can form part of a complex perfective verb as well (Isacenko 1960), as in (11).

(11) Durak v-lez v dom, po-otkry-va-l vse okna,
idiot in-broke.in in house DISTR-open-SI-PST all windows
po-rastvor-ja-l dveri, xodit po domu.
DISTR-open-SI-PST doors walk over house.DAT
'The idiot broke into the house, opened all the windows one by one, and is walking inside.'

Each of the conjuncts in (11) are perfective; in the second and third, the verb stem is still inflected with *-yva*. The character of the *-yva* suffix will also be elucidated below.

Russian verbs fall into five subcategories, based on their aspectual properties. The largest group of verbs lack any inherent aspectual specification. They are interpreted as imperfective, unless a prefix or semelfactive *-nu* is added to them. A small number of verbs are interpreted in the opposite way, i.e. as perfective, unless a secondary imperfective *-yva* is added to them. This group includes verbs like *dat'* 'give', *sest'* 'sit down', *rešit'* 'decide', *kupit'* 'buy', *xvatit'* 'grab', *obidet'* 'offend', *brosit'* 'throw', and about twenty others. There are a few verbs which employ suppletion to distinguish between imperfective and perfective senses. Examples of this third group include *brat'; vzjat'* 'take', *položit'; klast'* 'put' and *govorit'; skazat'* 'speak'.[3] The bi-aspectual verbs can be interpreted as either perfective or imperfective forms freely, with no accompanying change in their form. Many of these are borrowed forms.

Finally, there are verbs of motion, each of which employ two stems, in an apparently suppletive relationship. The choice of stem for motion verbs depends on whether they are "directional" or not, as well as on the tense and aspectual inflections.

The table in (12) summarizes the building blocks which Russian grammar has access to in expressing tense and aspectual distinctions.

(12)	Aux. verb	Prefix*	Verb	Asp	Tense
	future	natural	imperfective	semelfactive	past
	aspectual	superlexical	perfective	sec. imperfective	non-past
		intermediate	paired		
		lexical	bi-aspectual		

With these components now on the table, we turn to the presentation of a model which arranges these pieces to generate the range of actual possibilities in the language. Needless to say that multiple head-movement will play a central role in this model.

3.2 THE LOCUS OF PERFECTIVITY

While the Slavic grammatical tradition locates perfective aspect in the prefix (for prefixed perfectives) or the verb stem (for inherently perfective verbs), this cannot be correct. For one thing, such a premise would imply that verbs with both a prefix and a perfective verb stem should be doubly perfective. Adding a prefix to a semelfactive verb should have the same effect. Such forms are easy to find: (13). And the same would be expected of verbs with multiple prefixes, already seen in (10).

3. The copula *byt'; bud-* 'be' and *idti; šo-* 'go' presumably belong to the paired verb class, but with additional complications.

(13) a. Helder za-brosi-l mjač (Svenonius 2005b)
Helder into-threw-PST.m ball

v vorota angličan.
in goal English
'Helder kicked the ball into the English goal.'

b. do-dat' (Tatevosov 2014)
COMPL-give
'complete giving'

c. pere-rešit'
REPET-decide
'decide again'

d. pod-obidet'
PERD-offend
'offend slightly'

e. do-so-brat'
COMPL-with-take
'finish collecting'

f. pere-ki-nut' (Romanova 2007)
over-throw-SML
'throw something over'

But none of these forms display any complicated double perfectivity (whatever that would look like). In each case, the interpretation of the verb or sentence is simply perfective.

Tatevosov (2011) provides a second finding which undermines the idea that perfectivity resides in the verb and or a prefix. He shows that nominalizations formed from prefixed verbs lack any perfective meaning, as in (14). Compare (14a) with (14b).

(14) a. Vasja na-pisa-l pis'mo v dva časa i v tri časa.
Vasja PRF-write-PST.m letter in two hour and in three hour
'Vasja wrote a letter at 2 p.m. and at 3 p.m.'

b. na-pisa-nije pis'ma v dva časa i v tri časa
PRF-write-NOM letter.GEN in two hour and in three hour
'writing a letter at 2 p.m. and at 3 p.m.'

In (14a), the perfective aspect associated with the sentence ensures that there must be two distinct writing events—one at 2 p.m. and one at 3 p.m. But in (14b), the nominalization can be interpreted as referring to a "single event scenario whereby the writing continues from 2 p.m. to 3 p.m." Tatevosov concludes that there is no perfective meaning provided with the nominalized verb because if there was one, the interpretation of the two examples would be comparable.

If perfective meaning is not introduced as a lexical property of a "perfective" verb, then it must originate somewhere else, within a part of the sentence which lacks phonetic visibility. Fowler's (1994) proposal is that perfective verbs are combined with a silent perfective prefix, which functions as one of the set of natural perfective prefixes. It is the silent prefix which provides perfective meaning rather than the verb.

Of course, the problem then becomes how to constrain the distribution of the silent perfective prefix. Otherwise, every sentence should have a perfective interpretation freely, which is obviously not the case. Fowler and Tatevosov defer the question of how the zero perfective head is constrained. Fowler takes it to be the purest of the natural perfective prefixes.[4] Tatevosov is more syntactically circumspect, taking the silent category to be a perfective "operator" which is located somewhere outside the verb phrase and above the location of "secondary imperfective" inflection.

Whatever the syntactic location of this silent element may be, it is clear that there must be a bidirectional dependancy between the silent perfective category and an inherently perfective verb. If the silent head could appear by itself, then every clause should have the option of being interpreted as perfective. And if an inherently perfective verb did not need the silent head, then all such verbs should be freely found with imperfective meanings.

I therefore posit a morphosyntactic feature which distinguishes verbs of the inherently perfective group from regular imperfective verbs—the feature [AD] (for *aspectually dependent*).[5] Verbs like *kupit'* 'buy' or *rešit'* 'decide' bear [AD]; verbs like *čitat'* 'read' or *ljubit'* 'love' do not. More specifically, assuming verbs are made from the combination of an acategorial root with a categorizing v head, the root for perfective verbs must bear the [AD] feature. The question then becomes why verbs bearing [AD] must appear within the domain of a silent perfective head. The answer should be that such a configuration is necessary to allow a sentence like (15) to satisfy interface requirements.

(15) Pavel kupi-l xleb.
Pavel buy-PST.m bread
'Pavel bought bread.'

4. Fowler does not use the term "natural," but his text makes it clear that this is what he means.

5. Tatevosov (2011) uses the term "formally perfective" to express essentially the same idea. Here I prefer a notation which does not suggest that verbs which bear this feature have an inherent connection to the actual semantic notion of perfectivity.

The [AD] feature must be somehow active within the syntax, since its role is to connect the silent perfective head with the verb. But it should not be semantically visible, since the verb itself does not contribute aspectual meaning to the clause. It seems, therefore, that the [AD] feature must be deleted before it can cause problems at the semantic interface, and the silent perfective head is necessary to allow this feature deletion to take place.

Let us suppose, therefore, that the silent perfective head, henceforth Prf, also bears an unvalued [AD] feature, so that regular feature valuation operations may connect Prf and an [AD]-bearing verb root. Valuation of [*u*AD] occurs when Prf acts as a probe which finds the verb in its local c-command domain, and valuation allows both [AD] features to be deleted, as neither must be considered by the semantics. (Deletion does not eliminate the [AD] feature for morphological interpretation, so the [AD] feature on the verb will still be available for morphological rules of Vocabulary Insertion, as discussed below.) The structure for (15) will therefore be (16) at the C-T phase, before head-movement, labeling, and valuation.

(16)

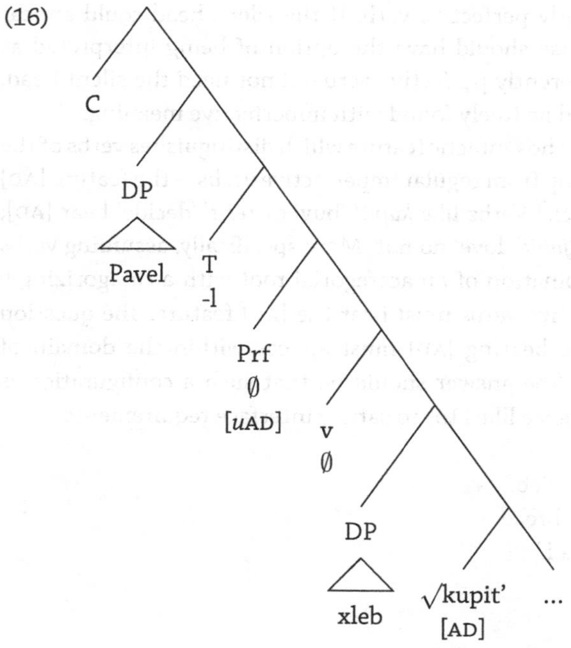

In most cases, the inherently perfective verbs are transitive, so they belong within a vP phase. One might therefore worry that the phase boundary for vP would insulate the root, preventing it from serving as a goal for the [*u*AD]-bearing Prf probe. But Chomsky's (2015) proposal that phase head status is transferred from v to the root eliminates this concern, as the root is then accessible to operations at the C-T phase level, including [*u*AD] valuation.

The [AD] feature on an inherently perfective verb distinguishes it from naturally imperfective verbs, as an arbitrary lexical property of the root. The same feature now allows us to derive the properties of paired aspectual verbs and bi-aspectual verbs. Regular imperfective verbs cannot bear [AD]. Inherently perfective verbs must bear [AD]. And bi-aspectual verbs and paired aspectual verbs are free to bear [AD] when inserted into the syntactic derivation, but they need not do so.

With bi-aspectual verbs, there must be two distinct structures available to allow for usages like (17), where *ispol'zovat'* 'use' is imperfective in (17a) and perfective in (17b).

(17) a. Vy ispol'zu-ete sejčas eti materialy?
you use-PRS.2s now these materials
'Are you using these materials now?'
(Čertkova & Chang 1998)

b. Vy ispol'zu-ete zavtra eti materialy?
you use-PRS.2s tomorrow these materials
'Will you use these materials tomorrow?'

The (17a) interpretation is expected if *ispol'zovat'* does not have to bear [AD], since the absence of [AD] on the verb entails the absence of a Prf with a [*u*AD] feature to value. But if *ispol'zovat'* does bear [AD], as an option, then silent Prf may be present too, and the perfective usage in (17b) results.

For paired aspectual verbs, the syntactic analysis is the same as for bi-aspectual verbs, but Vocabulary Insertion rules will apply differently. Compare (18a) and (18b).

(18) a. On vzja-l knigu.
he take-PST.m book
'He took the book (and now it's gone).'

b. On bra-l knigu.
he take-PST.m book
'He was taking the book; he used to take the book.'

The perfective interpretation of (18a) indicates that Prf is present; the [AD] feature which must therefore be found on the verb will be deleted when valuation of [*u*AD] on Prf takes place. In (19b), there is no [AD] feature on the verb and so Prf is both unnecessary and unavailable so the sentence is imperfective. In this case, though, the Vocabulary Insertion rules for the verb *brat'* are sensitive to the presence of [AD], as in (19).

(19) a. *brat'* → /vzja/ / $\left[\frac{-}{\text{AD}}\right]$

b. *brat'* → /bra/ (elsewhere)

The selection of stem forms for verbs of motion makes use of the same mechanisms, but adds two additional complexities which will fall into place after the secondary imperfective suffixes are examined.

The [AD] feature plays a larger role in the distribution and interpretation of the verbal prefixes. Let us begin with the natural prefixes—the prefixes which seem to contribute nothing to the clause beyond its perfective character. But if the silent Prf head is the true source of perfectivity, then natural prefixes cannot be, and we must find some other role for them to play. As natural perfective prefixes do appear when there is an imperfective verb stem, and such verbs do not bear [AD], the obvious conclusion is that natural perfective prefixes bear [AD] instead. For a sentence like (20), the structure will then be (21).

(20) Natasha pro-čita-la stat'ju.
Natasha PRF-read-PST.F article
'Natasha read the paper (through).'

(21)

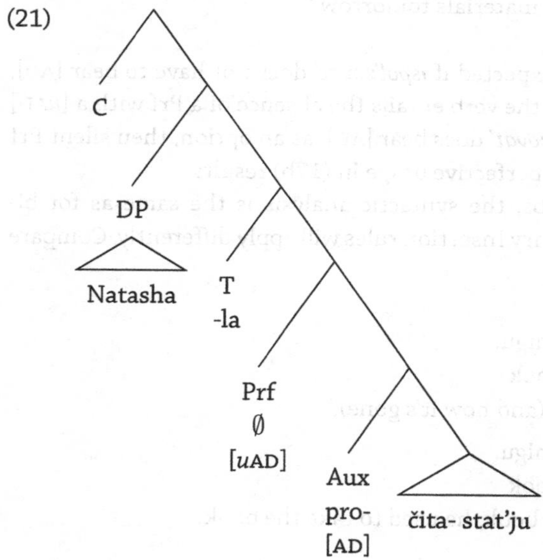

In other words, the natural perfective prefixes can be taken to be pure auxiliary elements, which appear in the sentence to allow its morphosyntactic demands to be met, but which do not otherwise add to the meaning. And the fact that different natural perfectives are required by different verbs may be attributed to arbitrary selectional restrictions, in which different auxiliary prefixes select verbs from distinct lexical classes. Auxiliary *na-* selects *pisat'* but not *delat'*, and so on.

The head-movement operations which will bring the appropriate terminal elements together must be driven by matching [STEM] features. If we annotate the appropriate [STEM] features on the structure in (21), we get (22).

(22)

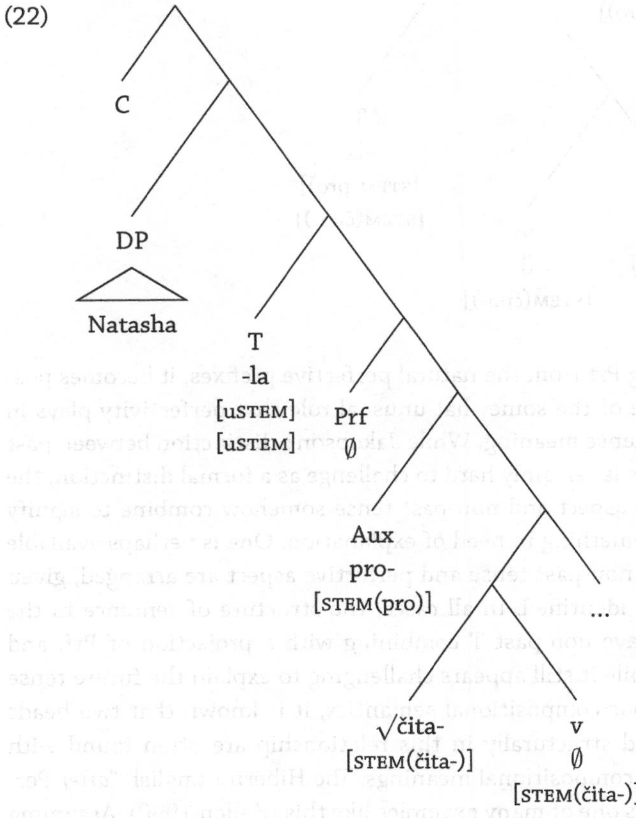

Notice that Prf has no [STEM] feature. As a silent category which does not attract a lower head, there is no evidence that it plays a part in [uSTEM] valuation in either direction. So probing T will simply ignore Prf in seeking matches for its [uSTEM] features.[6] T values its [uSTEM] features with *pro* and the verb in turn, and subsequent head-movement operations will bring both up to T, forming the morphological structure (23).

6. In fact, it would make little difference to the surface result if Prf were to bear a [STEM] feature. In that Case, T would simply have to bear an extra [uSTEM] feature in order to attract Prf before the next [STEM]-bearing head. But the concept of a [STEM] feature supplied by a fully silent head is problematic, and there is no empirical advantage to postulating one here.

(23)

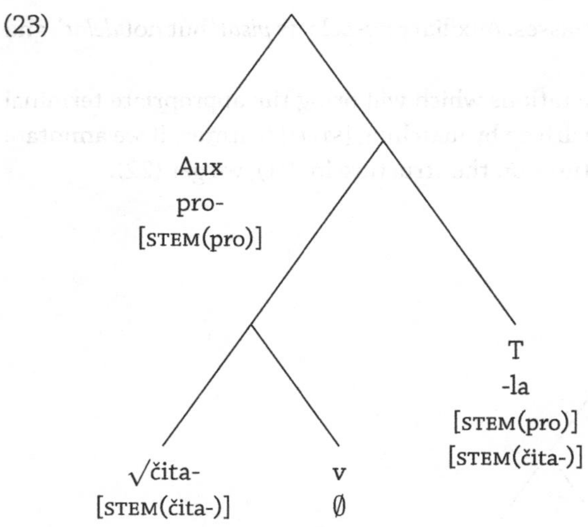

In distinguishing Prf from the natural perfective prefixes, it becomes possible to make sense of the somewhat unusual role that perfectivity plays in providing a future tense meaning. While Jakobson's distinction between past and non-past tenses is certainly hard to challenge as a formal distinction, the fact that perfective aspect and non-past tense somehow combine to signify the future is still something in need of explanation. One is perhaps available if we consider how non-past tense and perfective aspect are arranged, given the structures now identified. In all cases, the structure of sentence in the future tense will have non-past T combining with a projection of Prf, and Prf is invariant. While it still appears challenging to explain the future tense as a result of obvious compositional semantics, it is known that two heads which are organized structurally in this relationship are often found with unpredictable, non-compositional meanings. The Hiberno-English "*after* Perfect" form in (24a) is one of many examples like this (Kallen 1990). Assuming that *-ing* originates as a syntactic head (Chomsky 1957), the structure for (24a) which is interpreted at the C-I interface will be (24b).

(24) a. I'm after washing the car.
b. I [PRES] be after -ing [$_{vP}$ wash the car]
c. I'm washing the car.

In dialects of English which employ this construction, the combination of the progressive participle and a preceding (aspectual) particle *after* produces a perfective aspectual meaning, even though the progressive participle without *after* in (24c) is simply progressive. The future reading in Russian perfective present forms can be understood as entirely comparable, but only if the syntactic structure is also comparable, with two local heads working together semantically.

On the other hand, when T is a past tense suffix, the composition of the tense/aspect meaning is simply what one would expect, with T scoping over the aspectual head. In this case, the aspectual semantics are independent of that of the tense inflection. Perfective aspect will determine the "viewpoint" of the event in question, and the tense specification will situate that result in time.

Russian allows for a second, analytic, future tense construction, which employs the future auxiliary *budet* 'be', together with an uninflected imperfective verb, as in (25).

(25) Petja budet čitat' etu knigu zavtra.
Petja will read this book tomorrow
'Petja will read this book tomorrow.'

Examples like this are constructed by using the copula in place of a natural prefix in the Aux position below Prf. Like the natural perfective prefixes, the copular auxiliary must bear [AD]. The copula is one of the members of the paired aspectual verb group. When it bears [AD] and it appears with the non-past tense suffix, Vocabulary Insertion provides the suppletive stem /bud-/. Elsewhere, the copula uses the stem /by-/. So the structure of (25) will be (26).

(26)

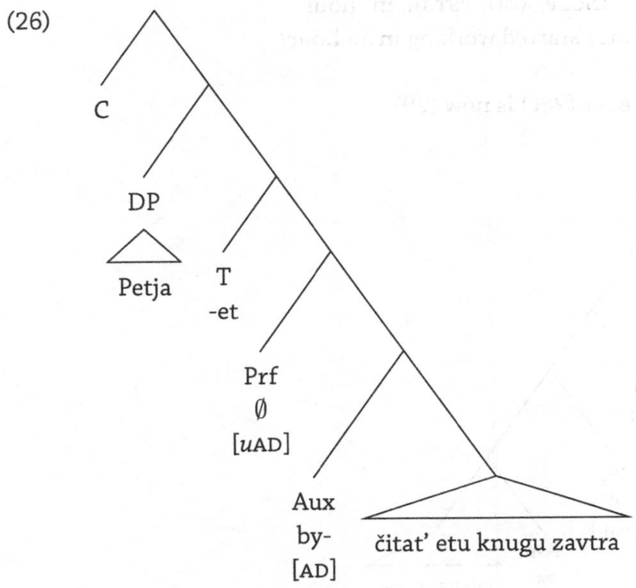

Again, the combination of non-past T and the Prf head as a non-compositional signifier of tense is what provides the future tense meaning here. And, in this case, no compositional alternative is possible, even if the T contains a past tense inflection. Without non-past T, Prf must be interpreted as truly perfective, and, in this case, that would require a perfective interpretation of the copular auxiliary. As no such interpretation is sensible, a non-future form of such a sentence is impossible.

(27) *Petja by-l čitat' etu knigu.
Petja read-PST.m this book
'Petja read this book (through).'

Turning now to the status of the superlexical prefixes, we can distinguish these from the natural prefixes on both semantic and structural grounds. A few examples of how superlexical prefixes are used appear in (28).

(28) a. On na-kolo-l orex-ov. (Svenonius 2005b)
he CUMUL-crack-PST.m nuts-GEN.PL
'He cracked a sufficiently large quantity of nuts.'

b. Ivan pro-side-l čas.
Ivan DUR-sit-PST.m hour
'Ivan sat for an hour.'

c. Kompjuter za-rabota-l za čas. (MacDonald 2008)
computer INCEP-work-PST.m in hour
'The computer started working in an hour.'

A plausible structure for (28c) is now (29).

(29)

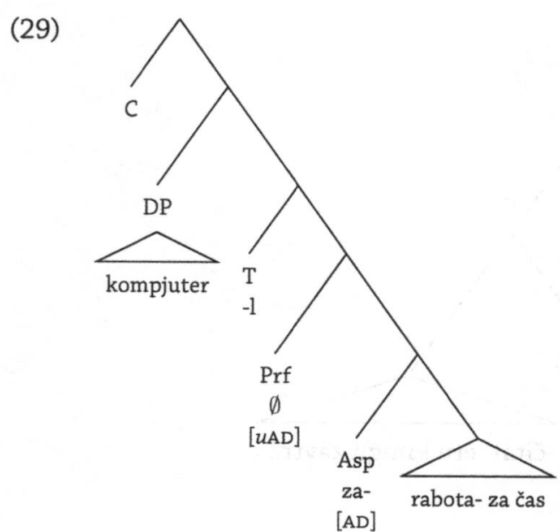

Semantically, the superlexical prefixes provide specific aspectual meanings other than perfectivity, listed in the table in (8). Perfective meaning still resides in Prf and not the prefix. These prefixes can be employed freely, although the result will be acceptable only to the extent that the semantic result is felicitous. Syntactically, the superlexical prefixes do not select a particular lexical class for their complement, unlike the natural prefixes in Aux. What the natural and superlexical prefixes have in common is that they both bear [AD], and therefore they both require a c-commanding Prf head to delete this feature. It follows that a single clause cannot contain both a natural prefix and a superlexical prefix. For the same reason, analytic futures built with the *budet* auxiliary cannot include a superlexical prefix on the infinitive: (30).

(30) *Kompjuter bud-et za-rabotat' za čas.
computer be-PRS.3m INCEP-work in hour
'The computer will start working in an hour.'

In (30), both *budet* and *za-* bear [AD], but the sentence does not have the resources it would need to delete both of them.[7]

At this point, let us briefly reconsider the "building blocks" which Russian makes use of in expressing tense and aspectual information with the verb. Given the analysis to this point, the summary table in (12) should be reformulated as (31).

(31) *Revised table of the Russian tense/aspect components*

Prf [*u*AD]	Aux [AD]	Asp [AD]	Prefix	Verb	Asp	Tense
∅	*byt'*	superlex.	**intermed.**	"imperf."	**semelfac.**	past
		nat. pref.	**lexical**	"perf." [AD]	**sec. impf.**	pres.
				bi-aspect. ([AD])		
				paired ([AD])		

As this table highlights, the difference between verb types has been settled—verbs differ in whether they bear [AD] when drawn from the lexicon and merged into the syntactic structure. The difference between natural and

7. If multiple head-movement is the mechanism which brings a prefix together with the verb, then there is a second reason why (30) is ungrammatical, since no head will attract both *za-* and *rabota-*. This problem will not occur in all cases of analytic futures containing "perfective" complements to *budet*, however.

superlexical prefixes has become clearer—both bear [AD], but the latter also provide aspectual meanings. Russian tense now distinguishes between past and present, with the future meanings coming from a non-compositional pairing of present tense and Prf. What still has to be established are the roles played by the aspectual suffixes and by the intermediate and lexical prefixes.

Of these remaining items in the (31) table, the aspectual suffixes fall into place most directly. Consider first how the properties of the semelfactive suffix *-nu* may be treated.

Semelfactive verbs formed with the *nu-* suffix behave essentially like inherently perfective verbs. They are interpreted as perfectives and they combine with superlexical prefixes without becoming doubly perfective.

(32) a. Dima tolk-nu-l Mašu. (Gribanova 2013)
Dima push-SML-PST Masha
'Dima pushed Masha.'

b. Podarki ljubimomu čeloveku neskol'ko
presents beloved person somewhat
po-šat-nu-li vaše, v principe neploxoe
DELIM-shake-SML-PAST.3P your in principal not.bad
finansovoe položenie
financial position
'Presents for the one you love have somewhat shaken up your otherwise fairly good financial situation.'
(Makarova & Janda 2009: citing Goroskop (1997))

c. I na šavku pri-cyk-nu-l, [. . .],
and on stray.dog ATTEN-cluck-SML-PAST
'He even shushed a stray dog, [. . .].'
(Makarova & Janda 2009: quoting Boris Eksimov in *Noviy Mir*, 2002)

These properties will follow if semelfactive verbs also bear the [AD] feature. But since semelfactives are formed from imperfective stems, the [AD] feature must be introduced with the *nu-* suffix, and not the verb stem. And since *nu-* itself provides the semelfactive meaning, which is itself an aspectual notion, the natural role for *nu-* is to serve as the head of an aspectual category (Markman 2008, Gribanova 2013). Since *-nu* bears [AD], it must serve as a goal for a Prf head so that the [AD] feature can be deleted. This leads us to the structure (33) for (32a).

(33)

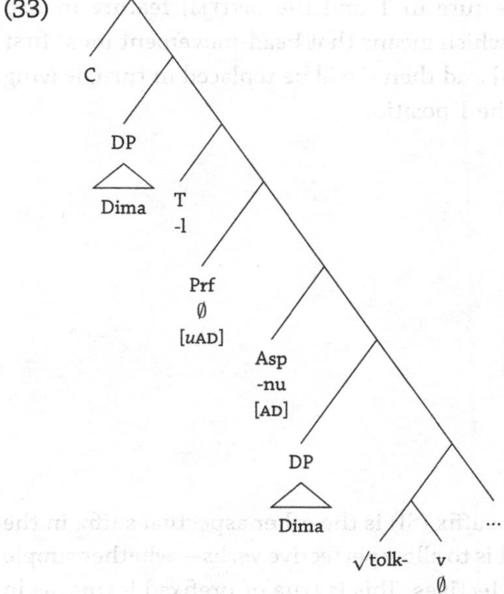

To clarify how the pieces of the complex verb are brought together in (32a), let us consider the same structure with the [STEM] features annotated in: (34).

(34)

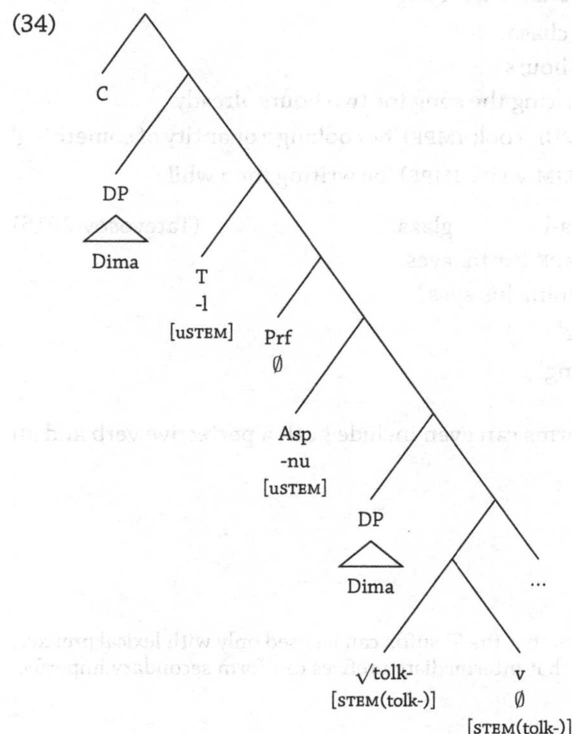

Given (34), both the [uSTEM] feature in T and the [uSTEM] feature in Asp will take the [STEM(tolk-)] value, which means that head-movement must first replace *-nu* with {{√tolk-, ∅}, *-nu*} and then *-l* will be replaced in turn, leaving the structure (35) linearized in the T position.

(35)

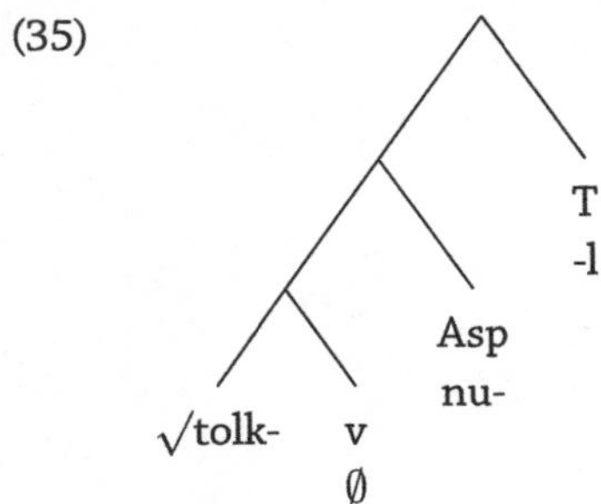

The "secondary imperfective" suffix (SI) is the other aspectual suffix in the system. The typical function of SI is to allow perfective verbs—whether simple or derived—to be used as imperfectives. This is true of prefixed forms, as in (36), and of inherently perfective verbs, as in (37).[8]

(36) a. Ja do-pis-yva-ju pesnju (Zinova & Filip 2013)
I COMPL-write-IMPF-1s song
uzhe dva chasa.
already two hours
'I'm finishing writing the song for two hours already.'

b. na-vari-vat' (CUMUL-cook-IMPF) 'be cooking a quantity of something'

c. po-pis-yvat' (DELIM-write-IMPF) 'be writing for a while'

(37) a. Volodja otkry-va-l glaza. (Tatevosov 2015)
Volodja open-IMPF-Pst.m eyes
'Volodja was opening his eyes.'

b. da-vat' 'be giving'

c. reš-at' 'be deciding'

Secondary imperfective forms can even include both a perfective verb and an intermediate prefix: (38).

8. Svenonius (2005a) claims that the SI suffix can be used only with lexical prefixes, but Tatevosov (2008) shows that intermediate prefixes can form secondary imperfective verbs.

(38) pere-kid-yvat'
DISTR-throw-IMPF
'be throwing one by one'

SI cannot, however, appear with semelfactive verbs. This follows immediately if the semelfactive suffix *nu-* and the SI suffix compete for the same syntactic Asp position, and cannot therefore appear on the same verb (Markman 2008, Gribanova 2013). In that case, the structure of (37) will be (39), before head-movement takes place.

(39)

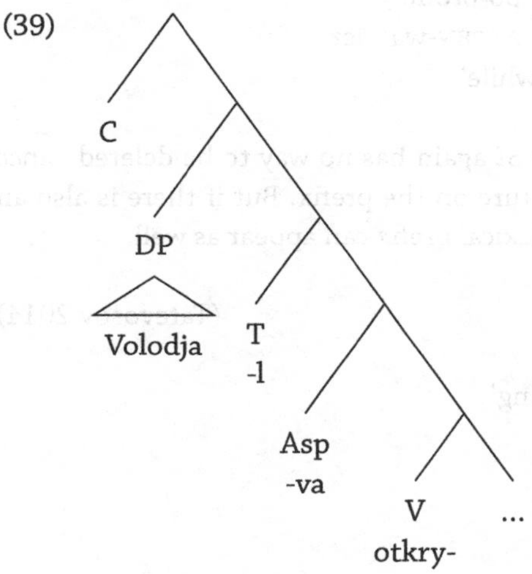

As for the interpretion of verbs inflected with SI, we need only consider how the [AD] features must be deleted in examples like (37a) and (36). In the former, a perfective verb bears [AD]; in the latter, a prefix does. But since none of these sentences are interpreted as perfective (or futures), the Prf head cannot be what deletes the [AD] feature. Instead, this job must fall to the SI suffix, which c-commands the [AD]-bearing terminal in all cases. And since the interpretation of a clause which does not contain Prf is imperfective, by default, SI does not actually have to contribute any aspectual meaning to the sentence. By taking away the need for Prf to appear, SI simply allows an imperfective meaning to be provided, even though it does not itself provide one. The only content SI needs to provide is a [*u*AD] feature, it seems.

The idea that SI bears [*u*AD] automatically ensures that this suffix cannot be freely attached to simple imperfectives: (40).

(40) *Anna čit-yva-la knigu.
Anna read-IMPF-PST.f book
'Anna was reading a book.'

In any case like (40), the [*u*AD] feature on SI would find no matching [AD] goal, so deletion of [*u*AD] could not occur, ensuring an illegible structure at the semantic interface. And if SI appears as a head in a position lower than the location of the superlexical prefixes, it follows that SI cannot appear in sentences like (41).

(41) a. *za-kuri-vat' (*vs.* za-kurit') (Svenonius 2005b)
INCEP-smoke-IMPF INCEP-smoke
'be starting smoking'

b. *po-braž-ivat' (*vs.* po-brodit')
ATTEN-wander-IMPF ATTEN-wander
'be wandering for a little while'

In these cases, the [*u*AD] feature on SI again has no way to be deleted, since it does not c-command the [AD] feature on the prefix. But if there is also an [AD]-bearing head below SI, a superlexical prefix can appear as well.

(42) a. na-da-vat' (Tatevosov 2014)
CUMUL-give-IMPF
'give a quantity of something'

b. za-otkry-vat'
INCEP-open-IMPF
'start opening'

The derivation of (42a) will require the structure (43), where for each [AD] feature, there is a corresponding c-commanding [*u*AD] feature, allowing all four to be deleted.

(43)

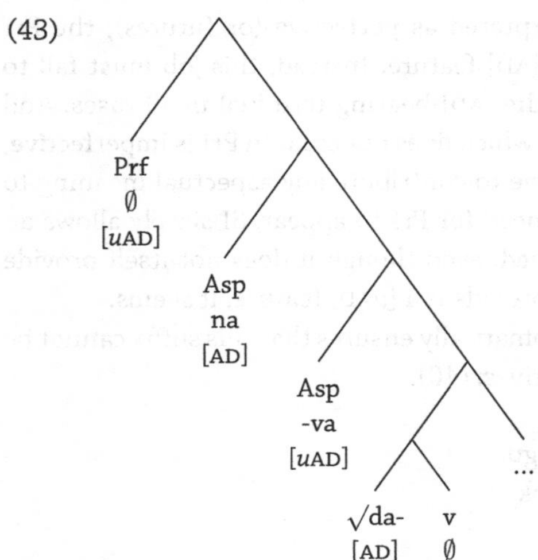

The interpretation of structures like (42) is necessarily perfective, since they must include a Prf head. This result also shows that SI does not make a perfective verb imperfective, because there is no imperfective sense in such examples. These are simply perfective, because SI does nothing other than allow an [AD] feature to be deleted.

On the other hand, Tatevosov (2014) finds some forms for which superlexical prefixes *za* and *po* appear to merge in a position below SI: (44).

(44) a. za-bole-vat'
INCEP-ail-IMPF
'be getting sick'

b. za-pe-vat'
INCEP-sing-IMPF
'be starting singing'

c. po-pis-yvat'
ATTEN-write-IMPF
'be writing for a while'

d. po-lež-ivat'
ATTEN-lie-IMPF
'be lying for a while'

For other superlexical prefixes, no such freedom of placement is available.[9]

The general idea that the uninterpretable [AD] feature is responsible for much of the behavior of individual heads in the Russian tense/aspect system allows a simple characterization of the secondary imperfective suffix, which is otherwise quite enigmatic. In terms of the overall clause structure, the relationships between SI and different [AD]-bearing heads also indicates that there can sometimes be two Asp heads in a clause (not including Prf), and that in some cases, they appear in different positions relative to each other.

Understanding the relationship between SI and the [AD] feature now makes it possible to capture the behavior of the remaining verb class: verbs of motion. In this group of verbs, the verb stems themselves fall into two semantic groups: directional and non-directional. The former signify motion towards

9. Tatevosov provides one example in which the apparent superlexical prefix *na* appears below SI and together with a perfective verb stem:

(i) na-dar-ivat
a.lot-give-IMPF
'give a lot of presents'

In this case, however, I suspect that *na-* is actually a lexical prefix, combining idiomatically with *dat'* to produce a meaning similar to what the cumulative superlexical prefix would provide.

a particular goal; the latter, motion which is less focused. Non-directional motion includes motion with no particular endpoint, but also repeated motion to the same location: (45)

(45) a. Maša xodi-la po lesu. (Gepner 2016)
Masha walk-PST.f on wood
'Masha used to walk in the woods; Masha was walking around in the woods.'

b. Ivan bega-l po magazinam, kogda my ego vstretili.
Ivan run-PST.m to shops when we him met
'Ivan was running from one shop to another when we met him.'

Motion verbs of both types often contain a lexical prefix, but here I focus only on the non-prefixed base forms. The full list of motion verb pairs appears in (46).

(46)

Non-directional	Directional	
begat'	bežat'	'run'
brodit'	bresti	'stroll'
ezdit'	exat'	'go (by vehicle)
gonjat'	gnat'	'drive'
katat'(sja)	katit'(sja)	'roll, push'
maskat'(sja)	maščit'(sja)	'drag'
lazat'	lest'	'climb'
letat'	letet'	'fly'
nosit'	nesti	'carry, wear'
plavat'	plyt'	'swim'
polzat'	polzti	'crawl'
taskat'	taščit'	'drag, pull'
vodit'(sja)	vesti(s')	'lead'
vozit'	vezti	'transport/carry (by vehicle)'
xodit'	idti (id-; šʊ-})	'go'

With Zalizniak (2017),[10] I take the non-directional verbs to be derived imperfective forms, in which the presence of a "secondary imperfective" suffix is sometimes opaque, and sometimes revealed by the stress pattern. For *begat'*, *gon'at'*, *katat'*, *lazat'*, *letat'*, *legat'*, *plyvat'*, *polzat'*, and *taskat'*, the stress-bearing suffix *-a* is clearly the secondary imperfective affix. For the remaining non-directional verbs, one must posit a zero allomorph for SI. The zero realization of SI is then associated with a stem belonging to the set: *brodit'*, *ezdit'*, *nosit'*, *vodit'*, *vozit'*, and *xodit'*.

10. Zalizniak bases her arguments in turn on Karcevsky (1927) and Isacenko (1960),

Non-directional verbs refer to actions which have no natural endpoint—they are anti-telic. As such, they are semantically resistant to a perfective interpretation, which means that they cannot co-occur with Prf within a clause. This is true both of the base forms of the non-directional verbs and of prefixed forms. The imperfective shape of these verbs then indicates that non-directional motion verbs always bear [AD] as a lexical property of the class. The [AD] feature is not itself semantically interpretable, but its presence allows the semantic feature(s) which imply non-directionality to be detected indirectly, sometimes, in the externalized output. SI is present because it provides the only available mechanism for ensuring that [AD] is deleted.

Directional verbs, in contrast, do not bear [AD] and they are semantically compatible with a Prf head, so they can be found in both perfective and imperfective clauses. Since they lack [AD], they "become" perfective only with the addition of a prefix, minimally the natural perfective prefix *po-*.

(47) Zavtra ja po-id-u v kino.
tomorrow I PRF-go-1s to cinema
'Tomorrow I'll go to the cinema.'

For a regular motion verb like *letet'* 'fly', this ensures four possibilities: (48).

(48)

	Imperfective past	Perfective past	Present	Future
3sf	lete-la	po-lete-la	let-it	po-let-it

When a non-natural prefix is employed to enrich the verb with more than just a perfective sense, it adds an [AD] feature which affects the morphological result in predictable ways. For the perfective forms, the stem takes the same shapes as in (48), i.e. *pri-letela* 'she flew here' and *pri-let-it* 'she will fly here'. For the imperfective forms, the [AD] in the prefix must be balanced by the addition of an SI suffix, producing the forms (49).

(49)

	Imperfective past	Perfective past	Present	Future
3sf	pri-let-a-la	pri-lete-la	pri-let-a-et	pri-let-it

The stems for the directional imperfective forms in (49) are identical to the non-directional past and present forms of *letat'*—not because of a blurred meaning of directionality in either case, but simply because the morphological result in both cases is due to the necessary presence of SI.

For the irregular directional forms (*bresti*, *exat'*, *lest'*, *polzti*, etc.) the stem forms which result when a prefix is combined with the stem to produce an imperfective verb will also coincide with the stem form for a non-directional verb, because again, the presence of SI ensures a specific stem shape. In these cases, what needs to be explained is the divergence of the perfective stems, which are suppletive. As with the paired aspectual stems discussed already, the suppletive motion verb stems can be handled by supposing a set of Vocabulary Insertion rules which are sensitive to the morphological context. In this case, what matters is not the presence of an [AD] feature in the stem, but simply the presence of a tense suffix to which the stem is attached. For example, the rules in (50)–(51) will ensure the correct output for the various uses of *begat'/bežat'* 'run' and *xodit'/idti* 'go'. For the reasons just laid out, a tense suffix will be directly attached to the verb stem only in limited circumstances: never with non-directional verbs, and not with prefixed directional verbs which are imperfective.

(50) a. bega- → /beža/ / _ + Tense
b. bega- → /bega/

(51) a. xodi- → /id/ / _ + Tense
b. xodi- → /xodi/

Crucially, the presence of a prefix plays no role in the application of rules like (51). The implication is that prefixes are attached more distantly than the tense suffix in the morphological structure to which (51) applies. This result is automatic if multiple head-movement is how the verb is formed. Consider the structure (52), which corresponds to example (47).

(52)

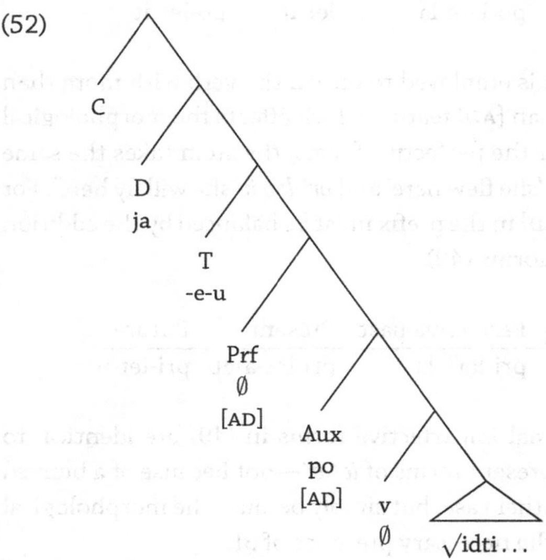

If *po-* and the verb root bear valued [STEM] features, v bears one [uSTEM] feature and T bears two [uSTEM] features, then feature valuation and head-movement will ultimately generate the structure (53) in T.

(53)

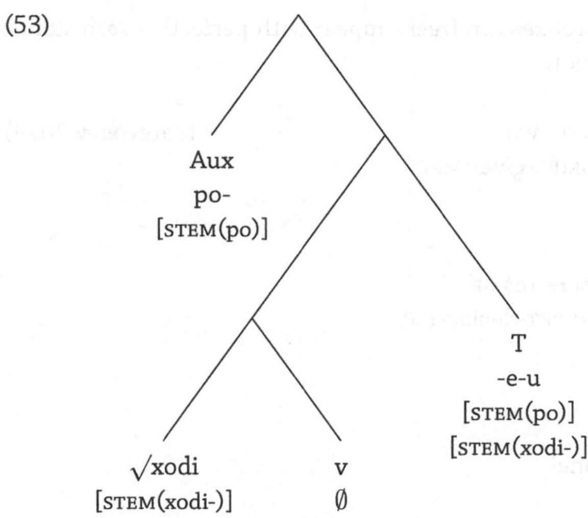

As zero v does not affect the operations, the tense suffix appears together with the verb root *xodi-* in this structure, ensuring that the suppletive stem *id-* will be used.

The central claim being advanced here is still that multiple head-movement is a necessary part of Russian morpho-syntax, and it is easy to lose track of this idea when the complexities of verb types and of aspectual interpretations are the immediate focus. And actually, the idea that a diacritic [AD] feature might distinguish classes of verbs and prefixes could certainly be deployed to advantage in an analysis in which multiple head-movement is not involved. The absolute necessity of multiple head-movement will become clearer when we look at the role valuation of [*u*AD] features plays in the distribution of the remaining two types of prefixes, a matter to which I now turn.

The intermediate prefixes completive *do-*, repetitive *pere-*, and perdurative *pod-* show three characteristics which distinguish them from superlexical prefixes. First, they appear closer to the verb than superlexical prefixes do, when circumstances allow both to be present. This will normally require that SI be included in the clause, so that Prf and SI can delete one [AD] feature each.

(54) a. na-do-pis-yvat' (Tatevosov 2014)
CUMUL-COMPL-write-IMPF
'accumulate a quantity of something as a result of completing writing it'

b. po-pod-rabat-yvat'
ATTEN-PERD-work-IMPF
'spend some time trying to gain some money'

Secondly, intermediate prefixes can freely appear with perfective verb stems, whether SI is present or not:

(55) a. do-dat'; do-da-vat' (Tatevosov 2014)
COMPL-give COMPL-give-IMPF

b. *na-dat'
CUMUL-give

c. pere-rešit; pere-reš-at'
REPET-decide REPET-decide-IMPF
'decide again'

d. *pere-otkryt'
DISTR-open
'open one by one'

Third, as already noted, intermediate prefixes commute freely, even with themselves, as in (56), repeated.[11]

(56) a. Vasja pere-do-pisa-l stat'ju. (Tatevosov 2008)
Vasja REPET-COMPL-write-PST.m paper
'Again, Vasja performed a final stage of writing a paper.'

b. Vasja do-pere-pisa-l stat'ju.
Vasja COMPL-REPET-write-PST.m paper
'Vasja completed re-writing a paper.'

c. Vasja do-do-pisa-l knigu.
Vasja COMPL-COMPL-write-PST.m paper
'Vasja completed finishing writing a book.'

11. An anonymous reviewer questions whether the two instances of *pere* or *do* are actually the same categories. For *pere*, for example, one might be equated to English *again*; the other, to English *re-*. In that case, the different interpretations of *pere-* might correspond to two distinct phrasal categories in which *pere-* would be situated. And much the same could be proposed for *do-*. In fact, even if this alternative analysis were upheld, the analysis of multiple head-movement developed here would remain the same. The claim that these intermediate prefixes are adverbial allows the properties of these prefixes to be derived along the same lines as prenominal adjectives in the English and Scandinavian constructions discussed in sections 2.6.4 and 2.6.3, respectively, but they would still fall into place if they were heads of phrasal categories immediately outside the verb phrase. In that case, they would still be the target for [uSTEM] valuation by a T or SI probe. On the other hand, if these are truly adverbial adjuncts, then nothing more needs to be said about them, and their analysis does not require the proliferation of new syntactic categories. More importantly, if the intermediate prefixes are treated as additional phrase heads, then it is not clear the [AD] features on multiple intermediate prefixes or on an intermediate prefix and a perfective verb can be deleted together.

d. Vasja pere-pere-pisa-l stat'ju.
Vasja REPET-REPET-write-PST.m paper
'Vasja re-wrote his paper again.'

This last property suggests what distinguishes intermediate prefixes from the others already discussed. While a series of heads are normally found in a specific order, each selecting the next, adverbial modifiers commute freely, with differing orders controlling their semantic scope. For example, in (57), *deliberately* and *quickly* can appear in either order, with no obvious structural difference but with consequences for their interpretations.

(57) a. Bourne deliberately quickly wiped the room.
b. Bourne quickly deliberately wiped the room.

Suppose the same is true for the intermediate prefixes in Russian. Then these are modifying adverbial elements instead of heads of phrases, and they attach to the verb phrase through adjunction. The structure of (56a) will be (58), in that case.

(58)

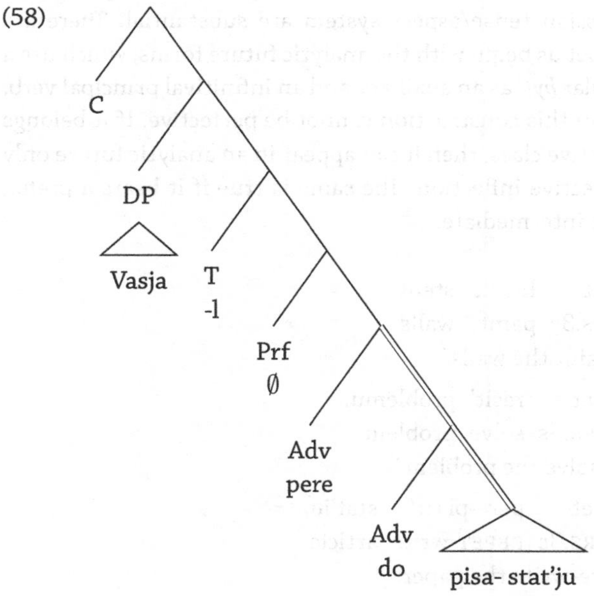

The adverbs in (58) can commute freely without altering the larger structure, and either could be replaced by the other, as long as the result is semantically felicitous, as the examples in (56) show they can be. And since these adverbs are adjoined to the verb phrase, they can be expected to show up closer to the verb than superlexical prefixes will be.

Now the question of how [AD] features are deleted in (58) comes up. Prf will bear [*u*AD] automatically, and that means it must find a goal which bears [AD]. Both *pere-* and *do-* must bear [AD], since the presence of either in a clause ensures a perfective interpretation, if SI is not involved. But then valuation of [*u*AD] should delete only the [AD] feature on the higher of the two adverbs, leaving one toxic feature behind to block convergence at the semantic interface. And yet these are grammatical sentences, so something must allow for deletion of the second [AD] feature.

The same problem actually arises in the (55) examples, where the intermediate prefix and the perfective stem both must bear [AD]. In this case, it is the [AD] feature on the verb which would not be deleted, since Prf would value [*u*AD] on the prefix instead.

The only conclusion we can draw is that Prf must be able to delete both [AD] features, which implies that Prf may bear multiple [*u*AD] features. It can then engage in feature valuation twice, matching first with the [AD] feature on *pere-* and next with the one on *do-*.

While there is nothing problematic in the premise that a head may bear multiple unvalued features—the entire model of head-movement developed in Chapter 2 depends on this idea, after all—the empirical consequences of this result for the Russian tense/aspect system are substantial. There are several consequences. Let us begin with the analytic future forms, which use a perfective form of copular *byt'* as an auxiliary and an infinitival principal verb. But the principal verb in this construction cannot be perfective. If it belongs to the inherently perfective class, then it can appear in an analytic future only with secondary imperfective inflection. The same is true if it bears a prefix, whether superlexical or intermediate.

(59) a. Maša bud-et kracit' steny.
Masha be-PRS.3s paint walls
'Masha will paint the walls.'

b. *Maša bud-et rešit' problemu.
Masha be-PRS.3s solve problem
'Masha will solve the problem.'

c. *Maša bud-et pere-pisat' stat'ju.
Masha be-PRS.3s REPET-write article
'Masha will re-write the paper.'

If Prf can freely delete any number of [AD] features in its domain, then all of the examples in (59) should be grammatical. With two [*u*AD] features, Prf could value and delete the first one with the [AD] feature on *budet* and then nothing prevents it from valuing and deleting the more remote one afterward. So both the [AD] on *rešit'* and the [AD] on *pere-* should be eliminated.

On similar grounds, ungrammatical forms where a superlexical prefix combines with a perfective verb or another prefix become hard to explain if Prf can bear multiple [*u*AD] features. Suppose example (55b) has the structure (60).

(60)

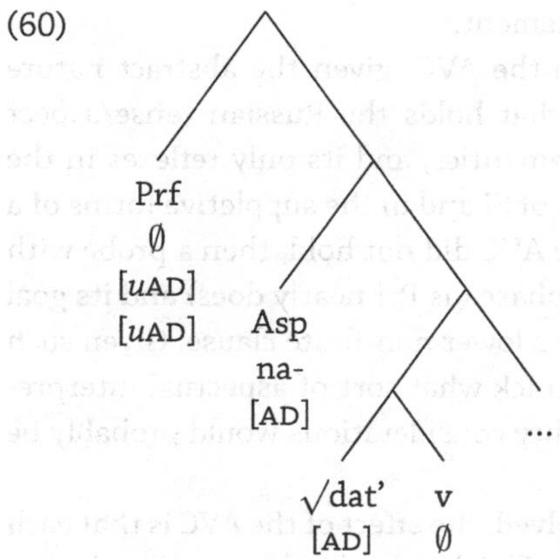

The two [AD] features should provide a value to the two [*u*AD] features in Prf, deleting all four in the process. Yet such forms are impossible.

Except for where intermediate prefixes are concerned, the pattern seems to be that Prf can value its [*u*AD] feature only by matching features on the head of its complement. This covers natural prefixes and *budet*, superlexical prefixes, and semelfactive *-nu* and perfective verbs, all of which can appear in isolation in a perfective clause. If multiple [*u*AD] features are necessarily available to Prf, then the valuation process must be restricted to a certain structural domain for this feature. And the same is true of SI, which also appears to value its [*u*AD] feature(s) only from the head of its complement (except with *do-*, *pere-*, and *pod-*).

The following constraint captures the general pattern: (61).[12]

(61) [AD] *Valuation Constraint* (AVC)
Valuation of [*u*AD] requires a contiguous goal.

12. Tatevosov's (2014) "selectional restriction" has much the same effect. In his phrasing, "the complement of a prefix [from a list of superlexical prefixes] cannot be grammatically perfective." While this does capture the general pattern, it does not constitute a real alternative to the AVC. First, the concept "grammatical perfective" is effectively equivalent to what I call the [AD] feature. It is a formal quality with no direct semantic content, as Tatevosov (2011) actually emphasizes. Second, the idea that the complement of a prefix can be required *not* to have some quality is difficult to implement without adding some powerful new notion of selection to the grammar. Third, the restriction of this rule to a particular set of prefixes lacks motivation, beyond getting the facts right. Alternatively, and less antagonistically, the AVC might simply be taken as a formal rephrasing of Tatevosov's descriptive generalization.

Syntactic contiguity will not equate to adjacency, but to an uninterrupted structural relationship between syntactic objects, in this case, a [*u*AD]-bearing probe and an [AD]-bearing goal. As both probe and goal are terminal elements, we can take this to mean a head-head relationship, such as is found between a selecting head and the head of its complement.

There is obvious functional value to the AVC, given the abstract nature of an [AD] feature. Although [AD] is what holds the Russian tense/aspect system together, it is invisible to the semantics, and its only reflexes in the morphophonology are in the expression of SI and in the suppletive forms of a handful of paired aspectual verbs. If the AVC did not hold, then a probe with [*u*AD] could appear at one extreme of a phase (as Prf nearly does) and its goal could appear at another, perhaps within a lower non-finite clause. Given such a grammar, it would be challenging to track what sort of aspectual interpretation should be available, and learnability considerations would probably be daunting as well.

Where no adjoined modifiers are involved, the effect of the AVC is that each head with a [*u*AD] feature—Prf and SI—will delete [AD] only on one goal, even if it has the capacity to bear multiple [*u*AD] features. The problems which arise by allowing extra [*u*AD] feature are thereby contained. Now consider what this means for the analysis of the adjoined intermediate prefixes. Let us return to the structure (58), now annotated with [AD] features.

(62)

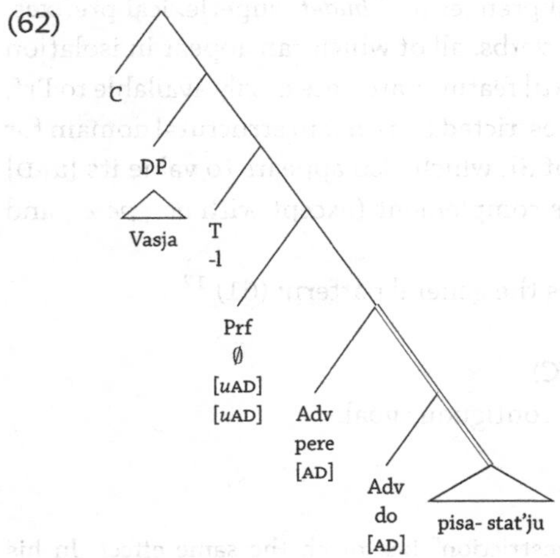

Given the AVC, the Prf probe should be able to take *pere-* and *do-* as goals only if they are contiguous, where contiguity means a hierarchical relationship no more remote than between a head and the head of its complement. In (62) though, the adjoined prefixes are actually closer to Prf than the head of its complement. Adjuncts are separated from the sister of the phrase which includes them only be a segment, and not by a full category. So the AVC must allow valuation of both [AD] features, as we require. In short, adjunction structures provide a loophole which allows a probe with multiple [*u*AD] features to delete multiple [AD] goals.

Of course, the same loophole is available when intermediate prefixes are adjoined to the projection of a perfective verb, as in (55). In that case, the adjoined prefix will be an accessible goal by virtue of the loophole, while the perfective verb is contiguous because of the head-head relation between the verb and the probe.

Multiple head-movement will take place with a structure like (62) like it does with Northern Swedish incorporated adjectives, by treating the adjoined element as a goal for [uSTEM] valuation, so that the head-movement step will produce a morphological structure (63) for T in (62).

(63)

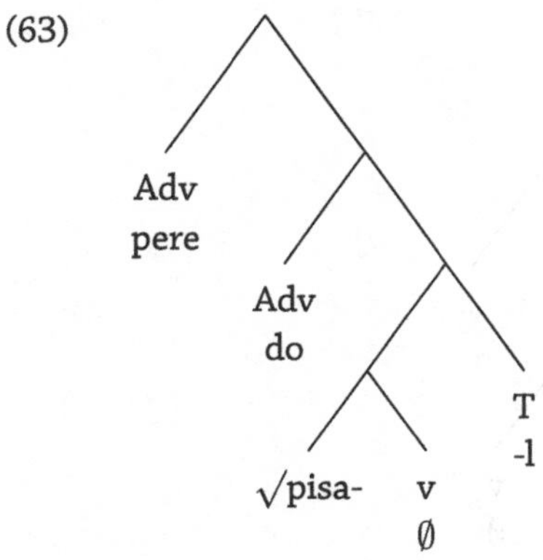

Because adverbial adjuncts adjoined to the verb phrase are subject to multiple head-movement, they cannot remain *in situ* while the verb raises past them. This accounts for the superficial resemblance between adverb placement in Russian and what is found in English, observed by Bailyn (1995, 2011). Adverbs in Russian cannot appear between the verb and direct objects, as seen in (64).

(64) a. *Ivan ubiraet často komnatu.
Ivan cleans often room
'Ivan often cleans his room.'

b. ?*Ivan celuet často Mashu.
Ivan kisses often Masha
'Ivan often kisses Masha.'

Bailyn maintains that this data shows that the verb does not raise out of the verb phrase in Russian, so that Russian and English pattern alike, despite the rich and regular agreement inflection in Russian finite verbs (Koeneman

& Zeijlstra 2012).[13] But the ungrammaticality in (64a) actually follows from how multiple head-movement operates, given structures like (65).

(65)

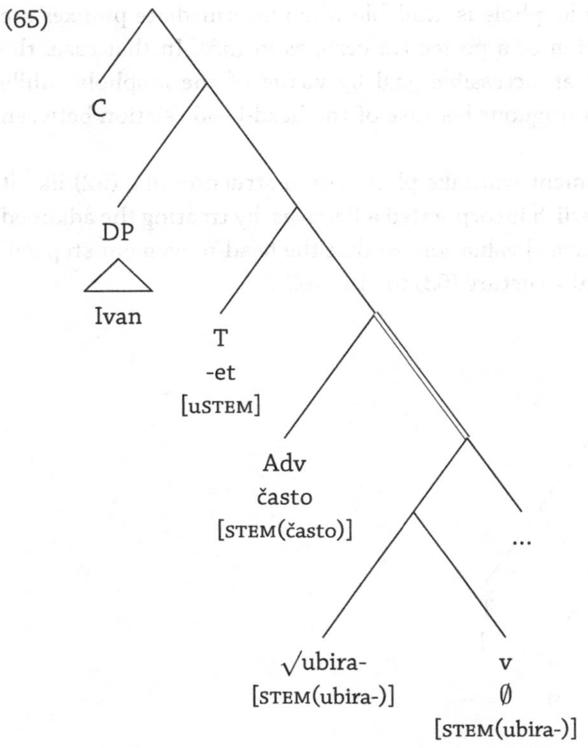

Since *často* must contain a [STEM] feature, it automatically blocks the T probe from accessing the more distance [STEM] feature on the verb. T must value its [uSTEM] feature in (65) with [STEM(často)], which will force head-movement to raise the adverb to the T position. But a full adverb like *často* cannot successfully combine with T, which requires a verbal stem.

13. Bailyn also observes that subjects cannot strand quantifiers in a position to the right of the verb in Russian:

(i) *My čitaem vse gazetu.
we read all newspaper
'We all read the newspaper.'

Bailyn treats this data as additional evidence that the verb does not raise to T. But if quantifiers are potential *intervenors* for [uSTEM] valuation, then they will not be allowed to remain inside the verb phrase either, for fear that they would block T from attracting ther verb. And since the actual position of stranded quantifiers is not conclusively established in the first place (Bobaljik 2003), it is difficult to judge whether they should expected to intervene in this context or not.

If the verb does not raise all the way to T, then adverbs can actually occupy an intermediate position freely. This is the case in compound futures, as in (66).

(66) a. Ne bud-u gromko pere-skaz-yvat' vse trevolneniya.
NEG be/PRF-1s loudly REPET-say-IMPF all troubles
'I will not loudly recount all the troubles.'

b. *Ne budu pere-skaz-yvat' gromko vse trevolneniya.
NEG be/PRF-1s REPET-say-IMPF loudly all troubles

In (66a), the principal verb raises only as high as the SI affix *-yva-*. The future auxiliary *budet* does not attract the principal verb at all, so the presence in (66a) of the adverb *gromko* between *budet* and the verb is acceptable. In (66b), however, the adverb is adjoined to the verb phrase and the verb must raise to SI, so once again, intervention of the adverb in valuation of the [uSTEM] feature on SI renders the structure morphologically unacceptable.

The analyses proposed here are fully consistent with the existence of two types of ellipsis in Russian: TP ellipsis, which takes place in answers to polar questions, and verb phrase ellipsis. In polar answers, the finite verb expresses a positive answer, as in (67).

(67) a. — Evgenija ot-pravi-la posylku v Moskvu?
Evgenija PRF-send-PST.f package to Moscow
'Did Evgenia send the package to Moscow?'
(Gribanova 2017a)

b. — Ot-pravi-la.
PRF-send-PST.f
'She did.'

Such answers are formed by raising the inflected verb from T to C in Russian (Gribanova 2017a), as in Finnish. TP is then elided, under identity with TP in the preceding polar question. In the model developed here, multiple head-movement places the verb and its prefixes in T in any simple finite clause, so that the subsequent T-to-C movement step carries the prefix along, unproblematically.

More interesting is the case of Russian VP-ellipsis, which depends more closely on the how prefixes are related to the verb in the final syntactic structure. Since natural, superlexical and intermediate prefixes are actually located outside the verb phrase—or outside one of its segments, in the case of intermediate prefixes—it follows that the prefix and the verb phrase might be independently involved in other syntactic operations. VP-ellipsis is one context where this expectation is upheld. In clauses with compound future tense, where the verb is clearly not raised to T, VP-ellipsis operates much as in English. Thus, the full verb phrase is omitted in the second conjunct, under identity with the first one in (68).

(68) Sonja bud-et zanimat'sja jogoj (Bailyn 2011)
Sonja be.FUT-3s occupy.self yoga
a Aleksandra ne bud-et.
but Alexandra NEG be.FUT-3s
'Sonya will do yoga but Alexandra won't.'

In contrast, in clauses with finite principal verbs, the second verb is actually pronounced in the position to which it raises,[14] although the remainder of the verb phrase is still omitted Gribanova (2013).[15]

What is more, Gribanova shows that ellipsis is sensitive to the structure of perfective clauses in a way that distinguishes the prefixes from the elided verb. Some of her data appears in (69).

(69) a. Ty po-znakomi-l Mašu s Petej? Konečno
you PRF-acquaint-PST.m Masha with Peter certainly
po-znakomi-l!
PRF-aquaint-PST.m
'Did you introduce Masha to Peter? Of course I did!'

b. Kažetsja, čto nikto ne podnja-l vazu kotoraja uže
seems that nobody NEG pick.up-PST vase which already
ne pervyj raz pada-ot. Naoborot, uže priše-l
NEG first time fall-PRS.3 on.contrary already come-PST
čelovek, kotoryj pere-ponjal.
person who REPET-pick.up-PST
'It seems that no one picked up the vase which fell more than once. On the contrary, a person who picked it up again already came.'

14. The idea that such ellipsis structures are possible has been challenged by Landau (2020), but Landau's alternative does not allow for structures like these, in which a verb root must be identical for an object to be omitted, but the prefix attached to be verb may be distinct. Moreover, the ellipsis contrasts discussed below between superlexical prefixes and intermediate prefixes, on the one hand, and lexical prefixes, on the other, would be entirely inexplicable if this type of VP-ellipsis is not possible. Simpson (2021) points out additional problems with Landau's critique.

15. Bailyn (2011) supposes that ellipsis of a finite verb phrase can also delete the verb, but the examples he provides include negator *njet* which functions somehow as a negative *do so*-like constituent, even though *njet* bears no finite inflection. It is unclear how strong Bailyn's argument can be, however, given the peculiar behavior of *njet* in this construction. It may be that *njet* is simply functioning as a (polar) verb phrase anaphor—like *so*—in which case his examples do not involve VP ellipsis in a finite clause at all.

c. Ty uže po-kormi-la malyš-a? Da, ja teper
you already PRF-feed-PST.f baby Yes I now
pere-karml-iva-ju, kažetsja.
EXCESS-feed-IMPF-1s seems
'Did you already feed the baby? Yes, it seems I'm overfeeding him now.'

What is striking about these data is not the extraction of the verb from the ellipsis site, but rather that the prefixes need not be involved in satisfying identity for the two verb phrases. While (69) employs the same natural prefix in both the non-elliding initial sentence in the elliding second one, in (69b), the first verb bears no prefix, but the second, which originates inside the elided verb phrase, does. And in (69c), the two sentences in employ different prefixes. If we consider the base structures for (69c), the fact that the prefix can vary without affecting the ellipsis makes sense. In both sentences, the verb stem *korm-* will appear initially within the verb phrase with no prefix attached, as in (70).

(70) a. [ty uže [$_{T}$ -la] [$_{Aux}$ po-] [$_{vP}$ korml- malyša]]
b. [ja teper [$_{T}$ -ju] [$_{Asp}$ pere-] [$_{vP}$ korml- malyša]]

In the model advanced here, multiple head-movement will situate the (audible copy of the) verb outside the verb phrase, when T attracts both the prefix and the verb. (The behavior of the 'secondary imperfective' suffix *-iva* is discussed below.) But what remains within the verb phrase—verb and object—matches the content of the verb phrase of the second sentence to that of the preceding sentence, which licences ellipsis. The syntactically independent prefixes *po-* and *pere-* continue to make their own distinct semantic contributions outside the verb phrase.

Now we can turn to the last class of prefixes: the lexical prefixes. Like natural, superlexical and intermediate prefixes, the lexical prefixes enforce a perfective meaning, so they must bear an [AD] feature. But these prefixes show much less semantic coherence than the superlexical and intermediate prefixes (Babko-Malaya 1999). Consider the following examples: (71).

(71) a. Lev pod-pisa-l pis'mo.
Lev under-write-PST.m letter
'Lev signed the letter.'

b. (Ja tam rabot-al 15 let) (Bailyn 2011)
I there work-PST 15 years
čtoby za-rabot-at' bol'šie den'gi.
in.order for-work-INF big money
'(I worked there for 15 years) in order to earn a lot of money.'

c. Ivan pere-kričal vsex ostal'nyx. (Flier 1984)
Ivan out-shout-PST.m all remaining
'Ivan outshouted all the rest.'

d. Helder za-brosi-l mjač v vorota angličan.
Helder into-threw ball-PST.m in goal English
'Helder kicked the ball into the English goal.'
(Svenonius 2005b)

e. David sovsem za-brosi-l futbol.
David completely into-threw-PST.m soccer
'David completely gave up soccer.'

f. Ona is-pisa-la svoju ručku. (Spencer & Zaretskaya 1998)
she out.of-write-PST.f her pen
'She has written her pen out of ink.'

As Svenonius shows, unlike the superlexical prefixes, lexical prefixes must originate inside the verb phrase, just as Germanic particles do, but they are are displaced out. In that respect, the (71) examples are comparable to an English sentence like (72a), with the base structure for the verb phrase (72b):

(72) a. Peter jotted the equation down.

b.

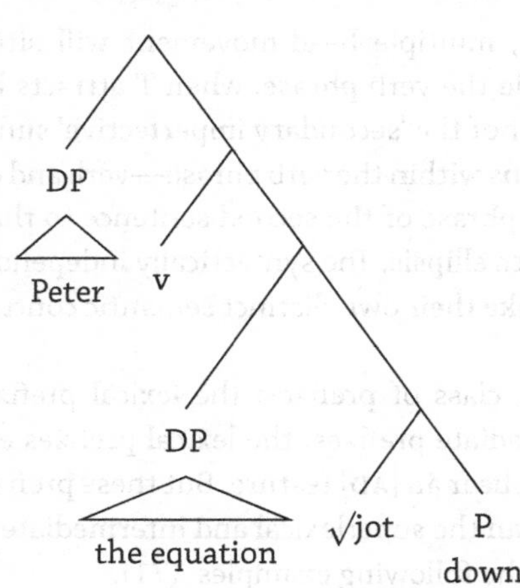

Like the particle *down* in (72), *pod-* in (71a) originates together with the verb root. Along the same lines, the base structure of the (71a) verb phrase will then be (73).

(73)

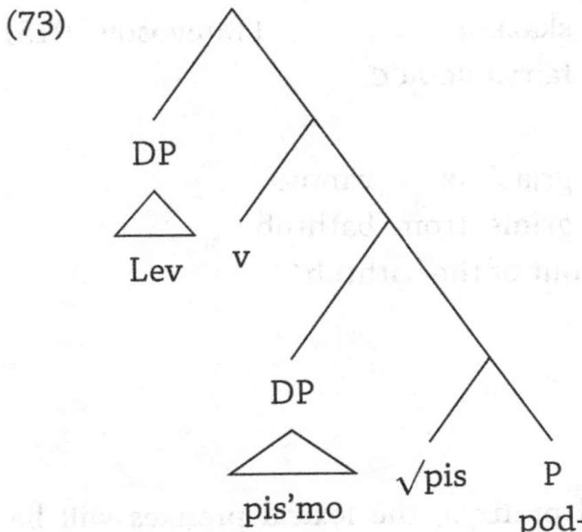

It is the combination of the verb root and *pod*—effectively a particle in this configuration—which produces the idiomatic meaning 'to sign'. Idioms are constructed from constituents in their base postion, so *pod* and the root of *pisat'* must originate sufficiently close together to allow for idiom formation.

In most respects, lexical prefixes behave identically to higher prefixes. Both lexical prefixes and superlexical prefixes (including intermediate ones) produce perfective interpretations for the clause, unless secondary imperfective morphology is employed to compensate. Like superlexical prefixes, lexical prefixes form verbs which cannot be used with a higher phase verb unless secondary imperfective morphology is also present. Lexical and superlexical prefixes are subject to similar morphophonological processes, as we will see. But unlike superlexical prefixes, lexical prefixes are not exempt from the matching requirement in VP ellipsis structures (Gribanova 2010), as (74) shows.

(74) *Kakaja-to ženščina pri-nes-la etu knigu, no potom
some woman at-bring-PST.f this book but later

pojavi-la-s' služanka, kotoraja u-nes-la.
appear-PST.f-REFL maid who away-bring-PST.f.

'Some woman brought over this book, but later there appeared a maid who took it away.'

The prefixes *pri-* and *u-* in (74) are lexical prefixes, and since they do not match, the verb phrase in the relative clause cannot be elided, so the object cannot be omitted from the surface string.

Like intermediate superlexical prefixes, Russian lexical prefixes can have [AD] deleted by the secondary imperfective Asp in place of Prf, as ilustrated in (75).

(75) a. Vasja ras-skaz-yva-l skazk-u. (Tatevosov 2015)
Vasja apart-say-IMPF-PST.m fairy.tale-ACC
'Vasja was telling a fairy tale.'

b. Ja sejčas vy-my-va-ju grjaz' iz vanny.
I now out-wash-IMPF-1s grime from bathtub
'I am now washing the grime out of the bathtub.'

c. za-pis-yvat'
behind-write-IMPF.INF
'to be recording'

As with the intermediate superlexical prefixes, the lexical prefixes will be attracted by SI, together with the verb. As with perfective forms with lexical prefixes, multiple head-movement is possible because the prefix will previously have adjoined to the verb phrase.

Both superlexical prefixes and lexical prefixes can appear on the same verb, as in (76):

(76) On pri-v-sta-l, čtoby popravit' kilt.
he ATTEN-in-stand-PST.m to smooth.INF kilt
'He stood up slightly to smoothen his kilt.'

The order of the preverbs is fixed, in such verbs; the lexical prefix must follow the superlexical one (Svenonius 2005b). This is to be expected, since the lexical prefix will always be adjoined to the verb phrase, while the superlexical one is a higher functional category which takes the verb phrase as its complement. When multiple head-movement displaces both upwards, the higher one will automatically end up further to the left in the resulting complex verb. It is also possible for an additional higher superlexical prefix to appear, outside a cluster of prefixes which are attracted by SI, as in (77).

(77) a. Vasja za čas po-vy-bras-yva-l vse lišnie šmotki.
Vasja in hour PRF-out-throw-IMPF-PST.m all excess belongings
'Vasja threw out all his extra belongings one by one in an hour.'

b. Vasja nemnogo po-pere-za-pis-yva-l (Tatevosov 2008)
Vasja for.a.while DELIM-REPET-behind-write-IMPF-PST.m

diski.
CDs
'Vasja spent some time re-recording CDs.'

Again, this is expected, since a higher Prf head may be introduced into the clause in any case.

So lexical prefixes must originate inside the verb phrase but they must be accessible for multiple head-movement operations in which T or SI attract them before the verb. Taken together, these imply that within the core syntactic derivation, the lexical prefixes must be displaced from their original position to a new position on the edge of the verb phrase. In their derived position, they are accessible for [*u*AD] and [*u*STEM] valuation operations, which determine what takes place in the process of externalization. What is more, since lexical prefixes appear to the right of intermediate prefixes, when both are found, the only option is that lexical prefixes must be adjoined to the verb phrase before intermediate prefixes are.

Part of the explanation for displacement of lexical prefixes is apparent if we consider the needs of [AD] features in verbal prefixes. Consider the structure in (73). Since transitive v is a phase head, the [AD] feature on *pod-* inside the vP phase cannot be accessed by a Prf probe to value its own [*u*AD] feature. This means that the [AD] feature on *pod-* cannot be deleted. Therefore *pod-* must be displaced to the phase edge, to be accessible from outside the phase. Since *pod-* is a preposition, it can adjoin to the verb phrase freely, by PP extraposition. (In most treatments in the literature, PP extraposition produces a word order in which the prepositional phrase appears at the right edge rather than the left, but this anticipated linear order will be moot, given later steps in the derivation of (71a).) At the C-T phase level, then, the structure for the same sentence will be (78), after *pod-* has adjoined to the verb phrase.

(78)

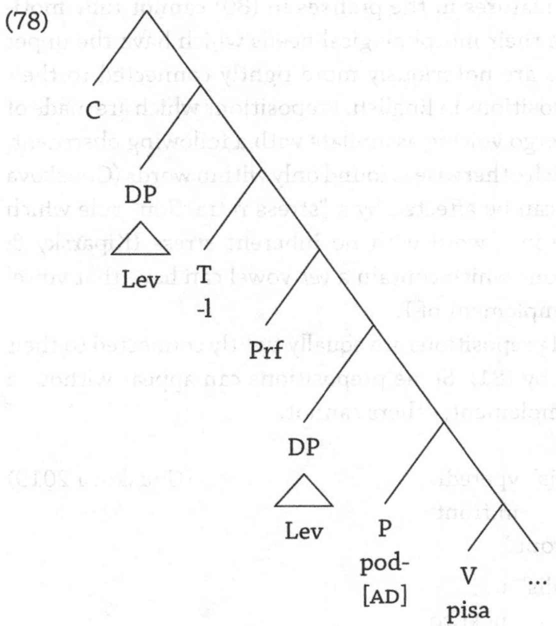

Since Prf c-commands *pod-* within this phase, the licencing requirements of [AD] feature will be met in (78).

For examples like (71a), the concepts and mechanisms which operate on other types of prefixes are now enough to provide a complete derivational account. The only part of the derivation which is unique to the lexical prefix case is the adjunction of a preposition to the verb phrase, an operation which is independently motivated on other grounds. In effect, the analysis of lexical prefixal verbs comes for free.

For lexical prefix structures in which the verb phrase is perhaps not phasal, however, something more must be said. If the [AD] feature can be deleted internal to the verb phrase, then some other motivation must be found to explain why the preposition/prefix must raise up. This will be the situation for the examples in (79), where the verb to which a lexical prefix attaches is passive (79) or middle (80):

(79) Èti voprosy by-li ob-sužd-eny. (Townsend 1967)
these questions be-PST.3p around-judge-PASS
'These questions were discussed.'

(80) Èti voprosy sejčas ob-suždaj-ut-sja.
these questions now around-judge-3p-REFL
'These questions are now being discussed.'

If the dependancy of [AD] features in the prefixes in (80) cannot fully motivate movement, it must be their morphological needs which have the upper hand. Russian prepositions are notoriously more tightly connected to their complements than are prepositions in English. Prepositions which are made of a single obstruent can undergo voicing assimilate with a following obstruent, an assimilation pattern which otherwise is found only within words (Gouskova 2019). Some prepositions can be affected by a "stress retraction" rule which accents the initial syllable in a word with no inherent stress (Kiparsky & Halle 1977). And prepositions which contain a *yer* vowel can have that vowel vocalized by a *yer* in the complement of P.

At the same time, not all prepositions are equally tightly connected to their complement, as evidenced by (81). Some prepositions can appear without a complement from their complement; others cannot.

(81) a. Oni priparkovalis' vperedi. (Gouskova 2019)
they parked in.front
'They parked in front.'

b. *Oni priparkovalis' u.
they parked next.to
'They parked next to (it/something).'

Gouskova (2019) distinguishes two classes of prepositions: "head prepositions" and "root prepositions." The latter are built from lexical roots; the former "consist of functional structure only." Root propositions tend not to interact phonologically with their nominal complement. They are often used adverbially, meaning they can be used with no nominal complement. They also do not have homophonous verbal prefixes, which means that they can be put aside for the purposes of identifying why lexical prefixes raise out of the verb phrase.

Although the details of the various phonological interactions are complex and controversial, for my purposes it is sufficient to observe that the class of "head prepositions" must normally be accompanied by a following nominal, and this appears to reflect prosodic properties of this category. The implication is that a head proposition which is not accompanied by a complement within the verb phrase can only satisfy its prosodic requirements if it finds some other substitute. This then suffices as a motivation for adjunction of P to the verb phrase: P may adjoin to the verb phrase in order to be realized in a position where it can function as a prosodically dependent element. The motivation is not direct, since it is not the adjunction structure which solves the prosodic problem. But the side effect of raising P to the edge of the verb phrase is that it is then in a position where it can be further displaced by multiple head-movement, and the effect of multiple head-movement is a new X^0 structure in which a prosodically dependent P *can* meet its needs.

(82) *Stress retractions in passive participles*
dó-pityj 'drunk up', *ná-n'atyj* 'hired', *pró-dannyj* 'sold'

(83) *Yer realization with lexical prefixes*
Ja uže ves' izo-žda-l-sja.
I already all from-wait-PST.m-REFL
'I am completely sick and tired of waiting for you!'

The superlexical and intermediate prefixes do not require the same motivating mechanism to end up in the right syntactic location for multiple head-movement. The former are always heads in a high position within the clause; the latter, adjuncts which must be located outside the verb phrase with a local, c-commanding probe to delete their [AD] feature. Neither belong to the P category, and so neither can be assumed to be prosodically dependent in the way lexical prefixes are. It then follows that a lexical prefix will have to appear adjacent to the verb stem, while intermediate prefixes and superlexical prefixes do not. The obligatory ordering of intermediate prefixes and lexical prefixes is a natural consequence, and need not be stipulated.

3.3 LIMITATIONS OF ALTERNATIVE MODELS OF RUSSIAN VERBAL STRUCTURES

The analysis developed above relies on two basic premises. One involves the role of the [AD] feature in determining the syntactic distribution of the parts of the Slavic verbal complex. The second is multiple head-movement. Together, they provide an explanation of a complex range of properties of Russian grammar. The question which must be asked, however, is how this analysis compares with other proposals in the literature.

Of course, the existing literature on this topic is massive, and it is not feasible to consider each model which it provides in isolation. But clusters of analytic models can be identified, and the different clusters can be evaluated in turn. In this next section, a comparison of the multiple head-movement model with a range of such general alternative is undertaken. The comparison will show that the alternatives are empirically and conceptually less effective in offering understanding of the grammatical principles on which Slavic verbal structures are based.

3.3.1 Verbs *in situ* models

Let us begin with the approach generally assumed in the vast traditional Slavic aspectological tradition, wherein verbal prefixes are derivational affixes added to the verb in the lexicon. In such an approach, prefixes play no direct role in the syntactic derivation, and can have no relevance to questions about the scope of syntactic head-movement. Within the generative literature, this same assumption is made by Pesetsky (1979, 1985), Babko-Malaya (1999), Mezhevich (2008), and by Bailyn (2011), whose arguments against verb-raising were discussed in section 3.2.

Svenonious's (2005b) model also counts as a model in which the verb remains *in situ*, although it does not situate verbal prefixes within the verb phrase. His treatment of the superlexical prefixes takes them to be full PPs situated as specifiers in an AspP projection outside the verb phrase. The combination of prefix and verb into a single prosodic unit is therefore a postsyntactic operation in this model, which involves "putting together of two 'word'-like units, each of which constitutes a minimal prosodic domain and is therefore minimally a foot, and bimoraic" (p. 241).

The first challenge faced by models in which the verb remains *in situ* is how to derive the tense/agreement inflection found on the verb in simple finite clauses. If prefixes are added to the verb within the verb phrase, then the explanation may be fairly simple. Assuming tense/agreement originates in T, then Russian might employ an affix-hopping operation to displace T onto the verb. This approach, however, ensures that the morpho-syntactic structure of the verb does not match what the morpho-phonology demands. In other words, an affix-hopping account leads directly to the "bracketing paradoxes" uncovered by Pesetsky (1979) and Fowler (1994).

One of these involves the formation of suppletive verb stems with finite verbs inflected for particular agreement forms. As Pesetsky (1979) notes "these irregularities are always preserved under prefixation, even when the meaning of the prefixed verb is idiosyncratic" (p. 41). The verb stem *dat'* 'give' is one such irregular form. Used with no prefix, suppletive stems appear with 1s, 3s, and 1p present tense inflections: (84).

(84) a. *dam* 'give;1s'
b. *dast* 'give;3s'
c. *dadim* 'give;1p'

And these same suppletive forms appear when lexical prefixes are added to the verb, forming new, non-compositional meanings for the derived verb: (85)–(86).

(85) a. *pro-dam* 'sell;1s'
b. *pro-dast* 'sell;3s'
c. *pro-dadim* 'sell;1p'

(86) a. *iz-dam* 'publish;1s'
b. *iz-dast* 'publish;3s'
c. *iz-dadim* 'publish;1p'

In Pesetsky's lexicalist model, the suppletive stems were "paradoxical" because the assumption was that non-compositional meanings should be the result of derivational morphology, operating prior to inflection. But that meant that the suppletion, which is triggered by the inflection, must operate only on a sub-part of the derived verb. This paradox evaporates under the approach taken here. Since the non-compositional meaning associated with lexical prefixes is determined syntactically—following Svenonius—there is no need to equate these structures with derivational morphology at all. All that is necessary to accommodate these forms is to provide an account of how the verb, the prefix, and the inflection are arranged into the actual verb form for a verb like *pro-dadim*, and this is already ensured in my model. The prefix *pro-* will originate inside the verb phrase, but it must raise to the edge of the phasal vP to have its [AD] feature licenced, and to find a prosodic host. In a perfective clause, a silent Prf head licences [AD] on *pro-*, and T then attracts Prf, *pro-*, and the verb to form a complex X^0 structure (87).

(87)

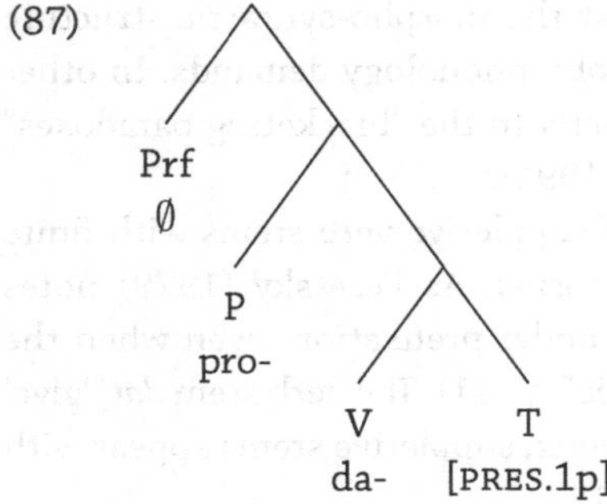

In the morphological component, the [V-T] constituent in (87) will be recognized as a unit which must be realized as a suppletive stem, just as an isolated verb *dadim* 'PRES.1p' must be. Since the prefix is not a part of this minimal unit, it plays no role in the suppletion.

The second of Pesetsky's bracketing paradoxes involves the realization of *yer* vowels in a handful of verbs with lexical prefixes.[16] Here, the phonology appears to require one structure but the semantics require a different one. As Pesetsky shows, the phonological processes *yer*-lowering and *yer*-deletion which affect these vowels interact in the following way. *yer*-deletion, a postcyclic rule, removes the high lax *yer* vowels from the postcyclic form of a Russian word. The rule is *bled*, however, by the earlier cyclic rule of *yer*-lowering, which lowers *yers* before a syllable which contains another *yer*. Once lowered, however, a former *yer* cannot trigger lowering of another *yer*. The effects can be seen in a comparison of the surface forms of the masculine and feminine past tenses of *podžech'* 'set fire to'.

(88)

Underlying feminine	*Surface feminine*	*Underlying masculine*	*Surface masculine*
[podʊ [[žʊg] la]]	podožgla	[podʊ [[žʊg] lʊ]]	podžog

In the derivation of the feminine form, the *yer* vowel in the verb root triggers lowering of the prefixal *yer* (cyclically), and then deletes (postcyclically). In the masculine form, the root *yer* is lowered by the presence of the *yer* in the past tense inflection, and cannot later trigger lowering in the prefixal *yer*, which must therefore delete. And without the structure indicated for these underlying forms, the same result cannot be obtained. (If the prefix were attached to the root first, then the *yer* in the masculine form would trigger lowering in the prefix before it could itself be lowered by the suffixal *yer*.) So

16. Pesetsky (p.c.) attributes the empirical observation to personal communication with Morris Halle.

the phonology shows that tense inflection must be attached more closely to the root than the superlexical prefix is.

(89) *podžeč'* 'set fire to'; *podžog* (M), *podožgla* (F) 'set fire to (preterite)'

The *pod(o)-* prefix is a lexical prefix, and must therefore originate within the verb phrase. If the verb were to combine first with *pod(o)-* before the verb raises to T, then the X^0 structures provided to the SM interface would be (90), for masculine and feminine past tense forms, respectively.

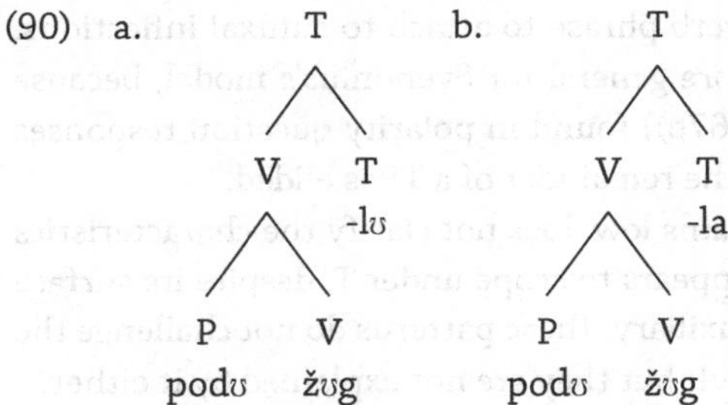

This result is avoided in a multiple head-movement analysis, where the prefix is further from the verb stem than T is. For *podžog*, the structure on which the various phonological rules will operate will be (91).

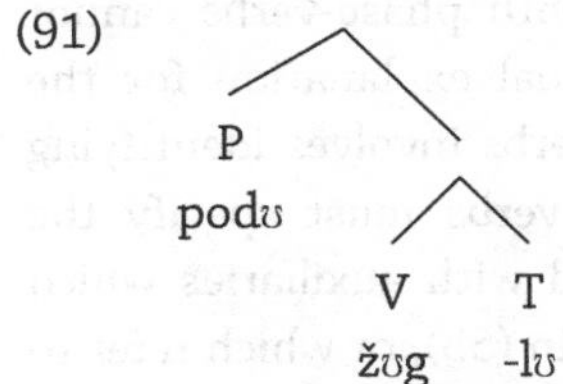

The *yer* vowel in the root is automatically lowered in the first cyclic, given this structure. No root *yer* will be available in the second cycle to trigger lowering of the prefixal *yer*, which must therefore be deleted. In short, everything works out as it should, given the structure generated in the multiple head-movement account.

If the prefixes remain in a position outside vP, as Svenonious proposes, then the bracketing paradoxes are avoided, but then it becomes difficult to explain the presence of tense inflection on the verb, since affix-hopping should not be able to take place. Affix-hopping appears to be subject to quite severe locality constraints which limit it to a head-head configuration (Embick & Noyer 2001). But there is no obvious alternative available, unless the location of tense/agreement features is not T at all in Russian. To my knowledge, nobody has offered a justification of this idea, which would apppear to necessitate a fairly comprehensive reanalysis of some well-established theoretical results.[17]

A related problem with any *verb-in-situ* models is that they have no ready way to accommodate the VP ellipsis patterns documented by Gribanova (2017b). Since the verb remains pronounced in VP ellipsis contexts, it must be the case that the verb is raised from the verb phrase. In itself, this does not show that prefixes are not attached to the verb within the verb phrase, but the finding that prefixes do not participate in establishing identity for ellipsis does show this. Gribanova's discovery that secondary imperfective and semelfactive suffixes also play no role in ellipsis identity further confirms that verbs must raise out of the verb phrase to attach to suffixal inflections. The ellipsis problem is slightly more general for Svenonius's model, because the TP-ellipsis patterns (seen in (67b)) found in polarity question responses retain a prefixed verb form when the remainder of a TP is elided.

A model in which the verb remains low does not clarify the characteristics of the *ne* negator. Recall that *ne* appears to scope under T, despite its surface position to the left of the future auxiliary. These patterns do not challenge the idea that the verb remains within vP, but they are not explained by it either.

On the plus side, Bailyn's observation that adverbs cannot apppear between a finite verb and its object does appear to follow from a *verb-in-situ* analysis, as it does in English, where the verb typically does remain low. But this result follows in the multiple head-movement analysis as well.

The idea that prefixes are pre-syntactic (derivational) components of the verb ensures that the lack of compound tenses with phase-verbs cannot be derived from the morpho-syntax. The traditional explanation for the incompatibility of perfective verbs with auxiliary verbs involves identifying a semantic clash (Jakobson 1957). If perfective verbs must specify the completion of an event, then they cannot be used with auxiliaries which themselves indicate that the event is completed, as in (5b), or which refer to the start of that event, as in (5c), or which require that the event be ongoing, as in (5d). A bit more work is required in this line of explanation to ensure that the periphrastic future form in (5a) cannot include a perfective form, though, since future tense is certainly semantically compatible with perfective aspect. But if the *budet* auxiliary is taken to mean 'become' rather than a simple future tense, then the perfectivity implied by the meaning of the auxiliary can again be said to clash with the perfectivity provided by a prefixal perfective principal verb.

17. Building on Pesetsky & Torrego (2007), Mezhevich (2008) develops a feature-sharing alternative to affix-hopping in which abstract tense features are transferred to the verb instead of an affixal tense suffix. It is not clear that this avoids the basic intervention problem, since T and the verb are still not sufficiently local whenever there are aspectual heads which separate them.

There are several reasons to be skeptical of this traditional semantic account. One problem is that it does not cover the full range of auxiliary verbs which reject combination with perfective verbs. For example, Romanova (2007) notes that 'abilitative' *umet'* combines only with imperfective verbs, as in (92).

(92) Ja umeju čitat'/*pro-čitat'.
I can read/PRF-read
'I can read.'

But there is no semantic clash between an auxiliary which means 'can' and a perfective in its domain. The English (93) appears to express exactly that type of idea, successfully, in fact.

(93) I can have read the book.

And even in the cases where there is some initial plausibility to the idea that incompatible meanings are the problem, the way speakers react to these forms is not what we would expect. Typically, semantic clashes can be resolved by speakers by finding contexts in which a bizarre or unlikely interpretation is suitable. But Russian speakers do not appear to find these acceptable at all, suggesting that this is a grammatical effect, rather than a semantic one. What is more, for the imperfective future forms built with *byt'*, Borik (2002) shows that this particular verb need not be perfective, since it can itself appear as the complement to another phase verb, as in (94).

(94) Prodolža-j byt' poslušnym!
continue-IMP be obedient
'Continue to be obedient!'

And if *byt'* need not be perfective, then the fact that it cannot combine directly with a perfective verb cannot be attributed to too much "perfectivity."

A more critical problem for the traditional account emerges from the existence of verb forms with multiple superlexical prefixes, as in (56b), repeated here.

(56b) Vasja do-pere-pisa-l stat'ju.
Vasja COMPL-re-write-PST.m paper
'Vasja completed re-writing a paper.'

The presence of either the *do-* or the *pere-* prefix would ensure that the aspect is perfective. Given perfective forms like (56b), then either multiple perfectivity is semantically acceptable, or there is a mechanism which allows the lower prefix, repetitive *pere-*, to lose its perfective meaning when necessary. But either conclusion robs the traditional explanation for data like (5) of its explanatory value. If multiple perfectivity is tolerable, then the prefixal forms in (5) should be tolerated. And if *pere-* can optionally become non-perfective, then it should be able to appear with a phase-verb auxiliary, which is not the case: (95).

(95) *Ne bud-u pere-skazat' vse trevolneniya.
NEG be.FUT-1s re-say all troubles
'I will not have recounted all the troubles.'

Overall, semantic explanations for the generalization that phase verbs cannot take prefixed complements are not persuasive. This is a limitation not just of models in which the verb remains within the verb phrase, but also of other alternative models to be considered next. But a semantic explanation for the contrasts in (5) is unnecessary if prefixes and verb stems are both attracted by T, because the empirical results which we require follow directly from the workings of the derivation.

Finally, a purely lexicalist account of Slavic prefixation will evidently have difficulty finding a principled account of the nuanced constraints on multiple prefixation, and the interactions between prefixes and suffixes such as the secondary imperfective *yva-* or semelfactive *-nu*. So models of this type are clearly not tenable, and cannot count as realistic alternatives to the multiple head-movement model offered here.

Multiple head-movement *vs.* no verb movement

Phenomena	Verb *in situ* (lexicalist)	(Svenonious)	Multiple head-movement
tense/agreement inflection	No	No	Yes
negation scope and location	—	—	Yes
VP ellipsis	No	No	Yes
morpho-phonological locality	No	—	Yes
adverb placement	Yes	—	Yes
aspectual constraints on phase verb complements	No	No	Yes

3.3.2 Compliant head-movement approaches

Consider now whether a model of the Russian verbal system can be constructed which employs standard head-movement operations only, and where the HMC remains fully in force. In order to make such a model maximally comparable to the multiple head-movement approach, let us assume that the mechanisms of [AD] deletion form a part of such a model, since many of the consequences of the [AD] feature are independent of how movement forms a complex verb. How would a sentence like (28a) be derived, with a base structure (96).

(96)

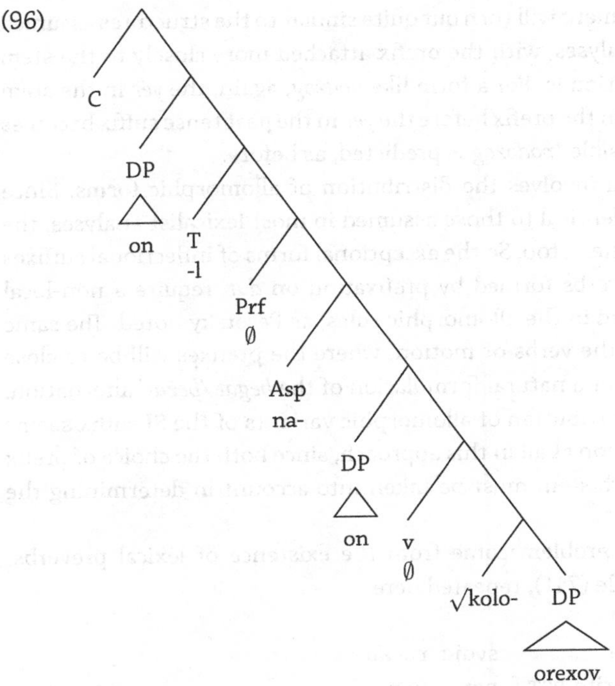

Since the verb must reach T and the head-movement constrains how it does so, *na-* and Prf must be taken to be strong affixes, with *na-* a prefix, alongside affixal T and v. Then the root can raise to v, v to Asp, Asp to Prf, and Prf to T, forming a complex X^0 (97) structure in T.

(97)

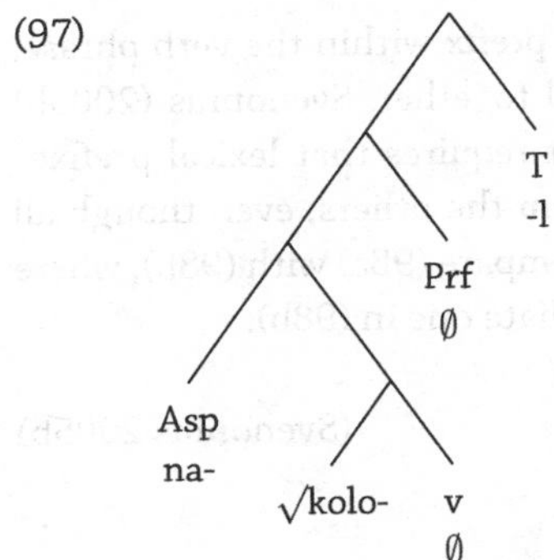

The first problem which arises is Bailyn's (1995) argument based on the placement of adverbs. Standard head-movement skips past adjoined categories, so the fact that adverbs cannot appear between a verb and its direct object counts against this approach.

The second problem comes from Pesetsky's bracketing paradox in the phonology of verb stems containing *yers*. As (97) shows, the X^0 output of standard head-movement will turn out quite similar to the structures assumed in most lexicalist analyses, with the prefix attached more closely to the stem than the tense inflection is. For a form like *podžog*, again, the *yer* in the stem should affect the *yer* in the prefix before the *yer* in the past tense suffix becomes visible, so the impossible **podožog* is predicted, as before.

The third problem involves the distribution of allomorphic forms. Since the X^0 structure is identical to those assumed in most lexicalist analyses, the same problems arise here, too. So the exceptional forms of inflectional suffixes with *dat'* 'give' and verbs formed by prefixation on *dat'* require a non-local context to be specified in the allomorphic rules, as Pesetsky noted. The same problem arises with the verbs of motion, where the prefixes will be to close to the stem to allow for a natural formulation of the *begat'/bežat'* alternation. Most tellingly, the distribution of allomorphic variants of the SI suffix seems to resist any explanation at all in this approach, since both the choice of prefix and the choice of verb stem must be taken into account in determining the form of SI.

The most serious problem come from the existence of lexical preverbs, however. Take example (71f), repeated here.

(71f) Ona is-pisa-la svoju ručku.
she out.of-write-PST.f her pen
'She has written her pen out of ink.'

As Svenonious shows, the prefix *is-* must originate as a particle within the verb phrase. In a standard head-movement theory, the verb must raise to T, and the prefix must therefore somehow be displaced past T, either with the verb or independently. What are the possibilities?

One is that the root might incorporate the prefix within the verb phrase, and then the two could raise to v and beyond together. Svenonius (2005b) is rightly critical of this possibility, because it requires that lexical prefixes have an entirely different set of properties from the others, even though all are drawn from the same prepositional pool. Compare (98a) with (98b), where *pere-* is a lexical prefix in (98a) and an intermediate one in (98b).

(98) a. Samoljot pere-letaj-et granicu. (Svenonius 2005b)
plane across-fly-3 border
'The plane is flying across the border.'

b. Vasja pere-pisa-l pis'mo. (Tatevosov 2008)
Vasja REPET-write-PST letter
'Vasja re-wrote the letter.'

In order for incorporation of a lexical prefix to take place, the verb root in (98a) would have to count as a strong affix, and the preposition *pere-*, as a root to be attracted. Head-movement would have to situate the root to the left of its attracting affix. But if another verb can combine with a homophonous intermediate prefix, as in (98b), the prefix must count as the strong affix, and the verb, as a root. And this contradiction multiplies through the entire system, with virtually every verb counting sometimes as root and other times as affix.

So incorporation is out. What possibilities remain? In this approach, *is-* cannot be adjoined to the verb phrase, because the verb would simply raise past it. And *is-* cannot undergo head-movement to a head position outside the verb phrase either, because this would violate the HMC. The only remaining possibility is phrasal movement to a specifier position outside the verb phrase. Suppose that this position is somewhere between T and the verb. Then the presence of the prefix should not affect head-movement of the verb, which would still raise past it to T. Alternatively, suppose that the prefix raises to some position above T, so that the verb ends up to its right after raising to T. Besides the explosion of unmotivated structure this would seem to require, it still would not get the order right, since the prefix would then appear to the left of the subject. And obviously the problem becomes still less tractable for examples in which a lexical prefix is preceded by some number of other prefixes, as in Tatevosov's (99) example.

(99) Vasja na-do-pere-za-pis-yva-l disk-ov.
Vasya CUMUL-COMPL-REPET-*za*-write-IMPF-PST.Ms DVD-GEN.p
'Vasya accumulated a quantity of DVDs, which he finished recording again.'

As the lexical prefix *za-* appears to the right of three other prefixes, then if it occupies a specifier position above T, then all the others must do so to, in positions to the right of the subject.

Finally, let us consider how a standard head-movement analysis will fare with the Russian grammatical patterns if supplemented by additional mechanisms like non-cyclic levels of morphology or morphological rebracketing operations.

Non-cyclic phonology is irrelevant to the how allomorphy is controlled, so the forms of *dat'* and *byt'* still require an account. In contrast, if rebracketing can take place before the forms of verb roots or inflections are determined, then both the *yer* phonology and the allomorphy observed by Pesetsky can be characterized.

But Bailyn's arguments against head-movement remain in force in such a model, because the internal structure of a verb has no bearing on whether it can raise past an adverb. The incompatibility of phase verbs with perfective forms remains a problem in such an enriched model. Most critically, the properties of lexical prefixes are still entirely inconsistent with compliant head-movement, and these are not affected by what happens in the morphophonology.

3.3.3 Partial head-movement models

Partial head-movement models are also conceivable, as offered by Gribanova (2013), Gribanova & Harizanov (2017), and Harizanov & Gribanova (2019).[18] In such an approach, the verb would continue to raise to a position outside the verb phrase, but not to T. If adverbs are precluded from adjoining to vP in Russian, but can appear in a higher position which is still lower than T, then the adverb placement issue is overcome. And the possibility of verb phrase ellipsis which does not affect the verb itself can then be allowed, as well. But the remaining problems all persist in such an approach. If the verb does not raise far enough, then there is no obvious mechanism which will combine it with a prefix situated outside the verb phrase. The position of lexical prefixes, which must originate inside the verb phrase, still require an explanation. The "bracketing paradoxes" obtain no explanation in such an account. And as Bailyn (2017) observes, the motivation for movement only to an intermediate position is unclear, particularly because T is still the locus for rich tense/agreement inflection.

3.3.4 Remnant movement

Finally, Caha & Zikova (n.d.) develop a fourth type of model of Slavic verbal prefix: one in which the order of prefixes, suffixes, roots, and sentential constituents reflects the output of remnant movement operations. Caha and Zikova suppose that the prefixes remain as independent syntactic constituents outside the verb phrase, out of which the verb does not raise. An AspP constituent containing the verb and prefixal PPs can raise higher, if the arguments of the verb first raise to a position outside the verb phrase. Together with

18. The analysis builds on Matushansky's (2006) earlier proposal, which also posits a phrasal movement of heads which feeds a subsequent word-formation operation.

an (unspecified) mechanism to attach tense morphology to the verb, this structure can allow the morphemes to end up in the right linear order.

Although Caha and Zikova do not discuss this, the positional restrictions on VP adverbs can perhaps be derived in a model like theirs, since the verb does not leave the verb phrase. So it will not be expected to precede external adverbs. But if the object is not a part of the verb phrase, then VP ellipsis should not elide the object, contrary to what Gribanova has found.

A remnant movement account will obviously have difficulty ensuring the correct morphophonology, since the heads with which a displaced phrase (VP, AspP, etc.) will always be further from the original stem than the categories (prefixes) which that phrase contains. The fact that phase verbs cannot combine with simple perfectives, prefixed or not, finds no obvious account in this model either. In short, a remnant movement account is perhaps the least attractive option of all, and does not constitute a viable alternative to the multiple head-movement account.

Remnant movement *vs.* multiple head-movement

	Remnant	Multiple head-movement
tense/agreement inflection	No	Yes
negation scope and location	—	Yes
VP ellipsis	No	Yes
morpho-phonological locality	No	Yes
adverb placement	No	Yes
aspectual constraints on phase verb complements	No	Yes

3.4 CONCLUSIONS

The remarkably rich array of data which Slavic prefixal morphology provides has proven resistant to systematic analysis in the existing literature. In models developed along generative premises, a large part of the difficulty is because the generalizations which need to be captured appear to point in two different directions. On one hand, morphophonological "bracketing paradoxes" and adverb placement patterns seem to show that the verb does not combine with prefixes by raising from the verb phrase. On the other hand, the morphosyntax of inflections, the VP-ellipsis patterns, and the formation of phase verb clusters indicates the opposite—that verbs do raise.

The analytic advantage that multiple head-movement provides is a way to capture both types of generalizations. Verbs seem not to raise because multiple head-movement allows verbs to raise only if other, higher material is also raised up in a way which preserves some of the base relations, i.e. some hierarchical assymetries between heads. And verbs seem to raise because in fact they do. And because the analytic challenges are so daunting in the Slavic verbal system, the significance of finding a way to resolve these paradox is greater. In that respect, the idea that multiple head-movement is truly a significant component of syntactic theory should seem quite viable at this point.

In comparison with the other multiple head-movement constructions identified in Perenakan Javanese, in Finnish, in northern Norwegian and Swedish, and in English, Russian grammar appears to assign a greater role to this type of grammatical operation. Not only does multiple head-movement take place in all types of clauses, it is also triggered by three different functional categories in this language. T, SI, and participial *-n* all attract prefixes before they attract a verbal stem. It appears that multiple head-movement is a type of grammatical operation which can be restricted to small pockets of the grammar or which can play a more central role, depending on the grammars in question.

CHAPTER 4

Multiple head-movement in Innu-aimûn

The examination of Slavic tense/aspect patterns in the previous chapter has shown that while similar multiple head-movement processes take place in different languages (Finnish, Perenakan Javanese, Russian), they apply minimally in some and more widely in others. This next chapter will make essentially the same point, but on a more dramatic scale. An examination of a wide range of word forms will show that multiple head-movement plays a still more significant role in the morphosyntax of Innu-aimûn (and in Algonquian languages generally). This finding is important in several ways. First, it will extend the empirical basis for my general claim that multiple head-movement is a robust phenomenon which must be incorporated into any theory of head-movement. Second, it provides a new testing ground for the specific proposals about the mechanism of head-movement from Chapter 2. And third, it raises important questions concerning the nature of parametric variation and language acquisition—questions which will then be addressed in Chapter 5.

It is important to start, though, with an appreciation of the complexity of the problems in Algonquian grammatical analysis. Although recent years have seen a marked increase in the number of generative studies of Algonquian languages, there is still considerable uncertainty about fundamental aspects of the syntax and the morphosyntax of these languages. Much of the difficulty involves the complex nominal and verbal morphology, in particular, the apparent *tripartite* structure of the complex words, as discussed in Chapter 1. The challenges posed by this unique morphological pattern are compounded by how the internal structure of verbs and nouns affects the syntactic behavior of other syntactic constituents, such as preverbs, quantifiers, and "relative root complements." There are also intricate interactions between verbal "conjunct" or "independent" orders, evidential suffixes, preverbs, and operations like wh-movement.

The Grammar of Multiple Head-Movement: A Comparative Study. Phil Branigan, Oxford University Press.
 DOI: 10.1093/oso/9780197677032.003.0004

More concretely, consider the list in (1), a partial selection of unresolved issues in Algonquian grammatical theory, and which all seem to be connected.

(1) a. the relationship between head-movement and verb inflections
b. the nature of two verbal "orders": conjunct and independent
c. the relationship between verbal orders and operator movement
d. the relationship between verbal orders and preverbs
e. the relationship between verbal orders and "initial change" ablaut
f. the relationship between preverbs and the "initial" in a tripartite verb
g. the relationship between preverbs and tense inflections
h. the relationship between preverbs and evidential verb suffixes
i. the relationship between "relative root" initials and relative root complements
j. the relationship between relative root complements and oblique arguments
k. the relationship between medials and initials
l. the relationship between medials and finals

This list includes only questions about the grammar of the clausal domain. A comparable one could be formulated involving the components of complex nominal expressions.

The point here is that there are many questions which should be answered together. An analysis which explains (1d) without addressing (1b) and (1c) may miss generalizations which are crucial to understand the full system. In analysis, we cherry-pick the pertinent questions at our peril.

And as with the Russian case, this means that the most transparent way to proceed is by first presenting a model in which a full set of answers is provided. Then a comparison with competitors in the existing literature can be made.

For example, Richards (2004) offers an account of the conjunct/independent distinction in which head-movement of the verb to T or to C is key. His analysis explains why the conjunct order is used with wh-movement, but says nothing about initial change, and why it occurs only with verbs in the conjunct order. Rhodes (2006) develops a detailed picture of relative roots and relative root complements in Anishnaabe, but this is not combined with new insights into the nature of other types of initials. Déchaine & Weber (2015a, b) construct a model where the relationship between initials and finals is more clearly delineated, but this does not address the nature of relative roots or between initials and preverbs. And Oxford (2018) provides a persuasive treatment of agreement inflections across the Algonquian family—on which I will draw quite extensively—but he says little about how the verbal orders are syntactically selected or the impact of preverbs on how evidential and agreement suffixes are expressed.

In contrast, if the concept of multiple head-movement forms part of the analysis, it is possible to answer all of these questions, and more. As such, these separate analyses cannot fruitfully be evaluated before the full multiple head-movement model is set out. (As we proceed through the latter, though, comparisons of specific points with the claims made by other orders will be provided.)

To that end, I now turn to the analysis of an extensive range of recurrent patterns in the grammar of Innu-aimûn, with multiple head-movement the common thread which unifies these patterns. To make the comparison with other languages already discussed more transparent, I proceed from top to bottom, starting with multiple head-movement operations at the C-T phase level in Innu-aimûn, then proceeding to v and applicative-like verbal affixes, and then examining multiple head-movement operations with heads in the nominal domain and the prepositional domain. When the full extent to which multiple head-movement is active in this language is established, the difficulty faced by alternative analysis which might hope to eschew the concept of multiple head-movement also becomes still clearer than before.

Many of the Innu-aimûn examples which appear in this chapter are drawn from textual sources, and include detail extraneous to the issue at hand. To isolate the most relevant portion of such data, I mark it with a wavy underline in the first line. Examples which are simple enough that no confusion is likely do not contain wavy underlines.

4.1 PREVERBS AND VERB COMPLEXES IN INNU-AIMÛN

4.1.1 General characteristics of preverbs

While the word order for major elements of the clause in Innu-aimûn is quite free, the opposite is true for ordering of the parts of a verbal cluster. The verbal cluster is composed of the verb itself and any number of "preverbs."[1] The preverb system provides a natural starting point for investigating how multiple head-movement operates in Innu-aimûn grammar, because Algonquian preverbs and Russian verbal prefixes display a number of similarites, and these

1. For convenience in presenting these forms in the Innu-aimûn examples, I will normally attach preverbs (when possible) to their verbal anchor in the second line with an = symbol, to distinguish them from the verbal 'initial', which is connected more tightly to the verbal components which follow (Leipzig glossing conventions employ the "=" junction marker to indicate attachment of a clitic element. It is not clear that cliticization is an accurate term for the prosodic relationship between a preverb and a verb. Innu-aimûn writing practice is not consistent on how preverbs are represented; some writers connect them to following verbs with a hyphen and others do not.) But *faute de mieux*, the "=" notation seems like the best available choice to indicate how preverbs and verbs are related in the surface string.

point to comparable derivations, in which preverbs and prefixes are brought together with a verb through multiple head-movement to a higher functional category.

As described in the appendix in section A.3.2, verbs in Innu-aimûn are inflected in different inflectional *orders*. The different orders employ affixal morphology which is quite distinct from each other, but verbs from both orders combine freely with preverbs. The preverbs and the inflected verb are often referred to as a "verb complex" in the Algonquianist grammatical tradition. Verbs in the independent order employ proclitic pronouns and three distinct agreement suffix positions to realize agreement features, while verbs in the conjunct order employ only a single agreement suffix for the same purpose, and they lack proclitics. The sample conjugations in (2) illustrate the morphological difference in simple cases.

(2) Inflectional orders: *nipâu* 'sleep'

	Independent	*(preterite)*	*Conjunct*	
	sg.	*pl.*	*sg.*	*pl.*
1	ni-nipâtî	ni-nipâtân	nipâiân	nipâiât
		tshi-nipâtân	nipâin	nipâiâk^u^
2	tshi-nipâtî	tshi-nipâtâu		nipâiek^u^
3	nipâpan	nipâpanat	nipât	nipâht

Among other semantic roles, preverbs can indicate tense, modality, and aspect. (I consider the range of preverb functions in more detail below.) Preverbs are uninflected morphemes which appear immediately before the verb. In (3), the verb complex is formed from the wavy underlined portions of the first line.

(3) a. *Nui natshi-kusseti nete Uashikutet.*
n-uî=nâtshi=kusse-tî nete Uâshikute-t.
1-want=go=fish-1.PRET there Washicoutai-LOC
'I wanted to go fishing at Washicoutai.'

b. *Shash ashitashkuapikateu nutatinun, apu tshika ut uepashtak.*
shâsh ashitâshkuâpikâte-u n-utâtinun,
already tie.to.pole-3 1-komatik
apû=tshika=ût=uepâsht-âk.
NEG=FUT=thither=blow.away-CJ.3
'My komatik is already tied to a pole, it won't be blown away.'

Semantic features of preverbs appear to control how preverbs are ordered, when multiple preverbs appear in a single clause. As a first approximation, preverbs can be divided into the following subclasses: tense markers, modals, aspect markers, and lexical preverbs, and these subclasses must appear in the order given. Assuming that linear order corresponds to hierarchical structure, the following abstract structure is then appropriate as a general template for clauses in Innu-aimûn.

(4)

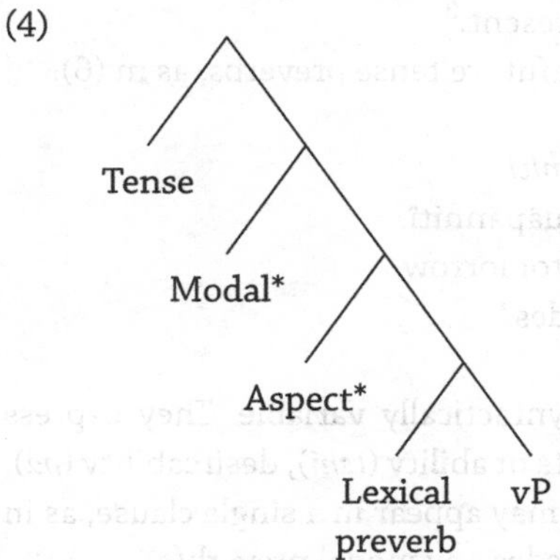

The asterisk on modal and aspect labels indicates that these may include multiple iterations of the same preverb category. With the exception of the lexical preverbs, the subclasses and semantic groupings of Algonquian preverbs are quite familiar from the study of comparable elements in any number of other languages, including English, where tense, modal, and aspectual information is organized in a similar fashion. The obvious implication is that at least some of the preverbs in Innu-aimûn should be equivalent to familiar functional heads, like English auxiliary verbs.

There are, however, complications. One involves how tense is expressed in specific contexts. There are two explicit tenses: future and preterite. Future tense is always expressed as a preverb *tshî*, *modulo* certain morphophonological changes, but preterite tense is a preverb *tût* in the conjunct order but a verbal suffix in the independent.

(5) a. *Tshîtûtepan.*
tshîtûte-∅-pan.
leave-3-PRET
'S/he left.'

b. *Apû tût tshîtûtet.*
apû=tût=tshîtûte-t.
NEG=PRET=leave-CJ.3
'S/he did not leave.'

One of the challenges a model of Innu-aimûn grammar must address is how to ensure the correct distribution of the two forms of the preterite marking.

In other words, we should hope to explain why preterite preverbs cannot be used in independent forms in Innu-aimûn, and why the conjunct order does not employ preterite suffixes.[2]

It is not grammatically necessary to specify any specific tense in a clause. Depending on the context of utterance, "neutral" tense inflection allows for an interpretation which is either past or present.[3]

Neutral tense marking is also used with future tense preverbs, as in (6).

(6) *Manakanet tshika uishkushaueu uapanniti.*
Mânakanet tshika=uîshkushâu-e-u uâpannitî.
Marguerite FUT=smoke.tan-FNL-3 tomorrow
'Tomorrow Marguerite will smoke hides.'

The modal preverbs are less morphosyntactically variable. They express cross-linguistically common modal concepts of ability (*tshî*), desireability (*pâ*), and volition (*uî*). Multiple modal preverbs may appear in a single clause, as in (7). If present, a tense preverb always precedes any modal preverb(s).

(7) a. *Ni-pâ tshî nipânâ-pan.*
ni-pâ=tshî=nipâ-nâ-pan.
1-should=can=sleep-1-PRET
'I should have been able to sleep.'

b. *Mânî tshika mashinâtâueu Shûshepa.*
Mânî tshika=mashinâtâu-e-u Shûshep-a.
Marie FUT=vote.for-DIR-3 Joseph-OBV
'Marie will vote for Joseph.'

c. *Apû tshika tshî ashamitân.*
apû=tshika=tshî=asham-it-ân.
NEG=FUT=can=feed-1⟩2-CJ.1s
'I can't give you any food.'

Aspectual preverbs are all available for use as a verb or as the initial component in one. For example, *nâtshi* 'go' functions sometimes as a preverb and sometimes as a verbal stem. The same is true of *tshîtshi*- 'start', *âshte*- 'stop', and *ashku*- 'await'. In each case, whether the aspectual element is verbal or

2. In the Pessamit dialect of Innu-aimûn, the preterite preverb *tshî* can actually appear with verbs in the independant order, a pattern which is common in East Cree, as well.

3. Drapeau (2014: p. 174) observes the role of neutral tense in narratives is to advance the action, while preterite forms in such contexts are used to establish the context for the events taking place.

preverbal depends on the properties of what succeeds it in the clause.[4] Thus, in each of the (a) examples in (8)–(11), the underlined item is the stem of a verb, but in the accompanying (b–e) examples, the same item serves as a preverb.

(8) a. *Netuakueuk, Shushep ninatshiau.*
IC/natu-âku-eu-k, Shûshep ni=nâtshi-â-u.
IC/fetch-porcupine-FNL-CJ.1 Joseph 1-meet-DIR-3
'When going after porcupine, I crossed paths with Joseph.'

b. *Pien natshitapeu uipushkau-mita nete Uashikutet.*
Pien nâtshi-tâpe-u uîpushkâu-mit-a nete Uâshikute-t.
Peter fetch.load-FNL-3 burnt.over-tree-PL there Washicoutai-LOC
'Peter goes to get a load of burnt wood at Washicoutai.'

c. *Nutaui tshe uitsheuk natshikutishuti.*
n-ûtâuî tshe uîtsheu-k
1-father FUTgo.with-CJ.1 go-retrieve.meat-CJ.3s-COND
natshi-kutishu-t-î.
'I will go with my father when he goes to get the meat of the caribou he killed.'

(9) a. *Tshitshitau.*
tshîtshi-tâ-u.
begin-FNL-3
'S/he begins to make it.'

b. *Eka uipat takushinini, eukuan tshe tshitshipuian.*
ekâ uîpat takushin-in-î, eukuan tshe=tshîtshi-pu-iân.
NEG without.delay arrive-CJ2s-COND then FUT=begin-eat-CJ.1s
'If you do not arrive soon, then I will start eating.'

(10) a. *tshitshi-atusseu.*
tshîtshi=atuss-e-u.
begin=work-FNL-3
'S/he begins to work.'

4. The logic here is that of Goddard (1988). Goddard's Meskwaki example (i), with enclitic *cha:h* and *meko*, is formed from two verbal roots, both of which could potentially serve as initials. But since *pesetaw-* is so realized, the only option for *wi:ke:chi* is to be a preverb, located "outside" the fully inflected verb.

(i) ke-wi:ke:chi=cha:h=meko pesetawa:petoke.
2-COMPLETE-SO/for-EMPH listen.to

b. *Uipat tekushinit, ekue tshitshipanit e atusset.*
uîpat IC/takushin-it, ekue tshîtshi-pan-it
without delay IC/arrive-CJ.3 then begin-move-CJ.3
e=atusse-t.
PREV=work-CJ.3
'As soon as he arrived, he started to work.'

(11) a. *Ashkatau.*
ashk-atâ-u.
await-V-3
'S/he waits for a person in order to harm him/her.'

b. *Ashku-mitshishu.*
ashku=mîtshish-u.
await-eat-3
'S/he is waiting to eat.'

c. *Ashku-passitsheu.*
ashku=pâssitsh-e-u.
await=shoot-FNL-3
'S/he stays ready to shoot.'

d. *Ashku-tshiueu.*
ashku=tshîu-e-u.
await=return.home-FNL-3
'S/he is ready to go back, to return home.'

For the more restricted comparable aspectual preverbs *ashte* 'stop' and *nâtshi* 'go', no purely verbal usage seems to be possible.

(12) a. *Ashteku.*
âshte-k-û-∅.
stop.running-FNL-3
'It stops running, flowing.'

b. *Ashtepanû.*
âshte-panû-∅.
stop-move-3
'It stops working.'

c. *Utshipitukupan nikuss, shash ashtepitiku kau.*
utshipitukupan nikuss, shâsh âshte-pitik-u kâu.
seize-PASS-3 1-son already stop=convulse-3 again
'My son was having convulsions; he has now stopped.'

(13) a. *Ashte-mishpun.*
âshte=mishpun-∅.
stop=snow-3
'It stops snowing.'

b. *Ashte-nutin.*
âshte=nûtin.
stop=be.windy-∅
'The wind stops.'

(14) a. *Natshikapaushtam*ᵘ.
nâtshi=kâpaûsht-am-u
go-stand.upright-FNL-3
'S/he approaches it, goes to stand up near it.'

b. *Natshi-unaitsheme ma.*
nâtshi=unaitsheme mâ
go-set.a.trap PRT
'Go and set some traps!'

c. *Natshi-kusseu.*
nâtshi=kusse-u
go=fish-3
'S/he goes fishing with a line.'

d. *Natshi-maushu.*
nâtshi-mâushû-∅
go-gather.berries-3
'S/he goes berry-picking.'

e. *Auassat mishta-mitshetuat niatshi-pakashimuht.*
auâss-at mishta-mîtshetu-at IC/nâtshi=pakâshim-u-ht.
child-p many-be.numerous-3p IC/go-swim-V-CJ.3p
'A lot of children go swimming.'

The use of specific stems sometimes as true verbs and sometimes as something more aspectual or functional is not uncommon in other languages. Cardinaletti & Shlonsky 2004 examine similar phenomena in Italian, and identify several classes of verbs which enable "restructuring" phenomena (Rizzi, 1976, 1978, Aissen & Perlmutter 1976, 1983) to occur, including modal/volitional verbs, aspectual verbs and quasi-functional verbs. The Italian aspectual verbs include *cominciare* 'begin' and *finire* 'finish', which matches the situation in Innu-aimûn. The quasi-functional category includes causative, motion, and perception verbs. The evidence they examine indicates that both types of verb may appear outside the verb phrase but lower than T, and when they are vP-external, they lack the argument structure of a true verb. In other words, they behave sometimes as normal verbs and other times as functional heads. Similarly, Aboh (2009) claims that some serial verb structures in Kwa and Khoisan languages are based on the use of a lexical verb as a functional head outside the verb phrase.

If we consider the Innu-aimûn counterparts to the various Italian restructuring verbs, we find that some—particularly the Italian modal and volitional cases—correspond to simple Innu-aimûn preverbs. But Italian aspectual and quasi-functional verbs have Innu-aimûn equivalents which are sometimes preverbs and sometimes initials. This suggests that the proper analysis of these in Innu-aimûn might also employ Cardinaletti and Shlonsky's insight that these verbs may appear either as the head of the verb phrase or in a higher functional position.

There is one additional aspectual element in Innu-aimûn which does not have the form of an independent verb or verb stem. *Continuative* aspect is expressed through a productive partial reduplication process, as in (15).[5]

(15) a. *Pâpu.* (Burgess 2009)
pâp-u.
laugh-3
'S/he is laughing.'

b. *Pâpâpu.*
pâ~pâp-u.
CNTN~laugh-3
'S/he keeps laughing.'

c. *Âtshipanu.*
âtshipan-u.
'S/he/it moves.'

d. *Âiâtshipanu.*
â~âtshipan-u.
CNTN~move-3
'It shakes, moves repeatedly.'

e. *Pîkupanu.*
pîkupan-u.
be.wrecked-3
'It breaks down.'

5. There are also several less productive types of reduplication in the verbal morphology, which I do not examine (Drapeau 2014).

f. *Pâpîkupanu.*
pâ~pîkupan-u.
CNTN~be.wrecked-3
'It's breaking down in different parts.'

Continuative reduplication only targets the verb. It cannot affect any higher member of the verb complex. Thus an example like (16b) is impossible.

(16) a. *Tatakushkateu.*
tâ~tâkush-kât-e-u.
CNTN~put.on-leg-*V*-3
'S/he tramples it.'

b. **Uaui takushkateu.*
uâ~uî=tâkush-kât-e-u.
CNTN~want-put.on-leg-*V*-3
'S/he is always wanting to put a foot on it.'

This restriction on the scope of reduplication follows if continuative reduplication reflects the presence of a more abstract "preverb," a reduplicant, which appears as an aspect head, in the same position where other aspectual preverbs may appear. Example (16a) will then have a base C-T structure: (17).

(17)

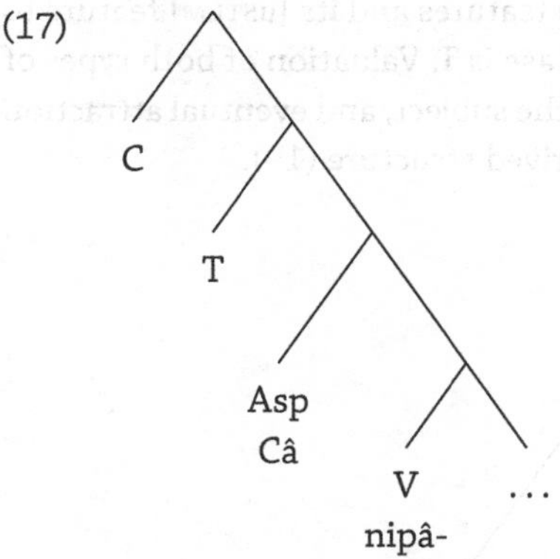

The class of lexical preverbs includes adverbial material, as well as non-functional preverbs which play a range of syntactic roles. These will be presented and analysed below, starting in section 4.3.1. The description of the other types of preverbs already provided is enough to suggest a basic clausal cartography of the upper range of the C-T phase, which is all that is necessary at this point.

With the basic characteristics of many Innu-aimûn preverbs now presented, we can turn to their analysis, beginning with clauses in the independent order, where T appears as a verbal suffix.

4.1.2 Multiple head-movement in the independent order

In the simplest case, the verb in a simple independent order root clause appears with no preverbs, as in (18a), where the base structure should then be (18b).

(18) a. *Pien nipâu.*
Pien nipâ-u.
Peter sleep-3

b.

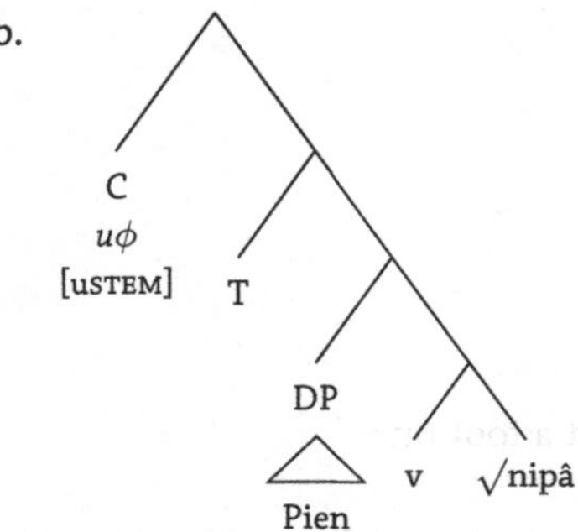

The verb root will raise to v, as always.

As C is the phase head in (18), the ϕ features realized in the verbal inflection can only be introduced in the C position. C bears a [uSTEM] feature, as well. And Feature Inheritance will transfer both its ϕ features and its [uSTEM] feature to the head of its complement, which in this case is T. Valuation of both types of features on T will produce agreement with the subject, and eventual attraction of the verb to T. The end result will be a derived structure (19).

(19)

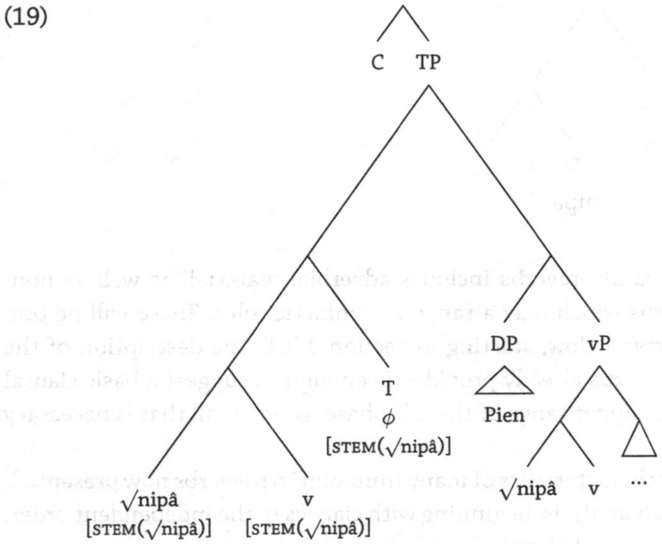

With this structure, Vocabulary Insertion for T and v in the complex inflected word will eventually provide a single word with the 3rd singular agreement suffix *-u*.

For clauses in which vP appears directly as the complement of T, the consequence of C-T Feature Inheritance will be superficially similar to analogous structures in French, for example. The [uSTEM] feature transferred on T will ensure verb-raising takes place, and then the inflectional features on T will be realized according to the specific morphological rules of the language.

The actual features transferred to T in Innu-aimûn will sometimes differ from those transferred in the analogous French situation, since Innu-aimûn allows for multiple agreement at the C-T phase level, as well as a set of evidential features. In (20a), the verbal suffix *-âu* realizes agreement with plural 2nd person features on the object. But in (20b), the suffix *-ân* realizes 1st person plural features on the subject in the same morphological position (as well as preterite tense). The choice of which features to express in this position—subject or object—is made on the basis of apparently arbitrary morphological rules, as discussed in the appendix section A.3.2, but contrasts like this show that both subject and object agreement feature sets are present on T at the S-M interface. In turn, this means that C must sometimes introduce two sets of ϕ features, depending on how much agreement is to take place.

(20) a. *Tshuitshititau.* (Baraby 2004)
tshi-uîtsh-iti-t-âu.
2-help-2⟩1-PRET-2p
'I help you (pl.).'

b. *Tshuitshititan.*
tshi-uîtsh-it-it-ân.
2-help-1⟩2-PRET-1e
'We help you (sg. or pl.).'

The exponence of past tense features is affected by the presence of evidential features. Intransitive verbs with evidential features have past tense realized with the *-pan* suffix, which appears to the right of the evidential exponent: (21).

(21) *Tshitakushinashapan.*
tshit-akushi-nâ-sha-pan.
2-be.sick-1i-INDIR-PRET
'(hearsay) You were sick.'

The presence of different ϕ features also affects how past tense features are realized in the suffixal inflection. With intransitive 3rd person verbs, and in transitive verbs with only 3rd person subject and object, the past tense exponent is again *-pan*: (22).

(22) a. *Atussepan.*
atusse-pan.
work-PRET
'S/he worked.'

b. *Petuepanat.*
petu-e-pan-at.
hear-DIR-3-PRET-3p
'S/he heard them.'

Besides the agreement inflection, the person features of subjects or objects are also indexed through proclitic pronouns. The use of such proclitics resembles patterns found in some variants of northern Italian, where subject doubling clitics are found (Brandi & Cordin 1989).

(23) a. *Fiorentino*
Mario e parla. (Suñer 1992)
Mario he speaks
'Mario speaks.'

b. *Trentino*
(Ti) te parli.
you you speak
'You speak.'

In both Innu-aimûn and in northern Italian, a subject clitic appears adjoined to T, regardless whether a lexical nominal subject or tonic subject pronoun also appears. In both, the suffixal agreement inflection also realizes features of the subject, often redundantly. And in both types of languages, there are gaps in the subject clitic paradigm. In Trentino, the subject clitic is not used for 1st person singular and 1st and 2nd person plural forms, while Innu-aimûn does not have a 3rd person subject clitic.[6]

Algonquian languages extend the clitic doubling pattern to object arguments, as well. Again, there are no 3rd person object clitics in Innu-aimûn. Thus, 1st or 2nd person object clitics are found adjoined to T, with or without an explicit nominal or tonic pronominal object in the clause.

6. Other Algonquian languages such as Nishnaabemwin do employ a 3rd person subject clitic in some contexts (Valentine 2001).

(24) a. *Nimûpishtik*ᵘ *(nin).*
ni=mûpisht-ik-u (nîn).
1=visit-INV-3
'She visits me.'

b. *Nikatshessimikunan kauapikuesht aiamieutshuapit.*
ni=katshessim-iku-nân kâuâpikuesht aiamieu-tshuâp-ît.
1=counsel-INV-1pe priest pray-house-LOC
'The priest gave us a sermon in church.'

When subject and object are both non-3rd person, then only one of the two is actually audible in the proclitic position, as seen in (20). I assume this to be a morphological restriction, which simply deletes one of the two clitics adjoined to T. It is always the 2nd person clitic which wins out in this case, and the 1st person clitic which is not pronounced.

With all that in mind, consider how the derivation proceeds for a sentence like (25).

(25) *Tshipetatinanashapan.*
tshi=petu-it-nânâ-sha-pan.
2=hear-1⟩2-1p-INDIR-PRET
'(hearsay) We heard you.'

When C is merged, forming the initial stage of the C-T phase, the structure for (25) will be (26).

(26)
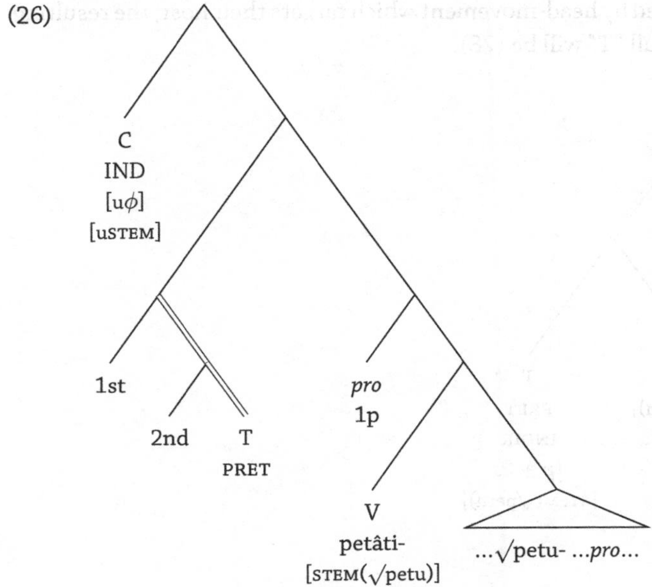

Feature Inheritance from the phase head will transfer features from C to T. Valuation of ϕ features and [uSTEM] features on T then produce the structure (27).

(27)

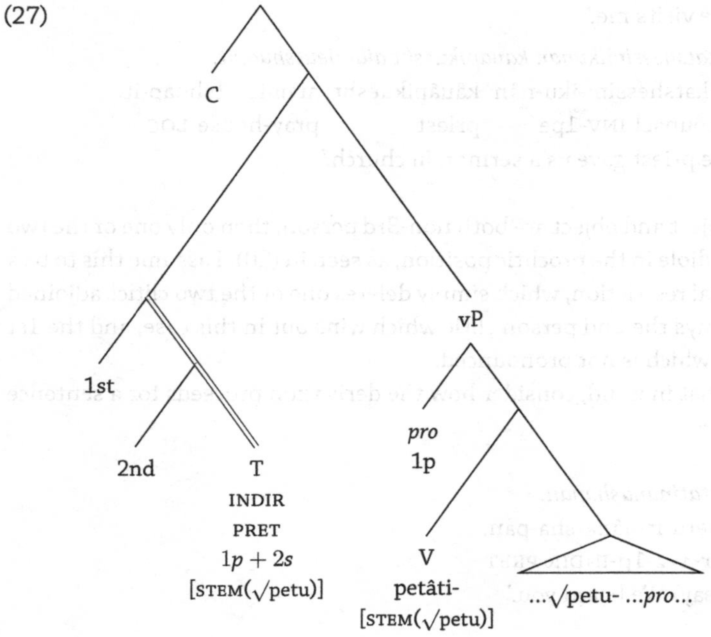

In the course of externalization, head-movement will take place, replacing the minimal T in (27) with a new structure containing T and the verb. Since clitics are unaffected by head-movement which targets their host, the resulting structure for the full "T" will be (28).

(28)

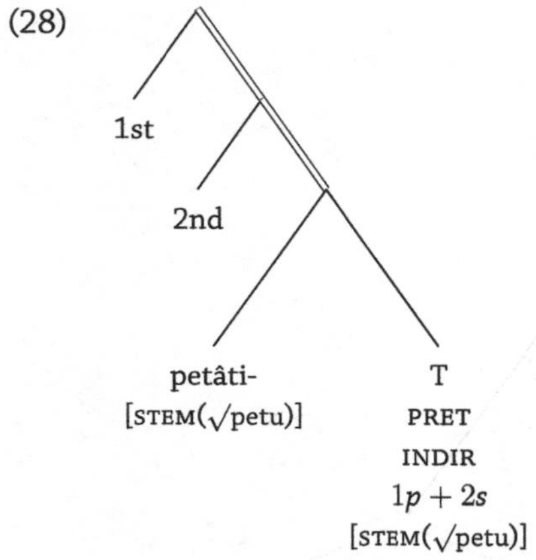

On the basis of this structure, clitic deletion, fission, and linearization rules can produce the structure (29) within the morphology.

(29) 2=petâti-1p-IND-PRET

And at this point, regular Vocabulary Insertion rules and regular morphophonology will produce the actual surface form.

Oxford (2014) observes that the 3rd person plural suffixes *-at* in the independent order resist explanation in terms of fission operations operating on a single T head, because /at/ follows everything else, and is often quite distant from the other exponence of agreement features. While this might indicate that 3rd person features are subject to some still more idiosyncratic morphological "magic," the structures derived through multiple head-movement to T make possible a less *ad hoc* approach. Since C is the origin of agreement features realized on T, we might suppose that some ϕ feature content is actually preserved in the C position. Chomsky (2013) suggests that this occurs in the agreeing complementizers found in West Flemish (Bennis & Haegeman 1984) and elsewhere. In that case, the following derivation becomes possible. If *-at* is the unique realization of 3p ϕ features in C, then T may simply not express 3p features in the morphology at all. The question then becomes how an affix in the C position might be displaced to T. In fact there is a familiar answer to this question, based on comparable phenomena in other languages: affix-hopping.[7] C-to-T affix-hopping is attested in Belfast English (with *for* in ECM structures; Henry (1995)), modern Hebrew (Shlonsky 1988), Irish (McCloskey 1996), and Basque allocutive forms (Benat Oyharcabal & Ortiz de Urbina 1993).

The structure for an affix-hopping derivation of (30a) then can be visualized with a structure (30b), where the presence of 3rd person features in T is seen in the ablauting influence they have on the realization of v as /e/ (rather than /â/). T attracts the verb to T, and affix-hopping of /at/ then ensures that the 3p suffix follows the tense suffix.

(30) a. *Uâpamepanat.*
uâpam-e-∅-pan-at.
see-DIR-3-PRET-3p
'They see her/him.'

7. The mechanics of affix-hopping of agreement morphology from C to T are discussed in the appendix section A.3.2.

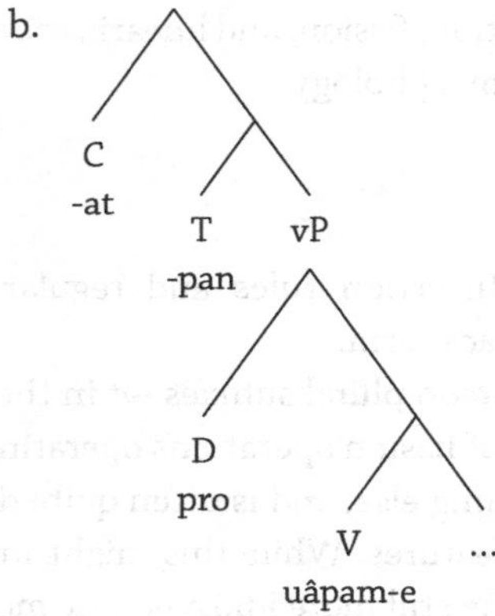

In derivation of a minimal verb complex like these, it makes no difference whether labeling takes place before or after [uSTEM] valuation—T will value its [uSTEM] feature with the verb in any case, and head-movement which brings the verb together with its inflection when the structure is externalized. But matters are different when preverbs are added in.

Suffixal tense inflections can co-occur with various types of (semantically compatible) preverbs: (31).

(31) a. *Nuî mûpishtuâ Ânî.*
N=uî=mûpishtu-â-∅ Ânî.
1=want=visit-DIR-PRET.1 Annie
'I wanted to visit Annie.'

b. *Pûn tshî ueueshtâpan nûtâpân.*
Pûn tshî=ueueshtâ-pan n-ûtâpân.
Paul can=repair-3.PRET 1-car
'Paul was able to fix my car.'

The immediate question for such examples is how to reconcile the position of the inflected verb with the position of the preverbs. An initial hypothesis for the derivation of such forms might be that the verb does not raise from the verb phrase, and that it appears to the right of the modal/auxiliary preverbs simply because this order reflects the base structures, which are preserved throughout the derivation. This hypothesis fails immediately, however, given the position of suffixal tense inflections, which are attached to the principal verb in each case. What is more, the past tense inflection takes wider scope semantically than the preverbs. For example, (31a) cannot mean that I want *to have visited* Annie, with the past temporal location being part of what I wish for. It means only that in the past, there was a time when I wanted to visit Annie. Tense is interpreted outside the preverbs in each case. And this is the crux of the problem. Morphologically, the tense inflection is more tightly bound to the verb than the preverbs are; semantically, the opposite is true, because the preverbs are more closely associated with the verb than tense is.

The meaning of these sentences requires that tense information occupies a higher syntactic position than the preverbs do. A syntactic structure like (32) would be appropriate to provide the actual meaning in (31b), for example.

(32)

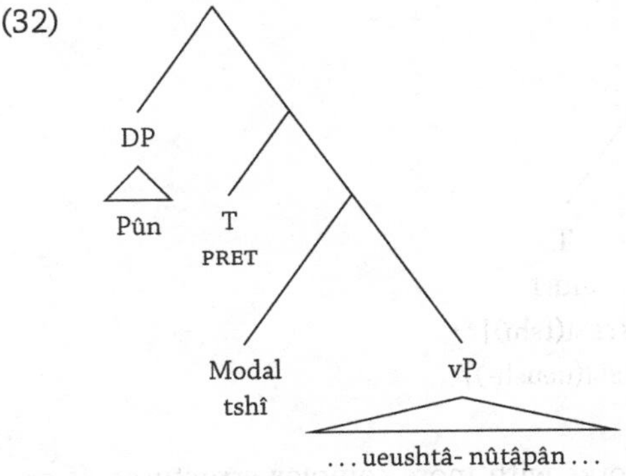

But this structure clearly does not present the component morphemes in their actual positions, since the *-pan* suffix is not attached to the verb in (32).

Suppose, therefore, that T may bear multiple [uSTEM] features (inherited from C), and that T values its [uSTEM] features before labeling takes place, just like in Russian. If both *tshî* and the verb bear [STEM] features, valuation of the features of T will produce the structure (33).

(33)

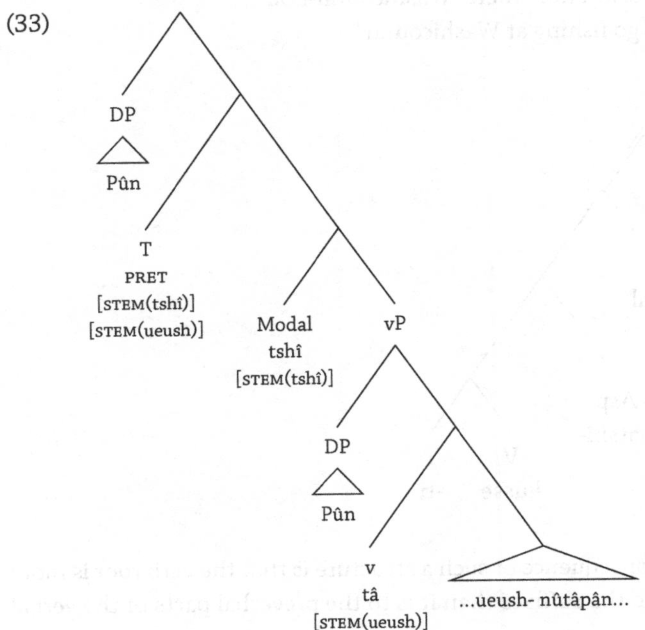

Given this structure, head-movement will then generate the required structure (34) in the position of T:

(34)

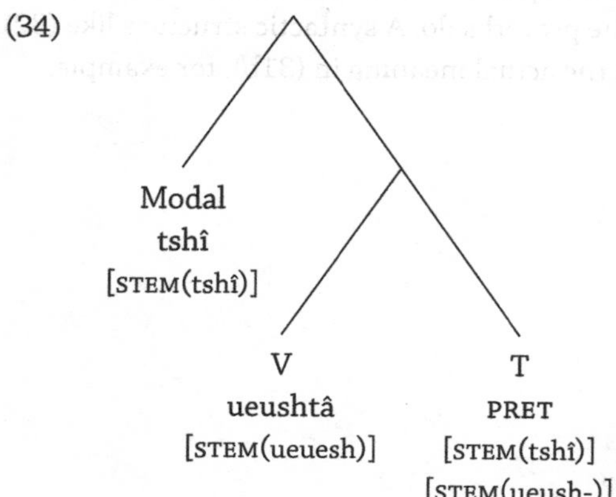

The same sort of derivation works with more complex structures. If one or more proclitics are adjoined to T, then head-movement will replace the innermost segment of T with successive sets of X^0 constituents, leaving the pronoun on the outside. For example, the structure provided for T in (3a) will be (36).

(3a) *Nui natshi-kusseti nete Uashikutet.*
n=ui=nâtshi=kusse-tî nete Uâshikute-t.
1=want=go=fish-PRET there Washicoutai-LOC
'I wanted to go fishing at Washicoutai.'

(35)

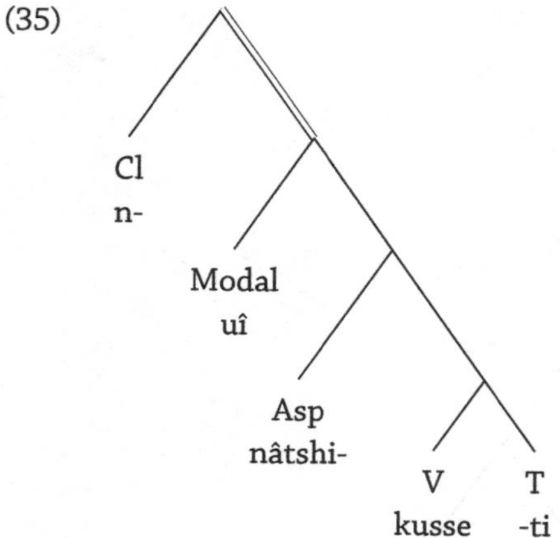

An immediate consequence of such a structure is that the verb root is more closely connected to the suffixes than it is to the preverbal parts of the verbal complex. It would therefore be expected that morphophonological processes might distinguish the two, with some cyclic phonology applying between verbs and suffixes which do not occur within the preverbs and the verb. In fact, a number of studies of the morphophonology in other Algonquian languages have found this to be the general situation (Wolfart 1996, Russell 1992, Russell 1999, Newell 2008, Weber 2020). For Innu-aimûn in particular, the domain of *j* epenthesis is limited to the domain between verb roots and suffixes, as discussed below in section 4.8.2.

4.1.3 Multiple head-movement in the conjunct order

As shown above, with independent order verb complexes, some tense inflection is realized through suffixation; this is impossible for verbs in the conjunct order.[8]

As Goddard (1974) observes, conjunct and independent orders differ overall in the degree to which they appear to compress inflectional information into individual morphemes. For most conjunct forms, in fact, subject and object agreement are simply realized as a single portmanteau suffix. (See section A.3.3 in the appendix for more details.) And while conjunct inflection can sometimes be broken into smaller morphological units, these are quite regular, and might be regarded as instances of morphological "fission," in the sense of Noyer (1992). For example, the "conjunct preterite dubitative form" in (36a) has suffixal inflection which includes two components: an agreement suffix *-itâ* and a dubitative preterite suffix *-(n)âkue*. Similarly, in (36b), the agreement suffix *-iân* and the subjunctive suffix *-î* can be distinguished from each other.

(36) a. *uâpamitânâkue*
uâpam-it-ânâkue
see-1⟩2-PRET.DUB
'if I had seen you'

b. *nipâiânî*
nipâ-iân-î
sleep-CJ.1s-SBJV
'if I am asleep'

8. In other Algonquian languages, tense contrasts can be found in conjunct order inflections, as well. Cree, for example, has both neutral and preterite conjunct paradigms (Ellis 1971). For languages like this, tense must evidently originate in the C position, and it simply stays there.

There is no obvious evidence that this morphological split has a syntactic correlate, though, and for my purposes, it would make little difference if it did. To streamline the discussion, I will describe conjunct order forms on the convenient assumption that conjunct inflection can be treated as a single functional head in the syntactic representation.

The suffixal morphology in verbs in the independent order is markedly less compressed, with up to four "slots" employed to realize the pertinent inflectional features. And in the independent order, the clitic pronoun which appears with 1st or 2nd person direct arguments attaches to the leftmost preverb, or to the verb when no preverb is found. A transitive verb like (37) examplifies these differences.

(37) *Tshuâpamâuâkupanat.*
tshi=uâpam-â-uâ-ku-pan-at.
2=see-DIR-2p-DUB-PRET-3p
'Perhaps you (plural) saw them.'

The existence of two parallel conjugations in any one language raises immediate questions about the function of verbal inflection in this language. While distinct inflectional paradigms are themselves not rare in other languages, they are normally paired with distinct meanings. Russian employs very different paradigms for the present and past tense, as does Arabic and Latin. Indicative and subjunctive conjugations are fully distinct in Basque. Hungarian makes use of distinct conjugation sets for definite and indefinite transitive verbs. So multiple dissimilar conjugations within a language are not uncommon.

What makes the Algonquian distinction between conjunct and independent orders different is that there is no clear semantic difference between the two. While they each have their own appropriate syntactic contexts, these do not directly reflect any obvious semantic motivation. In fact, the meanings expressed by verbs in the independent order constitute a subset of those expressed by verbs in the conjunct order. Independent verbs are used to form declarative root clauses, but conjunct verbs provide declaratives in both embedded and (negated) root contexts. Both are used to form questions. But conjunct order forms are used for a number of other purposes as well, as discussed below. If there is no semantic explanation available, then the existence of two distinct verbal conjugations in Innu-aimûn requires an explanation of another sort.

If the verbal cluster as a whole is considered, then the different functions of the conjunct order can more readily be associated with distinct forms. For example, irrealis-like meanings are expressed with conjunct forms which are used together with the *tshetshî-* preverb. (This is considered in more detail below.) But since *tshetshî-* always appears with conjunct verbs, there is no reason to associate this meaning with the conjunct inflection itself. It is simpler simply to associate the irrealis meaning directly with *tshetshî-*, particularly since the preverb can appear at a distance from the conjunct verb itself, if other preverbs appear between the two. The general problem of the distribution of the two verbal orders persists.

In other cases, the meaning of the conjunct verbal inflection depends on information situated at two opposite ends of the verbal cluster. For example, "iterative" forms (Clarke 1982) are constructed by combining a "subjunctive" form of the verb with a preverb which undergoes "internal change." Iterative forms are interpreted as referring to periodic events, as in the (38) examples. So-called subjunctive verbs include the neutral conjunct suffixes, followed by -*î*, and internal change is an ablaut operation which affects the first vowel in the first member of the verbal cluster. (An analysis of internal change is developed below.)

(38) a. *uipat tshekuânnu uîapatakî, tuiet tshika pimushinatam*ᵘ. (Drapeau 2014: p. 199)

uîpat	tshekuânnu	uîâpata-k-î,	tuiet
without delay	something	IC/see-CJ.3-COND	immediately

tshika=pimushinâtam-u.
FUT=throw.something-3
'Every time he sees something, he throws something at it right away.'

b. *Kum eshakuma nikuteu menu-tshishikaniti.*

Kûm	eshakuma	nikûte-u	menu=tshishkân-it-î.
Côme	every time	cut.firewood-3	IC/good=be.day-CJ.3-COND

'Every time that it is nice out, Côme cuts firewood.'

c. *Nimishta-ushinaman mani katshi-aimiti.*

ni=mishta-ushinam-ân	mâni	IC/kâtshî=aim-it-î.
1=much-laugh-1p	regularly	after=speak-CJ.3-COND

'We always have fun after he has spoken.'

Data like this raise further questions about how the two parts of a conditional meaning can be combined together, since they appear not to form a morphosyntactic constituent.

Simple conditional clauses also use conjunct order verb forms, but no overt Mood preverb appears at the edge of the verb cluster. Nevertheless, they do not permit an *apû* negator; nor do they allow IC to affect the leftmost vowel in the verb complex. Given the parallels between the effects of the different Mood preverbs and how conditional clauses behave, the obvious conclusion to draw is that conditional clauses also include a Mood preverb, but one which is phonologically null.

4.1.4 Deriving the conjunct order

The same general principals must apply to verbs in both inflectional orders, so the first question raised by these forms is why the independent order morphology is not employed in the specific contexts where conjunct order is found. The answer emerges from a single structural difference between the two orders. The base structure which I will justify for conjunct order clauses is minimally richer than before: (39). This differs from the structure for independent order clauses only in the presence of a Mood head between C and T.

(39)

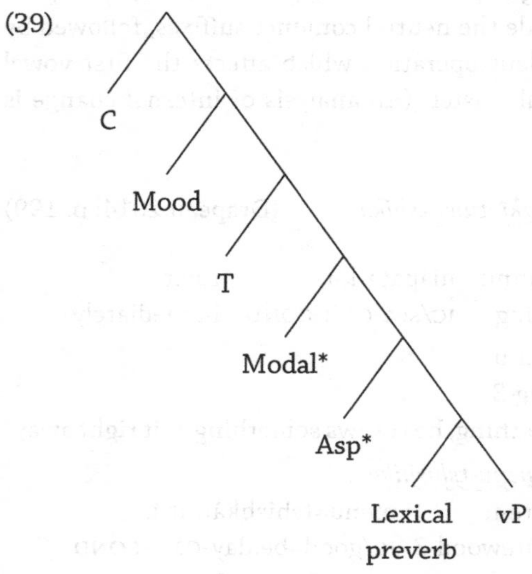

While the structure in (39) cannot be immediately matched up with any string of distinct words in Innu-aimûn, its components are found in more tightly connected morphosyntactic units—verb clusters—in this language. (The formation of these units is accomplished through multiple head-movement.) Once the motivation for the richer structures in (39) has been established, an explanation for the existence of the conjunct order can be provided. And again, the role of multiple head-movement in the derivation of conjunct order forms will become clear.

With conjunct order clauses, as usual, a simple clause will be completed with Merge of the C phase head, which introduces unvalued ϕ features, together with a variety of substantive features which contribute to the meaning of the clause. C is followed by a Mood head, which carries information about the overall "reality" of the clause. While the Mood head is less salient—if it exists at all—in English, it takes audible form in other languages. Some variants of Italian, for example, employ a double complementizer structure, where the lower complementizer appears to mark irrealis mood.[9] D'Alessandro & Ledgeway (2010) provide the Abruzzese example of this in (40).

(40) vedé che si illo non avesse lo consilho de Sidraç ca illu non
saw.3 *che* if ille not had the advice of Sidrac *ca* he not
potea nulla fare.
could nothing do
'He realized that, if he did not receive Sidrac's advice, he could not do anything.'

In (40), the *ca* complementizer is associated with the irrealis interpretation of the complement clause. And obviously, it is situated between the higher complementizer *che* and the tense-inflected verb *potea*. Thus, it occupies a position which corresponds to Mood in (39). The specific items which occupy Mood in Innu-aimûn are less directly visible, and I will return to the question of what belongs in Mood after some of the rest of the structure has been elucidated.

With this cartography in place, we can turn now to the specific characteristics of verbs and verb complexes in the conjunct order. Isolated verbs inflected in the conjunct order often bear two characteristic morphological markers: they carry conjunct inflectional suffixes, and the initial vowel in the verb undergoes an ablaut process of "internal change" (IC). The specific phonological effects of internal change are summarized in section A.2.2 of the appendix. My concern here is the syntactic environment in which it takes place.

The vowel which undergoes IC need not actually appear in the principal verb. IC targets the leftmost vowel in the verb complex, which may include a number of preverbs. For example, IC affects the initial vowel in the verb itself in the embedded clauses in (41), but it affects the vowel in the future tense-marking preverb *tshi-* in the embedded clause in (42).

(41) a. *Ni-mishkâtenimâu tshiâtûtet.*
Ni=mishkâtenim-â-u IC/tshîtûte-t.
1=be.surprise-DIR-1 IC/leave-CJ.3
'I am surprised that he left.'

b. *Tshân apû minuâtâk tshemuanit.*
Tshân apû minuâtâ-k IC/tshimuani-t.
John not like-CJ.3 IC/rain-CJ.3
'John doesn't like rain.'

9. D'Alessandro and Ledgeway employ Rizzi's (1997) Fin category label instead of Mood. Nothing turns on this terminological choice here.

(42) a. *Tshân tshissenitam*ᵘ *tshe-tât uâpanitî.*
Tshân tshissenitam-u IC/tshi=tât uâpanitî.
John know-3 IC/FUT-be-CJ.3 tomorrow
'John knows that he will be there tomorrow.'

b. *Ni-tshissenimâu tshe-pûshit uâpanitî.*
Ni=tshissenim-âu IC/tshi=pûshi-t uâpanitî.
1=know-DIR-3 IC/FUT-leave-CJ.3 tomorrow
'I know that he will leave tomorrow.'

Similarly, verbs in embedded clauses specified with perfective marking are introduced by the *kâ-* preverb, evidently the changed form of the perfective preverb *tshî-*.

(43) a. *Ni-mishkâtenimâu kâ-tshîtûtet.*
Ni=mishkâtenim-â-u IC/tshî=tshîtûte-t.
1=be.surprise-DIR-3 IC/PRF=leave-CJ.3
'I am surprised that he left.'

b. *Mishta-matshenitakuan-nu kâ-tûtâk.*
mishta-matshenitâkuannu IC/tshî=tûtâ-k.
very-be.unpleasant-?? IC/PRF-do-CJ.3
'It's too bad he's done it.'

When the conjunct verb appears with no tense-marking preverbs, then IC can freely be omitted, and an extra preverb *e-* then appears instead as the leftmost element in the verbal cluster (Brittain 2001).

(44) a. *Tshân apû minuâtâk e-tshimuanit.*
Tshân apû=minuâtâk e=tshimuan-it.
John NEG=like-CJ.3 PRV-rain-CJ.3
'John doesn't like rain.'

b. *Ni-mishkâtenimâu ê-tshîtutet.*
Ni=mishkâtenim-â-u ê=tshîtutet.
1=be.surprise-DIR-3 PRV-leave-CJ.3
'I am surprised that he left.'

Brittain concludes from this complementary distribution that IC and *e-* are two ways to realize a single lexical item, a conclusion that I accept. There is no clear difference in meaning between internally changed forms and *e-* forms, so the phonetic realization of this item is likely determined by some other component of grammar. Clarke (1982) and Brittain (2001) maintain that this is primarily a phonological matter, wherein the same underlying abstract element may be realized either as a prefixal *e-* or autosegmentally as a change in initial vocalic quality. If so, then the consequence is that verbs inflected in the conjunct order are frequently accompanied by a single IC preverb at the left edge of their verb cluster, a preverb which is realized (variably) in either of two ways. The presence of the IC preverb is one of the patterns which one would hope to explain in an analysis of the conjunct order.

One context in which this extra preverb—i.e. either IC or *e-*—is not found on conjunct verbs is in root negative sentences. Instead, the negator preverb *apû* is used.[10] Negator *apû* also appears as the left-most element of the verb cluster, as seen in several examples in (45).

(45) a. *Apû tût tshîtûtet.*
apû=tût=tshîtûte-t.
NEG=PRET=leave-CJ.3
'S/he did not leave.'

b. *Uapaki apu tshika ut pushian.*
uâpakî apû=tshika=ût=pûshi-ân.
tomorrow NEG=FUT=thither=leave-CJ.1s
'Tomorrow I will not go on a trip.'

c. *Anûtshîsh auâssat apû mîtshîht utîpinnu.*
anûtshîsh auâss-at apû=mîtshî-ht utîp-inu.
nowadays kid-PL NEG=eat-CJ.3p brain-OBV
'Young people today do not eat brain.'

d. *... apû mînât nenua umatshunishiminua nenua.*
... apû=mîn-ât nenua umatshunishim-inua nenua.
NEG=give-CJ.DIR that.OBV wear.clothes-CJ.3OBV that.OBV
'She did not give him the clothing.'
(LITP)

e. *Apu uapataman nene.*
apû=uâpâtam-ân nene.
NEG=see-CJ.1s that
'I do not see it.'

f. *Nunitan ninakapissinikan, apu tshi pitshikuenaman nimassina.*
n-unitâ-n ni-nâkâpissinikan, apû=tshî=pitshikuenam-ân
1-lose-1 1-thimble NEG=can=pleat-CJ.1s
ni-massin-a.
1-shoe-PL
'I mislaid my thimble; I cannot pleat my moccasins.'

10. The *apû* negator is also used for constituent negation, which I will not discuss.

Given that *apû* and the IC preverb cannot co-occur, it is likely that they occupy the same morpho-syntactic position. This now constitutes initial evidence for a Mood position, to the left of T, as a syntactic slot which can be occupied by two different items: IC or *apû*.

Other comparable cases of complementary distribution support the same conclusion. One involves the preverb *tshetshî*, which is used when a clause characterizes an "unrealized event."[11] Like *apû*, *tshetshî* appears at the left edge of a verb cluster, and it does not appear to be affected by IC.

Clauses which emply the *tshetshî* preverb are used in a broad range of contexts. They function as embedded polar questions: (46).

(46) a. *Apû tût uîtamut tshetshî tshîtûtet utâkûshit.*
apû=tût=uîtamu-t tshetshî=tshîtûte-t utâkûshit.
NEG-past-say-CJ.3 IRR=leave-CJ.3 tomorrow
'He didn't tell me whether he would be leaving tomorrow.'

b. *Apu tshissenitaman tshetshi mitshinanut utenniuashk^{u}.*
apû=tshissenitam-ân tshetshî=mîtshi-nânû-t utennî-uashk^{u}.
NEG=know-CJ.1s IRR=eat-PASS-3 tongue-bear
'I do not know if bear tongue is eaten.'

c. *Tuminik tatshinam^{u} utush, natau-tshissenitam^{u} tshetshi pashtenit.*
Tuminik tâtshinam-u ut-ûsh, natau=tshissenitam-u
Dominic touch-3 3-canoe hunt=know-3
tshetshî=pâshteni-t.
IRR=be.dry-CJ.3
'Dominic touches his canoe; he is checking to see if it is dry.'

With matrix predicates which select unrealized propositions as complements, *tshetshî*-clauses may be used. Such predicates may select subjunctive complements in a language like French, so *tshetshî* may be understood as providing a meaning similar to some uses of subjunctive inflections.

(47) a. *Tshika ishinâkuannu tshetshî tshîtûtet uâpaniti.*
tshika=ishinâkuann-u tshetshî=tshîtûte-t uâpanitî.
FUT=be.necessary-3 IRR=leave-CJ.3 tomorrow
'It will be necessary for him to leave tomorrow.'

b. *Nasht apu ushuniamian tshetshi aiaian mitshim.*
nâsht apû=ushuniâm-iân tshetshî=aiâ-iân mîtshim.
completely NEG=have.money-CJ.1s IRR=buy-CJ.1s food
'I have no money at all to buy food.'

11. Clarke (1982) classifies this preverb as a complementizer.

c. *Apu minuatak nikûpâniem tshetshî utikumit.*
apû=minuât-ak ni=kûpâni-em tshetshî=utîkumi-t.
NEG=like-CJ.1s 1-child-POSS IRR=have.lice-CJ.3
'I do not like for my child to have lice.'

Tshetshî-clauses are also frequently used as purpose clauses, as in (48).

(48) a. *Etien kushpitaieu ukussa tshetshi tshishkutamuat tshe ishi-natauniti.*
Etien kushpitai-e-u u-kuss-a tshetshî=tshishkutamu-ât
Etienne take.to.bush-DIR-3 3-son-OBV IRR=teach-CJ.3
IC/tshi=ishi-nataun-it-î.
IC/FUT=thus-hunt-CJ.3-COND
'Etienne takes his son in the bush to teach him how to hunt.'

b. *Ninapem natutikueti, uikua tshika manapashtau tshetshi tepatetsheian.*
ni-nâpe-m natutîkue-t-î, uîku-a
1-husband-POSS hunt.caribou-CJ.3-SBJV gland-PL
tshika=manâpash-tâ-u tshetshi=tepâtetshe-iân.
FUT=retrieve-V-3 IRR=make.pie-CJ.1s
'When my husband goes caribou hunting, he will recover the adrenal glands so that I can make some meat pies.'

Finally, *tshetshî*-clauses can serve as the complement to causative verbs: *tutueu* and *shîtshimeu*.

(49) a. *Tshi-tûtu-âu tshetshî pâpit Tûmâs.*
tshi=tûtu-â-u tshetshî=pâpi-t Tûmâs.
2=do.for-DIR-3 IRR=laugh-CJ.3 Thomas
'You made Tomas laugh.'

b. *Nishîtshimâu Tûmâs tshetshî minushtâshut mîtshuâpit.*
ni=shîtshim-â-u Tûmâs tshetshî=minushtâshu-t mîtshuâp-ît.
1=make-DIR-3 Thomas IRR=clean-CJ.3 house-LOC
'I made Thomas clean up the house.'

Given the type of clauses in which *tshetshî* appears, assigning it to the Mood preverb category seems appropriate. And *tshetshî* cannot co-occur with *apû* within a clause, which follows if they must compete for a single syntactic position. Instead, negation is realized within a *tshetshî* clause by means of an alternative negator: the preverb *ekâ*, seen in (50).

(50) a. *Shapatish anite ushkatshikutit e-tatak utatusseuna tshetshi eka unitat.*
Shâpâtîsh anite u-shkâtshikut-ît e=tâtâk
Jean-Baptiste there 3-canvas.bag-LOC IC/thus.do-CJ.3
ut-atusseun-a tshetshî=ekâ =unitâ-t.
3-tool-PL IRR-NEG-lose-3
'Jean-Baptiste puts his tools in his canvas bag so as not to lose them.'

b. *Etien nish^{u} pakashtueim^{u} upunishtashuna tshetshi eka uepainnit utush makainniti tipishkaniti.*
etien nîsh^{u} pakâshtu-eim-u u-pûnishtâshun-a
Etienne two submerge-*V*-3 3-anchor-PL
tshetshî=ekâ=uepainni-t ut-ûsh mâkain-nit-î
IRR=NEG=drift-CJ.3SG 3-boat be.choppy-CJ.3.OBV-SBJV
tipishkâniti.
tonight
'Etienne drops his two anchors in the water so that his boat does not drift away if there are waves tonight.'

When other preverbs are present, they also precede *ekâ*, as in (51).

(51) *Nitshissenimâu tshe ekâ takushint.*
ni=tshissenim-â-u IC/tshî=ekâ=takushin-t.
1=know IC/FUT=NEG=come-CJ.3
'I know he won't come.'

Since the *ekâ* negator follows *tshetshî* and other preverbs, it must occupy a lower position in clause structure, plausibly as an adverbial element adjoined to the verb phrase category between T and vP, as in (52).

(52)

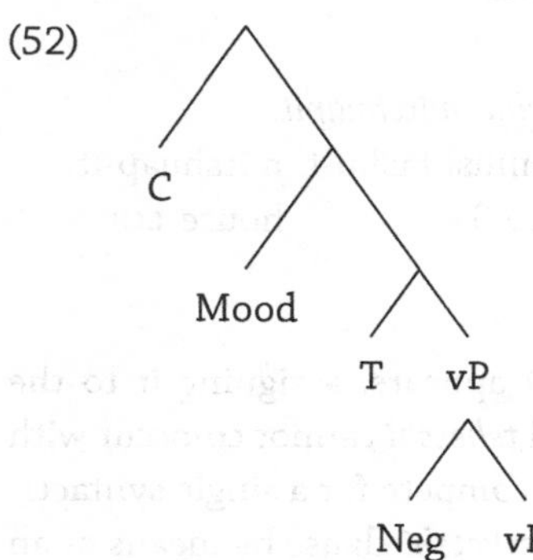

As a general description of the distribution of the two negators, it suffices to say that *apû* marks clausal negation in the Mood position when this position is not occupied by anything else. When Mood is occupied by something else, then *ekâ* must be used instead to express clausal negation.[12,13]

Sometimes, however, *ekâ* is found further to the left than would be expected, as in (53).

(53) *Tshitshue animishiu nikupaniem eka ua mitshit nutshimiu-mitshiminu.*
tshîtshue ânimishî-u ni-kûpânie-m ekâ IC/uî=mîtshi-t
truly be.difficult-3 1-helper-POSS NEG IC/want-eat-N-CJ.3
nutshimî-u-mitshî-m-inu.
bush-V=eat-N-OBV
'My child is quite tiresome because he does not want to eat bush food.'

For example, in (53), the modal preverb *uî* must clearly sit outside the verb phrase, so one would expect it to precede *ekâ*, which does not occur here. In such cases, it appears that the negative adverbial is displaced from its natural position into the clausal left periphery. This displacement can also be seen in examples like (54), where internal change affects the initial vowel of the verb, and not of *ekâ*.

(54) a. *Auen ekâ tshâtûtet?*
auen ekâ IC/tshîtûte-t?
who NEG IC/leave-CJ.3
'Who is not leaving?'

b. *Ni-tshissenimâu ekâ tiât mûsh nete.*
ni=tshissenim-â-u ekâ IC/tât mûsh nete.
1=know-DIR-3 NEG IC/be moose there
'I know there are not (any) moose there.'

If *ekâ* were simply adjoined to the verb phrase, then multiple head-movement would inevitably produce an X^0 structure like (55) for (54b), and internal change would apply to *ekâ* rather than *tât*.

12. *ekâ* is also the negator in imperatives, which would imply that imperative forms in this language employ a silent Mood head.
13. Particularly in narratives, *ekâ* can sometimes appear to the left of "higher" preverbs.

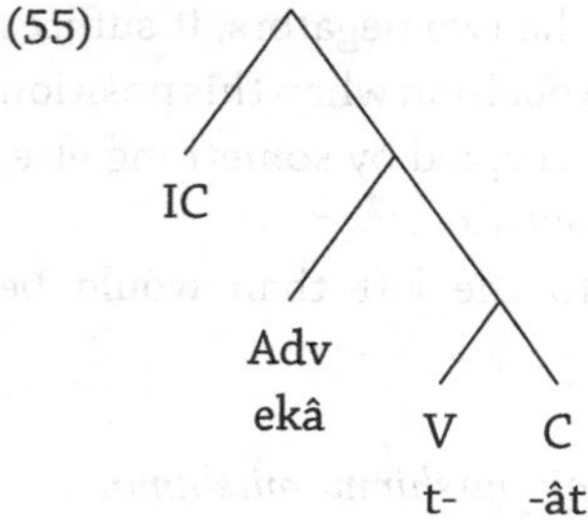

It seems that *ekâ* must raise in order to allow the derivation to succeed. And in fact, *ekâ* never undergoes internal change, unlike almost everything else which can appear low within a conjunct the verb cluster. This suggests that it is a lexical property of *ekâ* that it cannot tolerate this phonological operation, and so it must raise whenever it appears to the right of an IC Mood head. In that respect, *ekâ* behaves much like the Russian adverbials found in the same adjoined position, which also raise to avoid being implicated in multiple head-movement.

The *ekâ* negator is also sometimes found in clauses in the independent order, such as (56).

(56) *Ek^u ekâ nitâpuetuâua, nitânish iteu.*
ek^u ekâ ni=tâpuetu-â-u-a, ni-tânish, iteu.
then NEG 1=agree-DIR-3 1-daughter say-3
'"Then I did not give him my consent for my daughter," he said.'

Here again, however, *ekâ* cannot occupy the expected, verb phrase-adjoined position, since it appears to the left of the pronominal clitic *ni(t)*. Such clitics adjoin to T, to which the verb then raises. If *ekâ* were to remain adjoined to the verb phrase, it would appear outside the verb inside the derived X^0 inflected verb cluster, and the clitic would then attach to *ekâ*. But since *ekâ* is morphologically invariant, it avoids hosting a clitic, just as it avoids internal change. So, once again, *ekâ* undergoes movement to a position higher than T in a context where otherwise it would be involved in some morphology which it cannot tolerate.

So at least three different items can occupy the Mood position. (More will be introduced below.) And these items always occur together with conjunct order verb forms. It is impossible to combine *tshetshî* or *apû* with an independent order verb, and IC cannot affect a non-conjunct form: (57).

(57) a. **Âpû ni-mûpishtuâu nikâuî.*
    âpû=ni=mûpishtu-â-u n-ikâuî.
    NEG=1-visit-DIR-3 1-mother
    'I don't visit my mother.'

b. **Tshi-tûtuâu tshetshî pâpu.*
    tshi=tûtu-â-u tshetshî=pâp-u.
    2=make-DIR-3
    'You make her/him laugh.'

c. **Auen menuâtam*ᵘ *pinaku?*
    auen IC/minuâtam-u pinaku?
    who IC/like-3 bingo
    'Who likes bingo?'

Evidently the presence of Mood preverbs is intimately connected to the selection of a particular verbal order. The question I have been leading up to is how this relationship should be characterized. And now we are in a position to identify an answer.

Integrated into a phase theoretic model, a derivation which employs multiple head-movement provides a way to model the morphosyntax of conjunct order verb clusters. Suppose that conjunct order inflections are introduced in the C phase head position. Given that they realize ϕ features (and often little else), this is a natural supposition. Indeed, given Chomsky's (2001) claim that unvalued features are always introduced in a phase head, there is no alternative to this assumption. Since verbal agreement inflections always make use of the subject as one agreement target, phasal *v* cannot be the origin of these agreement features. And while T is the normal locus for realizing ϕ features, T is actually expressed as a preverb inside the verb cluster in many cases, and is quite remote from where the agreement morphology appears. So let us adopt the hypothesis that agreement is in C.[14] The base structure for the C-T phase in (45a), repeated, to take one instance, will then be (58).

14. An anonymous reviewer points out that the proposal that ϕ features reside in C is incompatible with the model of Béjar & Rezac (2009), which derives much of the Algonquian person hierarchy in a model where agreement is situated instead in the v head. The reviewer is correct, but the approach to agreement adopted here is instead based on the alternative analysis of Oxford (2018). In Oxford's model, v (or Voice) is the locus for Theme morphology, and the overt agreement in independant forms resides in T, which can agree with subjects and objects. Oxford does not address the nature of agreement in conjunct forms, but the logic of his analysis appears to carry over readily to the analysis of conjunct agreement proposed here.

(45a) *Apû tût tshîtûtet.*
apû=tût=tshîtûte-t.
NEG=PRET=leave-CJ.3
'S/he did not leave.'

(58)

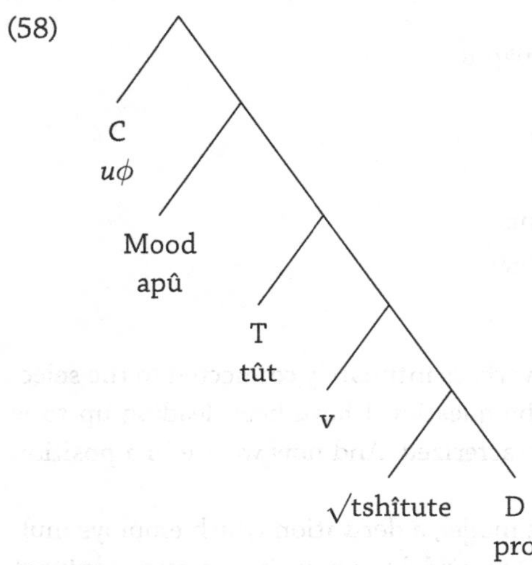

Depending on the type of clause being formed, C may contain substantive features in addition to ϕ. A conditional feature in this position will provide a conditional clause.[15] Dubitative evidential features may appear here as well. These extra features on C are reflected in the conjunct morphology, where they are realized as suffixes following the ϕ feature inflection. (I continue to assume that this reflects a post-syntactic fissioning of features into two adjacent morphological positions.)

Unvalued ϕ features originate in C in English, too, but in English, Feature Inheritance displaces them onto the head of the complement of C, i.e. onto T, where they find morphological expression. In the Innu-aimûn (58) structure, Feature Inheritance evidently cannot produce the same result, because all members of the Mood category are morphologically invariant. ϕ-features transferred to Mood cannot be realized at all. This does not imply that Feature Inheritance cannot take place in this structure—the contents of Mood may well represent specific semantic features which originate in C. But if ϕ features are to be expressed in this structure, it can only be in their original C position.[16] At the same time, agreement morphology in Innu-aimûn is affixal—in my terms, these ϕ feature clusters always carry a [uSTEM] feature, which forces

15. Ellis (1971) and Clarke (1982) call these forms "subjunctives."
16. In this respect, the ϕ featural inflection in the Algonquian conjunct order resembles the agreement morphology found on complementizers in a number of Germanic dialects (Bennis & Haegeman 1984, Goeman 1980, Zwart 1993).

them to find an appropriate stem to join with. And since only verbs and nouns can support affixes, the stem must be one of these. The only way for this to take place is through multiple head-movement. Preverbs in Innu-aimûn inherently bear [STEM] features, so C must always match its one [uSTEM] feature on the closest preverb, i.e. *apû* in (58). But the actual morphological demands of C require a verbal base, so C cannot settle for this result. Instead, C will value three separate [uSTEM] features, matching *apû*, *tût*, and the verb. And these newly matching pairs of [STEM] features will ultimately trigger three head-movement operations to bring the [STEM] features together. The end result will be the structure (59).

(59)

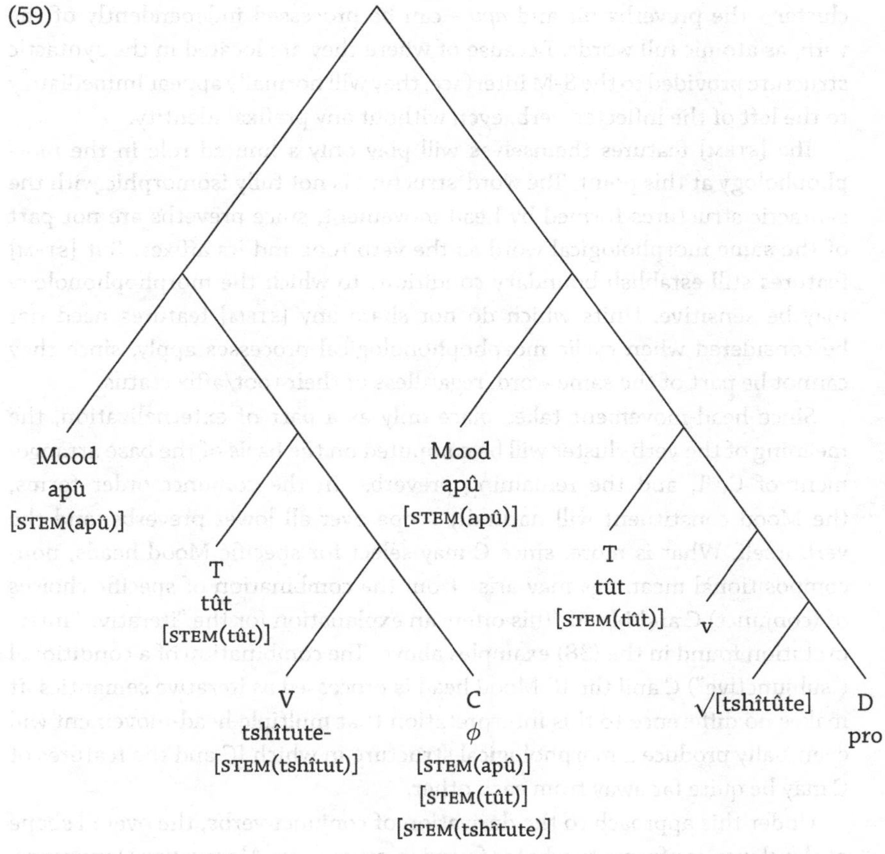

The ϕ features in C in (59) are ultimately pronounced as /t/, after valuation and externalization. Just as in the other multiple head-movement derivations identified in other languages, the copies pronounced after head-movement will be those in which [STEM] features are associated with their matches, so the (59) structure corresponds to the correct surface form.

Of course, in order for C to value multiple [uSTEM] features, C must be able to look beyond the first successful match. In other words, the parameter settings controlling valuation timing for C in Innu-aimûn allows [uSTEM] features to be valued before the labeling algorithm applies.

In order to provide an actual phonetic interpretation of the structures provided to the S-M interface, the morphophonology must be able to identify the component roots and affixes. In (59), the preverbs and the verb root √tshîtute- all constitute non-affixal units while the agreement suffix *-t* is an affix. Construction of the morphophonological structure therefore starts with the smallest root/affix pair, and processes *tshîtute-* and the agreement suffix to produce a complete inflected verb form. The remaining members of the verbal cluster—the preverbs *tût* and *apû*—can be processed independently of the verb, as atomic full words. Because of where they are located in the syntactic structure provided to the S-M interface, they will normally appear immediately to the left of the inflected verb, even without any prefixal identity.

The [STEM] features themselves will play only a limited role in the morphophology at this point. The word-structure is not fully isomorphic with the syntactic structures formed by head-movement, since preverbs are not part of the same morphological word as the verb root and its affixes. But [STEM] features still establish boundary conditions to which the morphophonology may be sensitive. Units which do not share any [STEM] features need not be considered when cyclic morphophonological processes apply, since they cannot be part of the same word, regardless of their root/affix status.

Since head-movement takes place only as a part of externalization, the meaning of the verb cluster will be computed on the basis of the base arrangement of C, T, and the remaining preverbs. In the conjunct order forms, the Mood constituent will naturally scope over all lower preverbs, and the verb itself. What is more, since C may select for specific Mood heads, non-compositional meanings may arise from the combination of specific choices of (conjunct) C and Mood. This offers an explanation for the "iterative" interpretation found in the (38) examples above. The combination of a conditional ("subjunctive") C and the IC Mood head is processed as iterative semantics. It makes no difference to this interpretation that multiple head-movement will eventually produce a morphological structure in which IC and the features of C may be quite far away from each other.

Under this approach to the derivation of conjunct verbs, the overall shape of the clause conforms to what is found in other (non-Algonquian) languages, and the morphosyntactic derivation matches what takes place in Finnish or Perenakan Javanese. Unlike what occurs in these other languages, multiple head-movement occurs in Innu-aimûn specifically because the presence of a Mood head blocks Feature Inheritance from realizing ϕ features on T. If Mood is absent, though, Feature Inheritance can relate C to T. This what takes place in the independent order forms.

The presence of two distinct inflectional orders in Innu-aimûn now reduces to two distinct categories in which agreement features are realized: C or T. Conjunct order inflection is C-inflection; independent order T-inflection.[17]

The different positions occupied by preterite markers in the two orders now follow, as well. In both orders, preterite markers will originate in T. In the independent order, ϕ features are transferred to T, along with a [uSTEM] feature. (Evidential features can be transferred to T in the same way, producing dubitative independent order verb forms.) T becomes a "strong affix" as a result, and when the verb then raises to T, the result is automatically interpreted morphologically as a verb stem with an attached (morphological) suffix. In contrast, in a conjunct context, C cannot transfer a [uSTEM] feature to T, so T can never attract the verb. Instead, multiple head-movement takes place and creates a structure in which (non-affixal) T is attached outside the V, C constituent. The morphological interpretation of T in this position can only be as a preverb.

Conjunct and independent order forms also differ in how they accommodate subject and object clitic pronouns. These are allowed only with independent order forms of the verb. This contrast between the two orders in whether they host such clitics can be derived from the different positions occupied by the verb in the two orders, i.e. C *versus* T. If the pronominal clitics in Innu-aimûn must adjoin to T, then they cannot appear attached to a conjunct order verb, which does not occupy that position.

Given such an approach, one might still raise the question why clitics cannot be attached to a preterite T realized as a preverb in the conjunct order. In fact, this is impossible, as evidenced by (60).

(60) *Apû (*ni-)tût-mûpishtût.*
apû=ni=tût-mûpishtû-t.
NEG=1=PRET=visit-CJ.3⟩1
'S/he doesn't visit me.'

This restriction on the appearance of clitic pronouns cannot be attributed directly to the position T occupies in a conjunct form. While conjunct T will always be preceded by another preverb—taking IC to be a preverb, as well—it is not the case that clitic pronouns cannot be placed inside a preverb cluster in Innu-aimûn. In the so-called *ka-...-ua* forms,[18] a clitic pronoun does appear to the right of the *ka-* preverb, as in (61).

17. Regrettably, the label for the category formerly known as Infl has changed in standard minimalist usage. If it had not, then conjunct and independent orders could simply be C and I inflections, respectively.
18. Baraby & Drapeau (1998: p. 184) call these *subjective* forms.

(61) a. *"Ek^u tshekuan ka-tshimamakapinaua shuk^u" itakanu Uapush.* (LITP)
"ek^u tshekuan kâ=tshî-mamâkâp-in-âu-a shuk^u" itâkanû
then what *ka*=2=have.big.eyes-V-2-UA so much say.to-PASS-3
Uâpush.
Hare
'"And how do you come to have such big eyes?" Hare was asked.'

b. *Ka-nuapatenaua tshekuan anite + nipa tetishikapaun.*
(Drapeau 2014: p. 187)
ka=n=uâpat-en-â-ua tshekuân anite
ka=1=see-V-1-UA what there
ni=pa=tetishikâpau-n.
1=would=stand.on.raised.surface-1
'I see something that I could stand up upon.'

I consider this construction in more detail below (section 4.2.3). In the meantime, it is sufficient to note that the pronominal clitics can appear within the verbal cluster under the right circumstances. So the question of why they cannot be a part of conjunct verbal clusters remains to be resolved.

Besides the affixal status of T in the independent order, T also bears ϕ features. In the approach taken here, C does not transfer ϕ features to T in the conjunct order. This difference provides another way to understand the lack of proclitic pronouns on conjunct T. Roberts (2010) provides fairly extensive evidence that pronominal clitic movement is dependent on the presence of ϕ features in the host. If so, then T in the conjunct forms will be unable to host proclitics in any case. In the *ka-...-ua* forms, the independent order inflections show that Feature Inheritance has actually transferred ϕ features to T, so the presence of a pronominal clitic in (61) is to be expected.

To sum up, the conjunct order will be derived whenever Feature Inheritance cannot apply between C and T, due to the blocking effect of an intervening head.[19] Agreement features and evidential features remain in C in this context, and can therefore be realized as suffixal inflection on the verb only if the verb raises to C. Given the presence of at least one non-verbal head between C and T, the verb can reach C only with a derivation which includes multiple head-movement.

In my view, the crucial syntactic difference between independent order structures and their conjunct order counterparts is that no Mood preverbs are found in the independent order. This has a number of immediate

19. Branigan (2020) develops a model of the left periphery in Romance and Germanic languages in which Feature Inheritance can transfer features to a sequence of adjacent heads, enabling C to transfer features past Mood to T. This possibility must be unavailable in Algonquian languages, suggesting that multiple Feature Inheritance must represent a parametrized option.

consequences. First, internal change never takes place within independent order forms, since internal change is triggered by the IC preverb, i.e. a Mood item. Clausal negation with *apû* cannot occur in independent order forms, since the *apû* negator belongs to the Mood category.[20]

The broader consequence of the absence of Mood is that C always has a TP complement in independent order structures. If we consider this together with the basic Chomsky/Richards premise that Feature Inheritance is a relationship between a head and the head of its complement, then it follows that Feature Inheritance between C and T is possible in independent order structures, while it is not in the conjunct order, where Mood intervenes. This suggests a cost-free explanation for the general question why Innu-aimûn should have two different inflectional "orders" in the first place. Conjunct order forms are necessary when C cannot transfer ϕ features to T; independent order forms are used when C succeeds in transferring ϕ features.

In that respect, Innu-aimûn is similar to those Germanic dialects in which agreement morphology can be found both in C and T positions, but where the actual realization of agreement features differs, depending on where they are situated. In East Netherlandic Dutch, for example, different verb endings are used for root clause verbs depending on whether a non-subject has undergone wh-movement.

(62) *East Netherlandic*

a. ... Wy speul-t (Zwart 1997)
we play-1PL

b. ... Waor speul-e wy?
where play we

This approach offers a new way to approach one of the persistent diachronic questions in the Algonquianist literature. As noted in the appendix, the agreement morphology in independent verb forms is essentially the same as one finds with possessed nominals. Previous literature, which classifies all verb endings simply as verbal morphology, has suggested two ways to account for this overlap between nominal morphology and that of independent verbs. Goddard (1974) proposed that the agreement in the independent order developed on the basis of the nominal endings, which were borrowed to inflect independent verbs. Goddard (2007) reverses the account, and maintains that nominal morphology must have taken endings from the verbal system. But if conjunct order verbal endings are associated with a category which is neither a noun nor a verb, then the relationship between independent order and

20. The *ekâ* negator is is occasionally found in independent order clauses, as discussed in section 4.1.4.

nominal morphology needs no *ad hoc* explanation. ϕ features retained in C are realized by a very specific set of morphological rules. But ϕ features realized in other categories, such as T and D, can be realized by a more general, category-neutral set of rules. In other words, nominal agreement and independent order verbal agreement are realized with 'elsewhere', default morphology, while C stands alone as the more specific case.

In both inflectional orders in Innu-aimûn, ϕ features are realized as suffixal inflection, which implies that the presence of agreement features on a head in Innu-aimûn correlates with that head being a suffix. More precisely, in this language, heads which bear ϕ features also bear a [uSTEM] feature. If C does not transfer ϕ features, then it also maintains its [uSTEM] feature; when ϕ features move to T, [uSTEM] goes with them.

(63) a. *Conjunct order* b. *Independent order*

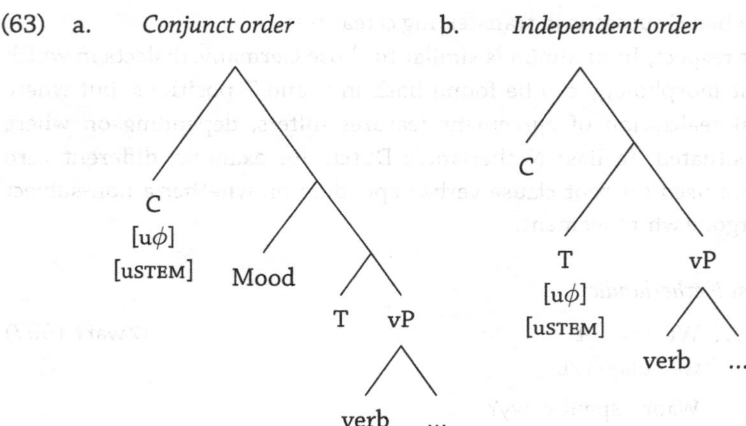

4.2 SOME NUANCES AND COMPLEXITIES

At this point, the main lines of a multiple head-movement analysis of Innu-aimûn clause structure have been presented. Before going on to compare this approach to potential alternative competitors, let us consider some complexities which any complete model should be able to accommodate. The point here is simply to show that a model incorporating multiple head-movement has sufficient empirical coverage that it can be taken seriously as a tool for characterizing real language. (We will return to the more abstract general questions after this parenthetical moment.)

4.2.1 Wh-questions in independent order

One of the environments which normally requires verbs in the conjunct order is wh-questions, as in (64).

(64) a. *Tân etîn anite?*
tân IC/it-î-n anite?
how IC/do-CJ.2s there
'What are you doing?'

b. *Tan etashtet tshitenepuanim?*
tân IC-itashte-t tshi=tenipuân-im?
how IC-CJ.3 2-phone-POSS
'What is your phone number?'

Besides the conjunct order inflection, the verb complex in wh-questions must realize internal change. In my terms, this means that the Mood position is occupied by the IC head. If wh-movement is a matter of matching features between a wh-phrase "specifier" and C, then the implication is that a C which bears WH feature must select IC as the head of its complement in this language.

Nothing in this model actually forces a [wh] C to select IC. Nothing prevents it, either. But there may be functional pressures in the language which would prefer that wh-questions be overtly signaled as such by the morphology. In many cases, the interrogative pronoun itself provides little indication that it is part of a question, since many of the wh-words are homophonous with indefinite pronouns. Only the use of conjunct morphology with internal change distinguishes between a question and a statement, as the minimal contrast in (65) shows.

(65) a. *Auen an neuaimu utinu?*
auen an IC/nuaim-u ût-inu?
who DEM chase-3 canoe-OBV
'Who is swimming after the canoe?'

b. *Auen eka shuku niaitak unitamu eimiakaniti.*
auen ekâ shûku IC/nait-âk unît-am-u
someone NEG only IC/hear.well-CJ.3 hear.poorly-V-3
IC/aimi-âkan-it-î.
speak-V-CJ.3-COND
'Someone who does not have very good hearing misunderstands when people speak to him.'

Since the difference between a question and a statement will often matter in communication, it is not surprising that Innu-aimûn grammar would find a means to disambiguate the two. Selection of IC by the [wh] C accomplishes this end.

One incidental difference between root and embedded clauses is that the interrogative pronoun itself is often omitted in the latter context (Clarke 1982), as in (66).

(66) a. *Tshissenitam*[u] *tiûtâk.* (Clarke 1982)
tshissenitam-u IC/tût-âk.
know-3 IC/do-CJ.1s
'He knows what he is doing.'

b. *Tshân tshitshissenimik*[u] *kâ=tûtaman.*
Tshân tshi=tshissenim-iku IC/tshî=tutam-an.
John 2=know-INV IC/PRET=do=CJ.2
'John knows what you did.'

Again, the fact that a [wh] C is able to signal the interrogative status of the clause by selecting IC makes the audible presence of the actual interrogative pronoun less significant, on communicative grounds at least.

While the use of conjunct forms with internal change in wh-questions is common in central Algonquian languages, Innu-aimûn allows for exceptions when the verb is in the preterite tense, as in (67).

(67) a. *Tshekuaneni tshui kukuetshimiti?*
tshekuân-eni tshî=uî=kukuetshim-it-î?
what-OBV 2=want=ask-2⟩1-SBJV
'What things did you want to ask me?'

b. *Nikuetshimau Shushep tshekuannu utshimama aimienipani.*
ni=kuetshim-â-u Shûshep tshekuân-nu u-tshimâm-a
1=ask-DIR-3 Joseph which-OBV 3-boss-OBV
aimie-nî-panî.
call-OBV-PRET-OBV
'I asked Joseph who his boss telephoned.'

I suppose this apparently unique departure from the cross-linguistic rule is a variant on the selectional properties of WH C. In Innu-aimûn, a WH C can evidently select either IC or a preterite T as the head of its complement. Since tense is situated lower than Mood, it follows that the verb can only be in the independent order if preterite T is selected.

Similar patterns can be seen in relative clauses, which also may involve wh-movement (Chomsky 1977). Relative clauses have no audible relative pronouns; instead, they are identified as such by the overall context, and sometimes by the use of a *kâ* preverb.[21] Relative preverb *kâ* is homophonous

21. Internally headed relative clauses seem also to exist in Innu-aimûn, as in (i).

(i) *Muk*[u] *auen uâ-mîtshishut tshika-mîtshishu.*
muk[u] auen IC/uî=mîtshishu-t tshika=mîtshish-u
only someone IC/want-eat-3 FUT=eat-3
'Anyone who wants to eat will eat.'

with the changed from of the past preverb, but its function is different enough that it is presumably a distinct functional item.[22] Relative *kâ* is another plausible candidate for the Mood position.

(68) a. *Ne nâpeu kâ-mishikât utâkushît nukumish an.*
ne nâpeu kâ=mishikâ-t utâkushît n-ûkumish an.
that man REL=arrive-3 yesterday 1-uncle DEM
'The man who arrived yesterday is my uncle.'

b. *Kauapikuesht akuneu ishkueua ka natuneniti mita.*
kâuâpikuesht akune-u ishkueua kâ=natune-nitî mita.
priest photograph-3 woman-OBV REL=fetch-OBV firewood
'The priest takes a photo of a woman who is gathering wood.'

4.2.2 Modal inflections and modal preverbs

Innu-aimûn verbs may employ a "dubitative" suffix to express the modal notion of possibility: (69).

(69) a. *Pâshtekupan.*
pâshte-∅-ku-pan.
be.dry-3-DUB-PRET
'Perhaps it was dry.'

b. *Tshitûtenâkupan.*
tshi=tûte-nâ-ku-pan.
2=do.it-2p-DUB-PRET
'You might have done it.'

c. *Tshiminuâshitânâkupan.*
tshi=minuâsh-i-tâ-nâ-ku-pan.
2=love-2⟩1-PRET.1p-DUB-PRET
'Perhaps I loved you.'

One effect of the presence of dubitative *-ku* is that the preterite feature in T is realized as /pan/. In simpler forms of the verb, the preterite suffix is given a zero realization when adjacent to SAP agreement morphology (in some dialects). In DM terms, this can be understood as a Vocabulary Insertion rule, which provides a ∅ exponent for preterite features in that context. The exponent *-pan* is then simply the elsewhere form for preterite features. And

22. Johansson's (2011) study of the cognate Blackfoot particle suggests this is the case.

the dubitative suffix ensures that the elsewhere form is realized by disrupting the adjacency between T and SAP agreement morphology.

Under the assumption that subject agreement inflection is located in T in the syntax (after Feature Inheritance puts it there), a corollary to this treatment of how *-pan* is realized is that Vocabulary Insertion must be preceded by Fission operations which separate SAP morphology and the dubitative suffix from T, attaching them to the verb stem in that order.[23]

The use of *-ku* to introduce one particular modal concept can be compared with the use of preverbs to express others, as described above. One striking fact about modal preverbs is that they also interfere with the zero realization of preterite features in T. For example, the preverb cluster *pâtshî-*, when used with a preterite verb, refers to a "non-realised past event" (Clarke 1982: p. 47).[24]

(70) *Nipâ tshî nipânapan.*
ni=pâ=tshî=nipâ-nâ-pan
1=should=can=sleep-1-PRET
'I should have been able to sleep.'

The morphological results are shown in (71), where the preterite feature is realized throughout in the *-pan* suffix.

(71) *"could have slept"*

1s	nipâtshî-nipânâpan	ni=pâtshî=nipâ-nâ-pan
2s	tshipâtshî-nipânâpan	tshi=pâtshî=nipâ-nâ-pan
3s	tshiâtshî-nipâpan	tshipâtshî=nipâ-pan
1pe	nipâtshî-nipânânâpan	ni=pâtshî=nipâ-nâ-nâ(n)-pan
1pi	tshipâtshî-nipânânâpan	tshi=pâtshî=nipâ-nâ-nâ(n)-pan
2s	tshipâtshî-nipânâuâpan	tshi=pâtshî=nipâ-nâ-uâ(u)-pan
3p	tshipâtshî-nipâpanat	tshipâtshî=nipâ-pan-at

Other modals, *pa=* and *uî=*, have the same effect on the form of preterite T. This is initially surprising. If the distribution of preterite forms were based strictly on morphological locality or adjacency, then we should not expect a preverb to have the same influence as a suffix.

23. Oxford (2019) proposes fission for the agreement morphology, but does not extend this to the dubitatitive suffix.

24. Clarke (p. 47) attributes the initial observation to Lemoine (1901). Clarke also observes that preterite temporal reference is canceled out in cases like this, where *-pan* and a modal preverb are used together for a more specific semantic purpose. Thus, she notes: "a form like *ni+uî+nipâpan* 'I would have slept' may be found with a present particle like *nutshish* 'now'."

On closer reflection, this morphological surprise is actually paired with a semantic oddity in the *-ku* dubitative forms. If modal concepts are located in a modal head, then the presence of *-ku* inside T makes no sense. Of course, one might draw the conclusion from these forms that *-ku is* a functional head located outside T, but then it becomes difficult to account for the interactions between SAP agreement, modality, and preterite T.

It appears we have two complementary problems. On the one hand, the morphology is sensitive to the presence of model heads which should be too far away to affect the morphology. On the other, a modal suffix appears in a position which should not correspond to its semantic role. Both problems can be resolved if we accept that modal forms of the verb complex always include two distinct elements: a modal head, which is not always given phonetic substance, and a "modal" suffix, which also can be silent.

Given these constituents in dubitative expressions, the pattern is the following. T in Innu-aimûn selects a modal complement only if it also bears an unvalued modal feature—call it *u*Mod. This feature takes its value from the selected complement. When the complement is *uî*, *pa*, or *patshî*, then the realization of the modal feature is zero. But the presence of this feature still makes a difference to how preterite features in T are realized. The silent modal suffix still blocks Vocabulary Insertion from translating preterite features to zero, and thereby allows the elsewhere form *-pan* to appear.

On the flip side, there is also a silent modal preverb which provides the "dubitative" meaning. When the modal feature in T takes its value from the dubitative preverb, it is given an audible realization as *-ku*. The suffix itself is semantically vacuous, but it functions to identify the presence of the associated modal preverb.

Both problems are now resolved. It is not a distant preverb which affects the realization of features within the verb, but always a local morphological component. And the semantics of modal verbs are always established by a modal preverb, which may be silent.

This treatment of the rather narrow question about how modal verbs are formed has implications for the larger issues. One of the arguments that multiple head-movement operations at C and T in Innu-aimûn is that such derivations are consistent with base structures in which T is higher than the preverbs. The main direct evidence given for those base structures is semantic; since T scopes over modal and aspectual preverbs, it should be higher. But now we have additional evidence for the same conclusion. We can explain the form of modal verbs only by supposing that T selects a modal complement. This requires that T be higher, which means that the syntactic derivation must somehow raise verbs to T even though there are closer, selected heads in between. In other words, modal verbs require a multiple head-movement derivation.

4.2.3 *ka-... -ua* verbs in Innu-aimûn

Clarke (1982) documents the growing use (in 1982) of *ka-... ua* verb forms in contexts, including embedded clauses, where conjunct verbs would otherwise be expected. (My own field notes are rife with such forms.) These forms are made of verbs in the independent order, to which a *ka-* preverb is added, together with a *-(a)ua* suffix. Some of Clarke's examples appear in (72).

(72) a. *Tshân apû minuâtâk ka-tshimuan-ua.*
Tshân apû=minuât-âk ka=tshimuan-ua.
John NEG=like-CJ.3s *ka*=rains-*ua*
'John doesn't like rain.'

b. *Ni-tshissenimâu ka-tshîtûteua.*
ni=tshissenim-â-u ka=tshîtûte-ua.
1=know-DIR-3 *ka*=leave-3-*ua*
'I know he is leaving.'

c. *Niminuâten ka-nimîtshishunâua.*
ni=minuâten ka=ni=mîtshishun-âu-a.
1=like *ka*=1=eat-1-UA
'I'm happy that I'm eating.'

d. *Ne nâpeu ka-tshîtûteua nukumish an.*
ne nâpeu ka=tshîtûte-∅-ua n-ûkumish an.
DEM man *ka*=leave-3-*ua* 1-uncle DEM
'The man who is leaving is my uncle.'

Clarke attributes to Ford (1979): the observation that *ka-... ua* forms emphasize the currently ongoing, progressive nature of the event in question, so that they are normally used in the present tense. Baraby & Drapeau (1998: p. 184) provides a different account of the nuanced semantics which accompany these forms, which she calls the "subjective mode." For her, this mode is used "dans la description des rêves, des souvenirs et dans les contextes de perception subjective, entre autres, pour exprimer l'étonnement." While intriguing, these differences in evaluating how the *ka-... ua* forms are used are probably not significant for understanding the underlying syntax.

The chief clue to what structure is appropriate for *ka-... ua*-clauses comes from examples like (72c), which contains the proclitic pronoun *ni*. Exceptionally, the proclitic is preceded in the verbal cluster by the *ka-* preverb. This tells us that the full independent form is actually in the domain of a higher functional head which includes *ka-*. And as *ka-* must occur together with a *-ua* suffix, the obvious hypothesis is a structure in which an independent order clause is in the domain of a structure like (73).

(73)

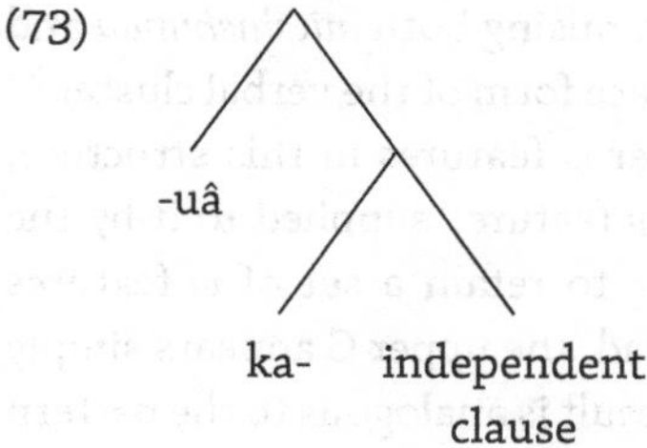

Since the independent order emerges when Feature Inheritance transfers features from C to T, this means that the *ka-* preverb in (73) must merge with a full CP structure. In other words, the *ka-... ua* clauses must be treated as CP recursion structures. This gives us (74) as an abstract structure for example (72c), after the verb raising to T has taken place.

(74)

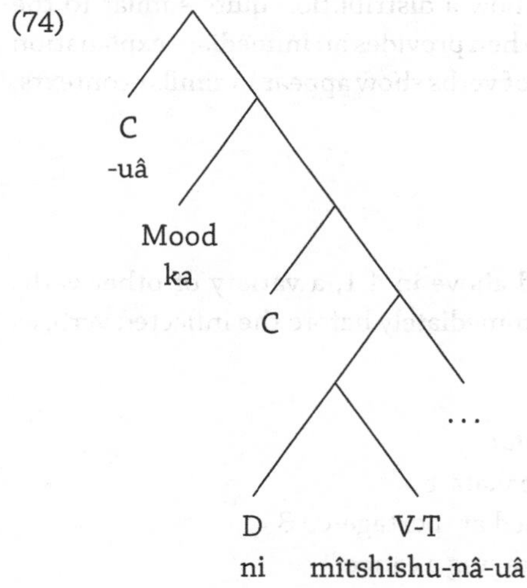

In the derivation preceding (74), Feature Inheritance will have transferred ϕ and evidential feature from the lower C to T, and at the completion of that phase, head-movement will have replaced the minimal T with a new $\{V, T\}$ structure. The question is what happens next, and why?

Chomsky (2015) proposes that C can sometimes undergo deletion after all of its features are transferred to T. One effect of the deletion operation is that C is eliminated as the head of the C-T phase, and T acquires phase head status instead. Suppose this takes place within the downstairs CP in a *ka-...-uâ* structure. Once C is deleted, then the inflected independent verb will become the new head of its phase, and therefore accessible for subsequent syntactic operations. Within the structure (74), the higher, non-deleted C *-uâ* can then find a match for its (second) [USTEM] feature in the inflected verb.

Later multiple head-movement can then apply, raising both *mîtshishunâu* and ka= to *uâ*, in that order, and producing the surface form of the verbal cluster.[25]

The higher C head will be unable to transfer ϕ features in this structure, since the independent verb will already have ϕ features supplied to it by the lower verb. Neither does the higher C appear to retain a set of ϕ features which are realized as conjunct inflection. Instead, the upper C appears simply to lack ϕ features in the *kâ-…-uâ* forms. This result is analogous to the pattern with CP recursion structures in some Germanic languages, where an explicit complementizer which appears in an embedded verb second clause is never allowed to show complementizer agreement morphology (Zwart 1997).

Despite the more complicated gymnastics of the derivation, the end result with a *kâ-…-uâ* form is a verbal cluster in which the first preverb is a Mood category, which is followed immediately by either other preverbs or by the verb itself. If *kâ-* is taken to have features similar to those of the IC preverb, then *kâ-…-uâ* forms will be expected to show a distribution quite similar to the default IC conjunct verb clusters. This then provides an immediate explanation for Clarke's finding that the two types of verbs show appear in similar contexts.

4.2.4 "Serial" verb structures

Besides the aspectual verbs discussed above in 4.1, a variety of other verbs can sometimes appear as "preverbs" immediately before the inflected verb, as in (75).

(75) a. *Nuitsheuakan apu nitau-pakatat.*
n-uîtsheuâkan apû=nitau=pakatâ-t.
1-friend NEG=be.skilled.at=portage-CJ.3
'My friend is no good at portaging a canoe.'

b. *nitau-pimuteu.* (Drapeau 2014: p. 397)
nitâu=pimute-u.
be.skilled-at=walk-3
'S/he knows how to walk.'

c. *kuetshi-tshishuaieu.*
kuetshi=tshishuâie-u.
try=anger-3
'S/he tries to anger him/her.'

25. Branigan & Wharram (2016) pursue a parallel approach in an analysis of noun-incorporation in Inuktitut, where deletion of a D phase head makes it possible for the noun to then be attracted by a higher verb.

d. *mishku-nipau.*
mishku=nipâ-u.
find=sleep-3
'S/he finds somewhere to sleep.'

e. *mueshtatshi-pituau.*
mueshtâtshi=pîtuâ-u.
be.tired.of=smoke-3
'S/he is tired of smoking.'

Unlike the aspectual verbs, the non-inflected verb stems in (75) provide information which is not limited to characterizing how the event unfolds in time. The verb on the left clearly adds lexical semantic substance, and the extra meaning is not that different from the meaning of the same verbs used simply as the principal verb in a clause.

The existing literature suggests one general approaches to verb complexes like these. Bloomfield (1962), and Drapeau (2014), and others classify these forms as compound verbs. This classification is consistent with the fact that the (non-clitic) inflection appears only on the second verb. But the structural details of the verb complex are not made explicit, which means that there is still work to be done in understanding these forms. (How compounding structures arise generally is hardly a settled question, so this is understandable.) Since I know of no reliable tools for unpacking the full structures, I will settle on showing how forms of this type may fit into a multiple head-movement-based analysis.

First, the meanings generated with the forms in (75) appear not to coincide with what one expects to find in compound verbs or serial verb structures in other languages. Take (75a), for example. The idea of walking here appears to relate to "knowing how" as if the former were the complement of the latter. The other examples in (75) admit of a comparable semantic relationship. In a compound verb, the relationship between the two verbs is typically different. English V-V compounds like *slam-dunk*, *push-start*, or *force-feed* lack an indication that the second verb is an argument of the first. Instead, the first verb seems to characterize the something about how the activity in question takes place, like a manner adverb.

In contrast, meanings like those in (75) are normally expressed in English with control structures, where a full non-finite clause appears with a matrix verb which selects it. And in fact, multiple head-movement offers a way that similar structures might give rise to these Innu-aimûn forms. Suppose that the first verb selects a clausal complement built with the second verb. Suppose as well that within the complement clause, the verb stem raises to C, as occurs in some Italian infinitival clauses (Rizzi 1982). For (75e), then, the structure of the matrix vP would be (76).

(76)

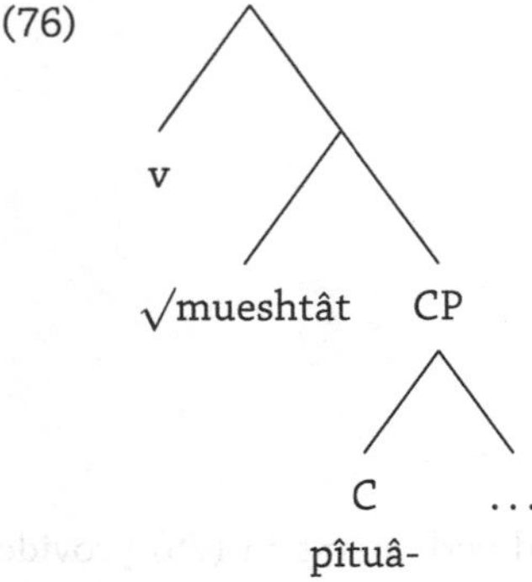

The derivation at the root C-T phase must now solve a number of problems. As usual, C or T will contain agreement suffixes which must find a verb to attach to. In addition, the two uninflected verbs in (76) must be made part of a full verb complex. If C provides two [USTEM] features to T, then multiple head-movement will displace both *mueshtat-* and *pita-* upwards, forming the complex verb (77).

(77)

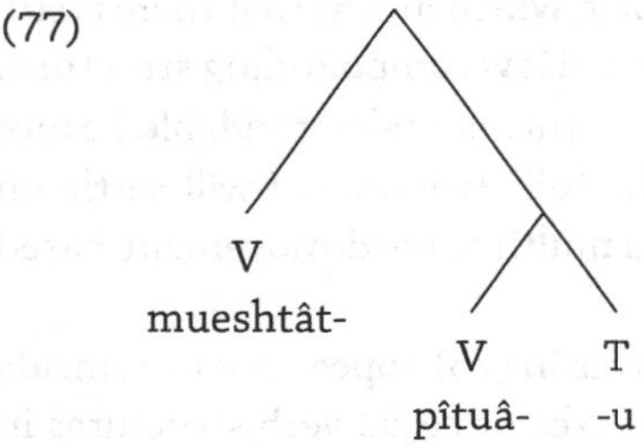

In a sense, I agree with the idea that these forms are like compounds; they are formed from two complete verbs. But the derivational glue which creates them is still multiple head-movement.

4.3 MULTIPLE HEAD-MOVEMENT WITH VERB PHRASE ADJUNCTS

The structure of wh-questions, *ka-...-ua* forms and apparent serial verb structures can be clarified with a multiple head-movement analysis, but these forms do not themselves force such an analysis. In contrast, structures in which an adjoined category is attracted from its base position in a multiple head-movement derivation can be understood only in the model presented here. Innu-aimûn grammar includes several constructions in which this takes place. The material adjoined to a verb phrase includes adverbials, quantifiers, and comitative applicatives, each of which is considered in this next section, in turn.

4.3.1 Manner adverbial initials and preverbs

One common type of verb *initials* are those which specify the manner of the event in question, and where the event type itself is characterized by a medial or a final. Typical examples of verbs with initials in this group are seen in (78).

(78) a. *Takuaikan minu-ashameu innua muk^u nasht apu minat atushkannu.*
takuaikan minu-asham-e-u innu-a muk^u nâsht apû=min-ât
government well=feed-DIR-3 Innu-PL only at.all NEG=give-CJ.3
atushkân-nu.
job-OBV
'The government feeds the Innu well, but it does not give them any work at all.'

b. *Ueshkat innuat muk^u atusha ishi-nipaiepanat atikua.*
ueshkat innu-at muk^u atush-a ishi=nipâi-e-pan-at
formerly innu-PL only arrowhead-PL so=kill-DIR-PRET-3p
atîku-a.
caribou-OBV
'The Innu of old killed caribou only with arrowheads.'

c. *minu-pinateu* 'kill it easily' (-pinateu 'kill')
d. *minu-puneu* 'sharpen (saw) correctly' (-puneu 'saw')
e. *manatshi-tueu* 'save it carefully for someone'
f. *akaneshau-shtau* 'write in English'
g. *kakusseshiu-tenueu* 'cook in the French Canadian way' (-tenueu 'cook')
h. *matsh-atusseu* 'work badly' (-atusseu 'work')
i. *matsh-ashtau* 'put it down badly; write it poorly'
j. *meshtikashu* 'burn up little by little' (*-kashu* 'burn')

In many cases, the same morphemes can also be found as preverbs, and as preverbs they can also signify the manner of an event.

(79) a. *minu=nipitatsheu* 'hunt well, successfully'
b. *akaneshau=aimu* 'speak English'
c. *kakusseshiu=pimishkau* 'paddle badly (like a white person)'
d. *matshi=papu* 'laugh in a nasty, bitter way'
e. *tshimut=autau* 'transport things on one's back secretly, illegally'
f. *meshti=atauatsheu* 'sell it all little by little'

The fact that these formatives are used as preverbs implies that their position is a syntactic matter. The use of the same elements as initials, for the same semantic function, suggests that even the initials should be accounted for syntactically. The multiple head-movement model developed here provides a mechanism for doing so.

Adverbial preverbs follow other preverbs, as seen in (80).

(80) *Tshitshue tshinaua nimassina, nasht apu tshi minu-pimuteian.*
tshîtshue tshînâu-a ni-massin-a, nâsht
really be.slippery-3p 1-boot-PL at.all
âpû=tshî=minu=pimûte-iân.
NEG=can=well=walk-CJ.1s
'My boots are really slippery; I cannot walk properly.'

In some cases, the modifier has the superficial form of a related noun, as in (81).

(81) a. *tshin kaupuai-nikamunau.* (Drapeau 2014: p. 396)
tshîn kaupuai=nikamû-nau.
you cowboy-sing-2p
'You sing western songs.'

b. *innu-pimipannua utauassima.*
innu-pimipan-nua ut-auâss-îm-a.
person-function-OBV 3-child-POSS-OBV
'His/her child has native status.'

c. *uapush-tipishkau.*
uâpush-tipishkâ-u.
rabbit-be.night-3
'It's a night propitious for rabbits.'

In such cases, however, the nominal is never given the referential semantic value of a θ-marked argument, and it seems appropriate to suppose that these nouns have been coerced into an adverbial semantic role. In that respect, they are comparable to English forms like *yesterday, today, tomorrow* which have the shape of a noun and which appear in nominal contexts, but which nevertheless function freely as adverbials.[26]

Similarly, some verbal forms serve as adverbial modifiers within a complex verb form: (82).

26. In Larson's (1985) treatment, nominals which function as adverbs are exceptionally endowed with inherent Case in the lexicon. I put aside the question whether there is a similar special feature which allows nominals to serve as adverbs in Innu-aimûn.

(82) a. *tshimush-apatam*ᵘ.
tshîmush=âpâtam-u.
steal=see-3
'S/he looks at it secretly, spies on it.'

b. *ashineu-mitshishu.* (Drapeau 2014: p. 398)
ashineu=mîtshish-u.
be.proud=eat-3
'S/he eats like a snob.'

Numerals too can be employed adverbially in the initial position. These are then most naturally interpreted as time adverbials, with the unit of measure determined by the pragmatic context.

(83) *nishtutipaikaneim*ᵘ.
nishtu=tipaikaneim-u.
three=hour.travel-3
'S/he takes 3 hours to travel a distance by canoe.'

Some adverbials which appear as preverbs or initials belong to the class of "relative roots," a category found across the Algonquian language family (Bloomfield 1962). Relative roots are anaphoric items which find their reference either locally, in a category located in a higher specifier position, or contextually. Compared to a language like Nishnaabemwin (Valentine 2001), Innu-aimûn has a fairly small set of relative roots (*ît-*, *îshi*, *ishpish*, *tatu-*, *ût*, *pet*), and only *îshi*, *ishpish*, and *ît-* are used adverbially, as preverb and initial, respectively.

(84) a. *Nimushum eukuan eshi-ashtunit.*
ni-mushu-m eukuan IC/ishi-ashtuni-t.
1-father.in.law-POSS this.way IC/so=make.canoe-CJ.3
'This is how my father-in-law makes canoes.'

b. *Tan ume nipa ishi-natukuitishun?* (Drapeau 2014: p. 305)
tân ume nipa=ishi=natuku-ît-îshu-n?
how this 1-would=so=cure-REFL-V-1
'How will I treat myself?'

c. *Ne eshi-aimit Mani apu nishtutuk.*
ne IC/ishi=aim-it Mânî âpû=nishtût-uk.
DEM IC/so=speak-3 Marie NEG=understand-INV
'The way Mary talks, I do not understand her.'

d. *Eukuan assiuashikuapui nitishi-natukuitishun.*
(Drapeau 2014: p. 330)
eukuan assîuâshiku-âpui nit=ishi=natuku-îtîshu-n.
this.way fir.tree-solution 1=so=cure-REFL-1
'I treat myself with a fir tree extract.'

e. *Eukuan nitishi-atussetan niǹan miam peikuan napeuat.*
eukuan nit=ishi=atusse-tâ-n nîǹân miâm peikuan
this.way 1=so=work-PRET-1p we like in.the.same.way
nâpeu-at.
man-p
'We worked like men do.'

f. *niǹ nipa tshi nataunapan tshishe-utshimau eka ishi-ueueshtatakue.*
nîǹ nipâ=tshî=nataunâpan tshishe-utshimâu
I 1.can=be.able=hunt-PRF big-chief
ekâ=ishi-ueueshtâ-tâkue.
NEG=so=repair-DUB
'I wouldn't be able to hunt if the government hadn't fixed it that way.'

g. *Nimitatauat eka katshi tshishkutamukau niǹ tshetshi ishi-atussetau miam niǹ ka ishi-atusseian.*
ni=mitât-â-u-at ekâ=kâtshî=tshishkutam-iku-âu nîǹ
1=regret-DIR-3-3p NEG=after=teach-INV-3p I
tshetshî=ishi=atusse-tâ-u miâm nîǹ ka=ishi-atusse-iân.
IRR=so-work-V-3 like I REL=so-work-CJ.1s
'I regret that I didn't teach them to work in the way that I work.'

(85) a. *Ishpish minu-tshishikanit kassinu pushuat.*
ishpish=minu=tshîshikân-it kassinu pûshu-at.
so.much=good=be.day-CJ.3 everyone embark-3p
'It is so nice out that everyone has gone out on the water.'

b. *Nuitsheuakan apu ishpish shapit miam nin ishpish shutshishiu.*
n-uîtsheuâkan apû=ishpish=shâpî-t miâm nîn
1-friend NEG=so.much=be.strong-CJ.3 like I
ishpish=shûtshishi-u.
so.much=be.strong-3
'My friend is not as strong as I am.'

c. *Katshi natauiani, nitaiatshimun kassinu tshekuan ka ishpish nipataian.*
kâtshî=natau-iân-î, nit=âiâ-tshim-un kassinu tshekuân
after=hunt=CJ.1s-COND 1=speak-REFL-1 every what
ka=ishpish=nipâtâ-iân.
REL=so-kill-CJ.1s
'When I return from hunting, I talk about how much game I killed.'

(86) a. *Eukuan eshi-tshishkutamakauian tshe itashtaiian nitassikumana.*
Eukuan IC/ishi=tshishkutam-âkau-iân tshî=it-ashtâ-iân
that.way IC/so=teach-PASS-CJ.1s IC/FUT=so-place-CJ.1s
nit-assîkumân-a.
1-metal.trap-PL
'It is in this way that I was taught to set my traps.'

b. *Kananin peikutau itashameu utauassima, kakakanuapekanniti etashamaushut.*
Kânânîn peikutâu it-asham-e-u ut-auâssîm-a,
Caroline in.the.same.way so-feed-DIR-3 3-child-PL
kâkakânuâpekan-nitî IC/it-ashamâushu-t.
spaghetti-OBV IC/so-feed.child-CJ.3
'Caroline always feeds her children in the same way; she gives them spaghetti to eat.'

In the analysis of these adverbial elements, the null hypothesis must be that they behave as adverbials because they occupy a syntactic position where adverbial interpretations are appropriate. For other languages, manner adverbials have traditionally been characterized as adjuncts in the verb phrase. As the role of manner adverbs is to provide ancillary information about the event characterized by the verb, this position is plausible on compositional grounds. Let us take this notion as a starting point.[27] And for the moment, I will consider only structures in which manner adverbials originate as vP adjuncts.

If manner adverbials are adjoined to vP, then the C-T structure for (82a) will be (87). Multiple head-movement then ensures the actual surface forms of the verb complexes which contain such adjuncts. T may contain multiple [uSTEM] features, which will ultimately drive movement. As usual, T must attract a verb to satisfy its morphological requirements, but since valuation of [uSTEM] features precedes labeling, T must attract the adverb *tshîmut-*, too. The result will be the X^0 structure (87b).

27. Déchaine & Weber (2015a) propose that some initials in Plains Cree and Blackfoot originate as vP adjuncts, as well. How their model relates to this one is discussed briefly in section 4.8.4.

(87)

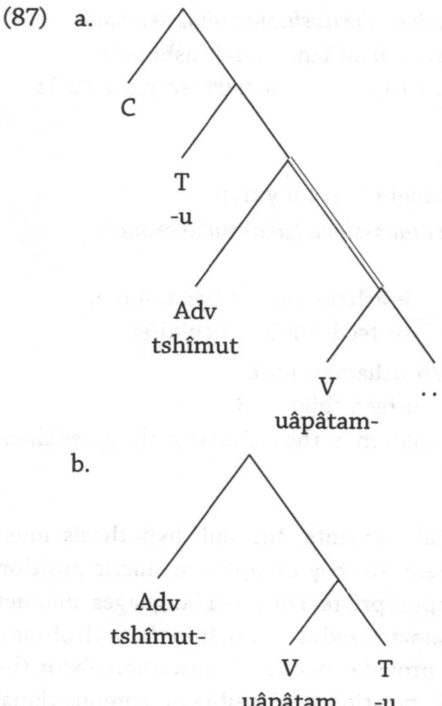

Nothing new is introduced to the model to obtain this result, which will apply generally to derive verbs with adverbial initials or preverbs. And no unusual semantic rules are required to interpret such adverbials, since adjunction of adverbials to vP is already a common structure in linguistic analyses of other languages.

4.3.2 Multiple head-movement with floated quantifiers

A second construction involving adjunction to the verb phrase and subsequent multiple head-movement involves some additional uses of quantificational initials. It has already been shown that some quantificational initials are interpreted as adverbial modifiers; the examples in (88) show that the same quantifiers have a non-adverbial interpretation in different syntactic contexts.

(88) a. *Ninapem nishuapitsheu kakua utakushit.*
ni-nâpe-m nîshu-âpitsh-e-u kâku-a utâkushît.
1-man-POSS two-stringlike-DIR-3 porcupine-PL yesterday
'My husband killed two porcupines yesterday.'

b. *Meshta-tshishinniti, nikuss apu nita nishushkuat utashtisha.*
IC/mishta=tshishin-nit-î, ni-kuss apû=nitâ=nîsh-ushku-ât
much=be.cold-3.OBV-COND 1-son NEG=ever=two-wear-CJ.3
ut-ashtish-a.
3-mitten-p
'If it is bitter cold, my son never wears two pairs of mittens one on top of the other.'

c. *Nishukutinnua nutaui ututa anite nashipetimit.*
nîshu-kutin-nua n-utaui ut-ut-a anite nashipetim-ît.
two-anchor-OBV.3p 1-father 3-boat-PL there near.shore-LOC
'My father has two boats anchored near the shore.'

d. *Shakuaki, nimishta-uapaten ushakai-pitakana anite nashipetimit.*
shâkuâki, ni=mishta=uâpât-en ushakai=pitakan-a anite
spring 1-many=see-1 cartridge.case-PL there
nâshipetim-ît.
shore-LOC
'In the spring, I see many cartridges on the shore.'

e. *Nipinut Shûshep ka nat-aut utassit mishta-nipaiepan amishkua.*
nîpinût Shûshep kâ=natâu-t ut-assî-t
last.summer Joseph REL=hunt-CJ.3 3-land-LOC
mishta=nipâi-e-∅-pan amishku-a.
many=kill-DIR-3-PRET beaver-PL
'Last summer, when Joseph went hunting in his territory, he killed a lot of beaver.'

In each case in (88), the pertinent complex verb or verb cluster contains a numeral or an expression of quantity which appears as an initial (88a–d) or as the lowest preverb in a cluster (88e). And the quantificational element applies to the internal nominal argument of the verb, either the object (88a,b,d,e) or an unaccusative subject (88c).

Since the quantifier in these examples applies to the object nominal, it is natural to suppose that it originates as part of the object. In order for the quantifier *neu* to reach its surface position, it must then be moved to the edge of the vP phase. Given the X^0 status of the complex D, it cannot simply Merge with vP, because the labeling algorithm would then force it to serve as the label/head of the {D, vP} structure. The only alternative is for D to be adjoined to vP within the syntactic derivation.

Movement of D away from the noun that it modifies is actaully common in Innu-aimûn even when the result is not one where the quantifier ends up within the verbal cluster, as seen in (89).

(89) a. *Kassinû nipâtshîtân uâua.* (Oxford 2008)
kassinû ni=pâtshî-tâ-n uâu-a.
each 1=drop-PRET-1 egg-PL
'I dropped all the eggs.'

b. *Neu nika ishkunashat muk^u.* LITP:4-3
neu ni=ka=ishkunash-at muk^u.
four 1-PRET=pull.up.by.hand-3p only
'I will only leave four small ones.'

c. *Nitashkushipan, muk^u tshiam nish^u ninipaiauat missipat.*
nit=ashkûsh-ipan, muk^u tshiâm nîsh^u ni=nipai-â-u-at
1=hunt.waterfowl-PRET only correctly two 1=kill-DIR-3-3p
missip-at.
eider.duck-PL
'I went waterfowl hunting but killed only two eider ducks.'

The distributive numerals in (90) show the same behavior.

(90) a. *Nanish^u mashinaimueuat uitsheuakanuau ishkuessat.*
nâ~nîsh^u mashin-aim-u-e-u-at uitsheuâkan-uâu-∅
DIST~two write-V-APPL-DIR-3-3p friend-PL-OBV
ishkue-ss-at.
woman-DIM-PL
'The girls wrote a letter to two friends each.'

b. *Ânî mâk Pûn nânîsh passuepanit atikua.*
Ânî mâk Pûn nâ~nîsh passu-e-pan-at atiku-a.
Annie and Paul DIST~two shoot-DIR-PRET-3p caribou-PL
'Annie and Paul shot two caribou each.'

And both plain and locative demonstratives can be displaced in this way, as in (91).[28]

(91) a. *Nenua kutâueu mishtikua.*
nenu-a kutâu-e-u mishtiku-a.
that-OBV knock.down-DIR-3 tree-OBV
'He knocked down that tree.'

28. In contrast, locative nominals in Swampy Cree do not typically allow their demonstratives to be displaced, but this is apparently a side-effect of the independent requirement in this language that oblique phrases appear clause-initially (Reinholtz 1999).

b. *Nete nititûtetân tshâinîsh-mîtshishûtshuâpît.*
nete nit=itûte-t-ân tshâinîsh-mîtshishû-tshuâp-ît.
there 1=go-PRET-1p Chinese-eat-house-LOC
'We went to the Chinese restaurant.'

It is clear from such examples that quantifiers and demonstratives can undergo leftward movement away from their nominal complements quite freely. For the quantifiers which end up as verb initials, it is natural then to suppose that the movement simply involves adjunction to the containing verb phrase. Adjunction of a determiner or quantificational item to the verb phrase is of course not uncommon in other languages. For example, Kayne's (1975) analysis of word order with French quantifiers establishes leftward movement of *tous* from within the verb phrase in sentences like (92a). And Holmberg (1986) shows that Swedish object pronouns raise out of the verb phrase in similar fashion, as occurs in (92).

(92) a. *French*
Elle a voulu tout vendre.
she has wanted all to.sell
'She wanted to sell everything.'
b. *Swedish*
Studenten läste den inte.
student.the read it not
'The student didn't read it.'

While the motivation for such movement remains contentious, what matters here is simply that it is evidently possible in other languages, so D movement to the edge of the verb phrase in Innu-aimûn should be possible as well.

If quantificational D can be adjoined to a vP, then nothing prevents an example like (88c), repeated here, from enjoying a derivation in which a base verb phrase (93a) gives rise to an intermediate structure (93b).

(88c) *Nishukutinnua nutaui ututa anite nashipetimit.*
nîshu-kutin-nua n-ûtâuî u-tût-a anite nâshipetim-ît.
2-anchor-OBV.3p 1-father 3-boat-PL there near.shore-LOC
'My father has two boats anchored near the shore.'

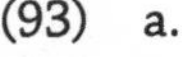

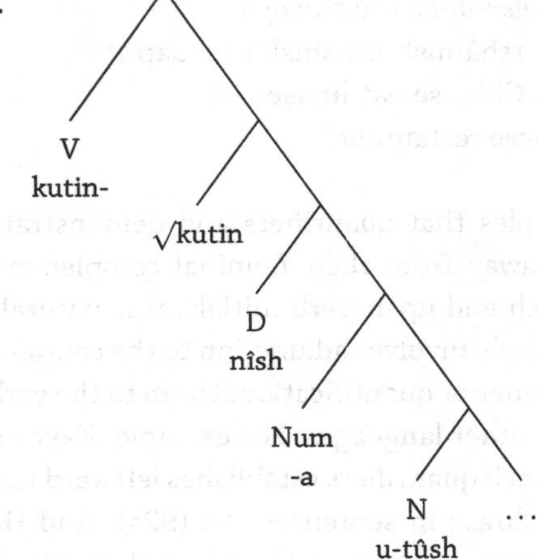

b.

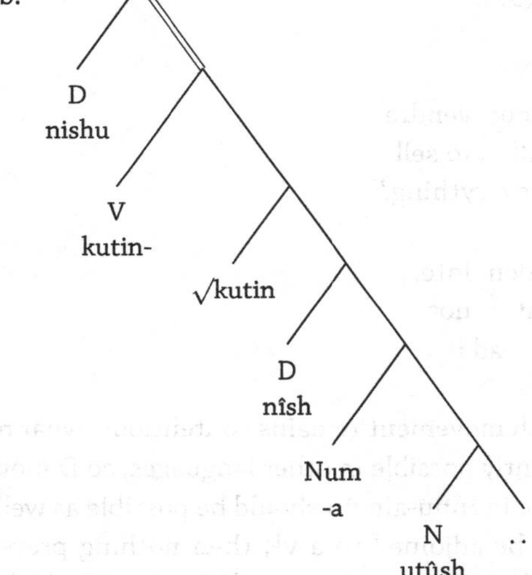

Given a structure like this, at the C-T phase level, T (or C) can attract D and V, as well as any higher preverbs which might be introduced at that phase level. In this case, as no additional preverbs are found, the result of [uSTEM] valuation and head-movement will be the verb complex (94).

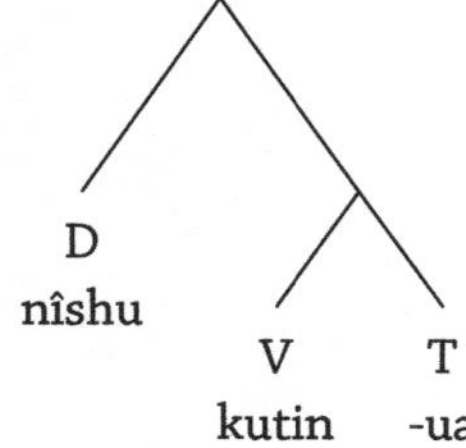

Again, as with adverbial adjuncts, nothing further needs to be stipulated in order to ensure the correct surface forms. Once adjunction of D to the verb phrase takes place, multiple head-movement takes care of the rest.

Structures in which D must have moved past the edge of the verb phrase still demand an explanation. It seems that determiners or quantifiers separated from their associated nominals appear in two locations: either within a complex verb cluster as the initial or to the left of the verb cluster. The former is possible only if the quantifier is small enough to fit morphologically within the derived verbal cluster, and it can be derived through adjunction of D to the verb phrases before multiple head-movement to T or C. Otherwise, it must move again, to escape serving as a goal in [uSTEM] valuation for T or C.[29] Exactly the same pattern has been seen in Chapter 3 (page 107), where the position of Russian adverbs is discussed. In Russian, adverbs adjoined to the verb phrase must raise to a position higher than the [uSTEM] bearing T probe, in order to avoid being part of the multiple head-movement process. For the demonstratives and large quantifiers in Innu-aimûn, the derivation requires the same response. The determiners and quantifiers which move to the left of independent T or conjunct C are unable to serve as initials within an inflected verb, either because D is invariant or too large, or because the verb itself cannot tolerate an extra category serving as the stem. Once again, movement to a higher position appears to be driven by the need to avoid an unacceptable morphological result.

4.3.3 Multiple head-movement with comitative verbs

Another Innu-aimûn construction in which a preverb or initial is obtained from within the verb phrase is found in comitative verb forms. In this construction, an intransitive verb is made formally transitive with the *uîtshi* preverb, which adds a comitative sense. The presence of the comitative preverb allows a comitative nominal argument to be introduced to the verb phrase, as well. The verb agrees with the comitative argument. Examples of the use of *uîtshi* appear in (95)–(97).

29. Reinholtz (1999) argues that the landing site for the displaced category in comparable Swampy Cree cases is the specifier position of a Focus phrase. The specifics of Reinholtz's analysis are somewhat dated, as she assumes Government-and-Binding premises. Thus, for her, nominals are NPs rather than DPs, and the ECP ensures that movement will take place only from properly governed positions. But in my experience, speakers of Innu-aimûn report no interpretations of these sentences which would suggest a focus-presupposition structure, and this suggests that the D-displacement does not take place to satisfy the requirements of left-peripheral discourse features.

(95) a. *pituau.*
pîtuâ-u.
smoke-3
'S/he smokes.'

b. *Uitshi-pituameu.*
uîtshi=pîtuâ-m-e-u.
with=smoke-V-DIR-3
'S/he smokes with somebody.'

(96) a. *Nikanutshen nanitamish.*
ni=kânutshe-n nânitam-ish.
1=play.cards-1 often-DIM
'We play cards pretty often.'

b. *Uitshe kanutshem-eu Maniua.*
uîtshi=kânutshe-m-e-u Mânî-ua.
with=play.cards-V-DIR-3 Marie-OBV
'She plays cards with Marie.'

(97) a. *Natumushueu.*
natûm-ûshue-u.
hunt-moose-3
'S/he goes after moose.'

b. *Uitshi-natumeu.*
uîtshi=natû-m-e-u.
with=hunt-V-DIR-3
'S/he hunts together with him/her.'

The verbs to which *uîtshi* is attached are typically intransitive, as here. The same verb root can often be found in a transitive verb, as well, but in such cases, a different *v* final will appear, as in (98).

(98) *Enut uiapamak Etien patuauatshet ushpuakana.*
Enut IC/uâpam-ak Etien IC/pîtuâ-uâtshe-t ushpuâkan-a.
first.time IC/see-CJ.1s Etienne IC/smoke-V-CJ.3s pipe-OBV
'It is the first time I see Etienne smoke a pipe.'

The object of such simple transitive verbs will bear a typical thematic role for objects, i.e. Patient or Theme, and not the role associated with the object in a comitative verb phrase.

When there is less verbal material in the verb phrase, *uîtshe* can also serve as the initial verbal component, as in (99).

(99) a. *Uîtsheueu.*
uîtsheu-e-u.
with-DIR-3
'S/he accompanies her; s/he goes around with someone (romantically).'

b. *Nanitam nunitshikumikakaun uatshetsheiani netuatshikuanuti.*
nanitam n-uni-tshiku-mika-kau-n IC/uîtshe-tshe-iân-î
sometimes 1-get-otter-give-PASS-1 IC/with-V-CJ.1S-COND
IC/natu-âtshik-uanu-t-î.
IC/await-otter-V-3-COND
'When there is an otter hunt and I am part of the group, I always receive an otter.'

Innu-aimûn comitative verb forms include a final suffix *-m* along with the *uîtshi* preverb. One does not appear without the other: (100).

(100) a. **Uitshi-pituau*
*uîtshi=pîtuâ-u
with=smoke-3

b. **Pituameu*
*pîtuâ-m-e-u
smoke-V-DIR-3

The pairing of a specific preverb with a specific final suffix would suggest that the two originate together in the base structure. At the same time, the presence of a grammatical object in a verb phrase in which the verb root is semantically intransitive requires that an argument position should be made available by some part of the comitative verb. Taken together, these observations imply a base structure like (101), for an example like (95b).

(101)

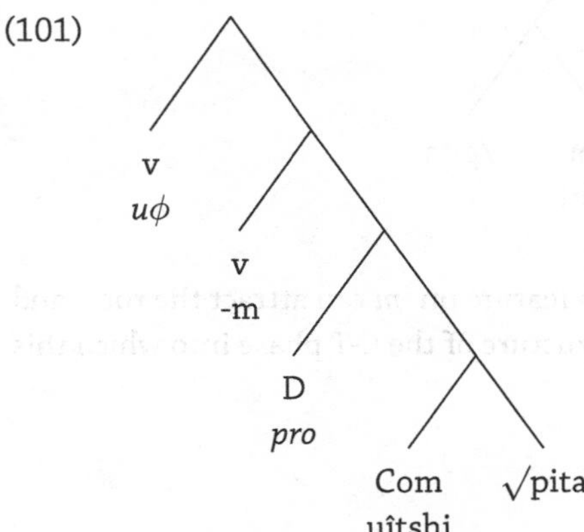

This structure provides an source for the grammatical object, which is assigned its θ-role by the comitative head *uîtshi.* The comitative phrase is evidently selected by a *-m* final, which is selected in turn by an agreeing phasal v head. The comitative head selects an animate specifier, and the animacy features then ensure that (phasal) v will then require animate agreement inflection.

But the derivational steps which unify the verb root, *uîtshi*, two v heads and tense into a single complex X^0 unit must still be identified. In particular, in the (101) structure, the root must raise to *-m*, and then to phase head v, despite the presence of *uîtshi* in between. Given the use of *uîtshi* elsewhere as a verb root, one would not expect it to bear a [uSTEM] feature—instead *uîtshi* presumably bears a [STEM(uîtshi)] feature. As such, *uîtshi* will be unable to attract the verb root. What is more, in this structure, *uîtshi* should intervene in the attraction of the root by *-m*.

Examination of the behavior of quantifiers has already shown that the head of a category inside the verb phrase can raise and adjoin to the verb phrase, as long as later multiple head-movement operations can make the adjoined head into a part of a higher complex word. Suppose that the same is true of *uîtshi*. In other words, suppose that *uîtshi* adjoins to the verb phrase, producing the structure (102).

(102)

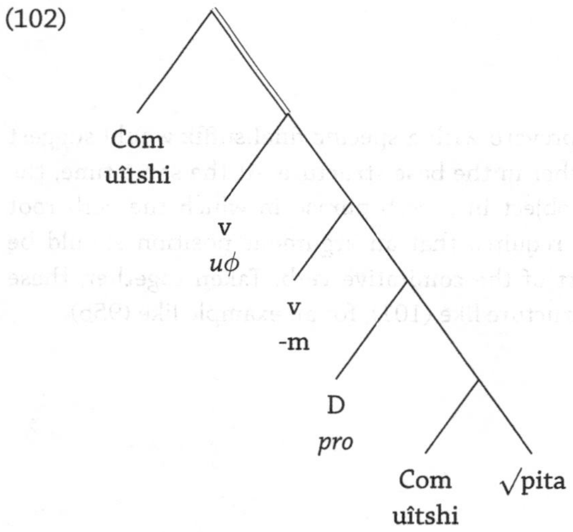

Given this derived structure, a [uSTEM] feature on *-m* can attract the root, and phasal v can then attract *pitam*. The structure of the C-T phase into which this enters will then be (103).

(103)

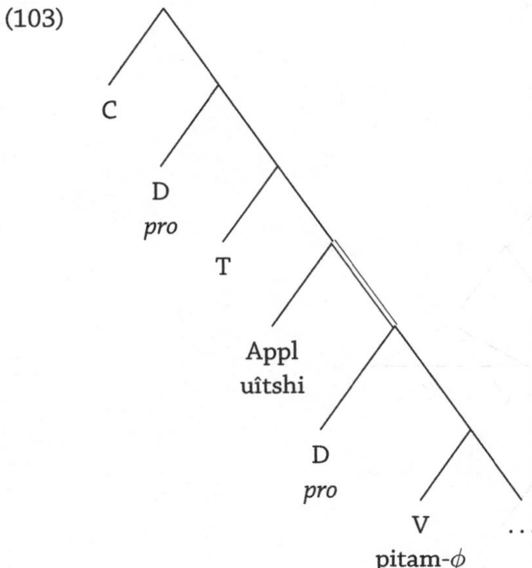

So the derivation of comitative verbs actually involves two phasal stages in which the timing of operations is critical. At the vP phase, the comitative affix must be raised out in order to avoid participating in multiple head-movement; at the C-T phase, where preverbs are processed, the comitative head adjoined to vP can serve as an acceptable part of the derived X^0 structure, so it remains in place for [uSTEM] valuation and later head-movement. This is the first indication that multiple head-movement also takes place within vP. This will be confirmed below, in section 4.4.

4.3.4 Multiple head-movement and symmetry-breaking derivations

Beyond the structures already examined, Innu-aimûn structures are also generated which resemble those which involve lexical prefixes in Russian. And as with other structures which involve multiple head-movement to C or T, Innu-aimûn grammar takes the ball and runs much further with it.

As in Russian, Innu-aimûn complex words can be formed when prior syntactic movement sets up the conditions in which valuation of multiple [uSTEM] features and subsequent head-movement can take place. Thus, a structure like (104a) will be altered to the structure (104b).

(104) a.

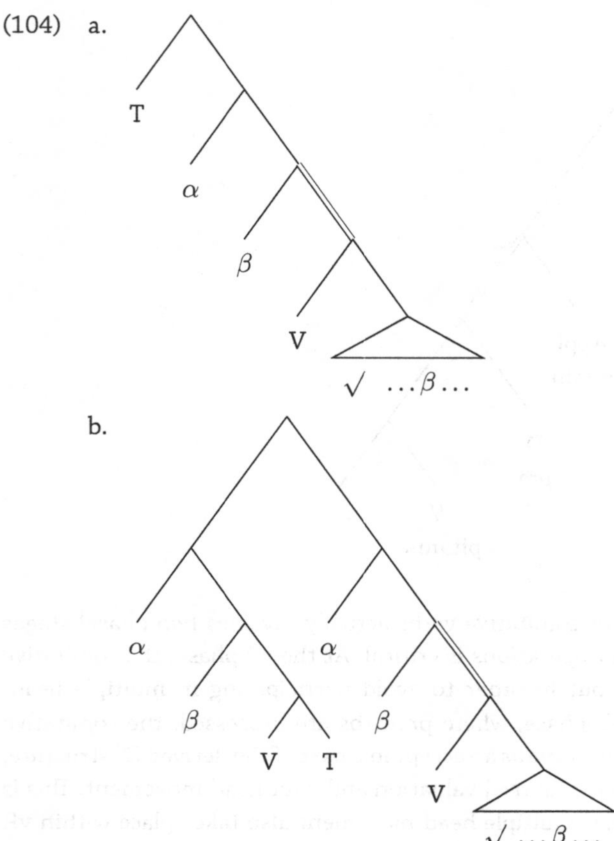

b.

From that point, the precise outcome depends on the individual morphological properties of β and the characteristics of the verb.

Locative initials

Russian lexical prefixal verbs are derived through adjunction of PP to the verb phrase, followed by multiple head-movement of the preposition and the verb to a higher functional head. In Innu-aimûn, the same combination of operations is used to construct a expressively rich set of complex verbs. Consider (105).

(105) a. *Shash tshekat nika kushpin.*
shâsh tshekat ni=ka=kushpî-n.
already almost 1=FUT=bushward-1
'I will soon leave for the bush.'

b. *Etien kushpitaieu ukussa tshetshi tshishkutamuat tshe ishi-natauniti.*
Etien kushpî-tâ-ie-u u-kuss-a
Etienne bushwards-accompany-DIR-3 3-son-OBV
tshetshî=tshishkut-amu-ât tshe=ishi-natau-niti.
IRR=teach-V-CJ.3 IC/FUT=so-hunt-CJ.3OBV
'Etienne takes his son in the bush to teach him how to hunt.'

c. *Shushep pakashtueshinu, nutim nipiutau utshimanima.*
Shûshep pakashtu-eshin-u, nûtim nipîutâ-u
Josheph into.water-fall-3 completely wet-3
u-tshiman-im-a.
3-match-POSS-PL
'Joseph fell in the water and got all his matches wet.'

d. *Etien nish[u] pakashtueim[u] upunishtashuna tshetshi eka uepainnit utush makainniti tipishkaniti.*
Etien nish[u] pakashtu-eim-u u-pûnishtâshun-a
Etienne 2 into.water-V-3 3-anchor-PL
tshetshî=ekâ=uepain-nit ut-ush makain-nit-î
IRR=NEG-drive-CJ.3.OBV 3-boat be.big.waves-CJ.3.OBV-COND
tipishkan-it-î.
be.night-CJ.3-COND
'Etienne drops both his anchors in the water so that his boat will not drift away if there are waves tonight.'

e. *Auâssat nunuîtishauâuat usham ashikueuat.*
auâss-at n=unuî-tishau-â-u-at usham âshîku-e-u-at
child-PL 1=outside-send-DIR-3p because yell-3-3p
'I send the children outside because they are yelling.'

f. Unuî-nâtshin-e-u.
outside-push-DIR-3
'S/he pushes him/her, it (anim) outside by hand.'

g. *Unuîpâtâu.*
unuî-pâtâ-u.
outside-run-3
'S/he, it (anim) rushes, runs outside.'

h. *Unuîtâtshishkam[u].*
unuî-tâtshishkam-u.
outside-kick-3
'S/he kicks it outside.'

i. *Nitauassim eshk^u ishpitapu anite utetapuakanissit.*
nit-auâss-im eshk^u ishpit-ap-u anite u-tetapu-akan-iss-ît.
1-child-poss still fit.in-sit-3 there 3-chair-NOM-DIM-LOC
'My child still fits into her little baby chair.'

The pertinent verbs in (105) all start with a locative initial, which is followed by one or more verb finals. The first verb final provides information about what type of motion is involved, a semantic role which one would associate with a root and not an affix.

The locative initial *kushpî* in the examples in (105a,b) identifies where the Theme argument ends up. The initial indicates the Goal argument for these verbs of motion; intransitive ∅ and transitive *tâ*-. Similarly, initial *pakashtu* is the Goal in (105c,d).

Given conventional assumptions about the syntax of Goal arguments, one would expect *kushpî*, for example, to originate together with the Theme argument inside the verb phrase. For example, the verb phrase in (105b) might start with a structure like (106).

(106)

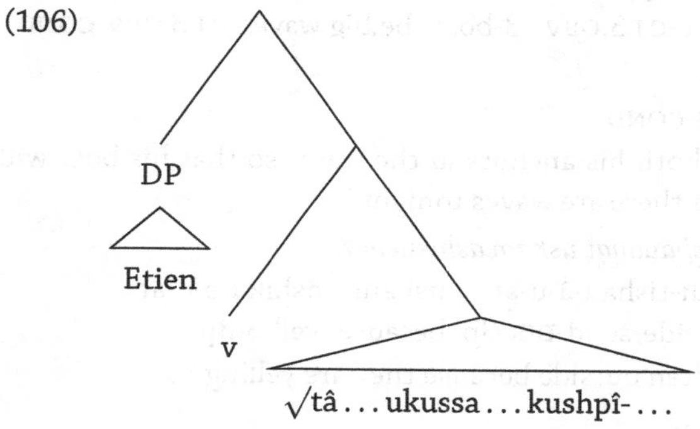

And then if *kushpî*- raises and adjoins to the verb phrase—like a Russian lexical prefix does—then multiple head-movement will create the actual verb form with no further complications.

Most Innu-aimûn verbs of motion behave similarly. They pair a locative prefix with one or more "concrete" finals. The former indicates the Goal; the latter, details about the motion itself. As a rule, the finals are not allowed to appear with no locative initial. When the meaning to be expressed is not specific about the endpoint of the movement, a vague locative initial *pim*- is sometimes employed.

(107) a. *Nika pimutaiau nitem.*
ni=ka=pim-ut-â-iâ-u ni-tem.
1=FUT=along-walk-V-V-3 1-dog
'I am going to walk my dog.'

b. *Mani mitshetipipuna eshpish pimipanitat utapannu.*
Mânî mîtshet-ipipun-a eshpish=pimi-pani-tâ-t
Mary many-year-PL so.much=along-motorized-V-CJ.3
u-tapann-u.
3-car-OBV
'Mary has been driving a car for many years.'

c. *Amishk^{u} pimaùneu ushkuaia.*
amishk^{u} pim-âun-e-u ushkuai-a.
beaver along-aquatic.carry-DIR-3 birch-PL
'A beaver is transporting birch trees in the water.'

It seems that Innu-aimûn motion verbs as a class select a Goal argument, obligatorily, and the Goal must always be displaced out of the verb phrase.

Continuative reduplication can apply to locative verbs: (108).

(108) a. *nanatapishtam^{u}.*
nâ~nat-ap-ishtam-u.
CNTN~closer-sit-V-3
'S/he moves closer to something little by little while sitting.'

b. *papimutakuatam^{u}.*
pâ~pîm-ûtakuâtam-u.
CNTN~along-shoot.arrows-3
'S/he shoots at it repeatedly with arrows.'

c. *aiatshipaniu.*
â~iâtshi-pan-iu.
CNTN~different-move-3
'S/he moves in place; swings/rocks him/herself for a period of time.'

Since such reduplication reflects the presence of a continuative Asp head immediately outside the verb phrase, these forms confirm that displaced Goal arguments are displaced only as high as the edge of vP. (One significant exception to this is discussed below, in section 4.3.4.) With this structure generated by core syntactic operations, the application of multiple head-movement can then produce an X^0 structure (109) for (108a), for example.

(109)

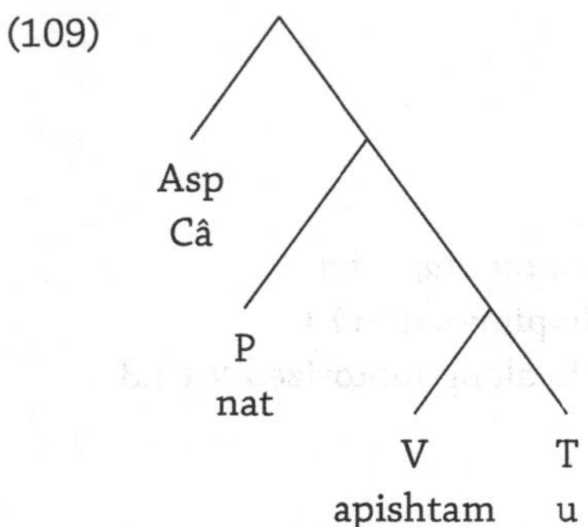

The obligatory adjunction of the Goal to the verb phrase in Innu-aimûn still requires an explanation. In the analogous Russian structures, the movement of the prefix from inside the verb phrase follows from both the prosodic requirements of the prefix and from the need to licence [AD]. In Innu-aimûn, neither factor plays a part. The locative prefix *asha* found in (110) can appear also outside the verb phrase as a freestanding particle, so it is not prosodically dependent on the verb. And there is no aspectual implication to the presence of the Goal, which appears in all possible tense/aspect contexts.

(110) a. *Nutaui ashaiapuku kuiakushit paushtikunu.*
n-ûtâuî ashâ-iâpuk-u IC/kuâkush-it
1-father backwards-move.by.current-3 IC/pole.boat-CJ.3
paushtiku-nu.
rapid-OBV
'My father goes back down with the current while poling up the rapids.'

b. *Nika shakassine-patan nitassik^{u}.*
ni=ka=shakassine-patâ-n nit-assîk^{u}.
1=FUT=fill-flow-1 1-pail
'I will fill my pail (with water).'

If the locative initial does not move to satisfy its own requirements, then movement must be forced by the larger context. Moro's (1997) analysis of of locative inversion structures suggests what the contextual motivation may be. Moro argues that locative Goals and nominal Themes originate as sisters within the verb phrase, in a symmetric structure which must be disrupted. For an example like (105b), the base structure of the verb phrase would then be (111).

(111)

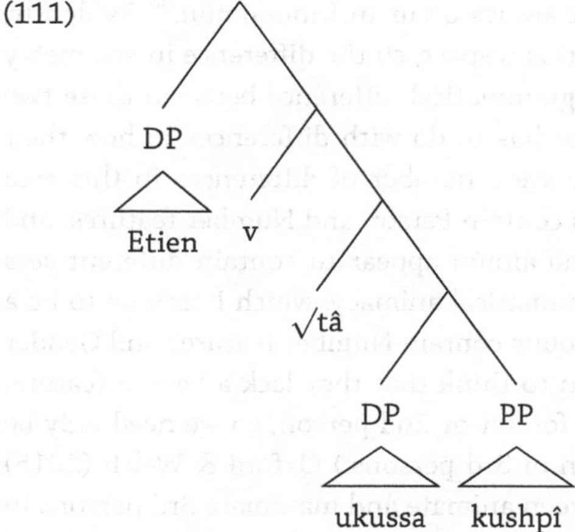

In labeling theoretic terms, this constitutes an exocentric structure which cannot be labeled without movement of either the DP or the PP. Adjunction of *kushpî* to the verb phrase breaks symmetry, as necessary. And subsequent multiple head-movement to T will produce the inflected X^0 (112).

(112)

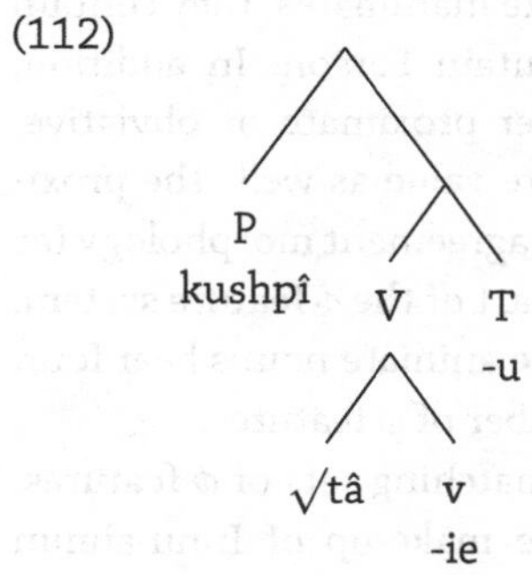

As there are two potential stems in this structure, v resolves the ambiguity by assigning [NR] to its sister *ta-*, and *kushpî* will end up as the actual morphological stem, with the remaining parts of the verb serving morphologically as affixes.

If Moro's structures are accurate, then the same general problem arises with symmetric arrangements of Theme and Goal arguments in Innu-aimûn and in English (or presumably Russian). English typically solves the problem by moving DP; the opposite must always occur in Innu-aimûn.[30] Evidently, English and Innu-aimûn differ in this respect, so the difference in symmetry breaking must follow from some grammatical difference between these two language types.[31] One likely factor has to do with differences in how their agreement systems behave. There are a number of differences in this area of the grammar. English nominals contain Person and Number features, and possibly Gender. Nominals in Innu-aimûn appear to contain different sets of features, depending on the grammatical animacy, which I assume to be a difference in Gender. Inanimate nouns contain Number features and Gender (by definition), but there is reason to think that they lack a Person feature. (They obviously lack specification for 1st or 2nd person, so we need only be concerned with the representation of 3rd persons.) Oxford & Welch (2015) note a number of differences between animate and inanimate 3rd persons in Algonquian languages which can be reduced to a difference in the presence of Person features in inanimate nominals, including their position in the person hierarchy, their involvement in inverse voice, and their participation in the proximate/obviative contrasts. If this is corrent—and I will assume it is—then inanimate nouns in Innu-aimûn will contain only Number and Gender features.

Animate nominals are more richly endowed. Like inanimates, they contain Number and Gender features, but they also contain Person. In addition, all animate nominals must be identified as either proximate or obviative, and this contrast must be represented as a feature value as well. The proximate/obviative distinction is realized in the verbal agreement morphology (as described in appendix A), so it must be treated as part of the ϕ feature system. So inanimate nouns bear only two ϕ features, while animate nouns bear four. In English, of course, all nouns bear the same number of ϕ features.

Since $<\phi, \phi>$ labels are constructed only from matching sets of ϕ features, it is plausible that relatively complicated feature make-up of Innu-aimûn nominals may make it more difficult to form such a label within the vP phase.

30. See also Branigan & Brittain (2018), who come to the same conclusion in their analysis of East Cree word order. Word order in East Cree appears to involve remnant movement of vP (which loses its verb) to a specifier position higher in the structure, which Branigan and Brittain argue also enables symmetry to be broken, but at the vP level. Multiple head-movement in such structures must involve relationships established on the "right branch," where T can access [uSTEM] features, and not on the left branch, where the remnant of vP is realized.

31. The lack of movement of object nominals to a specifier position within the verb phrase may also be related to the general freedom of extraction of quantifiers and demonstratives from within object. In languages like English, where such D-movement is evidently impossible, this could reflect a "criterial freezing" effect (Rizzi 2007, Chomsky 2015). In Innu-aimûn, if objects remain in their base position, no such freezing would be expected.

The immediate consequence would be that "object" nominals should not raise to the usual position between v and $\surd$.

Already documented properties of agreement with an animate "object" in Innu-aimûn confirm that this is the case. Branigan & MacKenzie (2002) show that animate agreement can traverse clause boundaries, like Ā-movement, and that the target of agreement actually remains within a complement clause. Some examples of this are seen in (113).

(113) a. *Ni-tshissenimânânat mûpishtuât Shûshepa Tshân mâk Mânî.*
(Branigan & MacKenzie 2002)
Ni=tshissenim-â-nân-at mûpishtu-ât Shûshep-a Tshân mâk
1=know-DIR-1p-3p visit-CJ.3p Joseph-OBV John and
Mânî.
Marie
'We know that John and Marie visited Joseph.'

b. *N'uî tshissenimâu tshetshî mûpishtâshkuenit kassinu kâuâpikueshîht.*
N=uî=tshissenim-â-u tshetshî=mûpisht-âshku-en-it kassinu
1=want=know-DIR-1s IRR=visit-INV-2-3p every
kâuâpikueshîht.
priest
'I want to know if every priest visited you.'

In (113a), the matrix verb agrees with the plural subject of the lower clause, which appears to the right of the downstairs verb. (113b) also has matrix agreement with a downstairs subject, which is located to the right of both the *tshetsî* preverb and the principal verb. In neither case can the subject be analysed as a sister to the complement of v.

According to Ritter & Rosen (2005), such data shows that Algonquian agreement is fully dissociated from A-movement. In their view, Algonquian agreement is always and only Ā-agreement. In labeling theoretic terms, this equates to the claim that Algonquian agreement cannot be employed to produce a <ϕ, ϕ> label.

With inimate objects, essentially the same conclusion is reasonable, although data comparable to (113) is unavailable. The only indication that verbs agree with an inanimate object at all is the use of TI verb forms in transitive contexts. But the Algonquianist terminology for classifying verbs actually presupposes that TI verb morphology is a reliable indicator of verbal transitivity, i.e. that they indicate the presence of a grammatical object. And Piggott (1989) and O'Meara (1990) have provided compelling alternatives to this premise—TI forms can be taken to be simply a verbal conjugation class, distinct from the AI verbal conjugation class. In that view, neither TI nor AI verbs show any evidence of agreeing with inanimate verbs, which might then indicate that no syntactic agreement takes place unless there is an animate target. This hypothesis becomes still more viable if Oxford & Welch (2015) are right about the absence of Person features in inanimate nouns—the absence of Person features would then coincide with a lack of agreement.[32] And obviously, if no agreement takes place, then no <ϕ, ϕ> label can be formed within vP, and no displacement of the object within vP will be possible (other than movement to the phase edge).

If locative initials move to break symmetry because their nominal sister cannot, then one might ask what happens when the nominal undergoes Ā-movement, as in wh-questions. The immediate answer is that the Goal argument still raises out of the verb phrase, as evidenced by the examples in (114).

(114) a. *Tshekuan tshe nakatamuin?*
tshekuân IC/tshi=nakatamu-în?
what IC/FUT=behind-2⟩1
'What will you leave me?'

b. *Tshekunnu nahi ka-pimutetaka?*
tsheku-nnu nahi ka=pim-ûte-tak-a?
which-Innu DSTL *ka*=along-walk-CJ.3s-*a*
'What kind of Innu is the one walking in the distance?'

One might expect that movement of the wh-phrase would eliminate the need for movement of the Goal in such sentences. But that depends on how wh-movement affects the structure, and in particular on the status of the lower copy of a wh-phrase. An ample literature shows that the "traces" created by wh-movement differ from those left behind with A-movement. In Innu-aimûn, it appears that wh-movement of a nominal does not disrupt symmetry in the necessary way.

Confirmation that the original copy of a wh-phrase retains its status is found in some non-compositional wh-expressions, seen in (115). The phrases *tshekuân uet* conveys a meaning similar to English *why*:[33]

32. Branigan & Wharram (2019) provide evidence that agreement is impossible in Inuktitut when a Person feature is lacking in D. The claim made by Oxford & Welch (2015) for Algonquian and Dene languages would then reflect a still more general cross-linguistic pattern.

33. As with questions where the interrogative pronoun alone identifies the question type, forms like *tshekuân uet* can permit the pronominal half to be omitted in indirect questions.

(i) a. *Tshissenitam eshi-tûtâk.* (Clarke 1982)
tshissenitam-u IC/ishi=tût-âk.
know-3 IC/thus=do-CJ.1s
'He knows how he is doing it.'

(115) a. *"Ekᵘ tshekuan uet ka-tshikakanuashkupuamenaua?" itakanu Uapush.* (LITP)

"Ekᵘ tshekuan IC/ut=kâ=tshi-kakânu-âshku-puâm-en-â-ua?"
"then what IC/hither=*kâ*=FUT-long-sticklike-thigh-V-2-*uâ*
itâ-kan-aU Uâpush.
say-PASS-3 Hare
'"And why do you have such long thighs?" Hare was asked.'

b. *Tshissenitam tshekuânnu uet tshîtûtet.*
tshissenitam tshekuân-nu IC/ut tshîtûte-t.
know-3 what-OBV IC/ut leave-CJ.3
'He knows why he left.'

c. *Tshekuannu ma uet minit umenu?*
tshekuânnu mâ IC/ût=mini-t umenu?
why Q IC/here=drink-CJ.3
'Why on earth did you make him drink that?'

In the surface form of such sentences, pronominal *tshekuân* is separated from locative *ut* by a range of other constituents. Minimally, the two are separated by the IC Mood head which produces the internal change ablaut, but additional material can appear between them as well. The idiomatic sense of this wh-phrase suggests that *tshekuân* and *ut* should originate together in their base position. The simplest structure consistent with these patterns would have *tshekuan ut* as an exocentric constitutent within the verb phrase, and then movement of *ut* can be derived if symmetry needs to be broken, as usual.

Returning to the structure (111), if neither animate nor inanimate objects can raise, then *ukussa* must remain in place. In that case, the only way to break the symmetry of {ukussa, kushpî} is with displacement of *kushpî*.[34]

With locative phrases which cannot be formed into a single X^0 element, no adjunction to the verb phrase is possible, because multiple head-movement at

b. *Tshissenitam tshe ishi-tûtâk.*
tshissenitam-u IC/=tshi=ishi=tût-âk.
know-3 IC/FUT=thus=do-CJ.1s

c. *Tshân tshissenitam uet iâkushit.*
Tshân tshissenit-am-u IC/ut=âkushi-t.
John know-V-3 IC/hither=IC/be.sick-CJ.3
'John knows why he is sick.'

34. See also Branigan & Brittain (2018), who come to the same conclusion in their analysis of East Cree word order. Word order in East Cree appears to involve remnant movement of vP (which loses its verb) to a specifier position higher in the structure, which Branigan and Brittain argue also enables symmetry to be broken, but at the vP level. Multiple head-movement in such structures must involve relationships established on the "right branch," where T can access [uSTEM] features, and not on the left branch, where the remnant of vP is realized.

the C-T phase cannot form a legitimate word (or cluster). But such phrases can still be employed by combining them with *ût*, a locative relative root.

(116) a. *Uipat kauikuaut utitaimupan natukunitshuapinu.*
uîpat kâuîkuâut ut-îtai-mû-∅-pan
without.delay helicopter thither-by.plane-V-3-PRET
natukuni-tshuâp-inu
heal-house-OBV
'The helicopter got to the hospital quickly.'

b. *Apu utitaman nete ua ituteian nete ka-uashetinaua.*
âpû=ût-ît-am-ân nete IC/uî=it-ûte-ân nete
NEG-thither-so-V-CJ.1 there IC/want=so-on.foot-CJ.1 there
ka=uashetinau-a.
KÂ-be.bald-plateau.at.summit-UA
'I have not reached the spot where I wanted to go, the place where there is a plateau with no trees at the summit of the mountain.'

c. *Uipat tshetshishep, kapiminaniti pushipan nituss, shash utitauetshe utanisha nutshimit.*
uîpat tshetshishep, kapiminâ-nitî pushi-∅-ipan ni-tuss, shâsh
early this.morning airplane-OBV leave-3-PRET 1-aunt already
ut-îtau-e-tshe utânisha nûtshim-ît.
thither-reach-DIR-DUB 3-daughter-OBV inland-LOC
'Early this morning, my aunt left by plane; she must have already reached her daughter inland.'

In that case, the larger locative phrase is not the actual Goal within the verb phrase, but only the antecedent for anaphoric *ût-*. It is *ût-* which originates as a sister to the Theme argument, and which therefore adjoins to the verb phrase to break symmetry.[35]

Goal predicates in Innu-aimûn

Locative arguments are not the only types of categories which can function as thematic Goals. Gruber's (1965) original model of thematic relations establishes the existence of a range of semantic fields, among which the *spatial* field employs locatives as Goals. In the *possessional* field, the Goal is the recipient in a transfer of ownership. In the *predicational* field, the Goal argument identifies properties which the Theme acquires as a result of the action of the verb.

35. This analysis of relative roots builds on work done together with Julie Brittain on the same construction in East Cree.

Just as locative Goals are frequently employed as verb initials, the use of Goal *predicates* as verb initials is also widespread in Innu-aimûn. Some examples appear in (117)–(121).

(117) *Minumûtâu.*
minu-mû-tâ-u.
good-arrange-V-3
'S/he arranges it properly.'

(118) a. *Tshishpaputâu.*
tshishpa-pu-tâ-u.
thick-saw-V-3
'S/he saws it thick.'

b. *Tshishpatshieu.*
tshishpa-tshie-u.
thick-V-3
'S/he thickens it (anim), makes it (anim) thick.'

c. *Tshishpatshishamᵘ.*
tshishpa-tshish-am-u.
thick-cut-V-3
'S/he cuts, slices it thick.'

(119) a. *Kashkatishueu.*
kashkat-ishu-e-u.
square-cut-V-3
'S/he cuts it (anim.) square.'

b. *Kashkatshiputâu.*
kashkatshi-pu-tâ-u.
square-saw-V-3
'S/he gives it a square shape with a saw or file.'

c. *Kashkatamûtâu.*
kashkat-amû-tâ-u.
square-arrange-V-3
'S/he set up, arranges things in a square.'

(120) a. *Kuishkukuashu tshikassipishun.*
kuîshku-kuâsh-u tshi-kassipishun.
straight-sew-3 2-pants
'Your pants are sewn straight.'

b. *kuishkuapikatamᵘ.*
kuîshku-âpikât-am-u.
straight-tie-V-3
'S/he ties it up straight.'

(121) a. *Nika shakassinepatan nitassik^{u}.*
ni=ka=shakassin-epâ-tâ-n nit-assîk^{u}.
1=FUT-fill-flow-V-1 1-pail
'I will fill my pail (with water).'

b. *innishiuieu.*
innishiu-ie-u.
intelligent-DIR-3
'S/he tames it.'

c. *Atshipeshaim^{u} mitshuap.*
âtshi-peshaim-u mîtshuâp.
different-paint-3 house
'S/he painted the house a different color.'

If Gruber is correct that the syntax expresses similar relationship in distinct semantic field with similar syntactic representations, then these forms can be readily derived in the same way as verbs of motion are. Take (119b), for example. Initial *kashkat* is predicated of the silent object as a result of the action of sawing. In other words *kashkat* is the Goal, and the corresponding base structure for the verb phrase should then be (122).

(122)

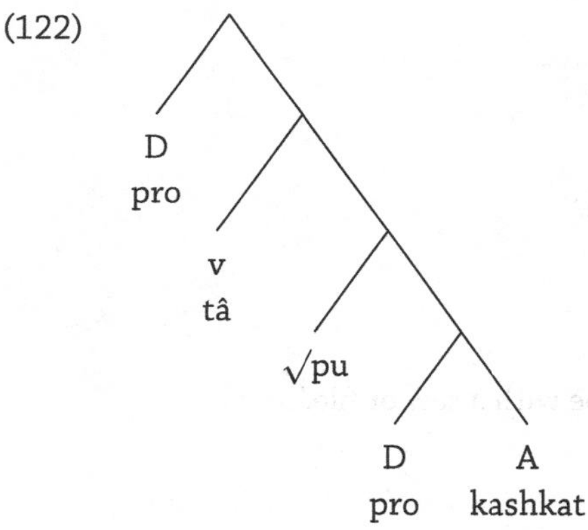

Just as in with motion verb phrases, the exocentric complement of the root must have symmetry broken in (122). And once again, the immobility of nominals in Innu-aimûn ensures that only the Goal argument can raise to do so. So *kashkat* must adjoin to the verb phrase, and multiple head-movement at the C-T phrase level will take care of constructing a complex verb from that configuration.

Similar conclusions can be drawn when numerals are used as resultative predicates. We have seen that *nîsh^{u}* 'two' is commonly used as quantifier within a nominal, but it may also appear as a verb initial with a Goal interpretation, as in (123).

(123) a. *nîshupuneu.*
nîshu-pû-n-e-u.
two-saw-V-DIR-3
'S/he saws it in two.'

b. *nîshuâpetshinam*ᵘ.
nîshu-âpe-tshin-am-u.
two-by.hand-tie-V-3
'S/he doubles it.'

c. *nîshuâpîkâteu.*
nîshu-âpîk-ât-e-u.
two-handle-V-DIR-3
'S/he ties them up together.'

Here too, the obvious syntactic analysis is one in which *nish*ᵘ breaks symmetry by adjoining to the verb phrase, setting up the conditions in which multiple head-movement at a higher phase will produce the attested verb forms.

Symmetry breaking adjunction in stative verb phrases

Adjunction of predicates to vP extends beyond the *telic*/resultative type of event in Innu-aimûn. In this respect, Innu-aimûn differs from Russian. Descriptive/stative predications also employ vP adjunction to break symmetry. These include simple copular verb forms and more complex predicative structures.

In the case of copular predications, the verb root itself is silent, so the simplest such forms will include a predicational initial, a *v* final, and the inflections: (124).

(124) a. *tshinuau.*
tshinu-â-u.
long-V-3
'It is long.'

b. *tshishenniu.*
tshishenn-i-u.
old-V-3
'S/he is old.'

c. *apishissishu.*
apish-îss-ish-u.
small-DIM-V-3
'S/he, it (anim) is small, little.'

d. *Passe katshishkutamâtsheshiht matshenitakushuat.*
passe kâtshishkutamâtshesh-îht matshen-tâku-sh-u-at.
some teacher-PL mean-present.self-V-3-3p
'Some teachers are disagreeable.'

Copular forms like (124) pattern with the resultative verbs. In both cases, the predicate will originate as a sister to the subject nominal inside an exocentric complement to the silent verb root. Symmetry will be broken by adjoining the predicate to the verb phrase.

As with other predicates, copular structures may be constructed with relative roots. As with non-anaphoric predicates, the relative root in such forms will originate as a sister to the nominal subject.

(125) a. *itapeu.*
it-âpeu-∅.
thus-man-3
'He is a man like that; he is that kind of man.'

b. *i'shikamau*
ishi-kam-â-u
certain.manner/type-lake-V-3
'The lake extends in a certain direction, has a certain look.'

More complex predicational contexts have a visible verb root which still selects a predicative complement structure. Examples of this type appear in (126):

(126) a. *apishinakuashu.*
apishi-nâku-ash-u.
small-look-V-3
'It looks small.'

b. *napeunakush-u.*
napeu-nâku-sh-u.
man-look-V-3
'He looks masculine.'

c. *tshîkâmâkuan.*
tshîkâ-mâku-an-∅.
raw-smell-V-3
'It releases a strong smell, odour; there is a strong smell.'

d. *matshimâkushû.*
matshi-mâku-shû-∅.
bad-smell-V-3
'S/he, it (anim) smells bad.'

e. *innishiutshenitakushu.*
innishîu-tsheni-tâku-shu-∅.
smart-V-present.self-V-3
'S/he looks intelligent, clever, smart.'

Here, of course, the structure will be essentially the same as with copular verbs, except that the verb root remains audible.

Similarly, verbs meaning to treat someone as something will fall into place (127), as do naming verbs (128). (The latter are constructed with relative root *ishi-*.) In both, there will be a base structure in which the object is sister to a predicative nominal, and where the predicate then adjoins to vP to break symmetry. So (127d) will be formed from the base structure (128), for example. In these transitive verbs, the nominal sister of the predicate is the target for object agreement, rather than subject agreement, but this does not alter how the base predication is formed, or how predicate adjunction breaks symmetry.

(127) a. *Uîtsheuâkanitutueu.*
uîtsheuâkan-îtutu-e-u.
friend-V-DIR-3
'S/he treats him/her as a friend.'

b. *Utshishennîmîtutueu.*
u-tshishenn-îm-îtutu-e-u.
3-father.in.law-POSS-do-DIR-3
'S/he has/treats him as her/his father-in-law.'

(128) a. *"Kapikueshit" ishinikatakanu nitem.*
"Kapikueshit" ishi-nîkât-akân-u ni-tem.
"Bushy" so-name-PASS-3 1-dog
'My dog is called "Bushy".'

b. *atshinikateu.*
âtshi-nîkât-e-u.
different-name-V-3
'S/he calls him/her by another name.'

Finally, depictive structures like those in (129) appear to be amenable to the same approach, with the depictive predicate fronted from its base position and adjoined to the verb phrase.

(129) *Aissimeuat tshikass ishi-mueuat namesha.*
Âissimeu-at tshikass ishi=mueu-at namesh-a.
Inuit-PL raw so=eat-3p fish-OBV
'The Inuit eat their fish raw.'

Comparing incorporation-based alternatives

The effect of adjunction of a locative or predicational category to the verb phrase is that it becomes available for multiple head-movement at the C-T phase. If so, then these structures offer perhaps the most compelling evidence for multiple head-movement in Algonquian languages. It is worth considering, therefore, if a simple alternative might be available, in which the initials are instead incorporated complements of the root. In that case, the derivation of (88e) could begin with the incorporation step in (131).

(88e) *Nipinut Shûshep ka nat-aut utassit mishta-nipaiepan amishkua.*

nîpinût	Shûshep	kâ=natâu-t	ut-assî-t
last.summer	Joseph	REL=hunt-CJ.3	3-land-LOC

mishta=nipâi-e-∅-pan	amishku-a.
many=kill-DIR-3-PRET	beaver-PL

'Last summer, when Joseph went hunting in his territory, he killed a lot of beaver.'

(130)

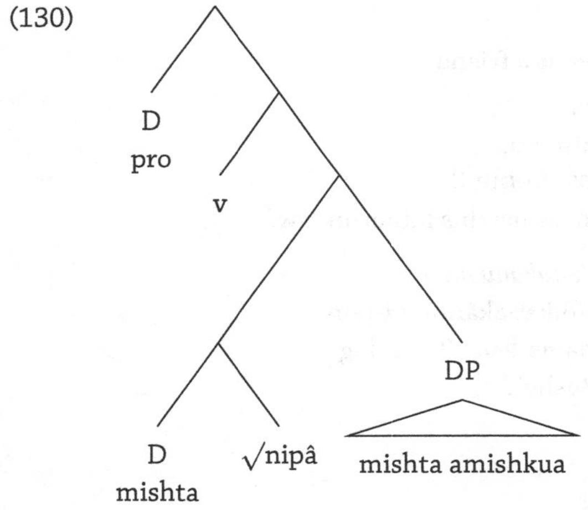

On the one hand, it would make little difference to my overall argument if this were the correct derivation of these locative/predicational verb forms, since the evidence in favor of multiple head-movement in other contexts in Innu-aimûn would remain. Nevertheless, there is evidence which still favors the analysis developed above over an incorporation-based one. This involves a departure from the regular pattern of continuative reduplication in some resultative verb forms. Consider how reduplication affects the form and interpretation in the following examples: (131).

(131) a. *Mânî peshaim^u^ mitshuâpinu metikat.*
Mânî peshaim-u mîtshuâp-inu metikât.
Marie paint-3 house-OBV carefully
'Marie painted the house carefully.'

b. *Atshipeshaim^u^ mitshuap.*
âtshi-peshaim-u mîtshuâp.
different-paint-3 house
'S/he painted the house a different color.'

c. *aiatshipeshaim^u^ mitshuapa.*
â~iâtshi-peshaim-u mîtshuâp-a.
CNTN~different-paint-3 house-PL
'S/he painted the houses a different color, one after another.'

Example (131a) does not include a resultative predicate. In (131b), though, resultative *âtshi-* 'different' appears as a prefix on the complex verb. The addition of continuative reduplication in (131c) produces an extra syllable at the start of the verb. (Since *âtshi-* lacks an initial consonant and the vowel in continuative reduplication remains constant, nothing is actually copied in this case, but the morphosyntactic phenomena is still recognizable.) And the semantic effect is a plurality of house-painting events, as one would expect.

In some similar cases, however, reduplication does not affect the Goal argument, but is found on the verb root instead. Thus, if *âtshi-* in (131) is replaced by a specific color term predicate, the results are as in (132).

(132) a. *Pien shîpeku-peshaim^u^ mitshuâpinu.*
Pien shîpeku=peshaim-u mîtshuâp-inu.
Peter green=paint-3 house-OBV
'Peter painted the house green.'

b. *Ânî kashteu-peshaim^u^.*
Ânî kashteu=peshaim-u.
Annie black=paint-3
'Annie painted it black.'

Continuative reduplication in this case affects the verb *peshaim^u^* instead of the color term resultative predicate.

(133) *Shipeku-papeshaim^u^ (mitshuapa).*
shîpekû=pa~peshaim-u (mîtshuâp-a).
green=CNTN~paint-3 house-PL
'S/he painted the houses green, one after another.'

The crucial difference seems to be that *âtshi-* is a monomorphemic affixal element while *shîpekû* is internally complex, formed from a root *shîpe-* and a verbalizing (v) suffix *-ku*. As such, *shîpekû* can be used by itself as a full verb stem in other sentences: (134).

(134) *Nasht shipeku unaman pieshaikatsheian nitush.*
nâsht shîpe-kû-∅ unaman IC/pesh-aikâtshe-iân nit-ûsh.
completely green-V-3 paint IC/paint-V-CJ.1s 1-boat
'The paint I am using to paint my boat is of a very pure green.'

The fact that reduplication "skips" the Goal argument in (133) is an indication that *shîpekû* does not appear at the edge of the verb phrase. In that respect, this pattern is similar to the movement of some determiners/quantifiers and *ekâ* out of TP. But unlike those, *shîpekû* remains to the right of all the other functional preverbs: (135).

(135) a. *Ni-natshi peshaim^u mitshuap.*
ni=nâtshi=pesh-aim-u mitshuâp.
1=go=paint-V-1 house
'I went and painted the house.'

b. *Ni-natshi shipeku-peshaim^u mitshuap.*
ni=nâtshi=shîpekû=pesh-aim-u mîtshuâp.
1=go=green=paint-V-3 house
'I went and painted the house green.'

Evidently, the position to which the colour term Goal raises is still relatively low within the clause—just not low enough to be affected by continuative reduplication.

Goddard's discussion of 'preverb bumping' in other Algonquian languages presents a comparable situation in which the expected order of an aspectual preverb followed by a locative initial is reversed.[36] Goddard's Meskwaki example of this phenomenon is in (136):

(136) *pemi-we.p+ose.+wa* 'he starts walking along' (*we.pi-* 'begin' , *pem-* 'along', *-ose* 'walk')

36. Goddard attributes the observation of this unexpected order to Jones (1904).

Here too, the Goal argument fronted to break symmetry is expressed just a little further to the left than one one expect, and immediately to the left of an aspectual head.

In both cases, the explanation cannot be that the Goal is unable to fit within a complex verb cluster, since it demonstrably can. Instead, there seems to be a requirement that some Goal arguments should not appear between Asp and the principal verb stem, while others can.

Since the Innu-aimûn exceptions in (132) involve fully verbal Goals, one possibility might be that continuative aspect is interpreted as applying to the closest verb in its domain. Adjunction of *shîpeku* to the verb phrase would place it closer to Asp than the verb *peshaim*, since only a single segment would then separate the color term from Asp. Since a result predicate must be stative, it would be semantically problematic to seek to interpret *shîpeku* as a plurality of resulting colors. In that case, it might be necessary to displace *shîpeku* out of the domain of Asp to form a sensible result. The minimal solution would be to adjoin the predicate to the next phrase up, i.e. to AspP. A minor technical issue is what sorts of intermediate positions are employed for moving a predicate out of the verb phrase, since adjunction will be necessary only for the final step of movement. The simplest assumption seems to be that the first step in the movement of the resultative predicate—when it will move still higher—can simply be (set)-merge with the verb phrase. In that case, the derived structure in which multiple head-movement would take place would then be (137).

(137)

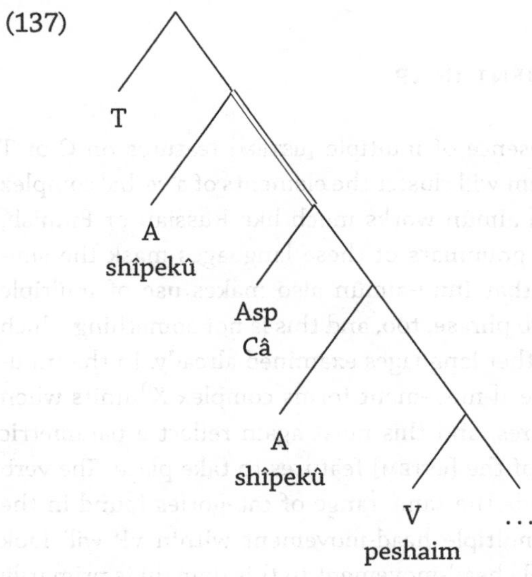

On this basis, [uSTEM] valuation and consequent head-movement to T would produce the correct forms. Given (137), T can value three [uSTEM] features, from *shîpekû*, Asp, and *peshaim* in turn. The eventual effect of head-movement operations will then be (138), as required.

(138)

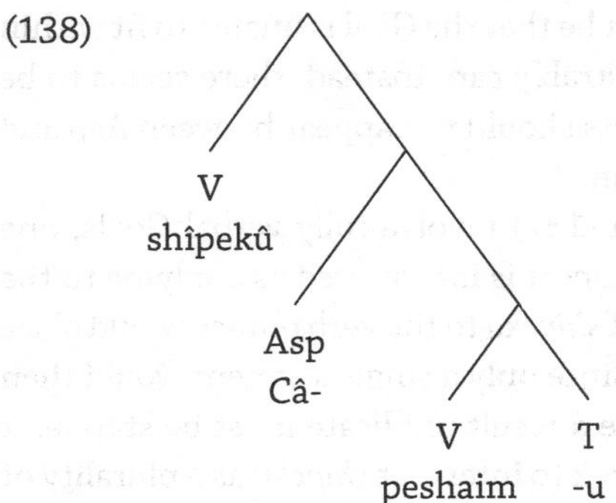

But regardless of whether a semantic explanation is appropriate for this pattern—and for the preverb bumping pattern generally—the fact that continuative reduplication does not always apply to a resultative predicate shows that the predicate cannot reach its surface position by an early incorporation operation. If it did, then *all* such predicates would be too deeply embedded within the complex verb to expect any exceptions to reduplication to be possible. As such, the analysis presented here, in which resultatives are displaced on their own, and not together with the verb, must be prefered.

4.4 MULTIPLE HEAD-MOVEMENT IN vP

Within the C-T phase, the presence of multiple [uSTEM] features on C or T ensures multiple head-movement will cluster the elements of a verbal complex together. In this respect, Innu-aimûn works much like Russian or Finnish, although other aspects of the grammars of these languages mask the similarities. It turns out though that Innu-aimûn also makes use of multiple head-movement within the verb phrase, too, and this is not something which appears to be possible in the other languages examined already. In the Innu-aimûn verb phrase, multiple head-movement forms complex X^0 units when v bears multiple [uSTEM] features, and this must again reflect a parametric choice which allows valuation of the [uSTEM] features to take place. The verb phrase does not typically include the same range of categories found in the C-T phase, so the effects of multiple head-movement within vP will look rather different. In fact, multiple head-movement in this domain is primarily involved in producing "noun incorporation" structures (of various types).

Let us begin with a descriptive overview of the pertinent cases. Innu-aimûn verbal forms include structures in which the "medial" component is nominal and the "initial" is verbal. Verbs with this shape are actually not frequently produced by speakers of younger generations in the Sheshatshiu dialect of Innu-aimûn, but they are found in texts and dictionary compilations provided by older speakers, and they are widely attested in other Algonquian languages. The nouns which are most frequently encountered in such a construction fall into a small number of semantic classes: animals, particularly those being hunted or ingested, people, body parts, and abstract nominals.[37] Examples of such verbs appear in (139a)–(143).

(139) a. *Etien kie ukussa natuatshikueuat niekate mamit.*
Etien kie u-kuss-a natu-âtshiku-V-u-at niekâte
Etienne and 3-son-OBV hunt-seal-DIR-3-3p over.there
mâmît.
downstream
'Etienne and his son went seal hunting over there, downstream.'

b. *Ninatuatshikueten nete Kapineiatshikunanit.* (INNUD)
ni=natu-âtshiku-et-en nete Kâpineiâtshikunân-ît.
1=hunt-seal-V-1 there Kapineiatshikuan-LOC
'I went otter hunting on foot at the Kapineiatshikunanit portage.'

c. *Nika natushatsheuen ikashteti.*
ni=ka=natu-shâtsh-eu-en ikashte-t-î.
1=FUT=hunt-lobster-V-1 low.tide-CJ.3-COND
'I will go after lobster when the tide has gone out.'

d. *Nui natumashinaitsheu atautshuapit, apu ushuniamit.*
Nui natu-mashinaitsh-e-u atâu-tshuâp-ît,
Louis hunt-write-V-3 shop-house-LOC
apû=ushûniâm-it.
NEG=have.money-CJ.3
'Louis asks for credit at the store, he has no money.'

(140) a. *Nitashkushipen, muk^u tshiam nish^u ninipaiauat missipat.*
nit-ashku-ship-e-n muk^u tshiâm nîsh^u ni=nipâ-iâ-u-at
1=wait-duck-V-1 only normally two 1=kill-DIR-3-3p
missip-at.
eider.duck-PL
'I went waterfowl hunting but killed only two eider ducks.'

37. In other Algonquian language which are spoken in regions where the traditional economy includes agriculture, food that is grown is also included in the lists of nouns which are "incorporated."

b. *Ashkamueu.*
ashk-amu-e-u.
await-V-DIR-3
'S/he waits for it (in hunting).'

c. ashku-mûaku-ep-û.
await-loon-sit-3
'S/he is stationed waiting for loon.'

d. *Ashkumûshuepû.*
ashku-mûshu-ep-û.
await-moose-sit-3
'S/he waits for moose.'

(141) *Atuan katshi nipaiati atikua, anakunakaim[u] uiashim.*
Atuân kâtshî=nipâ-iât-î atiku-a, ana-kûn-akaim-u
Anthony after=kill-3CJ-COND caribou-OBV cover-snow-V-3
u-iâsh-im.
3-meat-POSS
'After having killed a caribou, Anthony covers his meat with snow.'

(142) a. *nishtutu-akaneshauiu.*
nishtûtu-âkaneshâu-i-u.
recognize-English-V-3
'She understands English.'

b. *aimiashtikusheu.*
aimiâ-shtikush-e-u.
speak.to-French-V-3
'S/he talks to white people, to francophones; s/he interprets between Innu and French.'

(143) a. *mâshîshkueueu.*
mâsh-îshkueu-e-u.
beat-woman-V-3
'He hits, beats a woman; he is a woman beater.'

b. mu-âku-e-u.
eat-porcupine-V-3
'S/he eats porcupine.'

c. natu-âku-e-u.
hunt-porcupine-V-3
'S/he goes porcupine hunting.'

Nominal medials are sometimes used comitatively, as in (144).

(144) a. *papamuteishkueueu.*
pa~pimûte-ishkueu-e-u.
CNTN~walk-woman-V-3
'S/he is strolling along with a woman.'

b. *uapamishkueueu.*
uâpam-ishkueu-e-u.
see-woman-V-3
'S/he has a meeting with a woman.'

Examples like this, in which the verbal predicate is separated from final morphology by a form of a noun, have generally been treated as noun incorporation structures in the literature. But the order of morphemes in this Algonquian pattern bears little similarity to that found in noun incorporation in other language families. For one thing, the common situation in other polysynthetic languages is for incorporated nouns to precede the verb which incorporates them, as in the examples in (145) (from Baker (1988a)).

(145) a. *Mohawk*
Yao-wir-a?a ye-nuhs-nuhwe?-s.
PRE-baby-SUF 3FS/3N-house-like-ASP
'The baby likes a/the house.'

b. *Greenlandic Eskimo*
Nerrivi-liro-poq.
table-make-3SS
'He set the table.'

c. *Southern Tiwa* (Allen, Gardiner, & Frantz 1984)
Ti-seuan-mũ-ban.
1SS:A-man-see-PAST
'I saw the man.'

d. *Hiaki* (Haugen & Harley 2013)
Irene am=pan-hoo-ria.
Irene 3.PL=bread-make-APPL
'Irene is making bread for them.'

e. *Chukchi* (Polinsky 1990)
EtlEg-En qaa-nmE-g?e.
father-ABS reindeer-kill-AOR.3s
'The father killed a reindeer.'

Baker attributes this general pattern to the "Mirror Principle," whereby morphological ordering reflects the syntactic derivation behind it. In the case of noun incorporation, the N-V morpheme order results when a noun raises up and adjoins (to the left) to the verb which attracts it. In more elaborate contemporary verb phrase structures, the incorporated noun will adjoin to the verb root before the N-√ combination raises to v. But for Innu-aimûn, no consistent left-adjunction pattern can accommodate the actual order of morphemes. Suppose the base structure for (140d) to be (146).

(146)

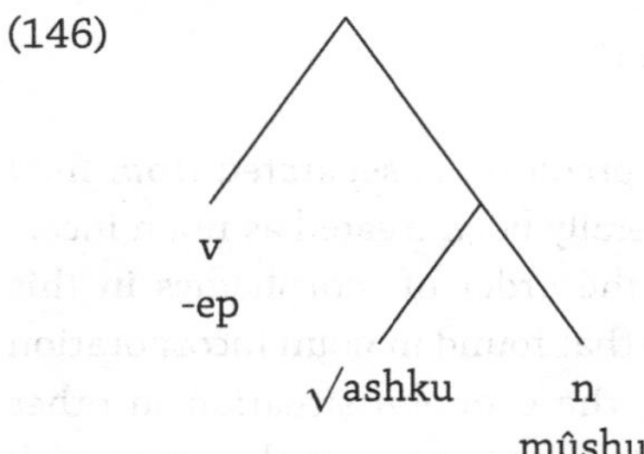

Incorporation of *mûshu* into *ashku* would have to involve right-adjunction, while the second step of √ to v movement would require left-adjunction.

While initially plausible, an analysis of this sort fails quickly when verbs with richer "initial" components are considered, an issue also noted for Ojibwe by Barrie & Mathieu (2016). Consider forms like (147a)–(149), each of which includes medial components *(n)apeu* 'man' or *-shkueu* 'woman; person of opposite sex'.

(147) a. *kanuenimapeueu.*
kanuenim-âpeu-e-u.
take.care-man-V-3
'She keeps/lives with a man.'

b. *kanuenimishkueueu.*
kanuenim-ishkueu-e-u.
take.care-woman-V-3
'He lives with a woman.'

(148) a. *shueniminapeueu.*
shuenimi-nâpeu-e-u.
caress-man-V-3
'She kisses a man.'

b. *shuenimishkueueu.*
shuenim-ishkueu-e-u.
caress-woman-V-u
'He kisses a woman.'

(149) *mamitunenimishkueueu.*
mâ~mitunenim-ishkueu-e-u.
CNTN~think.about-woman-V-3
'S/he thinks about someone of the opposite sex.'

In each of these forms, the medial is preceded by a verbal initial and followed by the *-e* intransitive final. But the initial components in these forms are transparently polymorphemic, so they cannot be treated as simple verb roots. For (147a), for example, the initial *kanuenim-* is also found in a non-incorporating verb like *kanuenimeu*, found in (150).

(150) *Shanut kanuenimeu ukuma.*
Shânut kanuenim-e-u û-kum-a.
Shanut take.care-V-3 3-stepmom-OBV
'Charlotte takes care of her stepmother.'

But this verb actually belongs to a large class of verbs ending in *-enim-*, verbs which refer to some kind of social or psychological action.[38] But then *-enim-* must also constitute a final component, and the internal structure of *kanuenimeu* will be (151).

(151) kanu-enim-e-u
take.care-mindfully-DIR-3

Continuing to assume a single generative engine for morphology and syntax, the implication is that *kanuenimeu* is one of the (many) verbs in this language in which v selects a second "final" v in its complement. In other words, *kanuenimeu* must arise from a base structure (152):

(152)

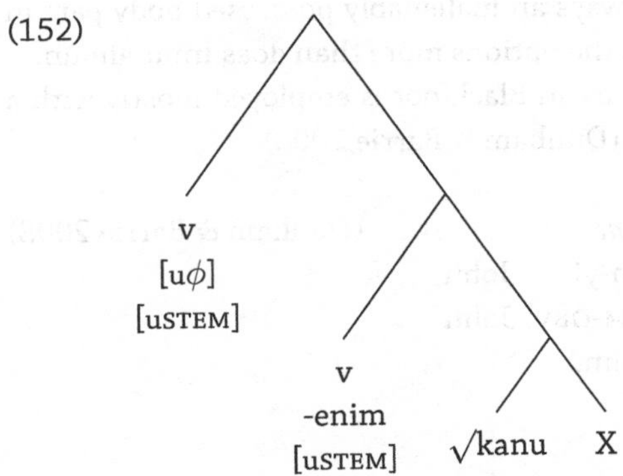

38. The form *-enim-* may well itself be bimorphemic, and composed of the two finals *-en* and *-im*, the latter of which has wider usage (M. MacKenzie, personal communication). The point being made here is not affected by this possibility.

Head movement of the root to the lower v, and then of *kanu-enim-* to the next v will generate the actual verb stem in vP. But if X is a nominal object to be incorporated within the same structure, then this same structure cannot give rise to forms like (147a)–(149) by head-movement of the nominal up to the root, because the end result has the medial separated from the verb root by the *-enim-* final. And it makes no difference in this case whether adjunction of the nominal is to the right of the root or to the left. The result comes out wrong either way. Nor is it critical for this argument that *-enim-* is classified as belonging to the v category, since any other categorial label will still ensure the same result.

Another reason to suspect that nominal medials are not comparable to familiar noun incorporation structures is the fact that some Algonquian languages appear to contain two distinct "noun incorporation" structures. In Blackfoot, for example, there are two distinct verbal structures which include visibal nominal and verbal components.[39] One patterns with the Innu-aimûn structures, as seen in the (153) examples. The other behaves like familiar, Bakerian incorporation: (154).

(153) *Blackfoot*

a. *anná Conrad áíssiikawatsii.* (Dunham & Barrie 2008)
ann-wa Conrad á-ssi-ika-atsi.
DEM-PROX Conrad IMPF-wipe-foot-V
'Conrad is washing his feet.'

b. *anná Meagan ísapaapino'toyii anní Patrick.*
ann-wa Meagan sap-aapin-o't-o-yii ann-yi Patrick.
DEM-PROX Meagan in-eye-grasp-TA-DIR dem-OBV Patrick
'Meagan poked Patrick's eye.'

The nominal medial in (153) is always an inalienably possessed body part in Blackfoot; this languages restricts the options more than does Innu-aimûn.

The other incorporation structure in Blackfoot is employed mostly with a small set of "defective" verb roots (Dunham & Barrie 2008).

(154) a. *iihpokónsskoyii anní John.* (Dunham & Barrie 2008)
pokón-hko-yii ann-yi John.
ball-provide.to-DIR DEM-OBV John
'He bought a ball for John.'

39. Mellow (1990) discusses Plains Cree cases similar to these. For him, the forms where a nominal appears to the left of the rest of the verb are to be analysed as compound structures.

b. *áátapíyooyi.*
á-matápi-ooyi.
IMPF-person-eat
'He eats people.'

c. *Anna Leo áínnokaikskimaa annohk.*
ann-wa Leo a-innoka-ikskim-aa-wa annohk.
DEM-PROX Leo IMPF-elk-hunt-AI-PROX now
'Leo is elk-hunting today.' (H. Bliss, personal communication)

In this structure, the set of incorporated nominals is relatively large, in contrast. The point here is that incorporation of the second type behaves entirely as one would expect, if the verbal root incorporates (the head of) a nominal complement. Thus, the properties of sentence (154b) are fully accommodated by an analysis in which the base structure (155) is manipulated by regular head-movement operations, raising n to the verbal root, then the complex n-√ to v, where left-adjunction applies each time.

(155)

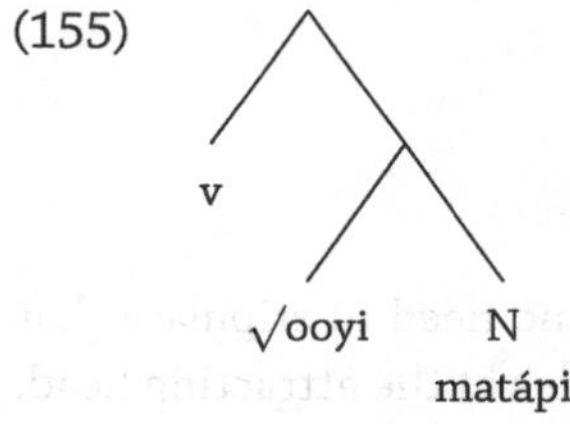

But if familiar noun incorporation in Blackfoot always produces an output with the order *noun–verb.root–v*, then the other—more characteristocally Algonquian—structure must be generated in some other way.

The implication is that the process which creates complex verbs with a nominal medial component is not adjunction of the noun to the verb root. This is not noun incorporation, in the Bakerian sense. In order to limit terminological confusion, I will refer to the Algonquian process in question as "noun accommodation" (NA) instead. (The Algonquianist literature frequently employs the term noun incorporation for these phenomena, and this usage predates generative analyses, but since I work in a generative context, it seems more important here to avoid the confusion which can arise in the more limited technical context.)

The question now is how to model Algonquian noun accommodation. A derivation incorporating multiple head-movement offers the results we need. If v can attract multiple heads, just as T and C do, then the following derivation of (140d) becomes possible starting from (146). As usual, v bears a [uSTEM] feature, which it values with the [STEM] feature on the root *ashku-*. But now suppose that v may also take on an additional [uSTEM] feature, and the second valuation takes *mûshu* as its goal. When the derivation approaches the point for externalization to the S-M interface, all the matching [STEM] features must be brought together, so head-movement must take place, starting with the outermost [STEM] feature on v. The nominal *mûshu* is used to supplement v, forming the new structure {v, mûshu}, and then *ashku* is added in turn. The result will be the structure (156).

(156)

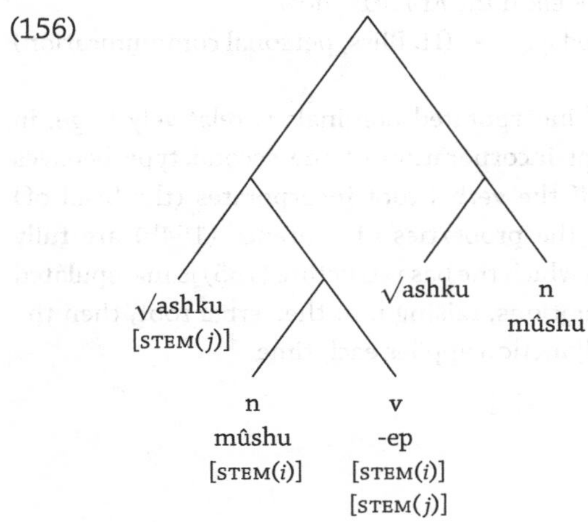

The correct result follows in this approach with no need to stipulate that different categories adjoin to arbitrarily different sides of the attracting head. All head-movement in Innu-aimûn simply undergoes linearization of the lower head to the left of the attracting head.

The same approach accommodates verb forms in which the initial component includes a v final, such as *kanuenimishkueueu*, with an initial structure for the full verb phrase as in (157).

(157)

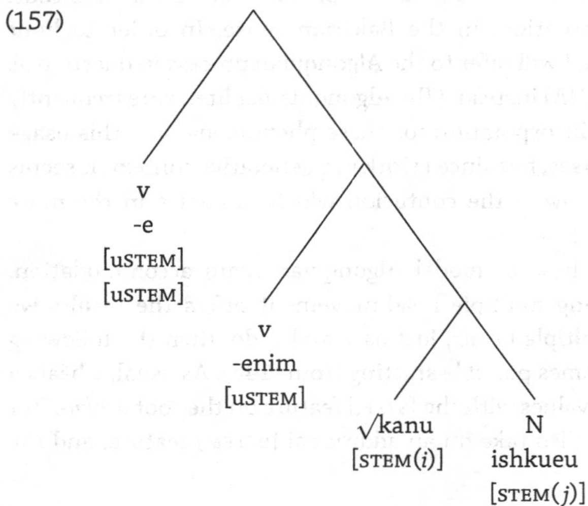

In this case, the values for the [uSTEM] features in the upper v are supplied by *kanu-* and *ishkueu*, in turn. The lower v *-enim* bears only a single, inherent [uSTEM] feature, which is valued by *kanu-*. And when the time is right, separate head-movement operations will displace the lower X^0 structures to form the only morphologically interpretable complex verb form: (158).

(158) a. *-enim* is replaced by {*kanu-*, *-enim*}
b. *-e* is replaced by {{*kanu-*, *-enim*} , *-e*}
c. *-e* is replaced by {*ishkueu*, *-e*}

A comparable set of derivational steps will apply in the case of comitative verbs with accommodated nouns, such as (159).

(159) *Uitshi-natutikuemeu.*
uîtshi-natû-tîku-e-m-e-u.
with-hunt-caribou-V-V-DIR-3
'S/he hunts caribou with him/her.'

In this case, adjunction of *uîtshi* to the verb phrase will generate the vP phase structure (160).

(160)

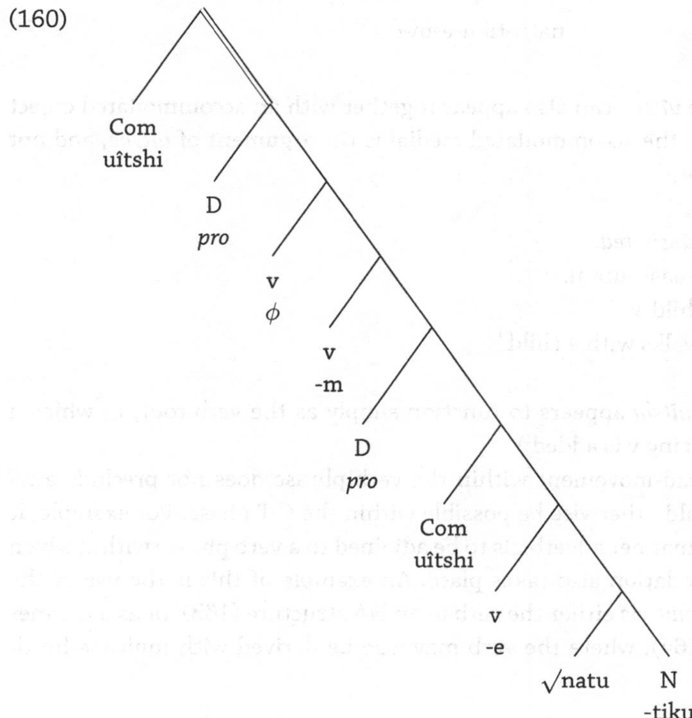

Given [uSTEM] features on each v head in (160), adjunction of *uîtshi* to the verb phrase will allow the root to raise to *-e*, then to *-m*. At that point, if phasal v has multiple [uSTEM] features, it can attract both the verb and the object *-tiku*, ensuring the structure (161) will be produced at the C-T phase level.

(161)

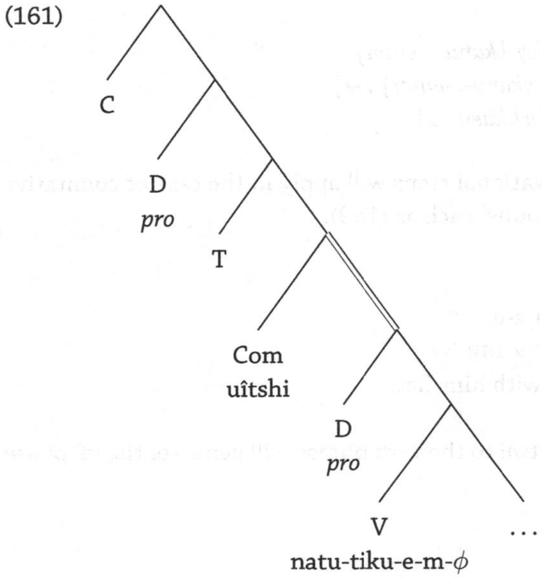

(Comitative *uîtshe* can also appear together with an accommodated object nominal where the accommodated medial is the argument of *uîtshe*, and not of the verb root.

(162) *Uîtshuâushûteu.*
uîtshe-uâsh-ûte-u.
with-child-V-3
'S/he walks with a child.'

In thse cases, *uîtshi* appears to function simply as the verb root, to which a regular verbalizing v is added.)

Multiple head-movement within the verb phrase does not preclude anything that would otherwise be possible within the C-T phase. For example, it is possible for manner adverbials to be adjoined to a verb phrase within which noun accommodation also takes place. An example of this is the use of the verb stem *tshimut-* as either the verb in an NA structure (163), or as a manner adverbial in (164), where the verb may also be derived with multiple head-movement.

(163) *tshimutamesheu.*
tshîmut-amesh-e-u.
steal-fish-V-3
'S/he steals a fish from a net.'

(164) a. *Tshimushapatam*ᵘ.
tshîmush-âpâ-tam-u.
secretly-see-V-3
'S/he looks at it secretly, spies on it.'

b. *Tshimushapaminapeueu.*
tshîmush-âpami-nâpeu-e-u.
secretly-see-man-V-3
'S/he watches, spies on a man secretly.'

c. *Tshimushapamishkueueu.*
tshîmûsh-âpam-ishkueu-e-u
secretly-see-woman-V-3
'S/he watches, spies on a woman in secret.'

4.4.1 Noun accommodation and tripartite stem structures

As discussed already inflected words in Algonquian languages have been traditionally analysed as conforming to a tripartite stem structure. The classification of the components of Algonquian verbs as initials, medials, or finals reflects this understanding that such structures are real. And the traditional approach has considerable descriptive value. For one thing, it provides a framework which can capture the fact that stems in initial position are often realized differently from stems in medial position. This phenomenon is common in noun accommodation structures; compare the forms of *atik*ᵘ 'caribou' in (165a) and (165b).

(165) a. *Atik*ᵘ *nipaiku maikana.*
atîkᵘ nipa-ik-u maikan-a.
caribou kill-INV-3 wolf-OBV
'The caribou got killed by a wolf.'

b. *Natutikueu.*
natu-tîku-e-u.
hunt-caribou-V-3
'S/he hunts caribou.'

As a full noun, the noun takes the form *atik*ᵘ; as a medial, it lacks the initial vowel. Alternating forms of this sort are essentially idiosyncratic (Drapeau 2014), and common. Some examples are listed in (166).

(166)

General stem	Medial form	
nâpeu	-âpeu	'man'
ishkueu	-shkueu	'woman'
kâkᵘ	-âku	'porcupine'
atim	-stim	'dog'
kûn	-âkun	'snow'

The question, however, is what the underlying basis for such superficial effects can be. The idea that initial-medial-final structures in complex verbs are formed through multiple head-movement offers a new way to address this question. In this analysis, the verb in (165b) is formed by multiple head-movement within the verb phrase, followed by multiple head-movement at the C-T phase level. (Of course, in this case, there is only one actual head-movement operation, but it still operates within the parameter settings which allow multiple head-movement.) Consider the vP phase structure initially formed for this sentence.

(167)

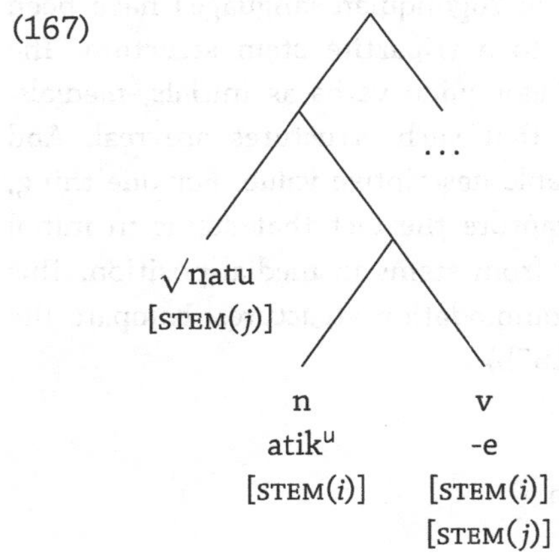

At earlier points in the derivation of this structure, two [uSTEM] features of v will have been valued, and two head-movement operations will have raised the verb root and the noun upwards to v in response, forming the complex X^0 structure seen here. In order for this structure to be successfully interpreted by the morphophonology, its root must be identifiable. Otherwise, any cyclic phonological processes will have no starting point. And the X^0 structure in (167) is problematically ambiguous in that respect, because both *natu-* and *atik*ᵘ are legitimate roots in other contexts, so there are two ways in which this structure could potentially be phonologically processed. If *atik*^{u} is taken to be the root, then the phonology will operate on a structure: [*natu* [[*atik*^{u}] *e*]]. On the other hand, if *natu-* is the root, then the structure interpreted by cyclic phonology will be [[*natu*] *atik*^{u} - *e*].

This problem will be potentially pervasive in any analysis based on multiple head-movement, of course. For many the cases already considered above, and in previous chapters, though, the problem does not actually arise. Russian prefixes are inherently unable to serve as morphological roots, just as are their cognate propositions. Morphemes can bear a (syntactic) value for the [STEM] feature and still count as non-roots for the morphophonology. What makes Algonquian noun accommodation different is that the nominal medial has a regular use as a root morpheme in other contexts.

The special form taken by some nouns in medial contexts can be taken as a reflex of a special morphophonological property associated with medial positions, *to wit* being unable to serve as an actual root. One way to operationalize this idea would be as follows. Suppose that root-sized elements which cannot serve as roots can be identified as such by a morphological feature [NR] (non-root). In that case we may introduce a rule which can disambiguate morphological structures which require it. In a context in which the structure does not suffice to allow a unique root to be identified for a complex X^0 structure, a head bearing multiple [STEM] features may assign [NR] to the closest potential root, leaving the more remote choice as the actual root for the morphonology to operate on. For a noun like *atik*^{u}, the addition of the [NR] feature is what ensures it is interpreted as *tiku-* instead.

More generally, if noun accommodation structures can find a legitimate interpretation in the morphophonology only if [NR] is assigned to the nominal medial, it will follow that only nouns which accept the [NR] assignment will be allowed to be accommodated. This then may serve as the formal distinction between the limited classes of nouns which are allowed to incorporate and those which cannot.

In such a model, many putative indicators of a tripartite structure can be derived from the operation of [NR]-assignment. This operation will always take place in noun accommodation in Innu-aimûn, but its effects can be seen in other contexts, too.

Goddard (1988) observes of Meskwaki that the same aspect-marking morphemes can be used as a preverb in some contexts and as the "initial" stem morpheme in a verb in others. The Meskwaki verb forms in (20)–(169) are examples of this. In (168b), *ki:š-* is a preverb; in (169b), it serves as the verb root.

(168) a. menowa 'he drinks'
b. ki:ši-menowa 'he has finished drinking'

(169) a. wi:seniwa 'he eats'
b. ki:šisenye:wa 'he has finished eating'

The difference, Goddard maintains, has to do with the availability of a non-root form for the verb which *ki:š-* is combined with.

> Whether or not a preverb is used in a particular stem is morphologically determined. Essentially, if an appropriate final exists, the initial combines with it to form a primary stem; if an appropriate final does not exist, the initial forms a preverb which is used to form a compound stem.

As (169) shows, there are two variants of the morpheme meaning "to eat" in Meskwaki: a root form *wi:seni-* and an affixal form *-isenye:*. It is because the affixal form exists that *ki:š-* can be combined with it to form (169b). In contrast, the morpheme meaning "to drink" has only a stem form, so *ki:š-* can only be used as a preverb. It is worth noting here that the difference between the affixal and stem forms has a phonological reflex; the affixal form lacks the consonant [w] which the stem form starts with. This pattern will be frequently seen in what follows.

The same type of contrast is found in Innu-aimûn, where *tshîshi* "finish" can be used either as a root or as a preverb. In (170b), it functions as a preverb, because the stem *nîtâutsh-* has no affixal form. But in (171b), it combines with the bound form *-kuât-* 'to sew' as the verb stem.

(170) a. *nitâutshu.*
nitâutsh-u.
grow-3
'S/he/it (anim) grows; s/he grows up.'

b. *Tshîshi-nitâutshu.*
tshîshi=nitâutsh-u.
finish=grow-3
'S/he, it (anim) finishes growing.'

(171) a. *tshishikuâtam*ᵘ.
tshîshi-kuât-am-u.
finish-sew-V-3
'S/he finishes sewing it.'

b. *tshîshikuâteu.*
tshîshi-kuât-e-u.
finish-sew-DIR-3
'S/he finishes sewing it (anim).'

The question then becomes how to characterize the difference between stems for which "an appropriate final" allomorph is available to allow other elements to usurp the initial position. Goddard's solution is to identify certain allomorphs as *finals*, which then may combine with *initials* in the usual way. I prefer to avoid this type of terminological finesse, which seems to recategorize the problem instead of resolving it. But I accept Goddard's implication that the problem centers around the difference between initials and finals. The deeper question is what this distinction itself involves. In that light, consider the relevant parts of the C-T phase structure formed by multiple head-movement for (171a), and the resulting complex X^0 structure formed by Feature Inheritance, [uSTEM]-valuation, and head-movement: (172a,b).

(172) a.

b.

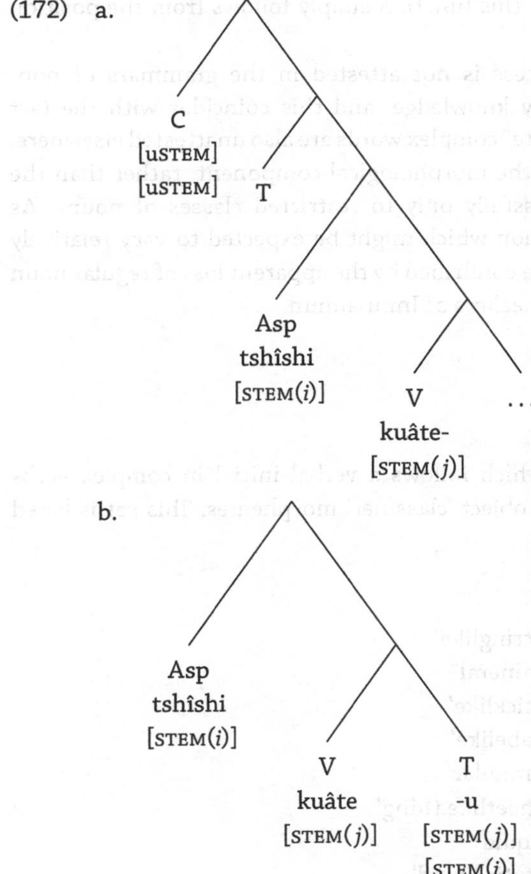

As with the "noun incorporation" structures, the derived X^0 form in (172b) has two potential roots—a problem which much be resolved for externalization to succeed. The problem can be solved by the mechanism of

[NR]-assignment, as before. Since T bears multiple [STEM] features, it can assign [NR] to *kuate-*, leaving *tshishi* as the only remaining possible root for the complex verb.

With the verbal cluster *tshîshi-nitâutshu* in (170b), the same problem must arise, since T will attract *tshîshi* and *nitâutsh-* in turn. But the stem *nitâutsh-* cannot tolerate the [NR] feature, so [NR]-assignment cannot take place in this context. The only alternative is to employ *tshîshi* as a preverb. Goddard's generalization then reflects a preference within the grammars of Innu-aimûn and Meskwaki for using aspectual heads as roots rather than preverbs whenever the derivation will allow this. In all cases, though, the basic syntactic structure remains the same. What is more, there is no need to maintain multiple categorial identities for preverbs which sometimes serve as verbal roots.[40] Their ability to serve this function simply follows from the position which they must occupy.

The [NR]-assignment process is not attested in the grammars of non-Algonquian languages, to my knowledge, and this coincides with the fact that Algonquian-like "tripartite" complex words are also unattested elsewhere. This process must belong to the morphological component, rather than the syntax, and it applies successfully only to restricted classes of nouns. As such, it is the type of operation which might be expected to vary relatively freely. This expectation may be confirmed by the apparent loss of regular noun accommodation in younger speakers of Innu-aimûn.

4.4.2 Classifier medials

Often the nominal medial which follows a verbal initial in complex verbs belongs to the limited set of object 'classifier' morphemes. This set is listed in (173).

(173) *Innu-aimûn classifiers*

-âpet	'stringlike'
-âpishk, -âpiss	'mineral'
*-âshk*ᵘ	'sticklike'
-aput	'tubelike'
-auak, -auatsh	'granular'
-et	'sheetlike thing'
-(i)p(e(k)), -ipetsh	'liquid'
-(i)kam, -akam	'static liquid'

40. At least in Meskwaki, most preverbs can function in this way (Goddard 1988, Dahlstrom 2000), so it is obviously a mistake to simply list them each as belonging to two separate categories.

The classifiers differ from regular accommodated nouns in at least two respects. First, they cannot appear alone, or in initial position in a verb, noun, locative, or adverbial particle, although they appear in each of these as medials. Second, their presence in a verb does not prevent the realization of a full argumental object (or unaccusative subject).

(174) a. *Ekue pituteiashkushimatshiht neu anitshenat mishtikuat anite.*
ekue pîtutei-ashku-shim-âtshiht neu anitshen-at mishtiku-at
then enter-sticklike-V-CJ.3p four those-PL dwelling-PL
anite.
there
'And then we put four of the trees in our tent.'

b. *anishkuapetshinam*[u].
anishku-âpetsh-inam-u.
pull-stringlike-V-3
'S/he lengthens it (a stringlike thing).'

c. *peikupekashtau.*
peiku-âpek-ashtâ-u.
one-stringlike-V-3
'S/he places it (a stringlike thing); s/he writes a single line.'

d. *tshishapissimu.*
tshish-âpiss-im-u.
brush-stonelike-V-3
'S/he brushes/rubs against it (a mineral thing).'

e. *shishupekaim*[u].
shishu-pek-aim-u.
rub-liquid-V-3
'She rubs it with a liquid.'

f. *Nishtesh nipimipatauau nipinu tanite ishkuatenua upishkueuna.*
ni-shtesh ni=pimi-pât-âu-â-u ni-pînu tânite
1-elder.brother 1=there-run.liquid-V-DIR-1 where
ishkuâtenua upishkueun-a.
burn-OBV raise.head-OBV
'I threw some water on my older brother for his hair was on fire.'

In some cases, medial classifiers serve to characterize features of an implied instrument.

(175) a. *ekue utinak atikuiana ekue matushtueiashkuauat.*
ekue utinak atiku-iân-a ekue matushtue-iâshku-âu-at.
then take caribou-skin-PL then throw.into.fire-sticklike-V-CJ.3s
'Then he took the caribou skin and threw it into the fire (with a stick/pole).'

b. *Sheshush tshishtashkuakanipan ekue nipit.*
Sheshush tshîsht-âshku-âkan-îpan ekue nipi-t.
Jesus pierce-sticklike-V-PRET then die-CJ.3
'Jesus was crucified, and so he died.'

c. *ekue mitshimapishkaik utetapuakan.*
ekue mitshim-âpishk-ai-k u-tetapuâkan.
then hold-mineral-V-CJ.3s 3-chair
'Then he put his chair back (with a metal instrument).'

With instrumental classifiers, no explicit extra nominal can be present as an overt instrumental phrase (Drapeau 2014: p. 436).

Instrument incorporation is attested in other languages (Mithun 1984). While the specific base position accorded to instrumental phrases will depend on one's theory of argument structure, the fact that incorporation does occur indicates that instruments may originate in a position lower than the verb root. And this means that instrumental classifiers should be able to start off in the same position. They cannot remain in their base position, and this presumably reflects their particular morphological characteristics, which prevent them from being realized outside of a verb. The analysis of (174a), then, will include multiple head-movement of the same sort, where v triggers movement of both the root and a lower nominal complement.

A more intricate analytic challenge is found with medial classifiers which do co-ocur with an overt object, as in (176). Take example (174a), for example. Here the object is *neu anitshenat* 'four of them' but the medial *ashku-* also characterizes the object as something with sticklike physical attributes. The question in this case is how both nominals can serve as "objects" at the same time.

Essentially the same problem is addressed in the generative literature on noun classifiers in languages like Japanese (Miyagawa & Arikawa 2007) or Mandarin (Cheng & Sybesma 1999), where the argument has been persuasively made that classifiers originate within constituents which also include the noun. It seems reasonable to consider that the same is true of classifiers in Innu-aimûn. In that case, a base structure for the verb phrase for (174a) would be something like (176).

(176)

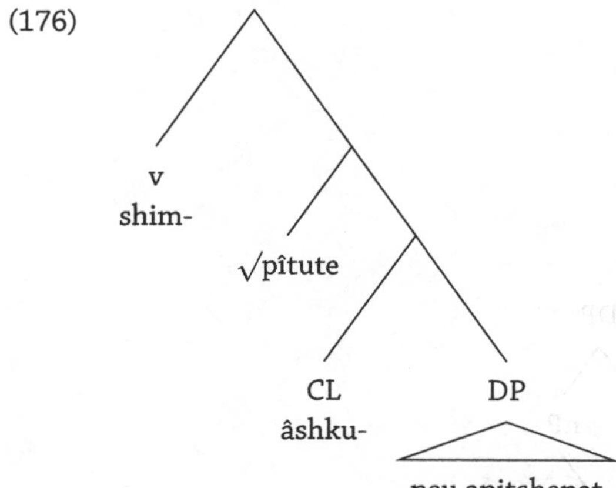

Given this structure, if v bears multiple [uSTEM] features and *ashku-* has a valued [STEM] feature, multiple head-movement will combine v with the verb root and the classifier to produce the attested complex verb. Classifiers must then pattern with other incorporating nominals in being able to accept a [NR] feature when assigned by the attracting v.

In fact, there is already reason to believe that Innu-aimûn classifiers must bear an [NR] feature as a lexical property. Departing from the usual pattern, where a single medial component is all that can appear within a verb, medial classifiers can be followed by a medial noun, when the latter is an inalienably possessed body part.

(177) a. *kakanuapetshishiteu.* (Baraby 2004)
ka~kânu-âpetsh-ishit-e-u.
CNTN~be.long-foot-V-3
'S/he has long feet.'

b. *uakashkutitsh-e-u.*
uâk-âshku-tîtsh-eu.
be.curved-sticklike-hand-V-3
'S/he has bent fingers.'

Again, the classifier and the classified nominal must originate as part of the same nominal constituent. But since inalienably possessed nouns can themselves be incorporated, multiple head-movement can affect both nominals in the (intermediate) structure (178) (for (177b)).

(178)

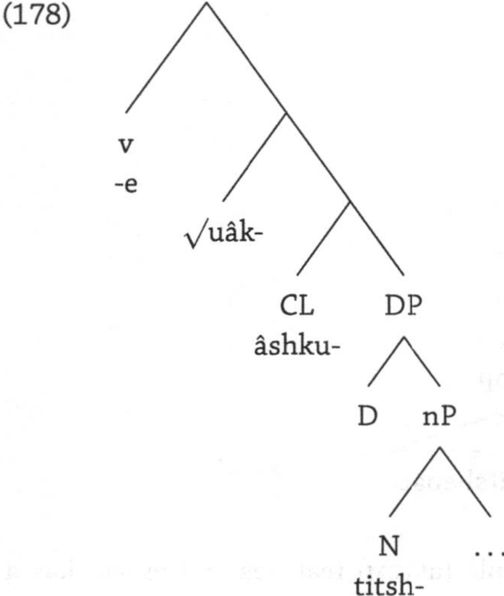

In other words, v will value three [uSTEM] features in turn, matching the root, the classifier, and the body part noun. At the point of externalization, head-movement then brings them together into the derived verbal form (179).

(179)

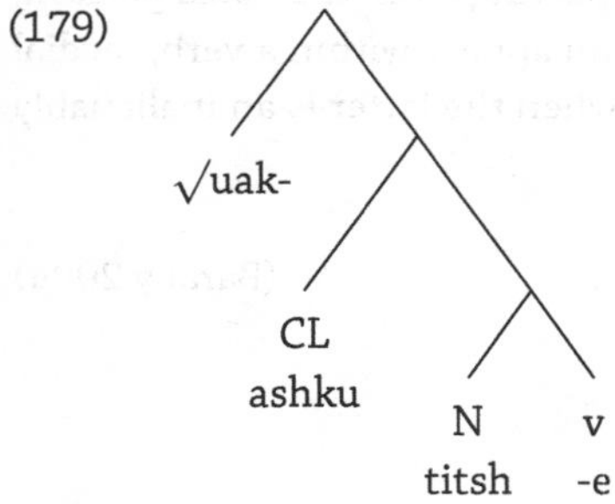

Given this structure, the problem of which potential root should serve as the actual root is compounded, since there are three candidates instead of two. The correct result must be that the verb root *uak* must be the morphological root. The [NR]-assignment operation will ensure that *titsh-* cannot be the root. But the classifier can be eliminated as an option only if it lacks the ability to serve as a root to begin with, which means that classifiers must bear [NR] as an inherent property.

4.4.3 Noun accommodation with silent verb roots

In Innu-aimûn verbs which express basic notions of possession or creation, there is no visible verbal root. Instead, the initial component appears to be an incorporated nominal, as in (180) (possession) and (181) (creation). (Predicational verb forms also incorporate a nominal stem with no visible verbal root, but the derivation of these forms is slightly different, and I will address these below.) For these cases, the analysis of noun accommodation already developed can be extended to understand how these forms are derived.

(180) a. *Shash nitanishkutapitshen.*
shâsh nit=ânishkutâpîtsh-e-n.
already 1-grandchild-V-1s
'I already have great grandchildren.'

b. *Mishta-katak[u] nipimuten uetashameiani.*
mishta=kâtâk[u] ni=pimûte-n IC/ut-ashâm-e-iâni.
great-far 1=walk-1 IC-Poss-snowshow-V-CJ.1s-COND
'I can walk very far when I have snowshoes.'

(181) a. *Uapaki nika utapanashkukashun.*
uâpâki ni=ka=utâpân-âshku-kâshu-n.
tomorrow 1=FUT=vehicle-sticklike-V-1
'Tomorrow, I will make myself a toboggan.'

b. *Tate anapitsheu unuitimit.*
Tâte ânapî-tshe-u unuîtim-ît.
Thaddeus net-V-3 outside-LOC
'Thaddeus is making a net outside.'

c. *Pinamen tshishineu ataia, ui ashtishitsheu.*
Pînâmen tshîshin-e-u atâi-a, uî=ashtish-îtshe-u.
Philomena tan-DIR-3 beaver.pelt-OBV want=mitten-V-3
'Philomena tans a beaver pelt, she wants to make mittens.'

d. *Niatshi-kusseiani, pitama nimanukashun ek[u] kuesseian.*
IC/nâtshi-kusse-iân-î, pitamâ ni=mânu-kâshu-n ek[u]
IC/go=fish=CJ.1s-COND first 1-dwelling-V-1 then
IC/kusse-iân.
fish-CJ.1
'When I go fishing, first of all I set up my tent and then I fish.'

e. *Numassinikuauat nitauassimat.* (Drapeau 2014)
n-u-massini-kuâu-at nit-auâss-îm-at.
1=3-shoe-V-3p 1-child-POSS-3p
'I'm making mocassins for my children.'

Consider first the possession structure, as for (180b). Besides the lack of a verbal initial, a verb like *uetashameiani* is noteworthy because it includes a possessive prefix with the nominal initial. While I have no detailed analysis to offer about the internal structure of possessed nominals, it is at least clear that such nominals must include a source for the possessive prefix, and must therefore be larger than a minimal noun. In fact, since possessive prefixes are presumably inflectional morphology—or clitics—the structure of possessed nominals must include extra functional structure. A base structure at least as complex as (182) seems necessary for the verb phrase for these cases.

(182)

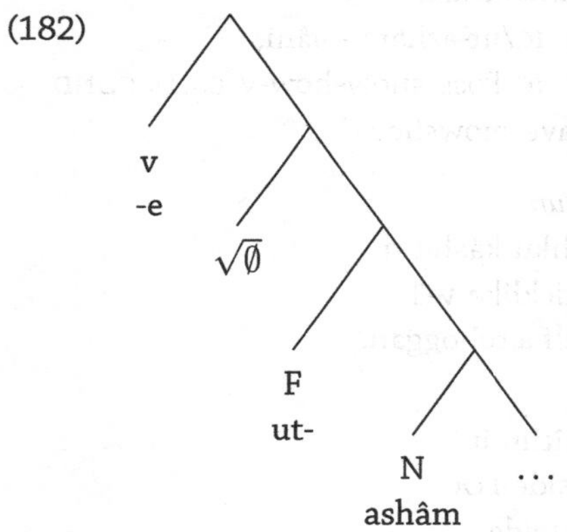

Suppose that the possessed noun *ashama* must raise to F to combine with the possessive prefix. Subsequent multiple head-movement to v will then generate the structure (183).

(183)

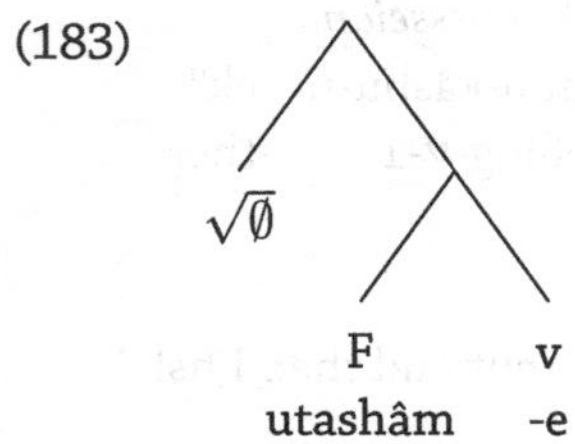

The abstract structure of these forms is comparable to noun accommodation structures, but the content of the terminal nodes makes a difference to how the morphology will react. Unlike regular NA structures, the question of which component will serve as the verb stem has only one answer here, because a silent verb root cannot be the stem. Only the accommodated nominal need be considered. What is more, in these forms, the rule which assigns [NR] to the closest possible stem need not and must not apply here, or there would be no stem left for v to adjoin to. Consequently, the shape of the nominal stem will not be altered, since it can never bear the [NR] feature in these forms. What is more, the fact that the nominal stem is allowed to carry possessive, inflectional morphology is less surprising in this case, simply because it is not identified (by [NR]) as a non-stem element.

The same logic should be applicable to the creation verbs, as well. Although the content of v is different for such verbs, the absence of a visible verb root will still ensure that the accommodated nominal will have all the properties of a full stem within these verbs.

On the other hand, if there is another way to find something which can substitute for the "missing" verb root, one might expect to see verbs of possession or creation in which there is no accommodated nominal object either. Such forms are attested, as in (184).

(184) *tshitshitau.*
tshîtsh-itâ-u.
begin-V-3
'S/he begins to make it.'

In (184), the aspectual head *tshit-* serves as the initial component and the stem, and verb final provides the idea of creation. Here there is no explicit verb root to serve as the actual stem of the verb. But the aspectual head *tshit-* is available to serve as the stem, so a legitimate verb can still be constructed for the morphophonology to interpret.

Another type of structure where something other than a verb compensates for the lack of a root as stem employs numerals as verb initials, as in (185).

(185) *Nishtesh neui-e-u utema.*

ni-shtesh	neu-e-u	utem-a.
1-older.brother	four-V-3	dog-PL

'My older brother has four dogs.'

Example (185a) shows how a possessed object may lose its numeral to the verb. In this case, the silence of the verb root is compensated by accommodation of the quantifier *neu*. The structure of the nominal object must be such as to permit the numeral to raise out, of course. If numerals originate as adjuncts to NumP, as in (186), then this can take place.

(186)

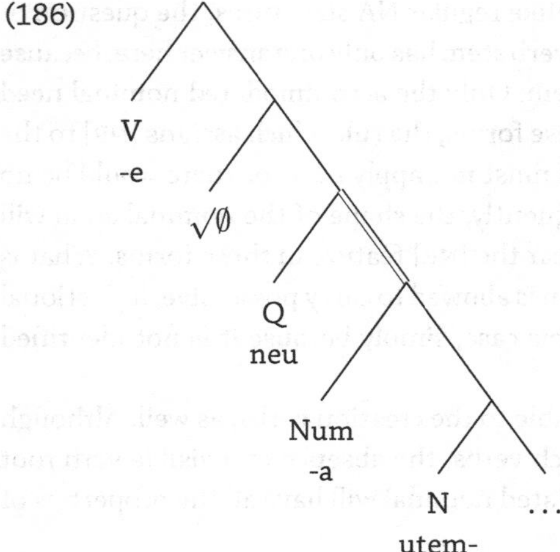

Given this base structure, v can attract both the silent root and *neu*, the latter of which will then serve as the verb stem.

Similarly, if an accommodated nominal has an attributive modifier, the modifier will take on the initial role, leaving the nominal itself to serve as the medial. The form in (187) is an example.

(187) *kâtshishuâpushitsheu.*
kâtshish-uâpush-îtshe-u.
partly.dry-rabbit-*v*-3
'S/he makes partly-dried hare.'

In this case, the base structure of the verb phrase must include an adjoined position for *katshish* 'partially dried', as in (188).

(188)

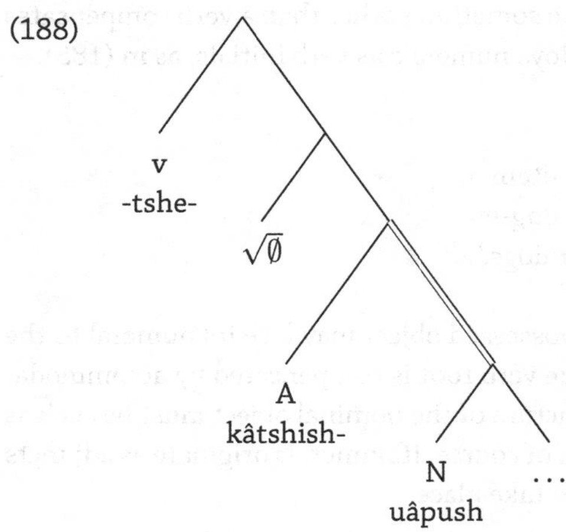

Just as T or C can attract an adverbial adjoined to vP, so v can attract a modifier adjoined to nP. With v attracting three lower [STEM]-bearing units, the derived X^0 structure will be (189).

(189)

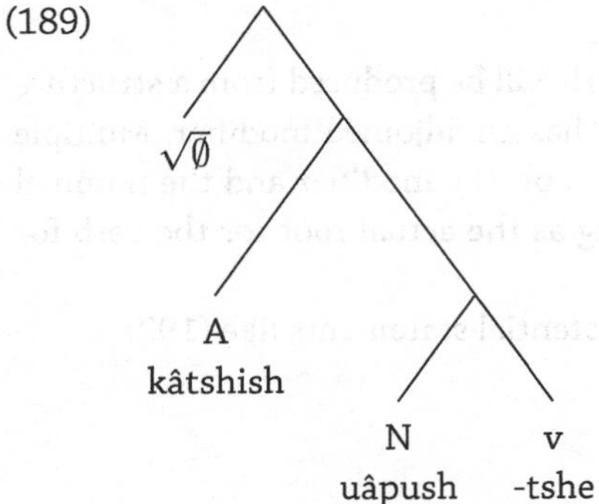

In this context, v must assign [NR] to *uapush*, leaving *katshish* as the unambiguous root for the complex verb.

The use of modifiers as initials is widespread in verbs of possession and in predicational verb forms, as seen in (190).

(190) a. *aieshkukateu.*
aieshku-kât-e-u.
tired-leg-*v*-3
'S/he has tired legs.'

b. *iapishishiteshû.*
iâpish-ishit-eshû-∅.
small-foot-*v*-3
'S/he has small feet.'

c. *apishishtikuaneshu.*
apishi-shtikuân-eshû-∅.
small-head-*v*-3
'S/he has a small head.'

d. *minukateshu.*
minu-kât-eshû-∅.
good-leg-*v*-3
'S/he has nice legs.'

(191) a. *apishishkueushû.*
apishi-shkueu-shû-∅.
small-woman-*v*-3
'She is a small woman.'

b. *minuapeushu.*
minu-apeu-shû-∅.
good-man-V-3
'He is a nice-looking man.'

Here again, the derived form of the verb will be produced from a structure in which the object of a silent verb root has an adjoined modifier. Multiple head-movement to v displaces the silent root, the modifier and the nominal in turn, and the modifier ends up serving as the actual root for the verb for morphophonological interpretation.

Similar derivations take place with existential statements like (192).

(192) a. *Nishtuat.*
nishtu-∅-at.
three-V-3p
'There are three of them.'

b. *Nîshuat ishkueuat.*
nîshu-∅-at ishkueu-at.
two-V-3p woman-PL
'There are two women.'

c. *Mitshetuat atikuat anite shipit.*
mîtshetu-at atîku-at anite shîp-ît.
many-3p caribou-PL there river-LOC
'There are many caribou at the river.'

Such statements express the proposition "there is/are X-many" of some nominal or quantifier. With quantifiers and with the numbers 1 through 4, the numeral is extracted from the object and appears as an initial on the verb. (The object itself may be silent and implied, as in (193a) or explicitly represented, as in (193b)).

The existential verb root here is clearly silent. If the numerals in (192) originate within the unaccusative subject of the verb, then they can be accommodated within the verb by multiple head-movement in the same way as with noun accommodation. For example, if (192b) has the base structure (193a), then v can attract both the silent root and numeral to generate the verb form (193b).

(193) a.

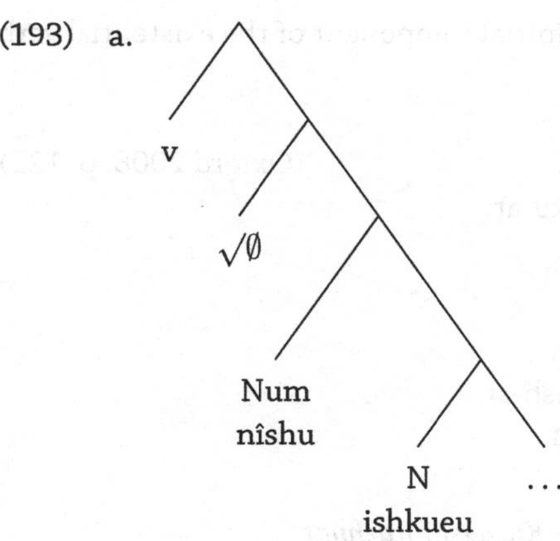

b.

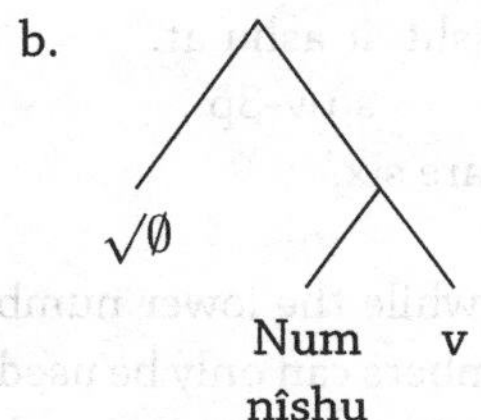

Not only may v attract the numeral in an existential sentence, but it may also look still further into the nominal complement and attract a noun (194a,b) or a classifier (194c).

(194) a. *Nishtûshkueuat.*
nishtu-shkueu-at.
three-woman-3p
'There are three women.'

b. *Nîshuâtâkanemakan.*
nîshu-âtâkan-emakan.
two-barrel-*V*
'There are two barrels of it.'

c. *Nishtuâshkuana.*
nishtu-âshku-an-a.
three-stick-*V*-3p
'There are three (sticklike) things.'

For the numbers 5 through 9, the initial component of the existential verb is the relative root *it*.

(195) a. *Patetât itashuat mishtikuat.* (Oxford 2008: p. 123)
patetât it-ashu-at mishtiku-at.
five so-V-3p tree-PL
'There are five trees.'

b. *Kutuâsht itashuat mînûshat.*
kutuâsht it-ashu-at mînûsh-at.
six thus-V-3p cat-PL
'There are six cats.'

c. — *Tan etashiht auassat?* — *Kutuasht itashuat.*
tân IC/it-ash-îht auâss-at? kutuâsht it-ashu-at.
how IC/V-3p child-PL six so-V-3p
'How many children are there? There are six.'

The higher numerals are phrasal, it appears, while the lower numbers are possible X^0 constituents. As such, the higher numbers can only be used in this context if the relative root serves as their proxy within the verb complex.

4.5 MULTIPLE ATTRACTION IN NOMINAL PHRASES

A substantial body of work has demonstrated the existence of of syntactic similarities between clausal structure and the structure of nominal expressions across a range of languages. In literature stemming from the 'DP hypothesis' of Abney (1987), explanations for such similarities typically entail similarly structured functional domains (DP and CP) which are subject to comparable transformational changes. For example, verb movement to T, which frequently occurs in clausal syntax, is formally similar to noun movement to D, which takes place in the nominal syntax.

In Algonquian grammar, too, the syntactic processes which I have identified in clausal syntax turn out to have their corresponding nominal counterparts. Just as C, T, and *v* attract multiple heads, so do D and *n*.

4.5.1 Multiple head-movement to D

While there are no overt determiners in Innu-aimûn, the grammar generates structures which appear to require multiple head-movement to the position where D would appear, if it were visible. These include structures where an abstract D head attracts both quantifiers and nouns, and structures where adjective-like modifiers are attracted together with the noun they modify.

Multiple head-movement with quantifiers

The most transparent examples of nominal structures with multiple head-movement to the edge of the phrase are complex nouns in which the initial component is a numeral, as in (196).

(196) a. *nîshuemîkuânîss*
nîshu-emîkuân-îss
two-spoonful-DIM
'two teaspoonfuls'

b. *nishtunâkan*
nishtu-nâkan
four-cupful
'three cupfuls'

c. *Neukuapikakan nimaushun.*
neu-kuâpikâkan ni=mâushu-n.
four-pail 1=pick.berries-1
'I picked four pailfuls of berries.'

These forms emerge naturally if numerals precede nouns in the base structure for nominals, and if D attracts each in turn. The structure (197a) can then form the source for the complex D in (197b).

(197) a.

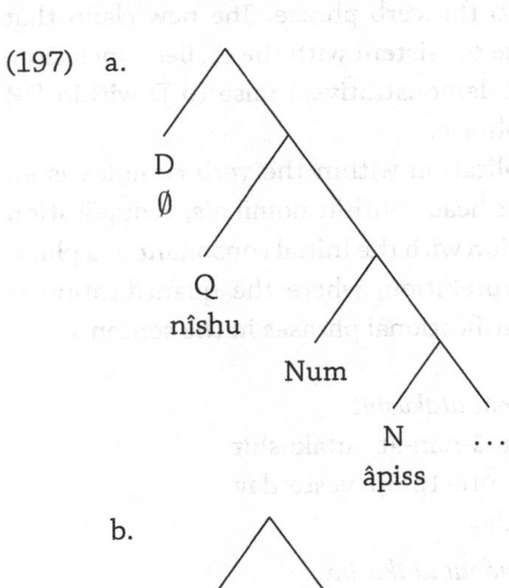

Such complex forms can also be used as adverbials initially adjoined to the verb phrase, as in (198).

(198) a. *neutipaikaneneu.* (Drapeau 2014: p. 446)
neu-tipaikan-ene-u.
four-measure-*V*-3
'S/he spent four hours doing it by hand.'

b. *mitshetutipishkueu.*
mîtshetu=tipishku-e-u.
many=be.night-*V*-3
'S/he has been gone for many nights.'

There is one notable difference between D and some of the other multiply-attracting heads in Innu-aimûn. Possibly because D itself is silent, D need not attract more than the first available target. As D is not a morphological affix, it is not looking for a particular category when it attracts. So while T must always trigger movement of everything up to the principal verb, D may displace Q and n but it also has the option of displacing Q alone, depending on the morphological context.

It has already been shown that quantifiers and demonstratives which originate in object nominals are prone to moving upwards in a syntactic structure. In section 4.3.2, it was shown that these movements start with adjunction of the quantifier or demonstrative to the verb phrase. The new claim that quantifiers originate below D has to be consistent with the earlier conclusion, and it is, as long as quantifiers (and demonstratives) raise to D within DP, before D raises to adjoin to the verb phrase.

As has already been noted, reduplication within the verb complex is an expression of the continuative aspect head. Within nominals, reduplication serves a different purpose. Reduplication with the initial consonant of a plural numeral ensures a distributive interpretation, where the quantification is given low scope relative to other quantificational phrases in the sentence.

(199) a. *Neu kânâkunâssat nimuânânat utâkushît.*
neu kânâkunâss-at ni=mu-â-nân-at utâkushît.
four cookie-PL 1=eat-DIR-1p-3p yesterday
'We ate four cookies yesterday.'

b. *Nâneu kânâkunâssat nimuânânat utâkushît.*
nâ~neu kânâkunâss-at ni=mu-â-nân-at utâkushît.
DIST~four cookie-PL 1=eat-DIR-1p-3p yesterday
'We ate four cookies each yesterday.'

c. *Ânî mâk Pûn pâssuepanat nîsh^u atikua.*
Ânî mâk Pûn pâssu-e-pan-at nîsh^u atîku-a.
Annie and Paul shoot-DIR-PRET-3p two caribou-PL
'Annie and Paul shot two caribou.'

d. *Ânî mâk Pûn pâssuepanat nânîsh^u atîkua.*
Ânî mâk Pûn pâssu-e-pan-at nâ~nîsh^u atîku-a.
Annie and Paul shoot-DIR-PRET-3p DIST~two caribou-PL
'Annie and Paul shot two caribou each.'

Given how verbal reduplication is analysed, a parallel syntactic derivation seems sensible for the nominal case. In other words, distributive numerals are formed with a reduplicant functional category located between D and the numeral: (200).

(200)

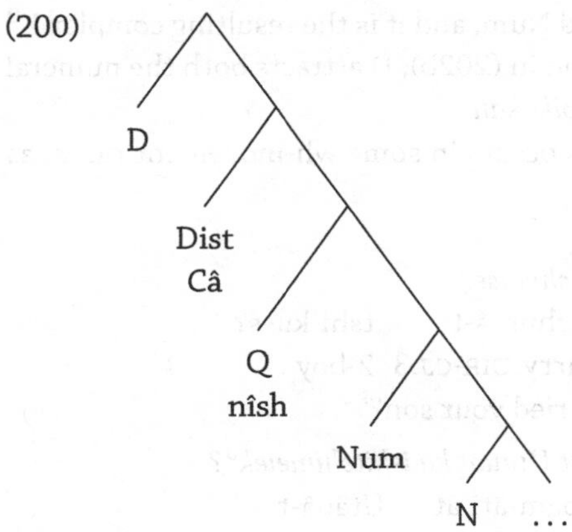

When D then attracts both Dist and the numeral, an X^0 structure (201) is formed in which reduplication can actually be effected, generating the actual forms we see.

(201)

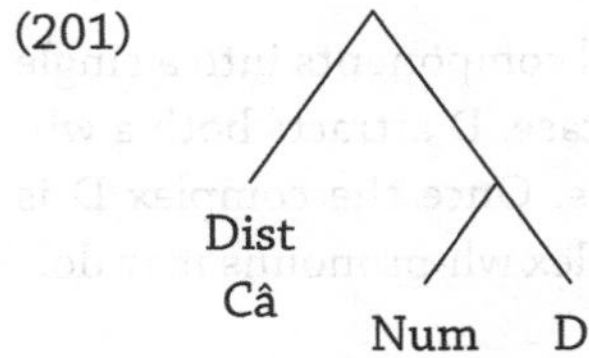

And the complex X^0 structure which (eventually) occupies D can then under further displacement in turn, such as adjunction to the verb phrase.

This means that the displaced category can itself be internally complex, as in the cases in (202).

(202) a. *Nanish*[u] *mashinaimueuat uitsheuakanuau ishkuessat.*
nâ~nîsh[u] mashinaim-u-e-u-at uîtsheuâkanu-âu ishkuess-at.
DIST~two write-APPL-DIR-3-3p friend-OBV girl-PL
'The girls wrote a letter to two friends each.'

b. *Neukuapikakan nimaushun.*
neu-kuâpikâkan ni=mâushu-n.
4-pail 1=pick.berries-1
'I gathered four pails of berries.'

The movement of complex X^0 categories follows if D attracts multiple heads before D is fronted. The distributive reduplication in (202a) necessitates a structure in which D attracts Dist and Num, and it is the resulting complex X^0 category which is moved leftward. And in (202b), D attracts both the numeral *neu* and an accommodated noun *kaupikakan*.

A similar set of derivational steps occurs in some wh-movement cases, as in (203).

(203) a. *Tshekushkueua uatshimat tshikuss?*
tsheku-shkueu-a IC/uîtshim-â-t tshi-kuss?
which-woman-OBV IC/marry-DIR-CJ.3 2-boy
'What type of woman married your son?'

b. *Tshekunnuat tshuapamatiat Utauat ka ishitshimeiek*[u]*?*
tsheku=innu-at tsh-uâpam-âti-ât Utâuâ-t
which-innu-3p 2=see-FNL-2p.3p Ottawa-LOC
kâ=îshitshime-iek[u]?
PRET=travel-CJ.2p
'From which region were the Amerindians you saw when you went to Ottawa?'

Here again, silent D appears to cluster two nominal components into a single complex X^0 form, which is then displaced. In this case, D attracts both a wh-morpheme *tshek*[u] and the noun which it classifies. Once the complex D is formed, it can undergo wh-movement, just as simplex wh-pronouns may do.

Multiple head-movement with attributive modifiers

Attributive modifiers apply to nouns in much the same way as manner adverbials apply to verbs. In a language like English, such modifiers are adjectives or PPs, but Innu-aimûn lacks free-standing adjectives.[41] Instead, attributive modifiers are typically expressed as prenominals (204), or as initial components in complex nouns (205).

(204) a. kâtshish-uâpush
partly.dried-rabbit
'partially dried rabbit'

b. matshi-ishkûteu
bad-fire
'hellfire'

c. Innu-aimun
Innu-speech
'Innu language'

(205) a. âish-innu
future-Innu
'Innu person of the future'

b. kashteu-âpishtân
black-marten
'black marten'

c. kashteu-âtsheshû
black-fox
'black fox'

The derivation of these nominal structures patterns with that of manner adverbials. Like adverbs, attributive modifiers in nominal structures can be assumed to originate as adjuncts attached to nP. The base structure for (205c) is then (206).

(206)

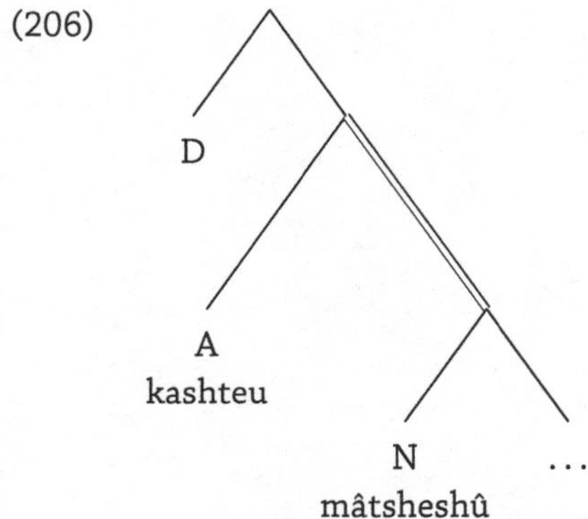

41. Oxford (2008) suggests that Innu-aimûn does include a single adjective, the word *kutâk* 'same'.

And just as T or C attracts adverbial adjuncts, and v attracts adjectival modifiers, D can also attract an adjoined constituent which functions adjectivally, before finally attracting the nominal root itself. The effect of this displacement on (206) will be the X^0 structure: (207).

(207)

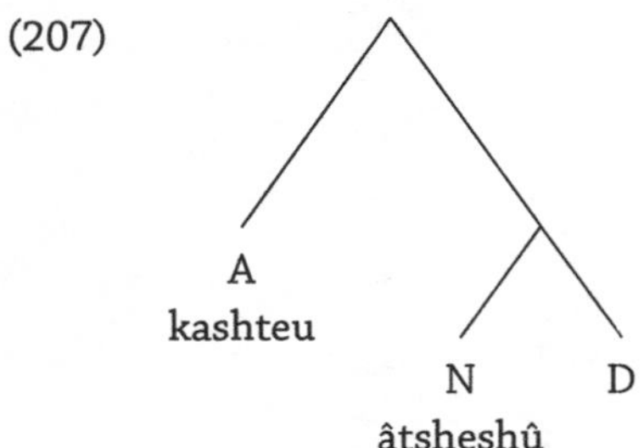

Notice that the derived nominal medial *âtsheshû* differs from the free-standing noun *mâtsheshû* by the loss of its initial consonant. This also matches what occurs in the derivation of complex verbs, and the explanation will be the same. With both *kashteu* and *mâtsheshû* presence in the complex noun, there are two many possible stems for the morphophonology to deal with. To resolve the ambiguity, D can assign [NR] to the closest possible stem, *mâtsheshû*, so that only *kashteu* will count as the actual stem. It is the presence of [NR] which then ensures that the allomorph *âtsheshû* is what is realized.

As there is no independent adjectival morphology in Innu-aimûn, the initial modifier will often resemble independent words from other categories. Thus, the modifiers in (208) are similar to free-standing nouns; those in (209), to verbs.

(208) a. *mashku-unaikan*
mashku-unaikan
'bear trap'

b. *pakâkuân-pimî*
pakâkuân-pimî
chicken-fat
'cooked chicken fat'

c. *pâssikanâpishk*^{u}
pâssikan-âpishk^{u}
gun-stick
'barrel of a shotgun or rifle'

(209) a. kusseu-tshuâp
fish-house
'fishing lodge'

b. ashinîu-pâssikan
be.mineral-gun
'pellet gun'

c. piminueu-ssîk[u]
cook-pan

d. pakâshimu-matshunish
swim-clothing.item
'bathing suit'

e. natûkun-ishkuess
heal-woman
'nurse'

In each case, however, the modifier will originate in a position adjoined to nP and be displaced as an X^0 constituent by the multiple [uSTEM] features of D.

The attributive modifier can itself be complex, due to prior internal operations in the modifier phrase before its head is attracted by n. In (210a), the modifier is *pâmâshkuaitsheu* 'play hockey', with internal structure which includes a verbal initial *pâm* 'move around', medial *âshku* 'stick,' and finals.

(210) a. *pâmâshkuaitsheumishtik[u]*
pâm-âshku-aitshe-u-mishtik[u]
'hockey stick'

b. *uâtshikatâshkuâshk[u]*
uâtshi-kat-âshku-âshku
pickaxe handle

For (210a), the initial component is formed from the complex stem for the verb in (211).

(211) *pâmâshkuaitsheu.*
pâm-âshku-aitshe-u.
go.around-sticklike-*V*-3
'S/he plays hockey.'

The verb in turn is formed through multiple head-movement from a base structure (212). The classifier in this case signifies the instrument of "going around," but the interpretation of the whole is idiomatic.

(212)

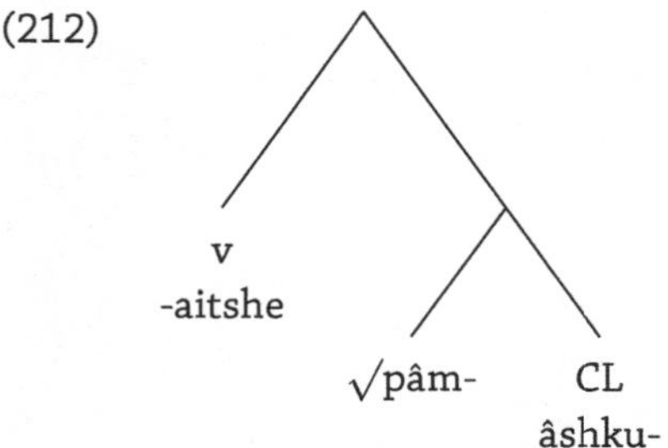

Given the complex verbal stem formed from (212), the structure which gives rise to the complex noun can now be (213).

(213)

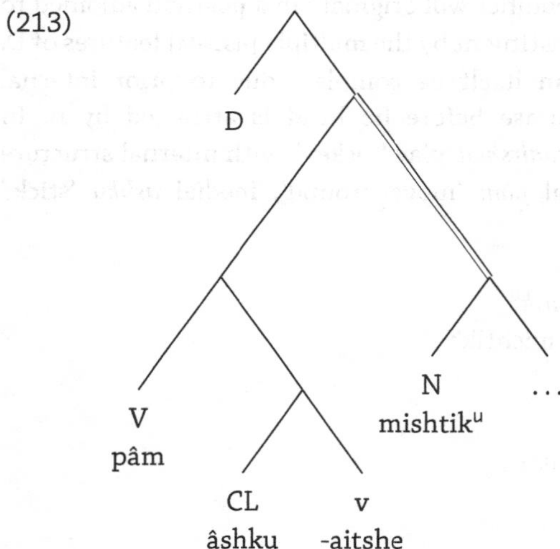

D will attract the complex head of the adjoined modifier, i.e. *pâmâshkuaitshe*, and then the noun *mishtik*^{u}.

Along the same lines, the modifier *uâtshikatâshku* 'pickaxe' in (211b) is formed from a modifier *uâtshikat* 'bent-legged' applied to the same noun *âshku* 'stick', with *uâtshekat* itself originating as a modification structure (*uâtshi-* 'curved (by heat)', *kat-* 'leg').

4.5.2 Multiple attraction by *n*

Just as verbs are formed with visible *v* 'finals' in Innu-aimûn, nouns are frequently formed with a visible *n* (Borer 2014). Often, in fact, there is a matching nominalization for given *v* finals. For example, verbs which refer to the use of a tool to accomplish an action are regularly formed with the (complex) *-aim* final.[42] And nouns referring to the instrument being used for a specific activity are formed with the *-aikan* ending.[43]

(214) a. kâshkâshkaim^u 's/he scrapes'
b. kâshkâshkaikan 'scraper'
c. akaim^u 's/he takes a shovelful'
d. akaikan 'dustpan'

Notice that the *-aikan* nouns are not formed from their verbal counterparts. Instead, both noun and verb take the same root (*kashkashk-* or *ak-* in (214)) and add distinct category-forming suffixes to form the full words.

And just as the *-aim* verbalizer can attract multiple heads, so can its nominalizing counterpart *-aikan*. Thus, simple verbs can be formed by adding *-aim* to *kuetip-* and *nak-* in (215). And the same *v* can attract multiple heads to form the more complex verbs in (216). (The classifier *-âshku* 'tree-/stick-like' is incorporated in these forms, as an object or instrument, respectively.)

(215) a. kuetipaim^u 'turn it over'
b. nakaim^u 'stop something from moving, using an object'

(216) a. kuetipâshkuaim^u 'turn it (tree-like) over'
b. nakaiâshkuaim^u 'hold something in place with a stick'

And *-aikan* does exactly the same, in (217).

(217) a. kuetipâshkuaikan 'hook for handling logs'
b. nakaiâshkuaikan 'end post support for a woodpile'

42. The underlying form of such finals is actually bimorphemic, with *-ah* 'tool-usage' and *-am* combined and altered by regular phonology to *-aim* (MacKenzie 1980).

43. Again, the underlying form is bimorphemic, with *-ah* joined to *akan*. The text discussion could in fact refer more accurately, but less transparently, to the alternation of verb-forming *-am* and noun-forming *-akan*.

The structure of nP for (217a) will then be (218).

(218)

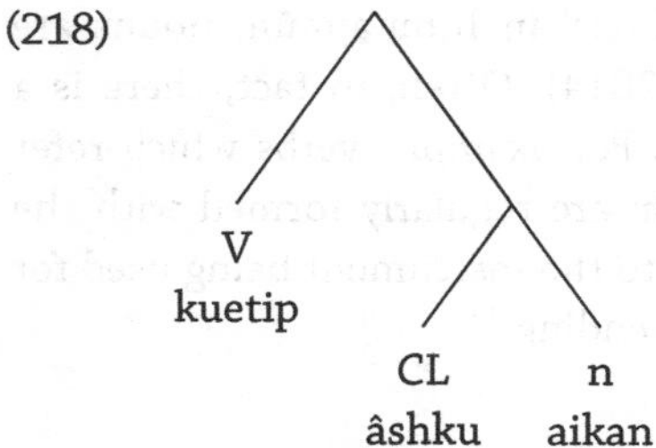

4.6 MULTIPLE HEAD MOVEMENT IN LOCATIVES

The problem of morphological structures which do not directly reflect semantic "closeness" is quite pervasive in Algonquian grammar, and it affects words of many grammatical categories. Locative expressions, for example, display the same seemingly paradoxical properties as tensed verbs do. Innu-aimûn nouns are marked with the locative suffix *-ît* when they are used to refer to a location, as in (219).

(219) a. *Natukunishkuess tshiueu nete Munianit.*
natûkun-ishkuess tshîu-e-u nete Mûniân-ît.
treat-woman return.by.air-V-3 there Montreal-LOC
'The nurse is flying home to Montreal.'

b. *Nimushum pashaishameu anite shipit.*
ni-mushum pashai-shâm-e-u anite shîpî-t.
1-grandfather cut.wood-snowshow-V-3 there river-LOC
'My grandfather is cutting wood at the river to make snowshoes.'

Nominals in medial position in a complex noun can also bear a locative suffix, as exemplified in (220), from Oxford (2008).

(220) a. *nîtâtshuanît* 'at the foot of the rapids' (*nîtâ-* 'at the foot' + *tshuan* 'rapids')

b. *âpitûtâtît* 'midway on a wooden thing' (*âpitû-* 'midway' + *tât* 'wood')

In these examples, though, the suffix is clearly semantically bound to the initial member of the complex morphological structure. The location in (220a) is not the rapids themselves, but rather what is gathered at their *foot*. And (220b) does not situate something at the piece of wood itself, but specifically at a point midway along it. So the locative suffix should not be located further from the initial than it is from the medial element in the structure in which the meanings of these phrases is determined. The structure must, in fact, be quite similar to that of the English translations, with a locative word taking a phrase which includes the anchoring nominal as its complement.

Oxford (2011) provides evidence that the locative suffix *-ît* should be treated as belonging to the *p* category, analogous to *v* in verb phrases or *n* in nominals. In that case, a derivation like that which we appear to find in verb phrases can be identified in complex prepositions, as well. As with complex verbs, these prepositions appear to incorporate a nominal which is then sandwitched between the prepositional root and a final suffix. If *p*, like *v*, is able to incorporate both the head of its own complement, and then the nominal head of the complement to P, then the underlying structure for (220a) will be (221a), with the derived structure (221b) formed by multiple incorporation.

(221) a. b.

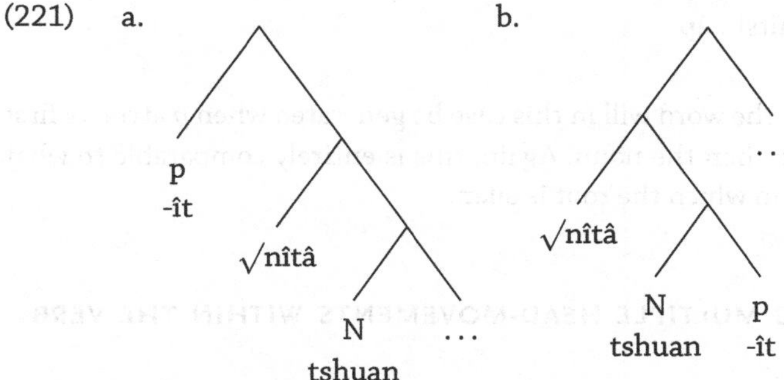

Quite often in Innu-aimûn, locative "particles" are formed with preposition-like initial and a nominal medial, but in which the *-ît* suffix is absent.

(222) a. mûshtishik[u] 'on the ice', nâtakâshik[u] 'near the shore on the ice', shekushik[u] 'under the ice', tshîtshishik[u] 'very close, right up against a cliff of ice'

b. pîtashuaim[u] 'inside a place, an enclosed object', pitshîkuenitsheu 'inside the mouth', (pîtakamît 'inside; indoors')

c. tshîtshit 'very near; close; on the edge', tshîtshikâm 'very close to shore', tshîtshîshipitam[u] 'right by the fire, right up against the fire'

Given the parity of morpheme ordering and meaning between the particles in (220) and those in (222), an analysis of the latter should not be too different from that seen in (221). In other words, we may suppose that for the (222) examples, too, the initial and medial elements should both be attracted by a higher head. That simply requires that we assume a silent allomorph of the *-ît* locative suffix in locative particles where it is not seen, and I will do so henceforth.

Alongside the silent allomorph of *-ît*, there is apparently a silent lexical preposition. In general, nouns in Innu-aimûn freely bear the *-ît* suffix if their function is locative. If *p* must take a locational complement, then the original structure for a word like *mitshuapît* 'at/in/to the house' will still include a prepositional root, as in (223).

(223)

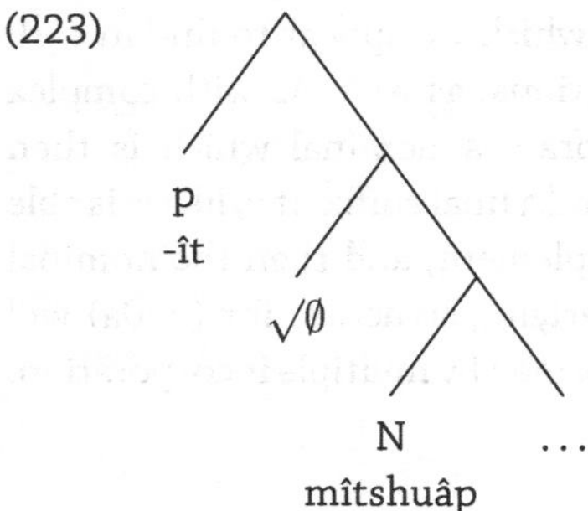

The actual form of the word will in this case be generated when *p* attracts first the silent root and then the noun. Again, this is entirely comparable to what is seen with verbs in which the root is silent.

4.7 INTERACTING MULTIPLE HEAD-MOVEMENTS WITHIN THE VERB PHRASE

As has now been shown, besides the multiple head-movement which is determined within the C-T phase, there are parallel multiple head-movement operations which take place inside vP, DP, nP, and pP. And these can each interact with the others, just as all of them can feed into the multiple head-movement at the C-T level. For example, a verb of motion, which always involves adjunction to vP, can include accommodated nouns, as well.

(224) a. *Atik^{u} nepaiakaniti, shaputue unuitatshishenakanu tshetshi eka uishautsheshinit.*
atîk^{u} IC/nipai-âkan-it-î, shâputue unuî-tâtshîsh-en-âkanû
caribou IC/kill-*V*-CJ.3-COND immediately out-tripe-*V*-PASS-3
tshetshî=ekâ=uîshau-tsheshin-it.
IRR=NEG=yellow-*V*-CJ.3
'When a caribou is killed, its guts are removed without delay to avoid having the meat around the intestines go yellow.'

b. *kushpitaishkueueu.*
kushpî-tâ-ishkueu-e-u.
bushwards-accompany-woman-*v*-3
'He goes into the bush with a woman.'

For the most part, accommodated nouns can appear in motion verbs only if the verb root is silent, as in (224a). This reflects how the language identifies which potential stem will provide the actual root. Since v assigns [NR] only to its adjacent sister, the presence of a locative initial, a visible root, and an accommodated medial becomes too much for the morphology to tolerate. But if the root is silent, then the medial can be assigned [NR] and the locative initial becomes the actual stem. In the exceptional case of (224b), the root *tâ-* must bear [NR] as a lexical property, so that it does not compete with *kushpî* in this way.

Such sentences arise naturally, given the derivation of the less complex verbs of motion. For example, (224b) will originate with *kushpî* and *ishkueu* (Goal and Theme arguments) as sisters within an exocentric complement to the root *tâ-*. With two [USTEM] features, v can attract *tâ-* and *ishkueu*. But as head-movement takes place only at the point of externalization of the syntactic structure, accommodation of *ishkueu* does not serve to break symmetry. Adjunction of *kushpî* to the verb phrase is still necessary. And at the C-T phase, T will attract *kushpî* and the complex verb *tâ-ishkueu-e*, deriving the actual form.

What is more, the locative initial need not be a simple monomorphemic element. Section 4.6 showed that locatives can be built up from smaller components, again employing multiple head-movement to do so. The same is true of locatives which appear at the front of a verb of motion, as illustrated in (225).

(225) a. *natakamassekaim*ᵘ.
nâtakâm-assek-aim-u.
towards-bog-V-3
'S/he goes towards the side of the muskeg by walking.'

b. *matapessekaim*ᵘ. (Drapeau 2014: p. 446)
matâp-essek-aim-u.
to.boundary-bog-V-3
'S/he arrives at a muskeg on foot.'

c. *apituakunatshinam*ᵘ.
âpîtu-âkun-atshinam-u.
halfway.into-snow-V-3
'S/he sinks halfway into the snow when walking.'

d. *Shekuakunepanu nutapan anite apitu.*
sheku-âkun-epan-u n-utâpân anite âpîtû.
underneath-snow-V-3 1-vehicle there halfway
'My snowmobile sank in the snow halfway along.'

Such forms arise if there is accommodation of the object of the preposition before the complex preposition raises and adjoins to the verb phrase to break symmetry. Within the complex preposition, it will be the attracting (silent) p which assigns [NR] to the accommodated nominals. This leaves v free to assign [NR] to its own sister, and the initial preposition ends up identified as the actual stem for the verb.

Resultative predicates are also displaced from their base position together with accommodation of a nominal object, as in (226). In most cases, such structures are constructed with silent verbal roots—whatever detailed lexical semantic information is not found in the Goal predicate comes from v.

(226) a. *kuishkuapitshepitam*ᵘ.
kuishku-âpitshe-pitam-u.
straight-stringlike-affect.quickly-3
'S/he straightens it (stringlike) quickly.'

b. *mikuapissam*ᵘ.
mîku-âpiss-am-u.
red-mineral-*v*-3
'S/he makes it become red (in the heat).'

c. *katshishumesheu.*
kâtshishu-mesh-e-u.
dried-fish-*v*-3
'S/he makes partly-dried fish.'

The incorporated medial may be a real noun or a classifier. In both cases, the base structure will be again be one in which the predicate originates as a sister to a nominal object. For (226a), for example, the base structure of the verb phrase will be (227).

(227)
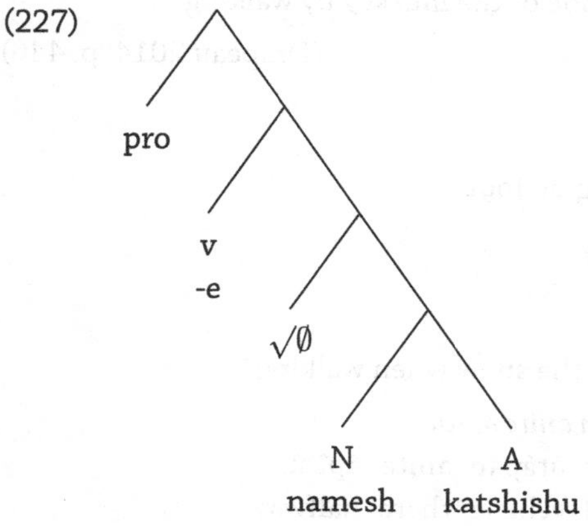

In order to break symmetry in the {n, A} structure, *katshishu* must adjoin at the phase edge. The accommodated nominal is displaced through normal multiple head-movement within the verb phrase. Head-movement operations cannot serve to break symmetry, of course, since they occur too late in the derivation, so movement of the predicate will always still be necessary. The combination of Goal adjunction and incorporation produces the structure (228) at the completion of the phase.

(228)

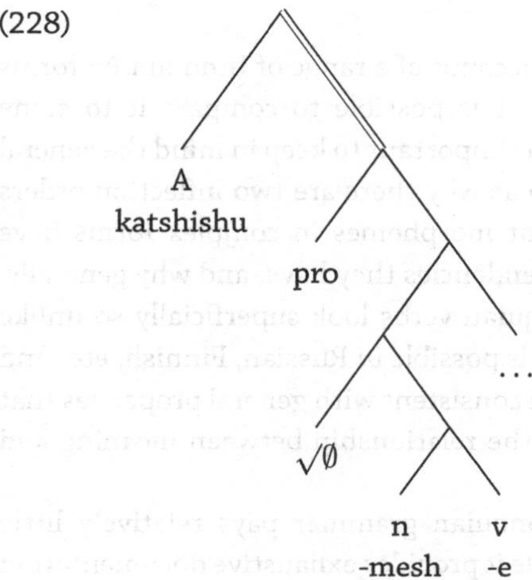

And once again, this structure will be subject to multiple head-movement at the next phase level, where T will attract both *katshishu* and *mesh-e* upwards.

Copular verbs can also accommodate a medial nominal or a classifier freely: (229).

(229) a. *apishtapeushu.*
apisht-âpeu-sh-u.
small-man-*V*-3
'He is a small man.'

b. *apishapissishu.*
apish-apiss-sh-u.
small-mineral-*V*-3
'It (anim, mineral) is small.'

Such noun accommodation structure patterns with the resultative verbs.

While the complex verbs formed from the interactions of multiple head-movement in different domains are remarkable linguistic creations, they are also simply what one expects to see if the grammar has the resources documented here. Relatively simple structures provided within one pocket of the grammar will always have the opportunity to combine with relatively simple structures within another. Ultimately, it cannot be a complex grammatical system that provides complex output, but a simple system employed recursively.

The general model developed here to characterize what we find in Innu-aimûn has that character.

4.8 NON-ALTERNATIVES TO MULTIPLE HEAD-MOVEMENT

Now that a multiple head-movement account of a range of Innu-aimûn forms and structures has been articulated, it is possible to compare it to some alternative approaches. In doing so, it is important to keep in mind the general questions raised by these forms, such as why there are two inflection orders in the first place, why the component morphemes in complex forms have the linear orders and hierarchical dependencies they have, and why generally, the morphological features of Algonquian verbs look superficially so unlike English, for example, but mirror what is possible in Russian, Finnish, etc. And the answer to these questions must be consistent with general properties that seem to hold universally concerning the relationship between meaning and base syntactic structures.

The traditional literature on Algonquian grammar pays relatively little attention to these questions, even while it provides exhaustive documentation of the contextual use and function of the different forms. Within the generative literature on Algonquian grammars, there are not so many studies which grapple with these questions either, although the number has been growing in recent years. For example, Brittain (1997) proposes that conjunct order inflection represents movement of the verb to C in Innu-aimûn, and I have adopted her proposal as one of the cornerstones of my analysis. Richards (2004) takes the opposite tack in his study of the two inflectional orders in Wampanoag, concluding that independent order verbs are in C and conjunct forms are in T. Unfortunately, the contexts in which conjunct and independent orders are used in Wampanoag are quite different from those of Innu-aimûn, which makes it difficult to compare arguments in detail. Embedded clauses in Wampanoag use the independent order freely, for example. And the focus of Richards's study is limited and avoids considering the interactions between internal change and conjunct inflection, or between the preverbs and the inflectional orders generally. Lacking comparative details, it is difficult to undertake a proper comparison of how the two orders should be analysed in these different languages, so I must defer a comparative analysis to later studies.

Instead, let us consider the general features of some obvious alternative approaches to the constructions which have been considered above. The goal of this final section will not be a comprehensive survey of the literature, but rather an summary of the difficulties which must be faced by analyses which eschew the idea of multiple head-movement. In addition, I briefly consider two specific recent approaches which attempt to treat some of the constructions examined here: Déchaine & Weber (2015a) and Roberts (2020). In all cases, it turns out that a multiple head-movement-based analyses is ultimately simpler and offers more empirical coverage of the facts.

4.8.1 Low verb approaches

To begin with, one might formulate the hypothesis that the verb does not raise from vP. This hypothesis is inherent in much of the earlier Algonquianist literature, starting with Bloomfield, for the simple reason that no concept of verb raising was available within the theoretical matrix of the time. But it remains a logical possibility, even within generative analysis. Given the apparent cross-linguistic correlation between rich inflection and verb raising (Koeneman & Zeijlstra 2012), this might seem unlikely, but let us consider it anyways. This hypothesis offers a simple explanation for the fact that the preverbs scope from left to right—if the verb does not raise, then if Innu-aimûn is systematically head-initial, then the preverbs might be supposed simply to occupy the head positions of a series of functional projections, i.e. TP, ModalP, AspP, etc. Under this type of analysis, the fact that preverbs are phonologically distant from the verb is ensured by their syntactic distance.[44]

Several critical problems arise almost immediately, however. The first is that the use of tense suffixes in the independent order is difficult to reconcile with a structure in which the verb remains low; then the content of T—both tense and agreement features—must somehow lower. (In conjunct order forms, this problem is moot for tense features, but remains for agreement features.) Affix-hopping is a potential mechanism to produce this result, but then any preverbs (*qua* heads) situated between T and the verb should either serve as the landing site for T or prevent affix-hopping from taking place. Neither result matches what actually happens, which is that independent order inflection appears on the verb whether or not there are preverbs in the verb complex.

The dependancies found between elements at the two extremes of the verb complex resist explanation in a model in which the verb remains low. These include iterative conjunct forms, discussed in section 4.1.3 and dubitative independent forms, discussed in 4.2.2. In these forms, the meaning or the morphological shape of the inflection cannot be determined without factoring

44. Goddard's (1988) treatment can be taken to represent an approach of this type, although the transformation terminology which Goddard employs is dated enough that his analysis does not translate directly into contemporary terms.

in what occurs in relatively high preverb positions. These dependances would have to ignore common locality constraints on semantic compositionality and morphological allomorphy, in a low verb analysis.

A model in which the verb does not raise offers no obvious explanation for the existence and properties of the two inflectional orders. Nor is the use of adverbial elements as a part of the verbal complex—either as preverbs or as verb initials—to be expected in this model.

Given Bloomfieldian premises, it is unsurprising that the semantic properties of complex verb clusters will receive only incomplete analysis in a model where the morphology is constructed entirely on the verb *in situ*. For example, consider how a lexicalist analysis of quantificational initials might work, given examples like (88b) and (88d), repeated.

(88b) *Meshta-tshishinniti, nikuss apu nita nishushkuat utashtisha.*
IC/mishta=tshishin-nit-î, ni-kuss apû=nitâ=nîsh-ushku-ât
much=be.cold-3.OBV-COND 1-son NEG=ever=two-wear-CJ.3
ut-ashtish-a.
3-mitten-P
'If it is bitter cold, my son never wears two pairs of mittens one on top of the other.'

(88d) *Shakuaki, nimishta-uapaten ushakai-pitakana anite nashipetimit.*
shâkuâki, ni=mishta=uâpât-en ushakai=pitakan-a anite
spring 1-many=see-1 cartridge.case-PL there
nâshipetim-ît.
shore-LOC
'In the spring, I see many cartridges on the shore.'

If *nish-* is attached as a prefix, pre-syntactically, then the lexical semantics must include an interpretive rule which allows such prefixes to apply to the syntactic object. This seems plausible.[45] But the preverb *mishta-* in (88d) should presumably be interpreted similarly, since it also applies to internal nominal arguments. Yet, as a preverb, *mishta-* will not be introduced into the structure pre-syntactically, so the rules interpreting quantifiers will have to be multiplied to cover both cases. With the multiple head-movement analysis, in comparison, the only semantics required are those which apply to quantifiers which appear within DP.

45. Branigan & Wharram (2019) propose a semantic analysis of Inuktitut antipassive constructions which has a character very similar to what a lexicalist approach to quantificational initials would require.

The Goal initials—locative or predicational—pose a different set of challenges. Once again, along with the process of combining the initial with the rest of the verb, specific rules of semantic interpretation will be required to ensure that the initial is related to an internal argument. In cases where the object is expressed as an incorporated noun, a distinct interpretive process will be necessary to treat the latter as Theme and the initial as Goal. Once again, the full range of possibilities will require more specific semantic rules than the multiple head-movement analysis does.

But even with the extra interpretive machinery, a lexicalist analysis will be unable to deal naturally with cases where the initial is "bumped" to the left of an aspectual head. If the verb is built by combining the initial with other components, then the resulting complex head should not be broken up by operations within or after the core syntax.[46]

In the end, if one starts from the position that verbs in Algonquian languages are not affected by syntactic movement, the structures which have received a unified treatment in the analyses developed here must instead be described by a grab-bag of more local, specific operations: non-local affix-hopping, morphological mergers without motivation, special semantic interpretation rules for medials, initial, and finals.

4.8.2 Compliant head-movement

Another possible general approach would rely on standard, compliant head-movement to form the full range of complex words which are attested in Innu-aimûn. There are clear advantages to such an approach, if it can be maintained. Compliant head-movement is certainly a real grammatical phenomenon, and one which plays a central role in building complex words in a host of languages (Baker 1988a).

For example, a derivation of the two orders in such an approach could start from base structures similar to what I have proposed, with preverbs situated between C and the verb phrase, and even perhaps including a Mood position immediately following C. Consider again example (42b), with the base structure for the complement clause in (230).

(42b) *Ni-tshissenimâu tshe-pûshit uâpanitî.*

ni=tshissenim-â-u	IC/kâ=pûshi-t	uâpanitî.
1=know-DIR-1	IC/FUT-leave-CJ.3	tomorrow

'I know that he will leave tomorrow.'

46. Infixation might constitute a counterexample to this claim, but aspectual heads in Innu-aimûn show none of the characteristics of incorporation operations.

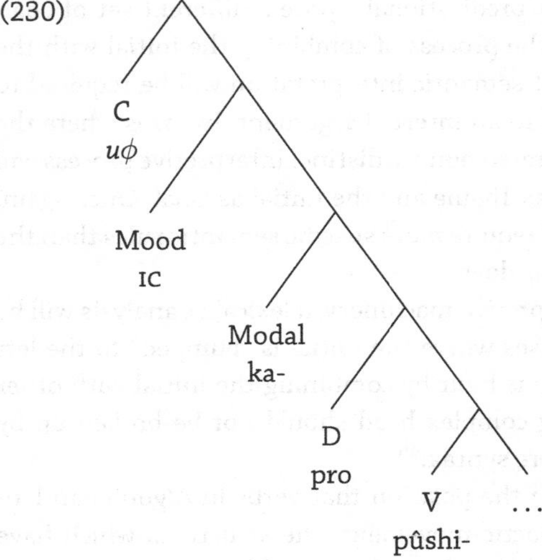

With this structure, a general account of the distribution of conjunct order forms can actually be derived along the same grounds as in the multiple head-movement model. And given the right distribution of [USTEM] features (or their equivalent in other models), the structure (230) could allow the verb to raise to *tshi=*, then *tshi-pûshi-* to IC, and finally IC-*tshi=pûshi* to C. If IC and *tshi-* are lexically specified as prefixes, and C as a suffix, then the linear order of morphemes in the resulting X^0 structure will be correct.

Although this approach may initially seem promising, it still faces a number of serious difficulties. The first is how to account for the realization of past tense inflection, which is prefixal in the conjunct order and suffixal in independent forms. If the verb simply raises to T in both orders, then there is no reason why T should be realized differently. In contrast, the multiple head-movement analysis ensures this result directly.

A second issue which compliant head-movement fails to accommodate is the disconnect between the internal structure of the verb complex and the structures which the morphophonology seems to require. Successive head-movement in the (230) context would produce an X^0 structure: (231).

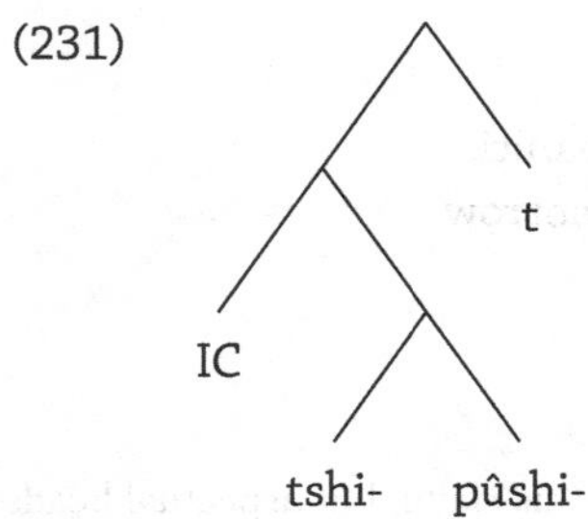

But the morphophonology requires that the suffix be within a morphological domain which includes the verb stem while the prefixes must be more distant, as Russell (1999) notes for the Plains Cree analog. For example, within the verb, adjacent vowels are broken up by introducing an epenthentic /i/, as discussed in section A.2.2. This process applies generally within the suffixal conjunct inflections, as in (232).

(232) a. *nipâiân* 'I sleep; CJ' (*nipâ-* 'sleep'; *-ân* 'CJ.1s')
b. *petuiekui* 'when you (pl.) listen (to him, her)' (*petu-* 'listen to'; *ek*ᵘ 'CJ.2p'; *-î* 'when')

But this process does not take place when adjacent vowels arise when preverbs and verbs combine. In the (233) examples, preverb *tshika* precedes a vowel-initial verb, and yet epenthetic /i/ does not appear.

(233) a. *Matiu tshika atashtau utassikumana.*
Mâtiu tshika=âtashtâ-u utassîkumâna.
Mathieu FUT=put.elsewhere-3 3-metal.trap-PL
'Matthew will move his traps to another place.'

b. *Eka natutamini, tshika utamautin.*
eka=natûtam-in-î, tshika=utâmau-t-in.
NEG=listen-CJ.2s-COND 2.FUT=hit-1⟩2-1
'If you don't listen, I will smack you.'

As noted in the analysis of Russian prefixes, a possible response to such a critique of a compliant head-movement analysis is that the structure of a verb complex can be adjusted in the morphology proper. More concretely, one might suppose that some "local dislocation" operations (Embick & Noyer 2001) could change the structure enough to ensure the correct surface forms. In particular, if suffixal inflections were lowered from their syntactic position, then the form of the inflection—and the phonological alterations it undergoes—might be determined in its derived lower position. To take a concrete case, consider the verbal complex in (234a). Under a compliant head-movement analysis, the verb's X^0 structure would be (234b) (after Vocabulary Insertion).

(234) a. *Apu tshi nipaian tepishkat.*
âpû=tshî=nipâ-iân tepishkât.
NEG=can=sleep-CJ.1s night
'I was not able to sleep last night.'

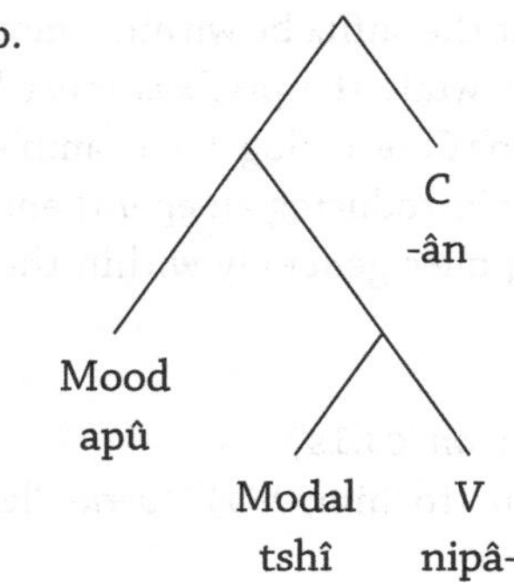

Given this structure, the suffix will be too far removed from the verb for /i/ epenthesis to take place, because this operation is word-level phonology. But if Local Dislocation can affect the hierarchical structure, then (234b) might be transformed to (235), and epenthesis would then take place, as required.

(235)

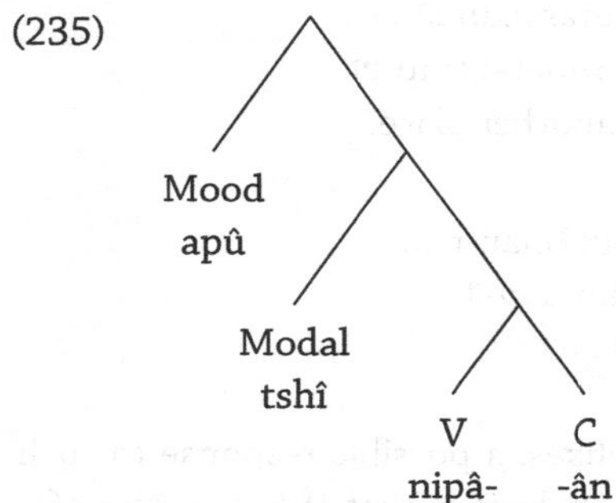

In fact, this solution does lead to the correct output, but at a cost. In order to match the surface facts, it must be stipulated that T is a suffix in the independent order but a prefix in the conjunct, and then that the former undergoes Local Dislocation while the latter does not. In effect, brute force mechanics is used entirely to match the data. The resulting analysis offers no insight into Innu-aimûn grammar, since the complexity of the data is matched by the complexity of the analysis.

My objection is not to morphological magic *per se*. The Distributed Morphology literature includes persuasive arguments that operations like *fusion* and *fission*, perhaps even *local dislocation* have a role to play in the derivation of complex morphological systems. And in fact, I have already suggested above that the evidential suffixes in conjunct order verbs are fissioned off from the agreement morphology in C. But in order to learn something about a grammar from the practice of analysis, these concepts must be used with care, and not simply to replicate the facts which a careful surface description already captures.

In contrast, an analysis based on multiple head-movement ensures the morphophonological domains which the data requires will be provided directly by the morphosyntax.

A further consequence of a compliant head-movement derivation is that the preverbs are necessarily buried within the derived structure. But there is evidence that some preverbs retain a degree of syntactic independance from their verbs. In textual transcriptions of natural language, preverbs and verbs are occasionally separated by other syntactic constituents, a pattern which is common in all Algonquian languages (Michelson 1917, Bloomfield 1946). Bannister (2005) provides the textual LITP examples of this in (236a); Oxford (2008) provides (236b) from the same textual source.

(236) a. *Apû tshî minekâsh nûkushiân.*
apû=tshî minekâsh nûkush-iân.
NEG=can long.time be.visible-CJ.1s
'I cannot show myself for long.'

b. . . . *shûk*ᵘ *uâ utshimâua nâtâukushit.*
. . . shûkᵘ IC/uî utshimâu-a nâtâukushit.
really IC/want chief-OBV be.met-CJ.3
'. . . since he really wants the chief to come fetch him.'

The grammatical status of examples like these is not entirely clear. This phenomenon is found more often in texts than in elicitation contexts. And while such examples certainly reflect speaker usage, speakers will often reject examples like this when asked to consider their well-formedness, in favor of sentences where the preverb cluster is not disrupted.[47] To the extent that these sentences are actually grammatical, however, there should be an explanation consistent with how the derivation proceeds. Since *minekâsh* in (236a) and *utshimâua* in (236b) are clearly words separate from the verbal complex, sentence of this type cannot be generated by simply adjoining the verb to a sequence of preverbs, and finally to T. What is more, since preverbs are buried within the complex head in any structure like (234b), they cannot themselves be displaced to the left of other words in the sentence. So examples like provide quite clear evidence that a compliant head-movement derivation will not provide a satisfactory account of the relationship between the verb, tense inflection, and modal preverbs.

Of course, the same reasoning entails that a successive alternative to a successive cyclic movement account will need to accommodate data like this. One possibility, assuming the structures defended here, is that an X^0 verbal constituent within the maximal X^0 verbal cluster is sometimes displaced to

47. Russell (1999) reports the same pattern of correction with Plains Cree speakers.

the right, past other phrasal constituents. For example, in (236b), the verbal cluster formed by multiple head-movement will have the structure (237), since conjunct C must attract T, the modal preverb *uâ* and the verb.

(237)

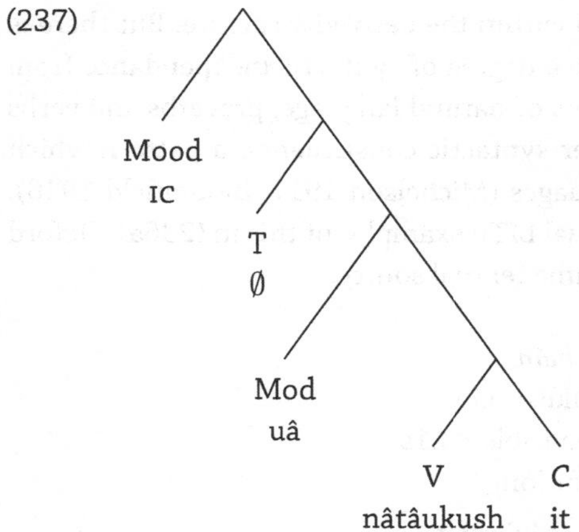

The bottom-most branch contains the verb and C, and this minimal constituent constitutes a legitimate word, whether or not it is combined morphologically with some number of preverbs. In (237b), it is this minimal constituent which is displaced to the right, past the nominal argument *utshimâua*. It remains unclear what purpose rightward movement serves in such a derivation, in part because of the difficulty in securing data of this sort, but the structure of the verbal complex is still such that it does not guarantee that such movement will be impossible. In contrast, any model in which the verb raises first to *uâ* and then to higher C-T functional positions should absolutely preclude movement of the verb which does not also displace the preverb.

A fourth problem for a compliant head-movement model of the Innu-aimûn verb complex is how to accommodate adverbials as preverbs and initials. This is probably the most challenging matter for such a model, in fact. As shown above, adverbials can serve as preverbs in a position between the verb and tense or modal preverbs. Consider the derivation which would be required for (80).

(80) *Tshitshue tshinaua nimassina, nasht apu tshi minu-pimuteian.*

tshîtshue	tshînâu-a	ni-massin-a,	nâsht
really	be.slippery-3p	1-boot-PL	at.all

âpû=tshî=minu=pimûte-iân.
NEG=can=well=walk-CJ.1s
'My boots are really slippery; I cannot walk properly.'

Suppose adverbs are adjuncts to vP. Since adverbial *minu-* is situated between modal *tshî-* and the verb, head-movement would have to first raise the verb up to the adjoined adverbial, in violation of the HMC. Afterwards, the adverb—now bearing the verb—would raise to *tshî-*, again violating the HMC. Only then could the correct form be derived by subsequent movement of the modal head up to the negator, and then to the conjunct suffix. But the double violation of the HMC means that this type of derivation lacks all plausibility.

The only way to avoid this conclusion is by stipulating that the adverbials which appear as preverbs are not adjuncts at all, but are instead combined with the verb through some sort of asyntactic derivational morphology or compounding operation. But this fails too, since the meaning of adverbial preverbs does not match what one would expect of a complex stem or compound. This is particularly clear in the case of relative root adverbials, since relative roots are anaphoric, and since anaphoric relationships cannot involve a subpart of a word (Postal 1969). In (84a), *îshi* takes its reference from demonstrative *eukuan*. Besides the anaphoric link, *îshi* provides no semantic substance which could be used to build a complex word.

(84a) *Nimushum eukuan eshi-ashtunit.*
ni-mushu-m eukuan IC/ishi-ashtuni-t.
1-father.in.law-POSS this.way IC/so=make.canoe-CJ.3
'This is how my father-in-law makes canoes.'

The anaphoric character of relative roots is still more evident in cases where the relative root refers to a wh-phrase, as in (84b).

(84b) *Tan ume nipa ishi-natukuitishun?* (Drapeau 2014: p. 305)
tân ume nipa=ishi=natuku-ît-îshu-n?
how this 1-would=so=cure-REFL-V-1
'How will I treat myself?'

Here *îshi* can only be interpreted as a variable bound by the wh-phrase. In that respect, (237) is comparable to sentence like (238), in which the pronoun is bound (indirectly) by the wh-phrase.

(238) Which niece decided that she likes walnuts?

The answer to a wh-phrase to which an adverbial relative root refers can also be an adverbial, in a location parallel within the clause, as in (239).

(239) — *Tan etikashuat Mani utauassima ka ishkuashuat?* — *Akuatikashueu.*
tân IC/it-ikashua-t Mânî ut-auâss-îm-a ka=ishkuashua-t?
how IC/so-burn-CJ.3 Marie 3-child-POSS-OBV PRET=burn-CJ.3
akuat-ikashu-e-u.
extremely-burn-DIR-3
'How much did Marie burn her child when she burned her? She burned her seriously.'

Since the meaning of the relative root is calculated only on the basis of the (non-local) syntactic context, it must not combine with the verb immediately in the base. But this means the problem of how to accommodate it within the verbal complex cannot be solved with compliant head-movement. In contrast, multiple head-movement accomplishes this with no additional stipulation.

The problem with adverbs is, of course, multiplied when quantificational, locative and predicational initials are considered. In fact, for these structures, the challenges faced by a compliant head-movement theory are far more daunting, since the option of treating such initials as base-generated above the verb is not available. Given their semantic functions, all of these must originate within the verb phrase and raise out. But then they cannot occupy a position to which a verb can raise through compliant head-movement. (This is exactly the problem which confounds compliant head-movement analyses of the Russian lexical prefixes, as Svenonius (2005b) recognizes.)

Within vP and nP, compliant head-movement fails to fully accommodate the facts of noun accommodation structures, as already noted above in section 4.4.1. Accommodated nouns cannot be attracted by the verb root, which appears in initial position, because of the extra "final" morphology which sometimes appears between the two. But without initial movement of an object to the verb root, there is no compliant account of noun incorporation.

Ultimately, then, compliant head-movement does not offer descriptive adequacy either. The Algonquian structures for which it works best require extra stipulation to work, and a number of common structures in these languages cannot fit into such an approach at all.

4.8.3 Remnant movement

For completeness, we can also consider a remnant movement theory as an option for analysis of the Algonquian verbal complex. It turns out that such a model fails rather quickly, given the issues already identified with models where the verb either does not raise or raises with compliant head-movement.

Given the size of the verbal complex, remnant movement would have to involve movement of quite large structures to order the component morphemes properly. Assuming the same base structures as above, prior to remnant movement, a sentence like (78b) will have a structure something like (241).

(78b) *Ueshkat innuat mukᵘ atusha ishi-nipaiepanat atikua.*
ueshkat innu-at mukᵘ atush-a ishi=nipâi-e-pan-at
formerly innu-PL only arrowhead-PL so=kill-DIR-PRET-3p
atîku-a.
caribou-OBV
'The Innu of old killed caribou only with arrowheads.'

(240)

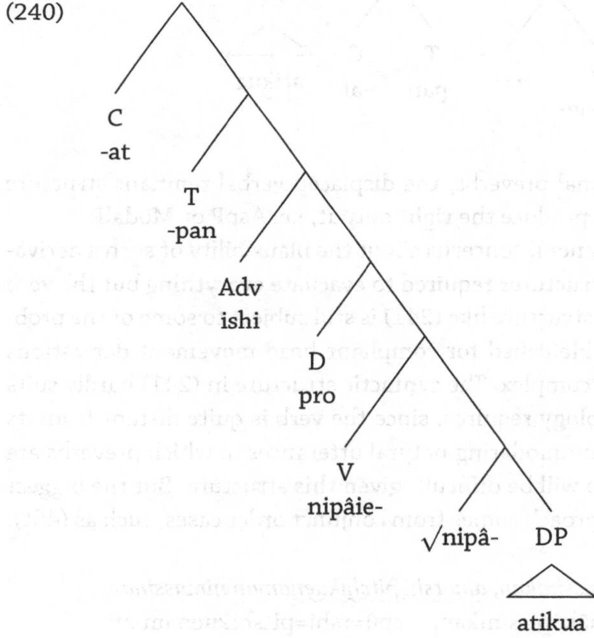

Remnant movement can produce the correct order of morphemes in the verbal complex if the object raises out of the verb phrase to some position between T and vP, and if vP then raises and merges with TP, and if affix-hopping then lowers C to T, producing (241).

(241)

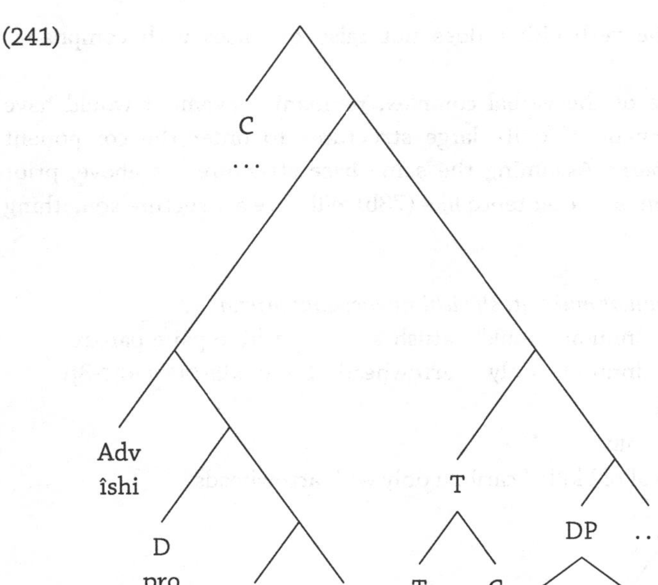

Of course, with additional preverbs, the displaced verbal remnant structure will have to be larger to produce the right output, i.e. AspP or ModalP.

Even putting aside general concerns about the plausibility of such a derivation, and of the extra structures required to evacuate everything but the verb from the verb phrase, a structure like (241) is still subject to some of the problems which have been identified for compliant head-movement derivations of the Algonquian verb complex. The syntactic structure in (241) hardly suits what the morphophonology requires, since the verb is quite distant from its suffixal inflections. Accommodating natural utterances in which preverbs are separated from the verb will be difficult, given this structure. But the biggest challenge to such an approach comes from conjunct order cases, such as (45f).

(45f) *Nunitan ninakapissinikan, apu tshi pitshikuenaman nimassina.*
n-unitâ-n ni-nâkâpissinikan, apû=tshî=pitshikuenam-ân
1-lose-1 1-thimble NEG=can=pleat-CJ.1s
ni-massin-a.
1-shoe-PL
'I mislaid my thimble; I cannot pleat my moccasins.'

For the second sentence in (241), the relevant structure before movement would presumably be (242).

(242)

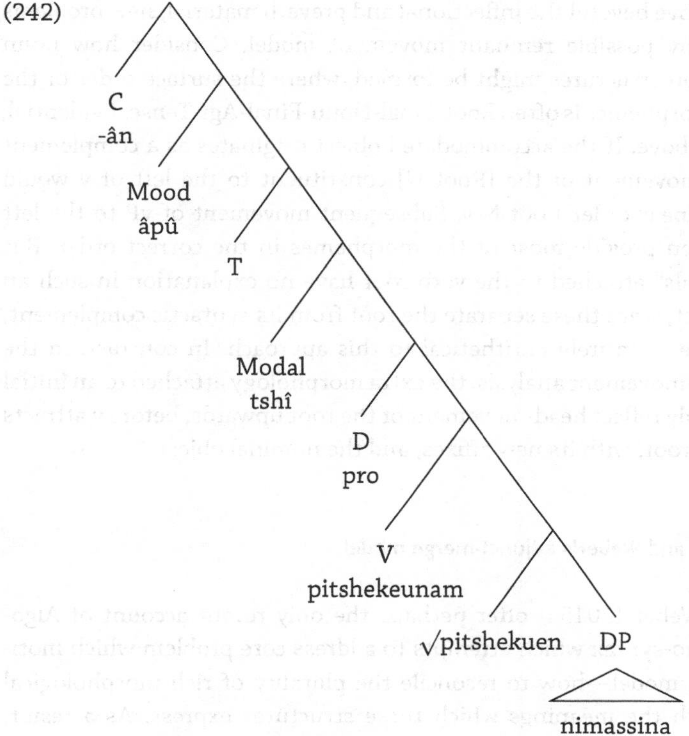

For such conjunct order forms, it will have to be a MoodP phrase which raises to Merge with CP, if conjunct inflection is indeed situated in C. But this means that the object must raise out of MoodP to escape the dislocated phrase. In turn, that means that there must be a new category between C and Mood which can host a specifier. But then C cannot select for Mood features, and it becomes impossible to capture the semantic dependencies between the conjunct suffixes and the content of Mood discussed above in section 4.2.2. These include the interative conjuncts and *tshetshî* irrealis clauses.

Quantificational initials are also a problem for a remnant movement account. Assuming that the quantifier originates as part of the object DP, it can only be separated with remnant movement if the object noun raises out of DP, and out of the verb phrase. If so, then the correct morpheme order could be ensured if the rest of DP—i.e. the quantifier—raises to be a specifier for the root, and then the complement of v raises to be a specifier in vP. These various phrasal movements will produce the correct order of morphemes, but at a cost. Movement of the noun from inside DP to a position outside the verb phrase is not attested elsewhere in the literature, to my knowledge, and it is unmotivated except as a way to get the right results.

Once we move beyond the inflectional and preverb material, new problems emerge for any possible remnant movement model. Consider how noun accommodation structures might be formed, where the surface order of the component morphemes is often Root-Final-Noun-Final-Agr-Tense/Evidential, as discussed above. If the accommodated object originates as a complement of the root, movement of the [Root N] constituent to the left of v would produce the linear order Root-N-v. Subsequent movement of vP to the left of T could then provide most of the morphemes in the correct order. But the extra "finals" attached to the verb root have no explanation in such an account. In fact, since these separate the root from its syntactic complement, their existence is entirely antithetical to this approach. In contrast, in the multiple head-movement analysis, the extra morphology attached to an initial verb root simply reflect head-movement of the root upwards, before v attracts both the verb root, with its new affixes, and the nominal object.

4.8.4 Dechaine and Weber's adjunct-merge model

Déchaine & Weber (2015a) offer perhaps the only recent account of Algonquian morpho-syntax which attempts to address core problem which motivates my own model—how to reconcile the plurality of rich morphological structures with the meanings which these structures express. As a result, there is some overlap in the structures posited in their model and what is proposed here.

Consider, for example the structure they propose for Plains Cree *miyo-n-am-(w)* 's/he improved it', which includes the initial *miyo-* 'good' and finals *-n* and *-am*. In the multiple head-movement model, such a verb is formed by displacement of the initial to adjoin to the verb phrase; Déchaine and Weber propose instead that *miyo-* is adjoined directly to vP with an "adjunct-merge" operation. In both models, the (temporary) effect is the same, since the result is category adjoined to the verb phrase which the morphophonology then interpret as the verbal root.

Similarly for nominal modifiers. Given a Blackfoot example like *i'naks-ipokaa-iksi* 'little child', Déchaine and Weber maintain that the modifier *inaks* 'little' is "adjunct-merged" to an nP containing *ipokaaa* 'child'. This matches the proposal made here, in section 4.5.1, where modifiers for nouns originate adjoined to nP.

So some comparable mechanisms are used in the two models to address similar questions about how syntactic structure gives rise to semantic interpretations. However, in contrast with the approach developed here, Déchaine and Weber do not offer a detailed explanation of how modifiers or "adjunct-merged" verb roots are combined into a single unit for the morphophonological interpretation. Nor do they consider the status of preverbs and how they interact with the complex verbs, on the one head, and the tense/evidential inflection, on the other. The characteristics which distinguish independent and conjunct inflectional orders are left unaddressed in this model, too. In short, while their model begins to address some of the issues which are covered here, it does not offer a complete enough picture of the overall morphosyntax to serve as a viable alternative to the multiple head-movement model.

4.8.5 Roberts's theory of multiple head-movement

Building upon an earlier presentation of the Innu-aimûn research reported here, Roberts (2020) proposes the following alternative analysis of multiple head-movement in Innu-aimûn. Roberts assumes that head-movement is constrained by Starke's (2001) *Featural Relativized Minimality*, whereby a potential goal for agreement and attraction to a probe can be skipped in favor of a more distant one as long as the more distant goal is more richly specified with the features driving movement. Schematically, in the context in (243), with F a probe and G and H, potential goals, F can agree with and attract H.

(243) $[\, F_{[X,Y]} \ldots G_{[X]} \ldots H_{[X,Y]} \ldots]$

In a case where F can attract multiple goals, the implication is that the more distant goal might be attracted first, followed by closer goals. For Roberts, this principle provides an account of the order in Italo-Romance clitic clusters, where the left-most clitic is the least richly specified one.

As Roberts shows, such an account can be extended to multiple head-movement if the right features are borne by the right displaced heads. In independent order verb clusters, for example, where T attracts preverbs and the verb, the right word order would result if verbs bear more features than preverbs, allowing T to attract a verb first and then a sequence of preverbs after.

This approach shares many of the empirical advantages with the approach to multiple head-movement developed here. The relationship between conjunct and independent orders might be derived in essentially the same manner—as a response to the presence of a Mood head between C and T. In the conjunct order, C would retain the features which attract heads, and C would then attract V first, and then preverbs, starting with the ones with the richest features.

On the other hand, if the order of head-movement operations is based on differences in how rich the feature specifications of the displaced heads are, then this implicates quite a large number of features in driving multiple head-movement. Assuming a maximally complex C-T phase structure like (244)—for a conjunct clause—V must be richer than Asp, which must be richer than modal preverbs (which must themselves be internally ordered by feature richness), and so on up.

(244) [C . . . Mood . . . T . . . Modal* . . . Asp . . . V . . .]

The problem with this implication is not the number of features which are required to make the multiple head-movement work out correctly, but rather that there is no independent motivation for the particularities. (Roberts does provide such motivation for the clitic cluster cases that he considers.) Consider Innu-aimûn sentences like (42a) or (7a), repeated here.

(42a) *Tshân tshissenitam tshe-tât uâpanitî.*
Tshân tshissenitam IC/ka=tât uâpanitî.
John know IC/FUT-be-CJ.3 tomorrow
'John knows that he will be there tomorrow.'

(7a) *Ni-pa tshî nipânâ-pan.*
ni=pa=tshî=nipâ-nâ-pan.
1=should=can=sleep-1-PRET
'I should have been able to sleep.'

For the verb in (42a) to be attracted to C before modal *tshi* and Mood IC, the verb must be richer than the modal, which is richer than IC, in turn. But the basis for claiming that *tshi* and IC have different levels of richness is simply the result which is desired here. And the problem is worse in (7a), where both modal preverbs are attracted by T (after the verb), but where the two have very similar semantic characteristics. Without an independent metric which establishes feature "richness" in such cases, an approach like the one Roberts proposes risks circularity.

A less abstract problem for this approach involves the derivation of verb complexes containing adverbial initials or preverbs, including relative root adverbials. This would have to have more features than higher preverbs, but fewer than the verbs they modify. But since the adverbial initials themselves are often verbal units adjoined to the verb phrase, it is difficult to see why they would be featurally less rich. And again, if the only answer is that this stipulation allows the model to obtain the right results, then this cannot count as a satisfactory alternative to a [STEM] valuation based model of multiple head-movement.

4.9 CONCLUSION

The survey of some morphosyntactic elements of Innu-aimûn grammar presented in this chapter is hardly comprehensive, but it should be clear at this point that multiple head-movement is indispensable. In fact, if there is a Sapirian "genius" to Algonquian grammars, the widespread use of multiple head-movement to form complex words seems like a fair candidate.

I have tried to demonstrate two things in this chapter. First, for a range of particular constructions, derivations involving multiple head-movement constitute a more viable form of analysis than any obvious alternatives. Such derivations allow us to make sense of a host of grammatical phenomena in this language, including the list in (245).

(245) a. the distribution of the inflectional orders
b. the position and distribution of negators
c. the interaction between elements at the extremes of the verb clusters
d. the derivation of *ka . . . uâ* verb forms
e. morpheme order in noun "incorporation" structures
f. the range of types of verb initials, in verbs with a silent root
g. parallels between tripartite verbs, nouns, and prepositions

The second thing follows from the first. Since multiple head-movement is triggered by multiple [uSTEM] features in C, T, v, D, n, and p, it only makes sense to conclude that this is the default character of the language. In other words, all categories which can trigger head-movement in Innu-aimûn may bear multiple [uSTEM] features, because all categories have a valuation timing parameter set to allow this. Innu-aimûn is a language for which the following holds for all categorial values of F: (246).

(246) Valuation of feature [uSTEM] in F precedes LA.

The significance of the generality of this parameter setting in Innu-aimûn, and in Algonquian languages generally, will be taken up in Chapter 5.

CHAPTER 5

Parameter setting with multiple head-movement

5.1 INTRODUCTION

The material covered in the last four chapters should now have made a persuasive case for a group of specific claims about the structure of Universal Grammar. Head-movement is a grammatical phenomenon which belongs to the system of externalization,[1] but one which is driven by prior, phase-level valuation operations, operating on [STEM] features. While the head-movement operation may operate identically in all languages, the [uSTEM] valuation operation produces different results, based on the values of the pertinent valuation timing parameters, which control whether [uSTEM] features are valued before or after labeling takes place. If labeling precedes [uSTEM] valuation, then the result is movement of a single head, subject (indirectly) to the HMC. But if labeling follows [uSTEM] valuation, then the result may be movement of multiple heads to a single probe position, resulting in what looks superficially like a "tucking-in" pattern of head-movement.

The evidence presented in these chapters should be sufficient to show that multiple head-movement is an essential part of the derivational systems in a range of languages. There is a substantial difference in how much each language resorts to multiple head-movement, though, since Innu-aimûn uses it everywhere and Russian, Finnish, English, etc. do so only in limited, specific grammatical contexts. To this point, it has been simply taken for granted that such variation can be reduced to differences in the settings for innate grammatical parameters. This assumption supposes that the concept of a suitable range of innate grammatical parameters is itself unproblematic. This

1. *Pace* Lechner (2006), Matyiku (2017), and other works cited there.

The Grammar of Multiple Head-Movement: A Comparative Study. Phil Branigan, Oxford University Press.
 DOI: 10.1093/oso/9780197677032.003.0005

supposition is challenged, however, by a substantial body of scholarly work and the challenges require some consideration if the analysis of multiple head-movement developed here is to be complete. For example, Newmeyer (2005) and Boeckx (2014) are properly skeptical of putative parameters for which no plausible ontological source is available. Clark (1988) shows that in many cases, there are multiple clusters of parameter settings which appear to be compatible with indivdual utterances in the linguistic environment of a child, so that no simple relationship between input data and individual parameter is feasible.[2]

My goal in this chapter will be more modest, however. Rather than confronting the full range of thorny issues in the theory of parameters, I focus on a particular subset of issues where the analysis of multiple head-movement can offer new perspectives. (Many of the other issues are already addressed—successfully in my opinion—in Biberauer et al. (2013) and Roberts (2020).) The specific characteristics of derivations which employ multiple head-movement offer new opportunities to proof theories of how parameter setting might be accomplished by children on the basis of the primary linguistic data (PLD) to which they are exposed.

In particular, the clear absence of isomorphy between the valuation timing parameter(s) which enable multiple head-movement and the linguistic forms which result[3] provides a novel testbed to examine how the PLD can be integrated in the parameter setting process. It will turn out that no direct, fully deterministic role for the PLD is feasible. Instead, I will conclude that the parameter setting process must include a stochastic core. The PLD provides data which is used by the learning process in two ways. First, it informs the learning process when it is trending in the right direction. Second, it sometimes provides impetus for the learning process to initiate a more richly articulated parameter space than the one it started with.

5.2 HOW EXISTING MODELS REACT TO THE PLD

The literature includes two broad approaches to the question how parameter setting makes use of the PLD. In what we can call *stochastic* models, random changes to parameter settings are triggered when the existing grammar is unable to successfully process utterances which appear in a child's linguistic environment. Eventually, after enough attempts, the learning algorithm must reach a set of parameter settings which succeed in processing enough

2. Fodor (2001) and Sakas & Fodor (2012) provide careful elucidation of the implications of this discovery, as well as a summary of many of the responses offered in the existing literature.
3. Dresher (1999) refers to this as the "Epistemological Problem" in learnability.

future utterances that they can be accepted as part of the final state of the mature grammar. Models which this general character include Gibson & Wexler (1994), Niyogi & Berwick (1996), Clark (1988), and Yang (2002).

In deterministic models, individual parameter settings are established by a relationship between the form of (some portion of) the utterances to which a child has access and a parameter setting decision. In other words, the data in some expressions provides enough information to immediately identify the correct setting for a specific parameter, and once the child has been exposed to enough of the right types of data, all parameters will be set correctly. This approach is advocated in Dresher & Kaye (1990), Dresher (1999) and extended in Westergaard (2009), Holmberg & Roberts (2014), Biberauer et al. (2013), and Roberts (2020).

To keep the discussion more focused, I will focus on how two specific models compare: Roberts's (2020) deterministic approach and Yang's (2002) stochastic one. Each of these builds on prior research to develop a learning model which avoids problematic features of earlier approaches. As such, they constitute reasonable examplars for how well deterministic or stochastic approaches can accommodate the grammatical patterns uncovered in the earlier chapters.

5.2.1 Triggers in Roberts's (2020) model

Roberts's model starts with the parameter ontology in (1).

(1) a. Terminal elements in a syntactic structure—elements of the lexicon—may initially be underspecified for Formal Features (FFs) to which the syntactic derivation is sensitive. Whether or not a specific such FF is present or absent constitutes a syntactic parameters. Parameter setting is a matter of filling in a FF's underspecified content, where required by the need to find a well-formed representation of expressions in a child's linguistic environment.

b. The existence of a parameter is dependent on a trigger which "expresses" it. An expression of a parameter is a substring of an expression in the linguistic experience of a child which can only be given a well-formed representation only if the parameter is present.[4]

The idea that parametric choices originate in underspecified formal features is a natural extension of the Borer-Chomsky Conjecture (Borer 1984, Chomsky 1995), which suggests that variation might be restricted to properties of individual syntactic heads. It is certainly possible to think of the Valuation

4. Roberts's formulation is drawn from Sakas & Fodor's (2012) characterization of "unambiguous triggers."

Timing parameters in such terms. (Indeed, it is difficult to think of syntactic parameters which cannot be characterized in such a way.) For example, the Northern Swedish dialects which allow for adjective incorporation (from section 2.6.3 must allow the definite article affix to value its [uSTEM] feature before labeling takes place within the DP phase. This is what allows multiple head-movement to collect adjoined adjectives and the noun together with D. The formulation of such a parametric choice provided in Chapter 2 would be (2).

(2) Valuation of [uSTEM] in D follows LA (F).

But this can certainly be framed as a formal feature of the D head. Assuming D is a phase head, the timing of operations in its phase must be controlled somehow, and this can be taken to be an underspecified property which will be necessary to flesh out for any phase head, as (3). Let us abbreviate this hypothetical feature as FF^{MHM} (for *formal feature for multiple head-movement*).

For Roberts, the absence of a parametric FF corresponds to the default, unmarked parametric value. Assuming binary parametric choices, this means that every parameter setting is actually a matter of the presence or absence of the FF involved. If we were to interpret a valuation timing parameter for multiple head-movement as such privative feature, then the absence of the feature FF^{MHM} would imply a specific ordering is the default for phase-level operations. This raises two immediate questions. Which of the two orderings is the default, and why? The fact that there is no obvious basis for an answer to either question is a matter of concern, but let us suppose that answers may be found. This will allow us to continue examining the suitability of this model for the multiple head-movement patterns. By convenient *fiat*, let us assume that that the default order, which obtains when no FF to the contrary is present, is the order in which [uSTEM] valuation precedes the Labeling Algorithm. Addition of the [uSTEM] valuation timing FF to a phase head will ensure that LA precedes valuation of [uSTEM] features within that phase.

Now consider how a deterministic, trigger-based model might accommodate the analyses in Chapters 2–4, beginning with the Innu-aimûn case. The end result must be that FF^{MHM} is assigned broadly to affixal categories in this language, so that C, T, v, etc. may trigger multiple head-movement. This means that triggers must be available in the PLD which justify assigning this feature to heads which (initially) lack it. More precisely, the PLD must include utterances containing substrings which can only be given a well-formed representation only if FF^{MHM} is present.

What might such triggers look like. Multiple head-movement allows a host of structures in Innu-aimûn to be generated, but many of them might also be generated by grammars which do not allow multiple head-movement. Utterances which can be generated with compliant head-movement alone cannot serve as triggers, so we should consider only those which cannot. Complex verb complexes and nominal structures in which an adjoined X^0 category is attracted by a higher head must involve multiple head-movement, so these are possible triggers which could lead to the assignment of FF^{MHM}. Examples like (3) belong to the right class of utterances, because each require multiple head-movement in their derivation.

(3) a. *Etien kushpitaieu ukussa tshetshi tshishkutamuat tshe ishi-natauniti.*
Etien kushpî-tâ-ie-u u-kuss-a
Etienne bushwards-accompany-DIR-3 3-son-OBV
tshetshî=tshishkut-amu-ât tshe=ishi-natau-niti.
IRR=teach-V-CJ.3 IC/FUT=so-hunt-CJ.3OBV
'Etienne takes his son in the bush to teach him how to hunt.'

b. *Amishk^{u} pimauneu ushkuaia.*
amishk^{u} pim-aun-e-u ushkuai-a.
beaver along-aquatic.carry-DIR-3 birch-PL
'A beaver is transporting birch trees in the water.'

c. *Nika shakassinepatan nitassik^{u}.*
ni=ka=shakassin-epata-n ni-tassik^{u}.
1-FUT-fill-V-1 1-pail
'I will fill my pail (with water).'

d. *Atshipeshaim^{u} mitshuap.*
atshi-peshaim-u mitshuâp.
different-paint-3 house
'S/he painted the house a different color.'

The problem in each case is that even such unambiguous "trigger" data is insufficient, as long as parameters are set one at a time. These types of structures are generated by a combination of adjunction of the Goal to vP and multiple head-movement. Without the former, the latter has no effect. And the adjunction itself is triggered by the need to break symmetry, because this is the only way for symmetry to be broken in the Theme+Goal exocentric structures within the verb phrase. So both the [uSTEM] valuation timing parameter and the parameter which controls how ϕ features interact with labeling must be set correctly to allow these data to be derived. No direct causal relationship between the data and parameter setting which enables multiple head-movement is defensible here.

The problem here is a case of the general issue which Clark (1988) already identified. Clark asked how a given set of parameters might respond to a failure to accommodate a new utterance, assuming "error-driven" learning. As Clark (p. 94) observes, in such circumstances "there is immediate information that at least one parameter in the hypothesis grammar is set to an incorrect value, but the learner may not be able to detect which parameter is at fault." As such, the learning procedure can make progress only if it can somehow consider all possible parameter settings at once to find a complete grammar which will successfully accommodate any new utterance data provided by the linguistic environment.

The computational resources necessary to compare full grammars—complete sets of parametric choices—will depend on the number of parameters which must be set. Assuming *n* independent binary parameters, the size of the parametric space to be considered will be 2^n. If there are only five parameters to set, then the learner must only consider thirty-two possible grammars to find one which works. With twenty-five parameters, though, 33,554,432 (2^{25}) will need to be considered. The former task can evidently be accomplished in a short period of time; it is less obvious that the latter can. And the potential intractability of the search for the correct grammar increases exponentially with a still larger set of parameters.

As Clark also notes, given any grammar with sufficient complexity—a large enough set of parameters—it is essential that a learner should have "some means of moving towards the target, based on experience" (p. 95). But the PLD in Innu-aimûn does not itself ensure that the learner will move far enough towards the target, in the absence of unambiguous triggers.

5.2.2 The role of PLD in Yang (2002)

Yang also starts from the assumption that UG provides an initial set of parametric choices which are to be fixed to form a mature grammar.

Yang's stochastic model does not suffer from the same problems, because it does not assume that the PLD provides any triggers (in the sense of Dresher (2016) or Roberts (2020)). Instead, Yang supposes that parameter settings are evaluated holistically, based on whether they allow a successful parse to be provided for an utterance provided in the PLD. It is not the fit of a single parameter which is evaluated for an utterance, but the fit of an entire parameterized grammar. The mechanism by which this takes place is provided by the premises in (4).

(4) *Parameter setting in Yang's model*

a. evaluation of parametric fit begins with selection of a full range of parametric choices, initially set arbitrarily.
b. the selected array of parametric choices is used to attempt to parse an utterance

c. if the parse is successful, each parametric choice in the array is recorded (individually) as successful
d. if the parse fails, each parametric choice is recorded as having failed
e. parametric choices with a record of success are *more likely* to be selected in subsequent evaluations than those which fail more often

As Yang shows, the effect of this algorithm is that over time, individual parametric choices which match the adult target language must emerge as the only option.[5] No one parameter need be associated with any substring trigger—instead, clusters of correct parameters will ultimately be reinforced by the appearance of "unambiguous triggers" in the utterances of the PLD.

So, for example, if a child is applying this algorithm in a Japanese PLD environment, then selection of a head-final value for the *head parameter* (however that is formulated), will lead sometimes to a successful parse, depending on how well suited the other parameter values are to the utterance in question, while selection of a head-initial value will rarely do so. The effect over time will then be that the head-final value for this parameter becomes more and more likely, until it is the only option considered by the learning process in formulating new tentative grammars. When all the correct parameter values have been favored sufficiently, then the mature grammar can be said to have been acquired.

Consider the Innu-aimûn verb forms with locative or predicational initials, for example, such as (5)–(6).

(105b) *Etien kushpitaieu ukussa tshetshi tshishkutamuat tshe ishi-natauniti.*
Etien kushpî-tâ-ie-u u-kuss-a
Etienne bushwards-accompany-DIR-3 3-son-OBV
tshetshî=tshishkut-amu-ât tshe=ishi-natau-niti.
IRR=teach-V-CJ.3 IC/FUT=so-hunt-CJ.3OBV
'Etienne takes his son in the bush to teach him how to hunt.'

(110b) *Nika shakassinepatan nitassik*^{u}.
ni-ka=shakassin-epata-n ni-tassik^{u}.
1-FUT-fill-V-1 1-pail
'I will fill my pail (with water).'

5. Yang also discusses the emergence of grammatical variation which persists in the adult grammar when a given parameter does not succeed enough to become inevitable. This possibility does not affect the analyses discussed here, so I will not consider it further.

The parameter settings specifically required to allow *kushpitaieu* and *nika shakassinapetan* to be generated are the timing parameter which allows T to value [uSTEM] before labeling takes place and the parameter which prevents nominals from bearing the ϕ features necessary to provide a label. The former allows multiple head-movement; the latter forces symmetry to be broken by moving the predicate rather than the nominal Theme, so that it adjoins to vP before multiple head-movement occurs. In Yang's model, the appearance of either of these examples in the PLD will trigger formation of an array of parametric choices which may include the correct settings for these to parameters, but which often will not, at least early in the learning process. If either parameter is set wrong, then both parametric choices will be marked as failures. But so will arrays in which both parameters are set wrong. The only circumstance in which a record of success can be built up (for such utterances) will be when both parameters are set correctly. So over time, the correct settings must be preferred, together with the other parameter settings which Innu-aimûn actually requires.

Yang has shown that this general process can ensure a successful acquisition path from the initial state to a mature grammar, and that this model does not suffer from the same vulnerability to *local maxima* (Gibson & Wexler, 1994) as other models do. But the model relies, as it stands, on the existence of an initial array of parameters which is rich enough to characterize all syntactic variation. In other words, it entails a full set of innate microparameters, each of which is an independent component of UG.

But while the correct parameter settings are guaranteed to emerge eventually in this model, there is no (mathematical) guarantee that they will emerge quickly. While Roberts's model has difficulty in dealing with grammars where there is no direct relationship between triggers and individual parameters, it at least captures the actual speed of the acquisition of syntactic parameters. Yang's model—like other stochastic approaches—ensures that the course of acquisition will be slower, the more parameters the grammar includes. Since the algorithm must construct each new trial array of parametric choices by setting values for each individual parameter, the number of potential grammars increases exponentially as the number of grammars increases. With three parameters, there are eight potential grammars to choose between (assuming binary parameters). With twenty parameters, there will be 2^{20} (=1,048,576) grammars. And so on. This does not affect the mathematical result: a single mature grammar can be isolated by this process no matter how many parameters there are. But it should be clear that a larger number of potential grammars will take longer to filter, and that the quantity of utterances which must be processed will be proportionately larger as well.

For the timing parameter which enables multiple head-movement, one must expect progress towards the correct setting to be quite slow in this model. A large proportion of utterances will be susceptible to parsing with either settings of the parameter, because compliant head-movement can enable a parse when there is only verbal inflection to consider or if the head parameter allows modal or aspectual preverbs to be head-initial and T, head-final. And for the disambiguating "trigger" structures like (3)–(4), the fact that two crucial parameters must be set right at the same time means there are more ways to fail than to succeed. And yet Innu children do learn their language, and within the normal time frame.

5.2.3 Harmony in parameter space

The problem of exponential growth in parametric search space follows from two observations. The first is that descriptive adequacy appears to require a surprisingly large number of (micro-/nano-)parametric choices to be available, simply to accommodate the many ways that languages can differ morphosyntactically (Kayne 2000, and many others). The second—already discussed above—is that parameters cannot be set one at a time, but must generally work together to approach the demands of the data in the PLD. The latter seems inescapable, but the former is susceptible to qualification. While grammars can certainly differ in many respects which call for microparametric treatment, it is also the case that individual grammars tend not to show a random assortment of parameter settings of a single type.

For example, there appear not to be any languages in which a random selection of phrasal categories show head-initial ordering while the (random) remainder show head-final ordering (Biberauer et al. 2017). The distribution of head-initial and head-final structures can be fairly complex within a language, but the choices are not randomly distributed. Nor are languages found in which a random set of verbs raise to inflecting, affixal T, while the rest require affix-hopping to take place. And I know of no languages in which a nominative-accusative Case system is used for a random assortment of tense/aspect/ϕ features in T, while ergative-absolutive Case is used for the remaining clusters of such features in T. If parametric space were entirely composed of standalone parameters, each set in isolation from the rest, then such languages or grammars should be commonplace. Instead, however, grammars seem more often to harmonize parametric choices among like categories (Greenberg 1963, Hawkins 1983, Roberts 2020). So even though languages can show mixed head-initial/-final properties, it tends to be the case that the "extended verbal projections" (v, Asp, T) pattern alike. (Biberauer, Holmberg & Roberts 2014). And split ergative Case systems are certainly common, but the split is normally along predictable lines, such as past *vs.* present, speech act participants *vs.* 3rd person, etc.

The two approaches to parameter setting examined above (Roberts (2020) and Yang (2002)) differ in the resources they provide to model such parametric harmonization patterns. Yang's approach has little to say about these.[6] I take this to be a significant limitation of this model. Not only is parametric space prone to explosive exponential growth, but the atomistic character of that space seems not to correspond well to what is actually observed.

In contrast, Roberts's model is explicitly designed to capture parametric harmony as a fundamental property of grammar. It is worth examining how this theory works in general to characterize such patterns before we turn to the specific issue of harmonic parameter settings in grammars allowing multiple head-movement.

As discussed already, for Roberts, parameters are FFs which are either present or absent in the featural makeup of individual lexical items. This ensures that any micro-/nano-parametric setting is formulable. The tendency of grammars to express same parametric choice across an array of grammatical heads must then be do to a property of the learning process which prefers to assign the same FF to lexical items belonging to the same class. Roberts calls this "Input Generalization," formulated (p. 93) as (5).

(5) *Input Generalization (IG)*
If a functional head H_i of class C is assigned FF_i, assign FF_i to all functional heads $H_1 \ldots H_n$ in C.

The scope of IG depends on the identity of class C in (5), and this is where the PLD plays its second role in this model. (The first is that a given FF_i is assigned at all only if the PLD contains appropriate trigger data.) Initially, C will include all pertinent lexical items in the language. However, if the PLD provides triggers which are incompatible with FF_i (after FF_i has been introduced), then the learning procedure "retreats" from applying IG with full generality. Instead, it splits C, first identifying a set of heads which must not bear FF_i, and then taking the complement of this set as the new set C to which IG may apply for FF_i.

Exposure to subsequent triggers incompatible with FF will have the same effect, removing new subsets from the set of lexical elements to which IG applies. In short, starting from the premise that FF_i is assigned to all lexical items, successive exceptions to this premise are identified and hived off from this initial set until no further exceptions are found, at which point the various parametric values of FF_i are presumably accurately set.

As Roberts shows, this approach has advantages which go well beyond the typological generalizations it enables. In particular, it provides a means to drastically reduce the (initial) parametric search space which the learning procedure must traverse, because IG ensures that many parametric choices

6. In contrast, Yang's (2016) *Tolerance Principle* is carefuly formulated to account for comparable rule harmony in morphological patterning.

need not be made individually. Unless the PLD prevents it, a single trigger may lead to a parametric value being set and generalized widely, perhaps even everywhere in the grammar.

At first, Roberts's model appears to be a good candidate for the challenge of modeling how multiple head-movement might be acquired. It is a parametric model, and it provides the resources to distinguish between "macroparametric" expression of a parameter setting and less pervasive expressions of the same grammatical notion. Let us therefore consider how the various multiple head-movement patternings might look in such an account. We will see that this model offers real advantages in understanding how some of the multiple head-movement languages might be acquired. What is more, some broad predictinons which this model entails seem accurate, if diachronic stability is considered. But some limitations of this approach will be identified, and this will lead to a rethinking of how the parameter space should be conceptualized to better fit the data.

First, the parameter(s) in question must be characterized as emergent features, which may or may not be introduced into particular grammars, depending on the evidence available in the PLD. Roberts supposed that UG may provide default mechanisms to control the derivation when no actual parametric features are found. For example, head-initial word order might be a default—as in Kayne (1995)—when no head parameter features are found in a given grammar. Along the same lines, one might suppose a default timing of labeling operations and valuation operations, where the former precedes the latter. In that case, head-movement would be compliant as a general rule, and positive evidence would be required to introduce multiple head-movement into the grammar. This might be sufficient for many languages. In French, for example, where no multiple head-movement constructions are obviously found, a default expression of the timing choices might be enough.

For Algonquian languages, multiple head-movement is pervasive, and "macroparametric." The implication is that children will have access to data which drives the emergence of a general timing parameter which reverses the default, by ordering [uSTEM] valuation before labeling. This parameter will be realized as a feature, borne by all "relevant" heads. Heads bearing [uSTEM] features will be the relevant ones, one would imagine.

Data which could ensure the emergence of such a feature will be readily available in an Algonquian language. In Innu-aimûn, for example, the noun accommodation patterns discussed in Chapter 4, section 4.4.1 cannot be processed without multiple head-movement being a part of the derivation, so the appearance of such forms in the PLD might trigger the necessary response by the LAD. Other triggers for such a feature might come from the different positions in which tense is expressed in conjunct and independent clauses, where the former employs a preverb and the latter, a suffix, even though the verb clearly raises in both types of clauses. As shown in Chapter 4, the complexities of these difference can only reflect the application of multiple head-movement, so such data might also serve to ensure that an appropriate parametric feature emerges in Innu-aimûn grammar.

In Roberts's model, the principle of Input Generalization applies once a feature is introduced by the LAD, providing a new default setting for the grammar in question. In an Algonquian language, the consequence is exactly what one would want, as Input Generalization will ensure that *all* (relevant) heads will employ the same value for the timing parameter, allowing multiple head-movement across the board. The implication is that acquisition of multiple head-movement patterns in Innu-aimûn should proceed very quickly, and minimal data should be sufficient to lead a child a long ways towards a full grammar, at least in this grammatical domain.

In contrast, in a language like French, where multiple head-movement appears to play no role in the derivation, the presence of a single trigger which requires that labeling preceded [uSTEM] valuation should be sufficient to establish the lack of FF^{MHM} from all heads in the language, given Input Generalization.

Roberts's model covers how the correct valuation timing settings might be established for Innu-aimûn, on the one hand, or French, on the other. In both cases, the generality of the correct setting ensures that any information available in the PLD which points in the right direction will quickly allow the right parameter conclusions to be drawn throughout the grammar.

As for the specific data which might justify a parametric choice in French on Innu-aimûn, possible "triggers" are fairly easy to find. For French, the fact that heads readily arise past their modifiers is significant. Conventional verb movement to T can be seen in the placement of adverbs and in the "complex inversion" construction. Noun movement past adjectives is also commonplace (Valois 1991). In both cases, only the correct setting where LA precedes [uSTEM] valuation will accommodate the data, as long as other parameter settings are also set correctly.[7]

As for the Innu-aimûn situation, the appearance of tense/agreement inflection on the verb inside preverbs over which tense scopes may serve as a trigger, although the possibility of a more complex competing grammar in which T is sometimes an affix, sometimes a prefix and morphological rebracketing occurs cannot be discounted. Noun-accommodating verbs, nouns and locatives might also count as triggers, but the same caveat obtains—if the learning procedure permits this, a grammar might be considered in which roots can incorporate

7. As an anonymous reviewer notes, not all modifiers are raised past in French. High adjectives in DP and high adverbs in the clause are not skipped freely. But the existence of some modifiers which can be skipped is sufficient to provide evidence for compliant head-movement in this language.

nouns to the right, while categorizing v, n, and p attract roots which attach to the left.

But adjuncts which appear *within* a complex verb have no analysis beyond what a multiple head-movement model provides. Verbs with adverbial initials, or with Theme-oriented locative or predicational initials can therefore be identified as triggers with some certainty. And in Roberts's model, one trigger type is enough, since Input Generalization ensures that the ripples from a single grammatical context will spread throughout the grammar.

For these fully harmonic languages then, Roberts's approach is both intuitive and empirically defensible. However, when we consider languages in which the use of multiple head-movement is confined to specific contexts, difficulties arise. The general problem is that Input Generalization should ensure that multiple head-movement is possible in a wider range of contexts that are actually possible.

Consider the Finnish polar question/answer structures, as in (6), repeated from page 61. In this language, a single auxiliary raises to C in a polar question, but multiple auxiliaries may do so in a polar answer, often together with TP ellipsis. In Chapter 2, it is concluded that multiple head-movement is possible only for the (silent) polar answer C. For its interrogative counterpart, valuation of a [uSTEM] feature must follow labeling.

In Roberts's model, such a grammar must be acquired as follows. First, the presence of a formal feature which enables Val([uSTEM]) > LA must be motivated by a trigger in the PLD. The trigger in this case must be the polar answers themselves, either with or without TP ellipsis. Then Input Generalization must be prevented from assigning the same FF to all other affixal heads in Finnish, and a smaller subset must be identified to which Input Generalization can apply. This is where the notion of a parameter hierarchy comes into play. For Roberts, the trajectory through parameter space necessitates considering larger sets before smaller ones. For example, the natural class {C, T, v} will be considered as a possible ("mesoparametric") group to which Input Generalization can apply before T or C alone is hypothesized as the subset to which the appropriate FF should be assigned.

Presumably the PLD in Finnish will provide evidence to allow the procedure to rule our T or v as heads which can bear FF^{MHM}. But here a problem arises. Only the polar answer C should end up with FF^{MHM} by this procedure, but there must be an earlier point at which all affixal members of the C category are considered. And Input Generalization will ensure that FF^{MHM} is assigned to C generally unless evidence is found which motivates a further division of the search space into individual members of C. But it is not clear what such evidence would look like for polar questions. Consider (6), repeated from page 62.

(6) a. — Onko Matti koskaan halannut käydä Roomassa?
has Matti ever wanted to.go to-Rome
'Has Matti ever wanted to go to Rome?'

b. — On halunnut käydä.
has wanted to.go
'Yes, he has.'

The *-ko* complementizer in (6a) is affixal and attracts an auxiliary. The same is true of the silent polar answer C in (6b), which must bear FF^{MHM}. Critically, however, the polar answer C is not required to bear multiple [uSTEM] features—it can bear a single one, as an acceptable option.

Suppose, therefore, that the learning algorithm were to posit the natural class of polar C as the group which should all be assigned FF^{MHM}. This hypothesis would appear to be consistent with the available data, since it would work for polar answers, whether C attracts one or more auxiliaries, and it would also accommodate polar questions in which C attracts only once. And even though the PLD will not contain utterances which require multiple head-movement to *-ko*, the absence of such data cannot be evidence that these are the wrong parameter settings. And because the relevant data are utterances rather than single words, even a statistical comparison of derivations with multiple head-movement to polar answer C and their absence with *-ko* is impossible—there can be no baseline quantitative expection for syntactic structures, which are infinitely generable.

This is the problem. Standard reasoning from the Poverty of the Stimulus leads to the conclusion that "superset traps" cannot be avoided in Roberts's model for cases like the Finnish polar answers, where the correct parameter settings and an (incorrect) superset grammar which contain them are both compatible with the positive evidence that children seem to rely on.

This problem is quite general. Consider the Russian multiple head-movement patterns, for example. T, the secondary imperfective suffix and participial *-n* trigger multiple head-movement in Russian, but C and v do not. As it happens, there is a polar focus C *li* in Russian which does attract verbs and auxiliaries, as in (7).

(7) a. Pročitala li Anna knigu? (King 1994)
read Q Anna book
'Did Anna read a book?'

b. Ja ne znaju, živet li on zdes'.
I NEG know lives Q he here
'I don't know whether he lives here.'

But *li* cannot attract more than one head, given the ungrammaticality of (8c).

(8) a. Žil li on v Moskve? (King 1993)
lived Q he in Moscow
'Did he live in Moscow?'

b. Budet li on žit' v Moskve?
will Q he live in Moscow
Will he live in Moscow?

c. *Budet zit' li on v Moskve?
will live Q he in Moscow
Will he live in Moscow?

Again, though, there is no obvious positive evidence available that shows that polar *-li* must not form utterances like (8), so there is no reason why the learning procedure should not assign FF^{MHM} to the superset {C, T, *-yva*, *-n*}.

Or consider the English *-ed* affix, which also triggers multiple head-movement. In this case, the trigger which shows multiple head-movement to be necessary must be the presence of an attributive adjective modifying the nominal root to which *-ed* attaches. Roberts's procedure which require some evidence for the lack of FF^{MHM} in larger supersets before the actual *-ed* affix alone is considered. In fact, just before the hypothesis space is restricted to *-ed*, the learning procedure should consider a superset which contains *-ed* and other adjective-forming suffixes, such as *-ous* (*disastrous, famous, mountainous*) or *-ic* (*artistic, athletic, metallic, energetic*). And since all members of this set can combine with a nominal stem, the grammar would be expected to generate structures in which an adjectival or adverbial modifier would be attracted before the stem, if *-ous* or *-ic* etc. were to attract more than once. This would then generate ungrammatical forms such as those in (9).

(9) a. *natural-disastrous
b. *jagged-mountainous
c. *aspiring-artistic
d. *nervous-energetic

The ungrammaticality of these forms implies that they will be absent from the PLD. But that cannot be evidence which allows the learning procedure to limit the scope of Input Generalization, for the same reasons as before. Again, the superset trap seems to be inescapable.

Roberts's model offers a means to express both the tendency of grammars to prefer harmonic clusters of microparameters and the possibility of exceptions to this tendency. But specific limitations of this model become evident when the grammatical patterns which multiple head-movement languages allow are examined closely. The appropriate conclusion to draw is that some refinements to this model are necessary, to avoid superset traps like these.

5.3 PARAMETER SETTING WITH EXCEPTIONS

Ultimately what we would like is a model of parameter setting which combines the mathematical inevitability of Yang's model with the speed of acquisition and typological nuance of Roberts's model. What does that look like? We can begin with Roberts's insight that the search space for the grammar in the initial stages should neglect nuance in favour of generalities. That means that rather than a model containing a large number of micro-parametric options we begin with a search space which contains only a small number of maximally general parameters. Such a search space will be unlikely to accurately characterize most mature grammars but it should limit the initial size of the search space to allow the general parameters to be set in a realistic period of time.

For example, if we take some of the most common parametric options, then the initial search might include a general parameter for head-placement, another controlling whether [uSTEM] features are present on affixes and zero heads, another which settles whether [uϕ] features are introduced by phase heads, a fourth which controls displacement of (clitic) pronouns or definite DPs within vP. There must be some parametric choices which control how Case operates in the grammar, perhaps one which distinguishes nominative-accusative systems from ergative-absolutive, and another which settles how ditransitive verb phrases work. The timing parameter which determines whether labeling takes place before [uSTEM] feature valuation belongs in the list as well.

(10) a. head-placement parameter
b. [uSTEM] assignment parameter
c. phase heads have [uϕ] parameter
d. object shift parameter
e. accusative/absolutive parameter
f. dative/accusative parameter
g. [uSTEM] valuation timing parameter

Any such list of initial parameters can only be preliminary, and is certainly incomplete, but my goal here is to examine the general properties of a synthetic model of parameter setting, so the details of which parameters are involved are not critical.[8] Some of these (10a,b,c,g) can be plausibly associated with "3rd factor" imperatives; for others (10d,e,f), the ontology remains more obscure. But the list does include a good deal of the types of differences which contemporary analyses rely on to characterize morphosyntactic variation.

8. Roberts (2020) far more exhaustive study proposes eleven general parameters, which entails an initial set of 2,048 options. Such a number is probably still tractable in the analysis developed here.

And significantly, it entails a relatively small number of ways that these few general parameters can be set. With seven parameters, there are 2^7 (=128) possible combinations, which is certainly a computationally tractable sum in this context.

Given this initial stage of the grammar, Yang's algorithm should produce an imperfect grammar which generates some of the sentences in an adult grammar, but which must fail on many. For example, if English sentences like (11) area found in the PLD, then target settings of (10a,c,d,e,g) will be systematically successful if they happen to coincide with other accurate settings for the utterance being processed, and so they should become associated with a high score fairly quickly. English is always head-initial, and there is almost always some sort of visible "subject" combined with TP. With pronouns, where Case distinctions can be seen, the form of an transitive subject is the same as the form of an intransitive subject, and different from that of a transitive object. Objects are never situated immediately before their verb.

(11) a. They have sent us two reminders already. (Triggers for 10a,c,d,e)
b. We usually keep cookies in this jar. (Triggers for 10a,b,d,e,g)
c. We are usually asleep by this time. (Triggers for 10a,b,c,d)

As with any stochastic model, the failure rate at the beginning of the learning process must be very high, since most guesses will contain at least one incorrect parameter setting which will prevent a successful parse. But the occasional correct combinations of (target) parameter settings will be rewarded, and some of the parameters in this list will build up a positive record fairly quickly. Once they have earned a high enough score, they become highly likely to be selected from then on, which effectively removes them from the search space for the parameter setting process.

So if (10a,c) are established as reliable with the settings head-initial and ϕ-feature bearing (forcing EPP effects), then the size of the search space drops from 2^7 to 2^5. Once a child can begin to track pronoun forms, then presumably the Case parameters can be settled by the same mechanism, eliminating (10e,f) from the search space and reducing its size to 2^3. But the PLD data which relates to the position of the finite verb requires the correct settings for (10b,d,g), and these certainly interact with each other. Whether the object has shifted to the left of the verb phrase cannot be established unless it is known whether the verb raises to a higher head, Asp, T, or C. And whether the verb raises to T—because of T's [uSTEM] feature—is hard to tell until it is known whether [uSTEM] features are valued before labeling takes place, because this controls whether an adverb can be skipped in such movement. And English provides contradictory evidence for the last of these, because copular *be* raises to T (past adverbs), but other verbs do not. There is no correct setting for (10b) in this grammar, and the target settings for (10d,g) cannot be found as a result.

Given this result, the acquisition process stalls. This is where Roberts's model suggests a way past the impasse. The only way for the learning process to make progress is to entertain the hypothesis that one of the parameters which remains is too general, and that some grammatical contexts require a different parametric choice than others. If that is an option, then the process can respond to an utterance like (11c) in a new way. If the (active) search space contains parameters which pertain to the position of the verb, then the presence of the verb *be* in this utterance might be taken to constitute an exception to the general pattern. In other words, if the general pattern is one in which affixal T lacks [uSTEM] features, then the presence of *be* might be associated with an exceptional pattern in which affixal T bears [uSTEM] features. This hypothesis then forms part of a new grammar, more richly specified than (10), with the form (12).

(12) a. head-placement parameter
b. i. [uSTEM] assignment parameter when *be* is selected
ii. [uSTEM] assignment parameter
c. phase heads have [uϕ] parameter
d. object shift parameter
e. accusative/absolutive parameter
f. dative/accusative parameter
g. [uSTEM] valuation timing parameter

In this new grammar, (12bi,bii) are controlled by elsewhere principles: (12bi) applies generally, but not when the structural description for (12bi) are satisfied by the utterance, then it applies instead.

The introduction of a new parameter enlarges the active search space from 2^3 to 2^4, but the result is a set of potential grammars, one of which responds better to the available data. This new set of parameters can progress towards an accurate target grammar, because when (12bii) provides a lack of [uSTEM] features on T with verbs other than *be*, success is possible, and when (12bi) is set to provide a [uSTEM] feature to T, the result can be success as well. So the new parameters in (12b) should earn positive scores quickly, and the target settings for (12d,g) should be dragged upwards in their wake.

Of course, even the set of parameters in (12) do not yet include the resources to accurately describe what heads raise to T in English. In my Canadian dialect of English, auxiliary *have* and *be* raise, just as copular *be* does (Pollock 1989). This means that a further refinement of the grammar must still take place, generalizing the exception in (12bi) to include a larger class: copular *be*, auxiliary *be*, auxiliary *have*. Notice, however, that even the inaccurate formulation in (12b) will allow the (12d,g) parameters to be set, since auxiliary verbs do not interact with shifted objects or vP-adjoined adverbs.

Returning to the multiple head-movement cases, let us consider how an approach of this new type might accommodate the patterns in Innu-aimûn, in Russian, in northern Swedish, etc. The Innu-aimûn situation is the easiest to characterize in this model. Let us start with the same hypothetical list of initial parameters (10).

(10) a. head-placement parameter
b. [uSTEM] assignment parameter
c. phase heads have [uϕ] parameter
d. object shift parameter
e. accusative/absolutive parameter
f. dative/accusative parameter
g. [uSTEM] valuation timing parameter

Since Innu-aimûn has fairly free word order, the status of (12a,d) will be difficult to determine from the data in the PLD (as it is for the linguist). The target grammar settings for (12e,f) are equally mysterious. I must put these aside, simply because of a pervasive lack of clarity about these aspects of Algonquian grammars. But the target values for the parameters in (12b,c,g) have been established in Chapter 4, so we can consider how the child might set these. Given the rich agreement morphology of Innu-aimûn verbs, in both orders, it seems that (12c) should be easy to set—certainly C, v, and D bear [uϕ], which is transferred with Feature Inheritance, and which appears in the nominal and verbal morphology. As for (12b,g), the data which can "trigger" the target settings is everywhere in the grammar. These parameter settings interact, so they must show up together with the target values for a parse to succeed, but verb clusters with preverbs and tense/agreement inflection, verbs with initial adverbials, locatives or predicates, nouns with initial adjectives, verbs with accommodated medials, will all require the target settings and so these settings should be rewarded quickly, and should actually disappear from the search space very early on. And since there are no exceptions to the general pattern in Innu-aimûn, the initial parameter settings in (12) do not need to be replaced by anything more intricate.

This picture suggests that the target settings for these two parameters will be set with ease and speed by Innu children, and that no variation should be expected. Diachronic and comparative evidence appears to support this result.

The Algonquian language family covers a vast geographic range, as shown by the map in (13).[9] Innu-aimûn (or Montagnais) is spoken in the northernmost area of this range, and belongs to the Central Algonquian group. The original proto-language for this family is estimated to have been spoken between

9. The map is taken from Oxford (to appear), based on an earlier map in Goddard (1996).

two and three thousand years ago. As Ian Roberts (personal communication) points out, this time depth can be further quantified in terms of generations of children acquiring these languages. If there's a new generation every twenty-five years, then there are 120 generations between the Proto-Algonquian period and the present time.

According to Goddard (1994), Alqonquian speakers spread from west to east, with the resulting languages differing largely on the basis of how long their populations have been separated. Blackfoot (the westernmost Algonquian language) is the most divergent, and the smallest differences are found within the Eastern Algonquian subgrouping.

(13) *The geographic range of Algonquian languages*

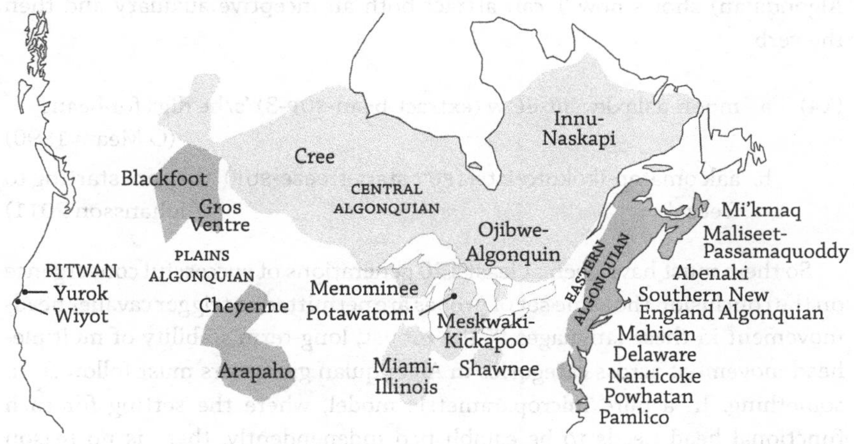

As one would expect, given the distances involved, the different groups of speakers of Algonquian languages have also occupied a wide range of ecological niches, both prior to and after the European invasion. Some Eastern Algonquian populations were agriculturalists. Cheyenne, Blackfoot, and Western Cree populations depended on bison hunting for much of their sustenance. Northern populations' economies have traditionally been of the inland hunter-gatherer variety. And populations in different regions have shared areal contact with very different types of other languages, from the Salish languages in the northwest, to Inuktitut in the north, and Souian and Iroquoian in large areas in the middle. In short, the groups of Algonquian speakers have lived in very different ecological and social environments, and they have been dispersed for a very long time.

This history is reflected in numerous ways in the histories of the languages. There are lexical differences between all Algonquian languages, and these appear generally to reflect the social and ecological histories in unsurprising ways. There are phonological differences, which one would also expect, given the passage of time from proto-Algonquian. There are also morphological differences, often involving the inflectional morphology.

It is therefore remarkable, given this diachronic context, that *all* Algonquian languages appear to make use of multiple head-movement in essentially the same ways. Every Algonquian language has complex words which follow the tripartite pattern: initial-medial-finals (Bloomfield 1946). And to the extent which can determined from existing descriptions, all of the Algonquian languages use these complex forms to express a similar range of complex ideas. It would take us far afield to examine these patterns in detail in a significant number of these languages, but the examples in (14) suggest how similar they are. Example (14a) comes from Delaware, an Eastern Algonquian language, and reflects multiple attraction by *v*, while (14b), from Blackfoot (Western Algonquian) shows how T can attract both an inceptive auxiliary and then the verb.

(14) a. moon-aalaxkwsiit-ee-w (extract-bean-SUF-3) 's/he digs for beans' (O'Meara 1990)

b. áak omatap-ikokoto-istsi (FUT start-freeze-SUF) 'they are starting to freeze' (Johansson 2011)

So there must have been at least 120 generations of successful convergence on the conclusion the same set of probes are permitted to trigger cavalier head-movement in these languages.[10] The robust, long-term stability of multiple-head movement across categories in Algonquian grammars must follow from something. In a pure microparametric model, where the setting for each functional head needs to be established independently, there is no reason to expect this degree of grammatical stability. What we would expect is the opposite—some microparameters might take on different settings over time, while others might remain the same. But in the model proposed here, where the initial parameter settings considered by the learning process are fully general, the value of the [uSTEM] timing parameter can be set early and with a high degree of confidence, and this result will resist exceptions, both in the course of acquisition and diachronically, as one generation succeeds another.

Because multiple head-movement is pervasive in Algonquian grammars, these constitute the easy cases. Something more complex must take place in the other multiple head-movement languages. So consider the northern Scandinavian "adjective incorporation" structures, and how they might be acquired in this model. On the whole, these languages appear not to embrace multiple head-movement, so the question is how this becomes a part of the

10. I am indebted to Ian Roberts for this observation.

grammar for the nominal structures in which it is possible. Presumably, this will reflect the presence of data like (72) (repeated here) in the PLD.

(72) Ser du star-svart-bil-en jänna?
see you big-black-car-DEF there
'Do you see that big, black, car?'

Notice that the verb appears in C in (14), and this is part of the general Germanic verb-second pattern. What is more, verbs which raise to second position skip freely past intervening adverbs, as in (15), where *hoppas* raises out of the verb phrase past *givetvis*. This shows that labeling must precede [uSTEM] valuation in this context.

(15) Jag hoppas givetvis på sportslig rättvisa.
I hope of.course for sporting justice

Given the pervasive use of verb-second word order in simple finite clauses in Scandinavian, the PLD will presumably contain ample trigger data to support a general parameter setting which orders labeling before [uSTEM] valuation. At some point, however, data like (14) will need to be dealt with, and this does not fall under the general pattern. So the learning process must posit an exception to the general parameter setting to reflect that [uSTEM] features in affixal (definite) D require the opposite ordering. This introduces a new timing parameter alongside the general one: (16).

(16) a. [uSTEM] valuation timing parameter for D
b. [uSTEM] valuation timing parameter

If parameter (16a) is set to allow valuation before labeling, then data like (72) can be processed successfully. The default parameter setting in (16b) will still cover the general case, allowing verb movement to second position(s) to continue to skip intervening adverbs.

The exceptional parameter must be formulated conservatively to avoid introducing new superset traps. In the norther Scandinavian case, it is enough to limit it to contexts where D bears a [uSTEM] feature—definite affixal D—because indefinite D does not attract anyways. In other contexts, the precise formulation of an exception parameter could be more consequential. This is the case for English *-ed*, for example. Like northern Scandinavian D, the possessive *-ed* affix must constitute an exception to the general English pattern, where labeling precedes [uSTEM] valuation. This means that the learning process must introduce a new parameter at some point, fracturing the [uSTEM] valuation timing parameter into a special case and a default case: (17).

(17) a. [uSTEM] valuation timing parameter for possessive *-ed*
b. [uSTEM] valuation timing parameter

The exceptional parameter in this case is nano-parametric, the scope of which is limited to a single exceptional morpheme. If the parameter were formulated with a larget scope of application, the sort of superset trap already discussed would result. For example, (17a) cannot be safely replaced with a formulation which characterizes the timing of [uSTEM] valuation operations in denominal adjectival suffixes like *-ous* or *-ic*. The right results obtain only if the exceptional parameter is formulated as conservatively as possible.

In Russian, the situation is slightly more complex, since the exception to the general rule must be made to cover T, *-yva*, and participial *-n*. As with Swedish or English, the general setting for the [uSTEM] timing parameter will order labeling before valuation. And many of the perfective prefixes are potentially compatible with multiple parametric analyses, so they may not count as effective triggers. Natural and superlexical prefixes might be treated as prefixes to which the verb raises, or in many cases, simply as particles appearing to the left of a verb which remains *in situ*. Intermediate prefixes may also represent agnostic elements, if they can be analysed as heads to the left of the verb phrase. (Such an analysis is inconsistent with the use of multiple intermediate prefixes in a single clause, but such structures may be in short supply in the PLD.) The most accessible evidence for the multiple head-movement analysis comes from the lexical prefixes, but these require that the children should already have a sophisticated understanding of how argument structure is syntactically expressed, and a confident theory of when the superlexical and natural prefixes are used, so that the presence of a lexical prefix can be seen to be significantly different. Once *some* lexical prefixes can be identified by the child as appropriate constituents of the verb phrase, utterances containing such prefixes come to constitute triggers for the [uSTEM] valuation timing parameter. And this can lead to a factoring of the general parameter into two subparameters: the general one, and a specific one which applies to [uSTEM] features in T.

(18) a. [uSTEM] valuation timing parameter for T
b. [uSTEM] valuation timing parameter

The new microparameter will cover both the lexical prefixes and the natural, superlexical and intermediate prefixes, automatically, so confirmation of this factoring should be rapid.

The formulation of (18a) as a microparameter which applies specifically to T raises questions about whether the scope of application is broader than one might expect, since past and present tenses can be distinguished in Russian, as can finite and infinitival T. In this case, however, these distinctions are presumably not inherent properties of T, but are obtained from C through the effects of Feature Inheritance. For the purposes of the formulation of parameter (18a), T may be taken to be a single lexical item, which means that this exceptional parameter is actually formulated as conservatively as possible.

Once the intermediate and lexical prefixes are established as vP adjuncts in the syntactic representation, which is possible only given multiple head-movement, the analysis of *-yva* and of participial *-n* will require a further factoring of the default parameter in (18b), to provide the mature parametric options (19).

(19) a. [uSTEM] valuation timing parameter for T
b. [uSTEM] valuation timing parameter for *-yva*
c. [uSTEM] valuation timing parameter for *-n*
d. [uSTEM] valuation timing parameter

5.4 FORMALIZATION OF A LEARNING ALGORITHM

It sometimes proves helpful to test an informal set of ideas with a more rigorous formal implementation. The LAD just sketched out is a pretty rough outline of what a proper proposal would involve, so the following is a more carefully articulated model of the same notions.

At a minimum, the syntactic component of a grammar consists of a set of syntactic categories and a set of rules which characterize the behavior of those categories in a syntactic derivation. Some rules (i.e. Merge, Feature Inheritance) are presumably invariant; others establish different behaviors for different categories in different languages. Let us refer to the set of variant rules (parameter) as *P*. Then development of a mature grammar requires the formation of a complete parameter set Γ_m: {*p* : *p* is a fixed value for a variant rule in P}. If the set of invariant rules is Ω, then $\Gamma \cup \Omega$ comprises the full set of syntactic rules for a grammar.

The ontological status of such rules remains subject to debate. It remains a logical possibility that UG—a language-specific component of cognition—provides each invariant rule in Ω and each variant option in Γ. A less bewildering possibility is that the some, and ideally all, of the rules in Ω and Γ arise from third factor effects, as discussed above. In any case, though, the mature grammar of an individual speaker must arise from the interaction of the initial state of the grammar, biological maturation, and the linguistic environment to which a child is exposed (PLD). The focus here will be on the process which produces a mature state for Γ: Γ_m.

The mechanism which forms Γ_m on the basis of the PLD is the LAD. The LAD must include at least two components: an initial set of variant rules Γ_0

for which values are to be fixed, and an algorithm LT which converts Γ_0 to Γ_m on the basis of the PLD.

(20) $\text{LT}(\Gamma_0, \text{PLD}) = \Gamma_m$

Γ_0 must be minimal, if we are to avoid a richly specified microparametric innate endowment. Ideally, Γ_0 will consist only of '3rd factor' options, which emerge from the computational mechanisms used to process grammatical derivations (Chomsky 2005, Biberauer et al. 2013). But given the subtleties in syntactic variation which have been so carefully documented by Kayne 2013 and many others, this means that LT must be able to generate 'microparameters' in formation of Γ_m.

In contrast, LT does not need necessarily to be limited by the same evolutionary considerations, since it presumably can draw on whatever general cognitive capacities are available outside the linguistic core.

Yang's (2002) stochastic learning model will serve here as the foundation for LT. Let us recapitulate how this model works. The mechanism which Yang proposes is one in which the child, on receiving PLD input, attempts to parse the sound stream into a grammatical structure. She does so initially by assigning random values for each parameter in her inventory, to form a tentative grammar: H_0.[11] This tentative grammar is then employed to attempt to parse the sound stream. If the parse is successfully accomplished, then the success is recorded in *each* of the component parameter settings in H_0. If the parse fails, then the opposite occurs—a failure is registered with each parameter setting.

The effect of this initial step is felt in subsequent attempts by the child to process a new utterance. With the next input sound stream, a new tentative grammar, H_1 is formed by establishing values for each parameter, and H_1 will be employed in the same way as H_1 was. But unlike what ocurred with H_0, the formulation of grammar H_1 takes the previous results into account in assigning parameter values. If the H_0 parse was successful, then each parameter is *more likely* to be assigned the value it had in H_0 than the contrasting value. This probability weighting is slight at first, but in Yang's model, it increases with each successful parse using the same parameter value, until that becomes the only value available.

Unlike Yang, I view the members of Γ_0 as rules which apply with maximal generality. Γ_0 cannot include variant rules which describe how verbs behave, or finite T, or nonspecific indefinite D. Instead, Γ_0 can identify a specific property,

11. Yang does not reject the possibility that even the initial values are influenced by considerations of markedness, but this option plays no role in how the learning model ensures its final result.

like head-finality, for **all** heads, whatever their categorial (or other) features happen to be. This ensures the size of Γ_0 will be small.

My implementation of these ideas starts with the relationship between the initial arracy of (innate) parameters and the mechanism used to record successful parameter choices. If Γ_0 provides both positive and negative options for each parameter it contains, then this should determine the form of Γ.

Rather than providing a positive or negative value for a parametric choice, let us suppose that both positive and negative values appear within Γ to begin with.[12] In other words, for the Head Parameter, Γ_0 will contain both statements in (21), together with a probability index which identifies how likely one is to be chosen over the other. And the same will be true for the [uSTEM] valuation timing parameter.

(21) Γ_0:

$p_1(x)$	0
$p_1(\overline{x})$	0
$p_2(y)$	0
$p_2(\overline{y})$	0
⋮	
Head precedes complements	0
Head follows complements	0
⋮	
[uSTEM] valuation precedes labeling	0
[uSTEM] valuation follows labeling	0
⋮	
$p_n(x')$	3
$p_n(\overline{x'})$	1

Exposed to a new utterance Σ, the child simply selects a list of rules from Γ_0, forming H_0. The list must be exhaustive—each possible parametric option must be represented in H, so either the head-initial or the head-final option must be represented, and the same will hold of the [uSTEM] valuation timing options.

12. The formulation presented here is deliberately agnostic as to whether or not parametric options should be associated directly with individual lexical items, i.e. the Borer-Chomsky hypothesis. One could certainly interpret what is proposed here as a procedure in which association of heads with particular parameters is implicated. For example, the composition of the tentative grammars H_i might be a matter of associating selections from Γ_i with elements drawn from the lexical. Whether this is a desirable detail appears to me to be orthogonal to the main issues considered here, so I leave it to the side.

(22) *Parameter Exhaustivity Principle* (PEP)
When selecting parametric values for a new parameter array, the result must exhaustively characterize all possible categories in the language with the parametric values chosen.

(It is presumably redundant to further limit the choices made in formulating H by preventing the tentative grammar from containing both values for the head parameter in the same list, since such a grammar will always fail.) A possible H_o drawn from (21) would then be (23).

(23) H_0:

$$p_1(\overline{x})$$
$$p_2(y)$$
$$\vdots$$
Head precedes complements
$$\vdots$$
[uSTEM] valuation precedes labeling
$$\vdots$$
$$p_n(\overline{x'})$$

LT then employs H_0 to to try to parse Σ_0. If the parse is successful, then—as in Yang's model—the members of H_0 are recorded as successful by incrementing the probability index for each matching item in Γ_0, forming a new grammar Γ_1. If the parse fails, then Γ_0 is not immediately altered. And the next time an utterance appears in the PLD, it will be Γ_1 which serves as the basis for forming a new tentative grammar H_1. The effect of a successful parse is then that the individual parameter choices made in forming H_0 become more likely to be chosen in future iterations.

Where no exemptions to a general parametric choice are found in the PLD—where the grammar is fully harmonic in one respect—the effect of this procedure is that the right (target) parametric choice will be more successful over time than the wrong one, so its index of probability will increase, and at some point the option of making the wrong choice effectively disappears. So the index associated with the head-initial option will climb to some high value for English children, and the index associated with a head-final setting will not climb much past 0. Similarly, the index for [uSTEM] valuation preceding labeling will secure a high value for an Innu child, making this choice the only one which is actually employed in the mature grammar.

If the list of options initially recorded in Γ_0 are small enough, then this algorithm can ensure the selection of a mature grammar in the actual space of time in which we observe that children acquire their syntactic competence. In other words, with a small enough Γ, the exponential growth of the search space would not be a worry. But then one must ask how a child might learn the subtle syntactic differences which encourage a microparametric analysis.

To answer that question, I extend Yang's model by introducing the option to take an initial rule set and add to it by factoring individual rules into multiple rules with more focused domains of application. This will make it possible to characterize microparametric variation with a model where acquisition is still fast enough to be plausible in the necessary time span.

The implementation of this extension is as follows. Let i be some point in the series of learning operations which produce new versions of Γ on the basis of new utterances in the PLD. As before, a successful parse of an utterance Σ_i using H_i drawn from Γ_i will produce a new grammar Γ_{i+1}, with each of the members of H_i given an incremented probability index. But if the parse of Σ_i using H_i fails, then LT can take the step of seeking to refine Γ_i, rather than simply giving up.

To do so, LT forms a second array Γ_i', which differs from Γ_i only in the value of a randomly selected member of Γ_1. In other words, LT tries to replace a particular parametric choice with better option drawn (randomly) from Γ_i, but still subject to Parameter Exhaustivity. In other words, LT selects one parametric choice in Γ_1, and replaces its with the opposite parametric choice.[13] And then a second attempt to parse Σ_i is carried out with the new tentative grammar $H_{i'}$. If this succeeds, than Γ_{i+1} will record that result.

But if both H_i and $H_{i'}$ fail to enable a successful parse of Σ_1, then a new strategy is employed to try to find a better grammar. H_i and $H_{i'}$ differ in how a specific parameter p applies, and at this point neither option for p has improved the result. LT therefore constructs an *exception* which carves up the domain of application of p. The exception must be relevant to the contents of the Σ_i utterence currently being processed. If Σ_i does not contain any prepositions, for example, then the new, exceptional rule should not be one which specifically characterize how prepositions behave.

In fact, to ensure than no superset traps arise with the introduction of exceptions, the formulation of an exceptional rule must be as conservative as possible. Initially, at least, exceptions should be "nanoparametric," and should apply only to a single lexical item found in Σ_i.

For example, if p describes whether labeling precedes or follows [USTEM] valuation—and neither option for p p has enabled a successful parse, the LT

13. This is essentially an operation proposed by Gibson & Wexler 1994, although it is here incorporated into a probabilistic learning model, in place of their more immediately deterministic one. Niyogi & Berwick (1996) offer a more powerful variant of this approach, in which multiple parameters may be switched at once to attempt to improve on a failed parsing attempt. The latter approach could certainly also serve as a basis for implementing the parameter splitting idea which is presented in the text, but the less complex model specified here appears to provide the necessary results.

can intoduce a new rule into H_i, forming H_i'', where the new rule might specific that valuation of [uSTEM] *in polar response C* precedes labeling.

This new exception does not replace the more general statements already in place in H_i. The more general statements remain in place, but their role in parsing Σ_i becomes restricted by elsewhere application conventions. This, if $H_{i''}$ has the form (24), after the exception has been introduced, then multiple head-movement will be permitted (by the exception) with polar response C—as in Finnish—but adverbs will be skipped freely by head-movement when triggered by [uSTEM] features in T, v, Asp, and even polar interrogative C.

(24) $H_{i''}$: $p_1(x)$
$p_2(y)$
⋮
Head precedes complements
⋮
Valuation of [uSTEM] in polar response C precedes labeling
Valuation of [uSTEM] follows labeling
⋮
$p_n(x')$

It will be clear that the formulation of the exceptional rule will always differ from the value of the general statement which it complements. If in (24), the general statement also ordered [uSTEM] valuation before labeling, then there would be no role for the exception to play. In fact, the point at which such an exceptional rule would be invented by LT would never be reached, if the exception were to match the general rule, because a successful parse would already have been achieved with the general rule alone.

If this parse fails, too, then the new exceptional parametric choice is simply forgotten (although it may be recreated in a subsequent iteration).[14] If this parse succeeds, however, then that success is recorded in Γ_{i+1} for the members of $H_{i''}$. This means that Γ becomes larger at this point, by the addition to the original list Γ_0 of parameter options of the new exceptional rule.

The record of a successful parse in Γ_{i+1} must increment the probability index of the exceptional rule, which can never be 0. It should not, however, record a successful role played by the default parametric choice, because the success in parsing does not come from the general statement on its own, but only by the general statement operating in combination with the

14. In contrast, the initial variable rules in Γ_0 can never be lost entirely, although they can be suppressed in favor of competing sub-rules. This would follow if the initial rules are themselves reflections of 3rd factor considerations, which cannot disappear from the picture.

exception. The right result can be ensured if only the exceptional rule receives an incremented probability index when H contains both a specific rule and a general rule.

When the next utterance Σ_{i+1} is perceived, LT starts up the process once more, but this time with the results of evaluation of Σ_i in place. A new tentative grammar H_{i+1} must be generated to try to parse Σ_{i+1}. Suppose that Γ_{i+1} now contains both of the original valuation timing rules for [uSTEM], but also the new exception, as in (25).

(25) Γ_{i+1}:

$p_1(x)$	4
$p_1(\overline{x})$	1
$p_2(y)$	3
$p_2(\overline{y})$	19
⋮	
Valuation of [uSTEM] in polar response C precedes labeling	1
Valuation of [uSTEM] follows labeling	18
Valuation of [uSTEM] precedes labeling	3
⋮	
$p_n(x')$	3
$p_n(\overline{x'})$	1

H_{i+1} is drawn from the grammar subject to Parameter Exhaustivity, influenced by the probability indices of the choices. So the most likely choice for the [uSTEM] valuation timing parameters in (25) is that H_{i+1} will simply contain the rule which requires labeling before valuation of [uSTEM] features. The other options are not (yet) excluded, so any of the combinations in (26) might be selected.

(26) a. Valuation of [uSTEM] precedes labeling.
b. Valuation of [uSTEM] follows labeling.
c. i. Valuation of [uSTEM] in polar response C precedes labeling.
ii. Valuation of [uSTEM] follows labeling.

And from now on, all three choices will compete with each other according to Yang's logic. The exception has to perform well enough to win a higher probability index than the more general statements in order to earn a place in the mature grammar Γ_m

Consider what effect this procedure should have on the shape of the grammar as it evolves over time. Any rule which applies throughout the grammar with a single value will be reinforced regularly, and will then quickly emerge with a single possible value, which restricts the search space and makes it easier to identify values for the remaining rules. Any rule which does not apply generally in the target grammar will be less successful than the (right) exceptions, and so they will become dominant and the more general rule will atrophy. The exceptions themselves may be replaced by other exceptions, if specific formulations of for the latter enable successful parses more frequently. If the first exception happens to be correct, though, a second exception should never have a chance to emerge.

A schematic representation of this model of LT appears in (27).

(27) *LT schematic*

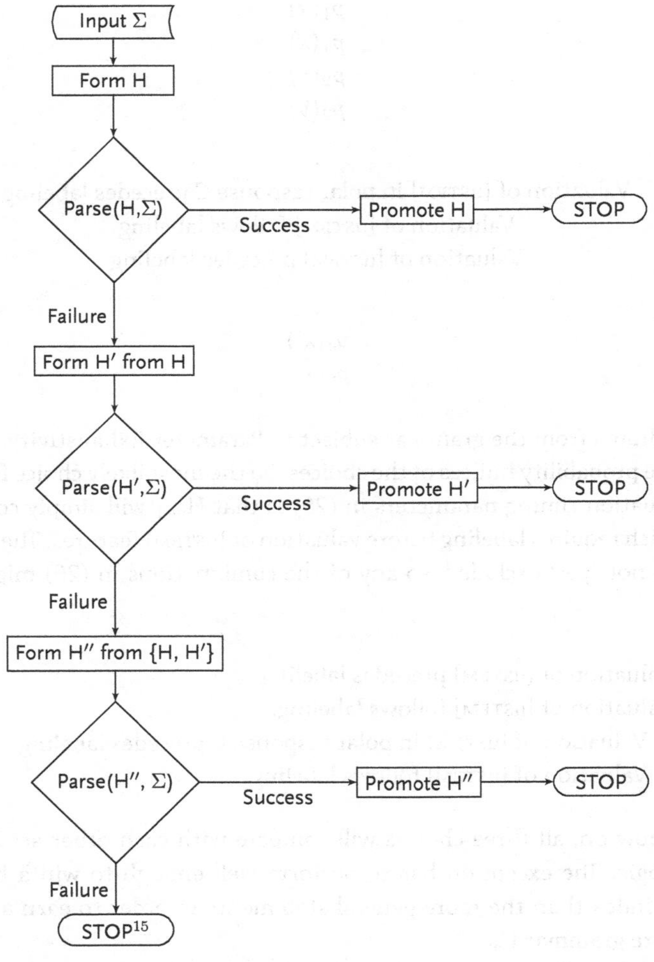

15. Strictly speaking, the final STOP in this flowchart need not reflect the end of the child's attempt to learn something from this string. There is no reason the entire process could not be rerun with the same input string, for as many times as the child's unconscious mind might want to do so. But at some point it will be nap time or lunch, or a distracting doggy might wander by.

In (27), the Form H operation is essentially Yang's proposal, but starting with a much smaller parameter space. If necessary, H is then replaced by H′ (Form H′ from H), and the result is checked for a better fit. And if this fails to improve the situation, then the option of expanding the grammar by adding an exception to the list of parameters in H is explored (Form H″ from H, H′).

At this point, the learning procedure has the resources to allow for quick acquisition of fully harmonic parameter settings, as in Innu-aimûn or French [uSTEM] valuation timing parameters, and for parameter settings which allow a single type of exception, as in Finnish, northern Scandinavian, or English. What remains is to isolate how such an approach can model the acquisition of mixed, micro- or meso-parametric systems, like Russian. In this case, of course, the target grammar must allow multiple head-movement to T (with all tenses and finiteness values), to SI *-yva* and to participial *-n*.

In fact, it appears that nothing new needs to be introduced in order to accommodate this type of situation, because the introduction of one exception into the grammar does not preclude a subsequent introduction of a second or third exception. All that is necessary is that the learning procedure should be exposed to data in the PLD which will resist parsing until the appropriate exceptions are introduced. Thus, an initial grammar like (21) might be enriched to (28) as a response to trigger data in which a lexical prefix appears to the left of a verb inflected with a past tense suffix.[16]

(28) Γ_j:

$p_1(x)$	4
$p_1(\overline{x})$	14
$p_2(y)$	7
$p_2(\overline{y})$	1
⋮	
Valuation of [uSTEM] in T precedes labeling	5
Valuation of [uSTEM] follows labeling	13
Valuation of [uSTEM] precedes labeling	2
⋮	
$p_n(x')$	3
$p_n(\overline{x'})$	1

But if a tentative grammar formed from Γ_j happens to contain both the general rule and the exception for T, and this grammar fails to provide a parse for an utterance containing *-yva*, then an exception can be formulated for this morpheme, too. And if the result is a newly successful parse, then a new parameter set (29) may be the result.

16. Different flavors of T need not be distinguished if Feature Inheritance from C provides tense and finiteness features.

(29) Γ_{j+1}:

$p_1(x)$	5
$p_1(\overline{x})$	14
$p_2(y)$	8
$p_2(\overline{y})$	1
⋮	
Valuation of [uSTEM] in T precedes labeling	6
Valuation of [uSTEM] in *-yva* precedes labeling	1
Valuation of [uSTEM] follows labeling	13
Valuation of [uSTEM] precedes labeling	2
⋮	
$p_n(x')$	4
$p_n(\overline{x'})$	1

For the Russian case, there is no particular reason to require that T, *-yva*, and *-n* should be treated as a natural class for the purposes of rule formulation. For other parameters, where a micro- or meso-parametric exception is required, one might will prefer that a group of exceptional rules should be brought together in one general formulation (but which is still more specific than a default rule). This would require an extra stage in the learning process. It may be that Yang's (2016) Tolerance Principle would play a role, if the number of exceptions to a general pattern climb past the threshold imposed by the Tolerance Principle.[17] It is beyond the scope of this study to examine exactly how this would work, particularly since no cases of multiple head-movement seen to demand such a treatment.

5.5 CONCLUSION

Science advances by examining the margins. The structures and derivations which I have examined in this work have largely remained at the margins in the history of generative studies of language. In some cases (Finnish, northern Scandinavian), this reflects the relatively small number of active researchers and the large number of languages which can be examined. In others (Russian and other Slavic languages), there is certainly a wealth of research which

17. The Tolerance Principle limits the number of exceptions to a general rule according to the following calculation. If x is the number of expressions of a certain type present in the PLD, then $\frac{x}{\ln x}$ is the number of exceptions which can be tolerated before a general rule must be hypothesized. This calculation assumes a Zipfian distribution of the relevant expressions in the PLD, and this criteria clearly eliminates full syntactic structures as expressions for which the Tolerance Principle might be applicable. It does not, however, appear to exclude the more abstract list of parametric choices from consideration.

addresses the empirical phenomena re-examined here, but the difficulty of reconciling the data with established generative models has kept this research, and the data that has been unearthed, at a remove from the main trends in generative morphosyntax.

In the case of Innu-aimûn and other Algonquian languages, there are a host of factors at play which have kept these grammatical phenomena at the margin. There are certainly ample practical challenges which impede theoretical research into these languages. And political and ethical considerations play a larger role in scholarly activities involving indigenous communities and languages than they normally do where languages of socially dominant, more powerful communities are concerned. But one factor which has certainly played a large part is the Bloomfieldian tradition in morphosyntactic analysis, which tends to make languages like Innu-aimûn appear more alien and less accessible than need be.

The analyses presented here, in Chapters 2–4, offer a means to bring these phenomena and these grammars into the grammatical mainstream, where they can inform the construction of more sophisticated, more enlightening generative models in the future. The examination of learnability implications of multiple head-movement structures is one example of the way that such a relationship between the center and these re-examined margins may prove fruitful. I am confident that there are others.

APPENDIX A
Selected notes on Innu-aimûn grammar

Besides the terminology associated with the tripartite analysis, there is a quantity of background information on Algonquian grammar which will be helpful for assessing the material presented here, particularly in Chapter 4. Those readers who are familiar with the fundamentals of Algonquian grammar can probably skim this appendix with impunity. I have tried to include only information which matters for the arguments and data presented in the body of this study. For those interested in more complete presentations of the grammar of Innu-aimûn, I suggest reading MacKenzie (1980), Clarke (1982), Oxford (2008), and particularly Drapeau's (2014) detailed grammar.

In the Algonquian grammatical tradition, words are classified as nouns, verbs, and particles, with the latter including any words which do not bear nominal or verbal inflections. However, recent scholarship has provided evidence for more categorial distinctions (Oxford 2008). I assume here, without argument, that Innu-aimûn is endowed with a full set of functional categories, including complementizers (C), determiners (P), tense (T), as well as adverbs, prepositions, and prepositional phrases. Adjectives do seem to be absent, however.

A.1 SOCIOLINGUISTIC CONTEXT

Innu-aimûn belongs to the Cree-Montagnais-Naskapi language continuum (MacKenzie 1980). It is spoken in several communities in northern Quebec and Labrador in Canada. The majority of the examples presented in this work represents the speech of Labradorian speakers from the community of Sheshatshiu.

I have drawn from disparate sources for Innu-aimûn data presented in this work. These include directed interviews with language consultants fluent in

Innu-aimûn, many conducted in the company of my colleague Marguerite MacKenzie. Besides the data provided by these interviews, the following sources have provided much of the examples used here. The Innu online dictionary, compiled by a research team under the direction of José Mailhot and Marguerite MacKenzie, includes both word lists and examples. The online Innu conjugation tool, provided at the same web site, has made the glossing of recalcitrant verb forms more tractable. Both have been provided and verified by fluent language consultants in the team. Data drawn from this database includes translations, to which I have added gloss information here. I have also added length diacritics. Some examples are drawn from traditional narrative texts compiled by the Labrador Innu Text Project, all of which have also been edited by fluent language consultants.

Verb conjugations for all conjugation classes, drawn from interviews with language consultants from a variety of dilects, are contained in Clarke (1982), in Baraby (2004), and in Drapeau (2014). I have borrowed heavily from these materials, regularizing the spelling on occasion when necessary for clarity.

Presentation of the Innu-aimûn data has required some notational compromises, since there is no common orthography to which every community or scholar wholly subscribes. And actually, surface forms can vary from community to community enough to justify variant writing conventions. Orthographic conventions which are widely accepted are described in this appendix, in section A.2.1.

For most of the examples presented, I have adopted a four-line format, in which the first line represents the data in the format presented in the source material. In most cases, this will not include diacritic representations of vowel length (*â, î, û*). Some schwa-like vowels are represented with different orthographies (*a, i*) in this line, as are some consonants, either because of surface variation (*l, i*) or because of differing orthographic choices made by different communities (*t, tsh*). The second line represents the same data, with morpheme breaks introduced following Leipzig conventions, and normalized as much as feasible. This normalization often includes the addition of vowel length marking diacritics, if this is not already present in the first line. I have also attempted to make the morphology more transparent in this line by unraveling some surface-level phonology. I replace the superscript ^{u} which indicates labialization of a preceding consonant with the /u/ which produces this labialization. The third and fourth lines provide glosses and free translations, as usual.

A.2 PERTINENT ORTHOGRAPHY AND PHONOLOGY

A.2.1 Orthographic conventions

The orthographic conventions commonly used for Innu-aimûn represent surface phonology fairly directly. Consonant voicing is not contrastive, so there is no orthographic need for *b*, *d*, *g*, and *z*, and *p*, *t*, *k*, *s* represents voiced and voiceless stops and fricatives. The single palatal affricates /č/ (and /ǰ/) is written as *tsh*, except in the obviative agreement suffice /nǰî/, which is often written as *-nitî*. Fricative /s/ is normally palatalized before a following obstruent, and written as *sh*. The glides /j/ and /w/ are written as *i* and *u*, respectively, as in Latin. The letter *n* also represents two distinct phonemes. It can stand for /n/, but it can also indicate the surface form of an underlying consonant which is realized in some regions as /n/, /l/, or /r/ instead (MacKenzie 1980). (In this work, the only significance of this involves data taken from Drapeau (2014), who documents a variant of Innu-aimûn where /l/ appears as the surface form of this phoneme. When data from Drapeau's grammar is used, in the source data line, this consonant is written as *ń*.)

Rounding of a syllable-final velar stop or labial nasal is shown with a superscript *u*. This normally reflects a late surface phonological rule which applies when a word-final /u/ follows labial /m/ or velar /k/; in that case the timing slot for the vowel is deleted, and the rounding feature of the vowel is transferred to the preceding consonant.

The orthography for vowels sometimes distinguishes long vowels (*â*, *î*, *û* from short vowels (*a*, *i*, *u*) except in the case of *e*, which is always long and never written with a diacritic. In 3rd person plural agreement inflection on verbs in the conjunct order, the orthographic string *Vht* is used to represent a tonal quality of the vowel or vowel lengthening, and not a pre-aspirated t. Elsewhere, though *h* means /h/.

A.2.2 Phonological rules

While research into the phonological systems of Innu-aimûn is far from exhaustive, the following processes have been established by MacKenzie (1980).

- Consonant clusters created by morphological processes (affixation) are broken into legitimate syllables by insertion of epenthetic /i/.
- Word-final /u/ is absorbed into a preceding obstruent, which becomes labial and rounded. The /u/ disappears.
- Progressive rounding assimilation affects both epenthetic and other /i/ vowels, when preceded by a labialized consonant.
- Velar and coronal stops are palatalized before /i/.
- /s/ is palatalized before obstruents.
- Nasal consonants are deleted before obstruents.
- Underlying liquids are realized differently in different dialects, i.e. as either /l/ or /n/. (In other languages in this family, the same underlying phoneme may also appear as /j/, /r/, or /θ/.)

These rules apply very generally. Other phonological and morphophonological rules with narrower scope will be described in the main text when necessary.

A.3 INFLECTION

A.3.1 Nominal inflections and their derivations

Free-standing nominals are inflected for ϕ features, for noun class, and for obviative status. These break down into the following distinctions: (1).

(1)

Feature class		
ϕ features	Number	singular *vs.* plural
	Person	1st, 2nd, 3rd
Noun class features	Gender	animate *vs.* inanimate
Obviation features		proximate *vs.* obviative

Noun class features are inherent to the noun root and are not expressed directly in the morphology, but they do influence the exponence of other features. For example, in animate nouns, obviation is expressed with an /-a/ suffix, but with zero morphology in inanimate nouns. (The presence of obviative features on inanimate nouns can still be inferred from how they influence verbal agreement inflections, as discussed below.) And plural features have an /-at/ exponent in animate nouns, but /-a/ in inanimate nouns. The distibution of nouns into animate and inanimate groups follows natural gender categories for the most part, but as is frequently the case with other gender systems, there are quite a few exceptions.

The distinction between obviative and proximate plays an important role in reference-tracking in complex discourse (Russell 1996, Branigan & MacKenzie 1999, Drapeau 2014), but the semantic function of these features has little direct relevance to the analyses presented in Chapter 4, so it is left to the side here.

For the most part, the ϕ features, noun class features, and obviation features are additive, with three exceptions. Obviation is fully neutralized in non-3rd person nominals. In obviative nominals, number contrasts are neutralized, so an obviative nominal can be interpreted as singular or plural, freely. And plural 1st and 2nd persons include an inclusive/exclusive distinction, so that there are three plural speech-act participants: 1st person exclusive (speaker and others), 1st person inclusive (speaker and hearer(s) (and others)), and 2nd person plural (hearers (and others)).

In possessed nominals, the possessed noun bears agreement inflection which reflects features of the possessor. This includes a prefix which expresses person features and a suffix which expresses person, noun class, number, and obviative features. If the possessor bears 3rd person proximate features, then an animate possessee is inflected as obviative. If the possessor is itself obviative, then the possessee includes obviation in its agreement inflection. With an inanimate possessee, obviative agreement /-nu/ appears alone, as in (2c). With an animate possessee, /-nu/ is followed by a second marker of obvation /-a/, as in (2d).

(2) a. nit-assî-nân
1-territory-1p
'our territory'

b. Pien u-shpuâkân-a
Peter 3-pipe-OBV
'Peter's pipe'

c. u-tâu-ia u-mûkumân-nu
3-father-OBV 3-knife-OBV
'his father's knife'

d. Ânî u-kâu-ia ut-ânapi-nu-a
Annie 3-mother-OBV 3-net-OBV-OBV

The double marking of obviation actually reflects the syntactic derivation which produces such forms, and in particular, the interaction of agreement, Feature Inheritance, and affix-hopping in possessed nominals, and in a way which mirrors the more complex inflection on verbs, discussed next. For a complex possessed structure like (2b), the base structure will be something like (3), where Poss is simply an agnostic label for whatever functional head introduces the possessor into the nominal structure.

(3)

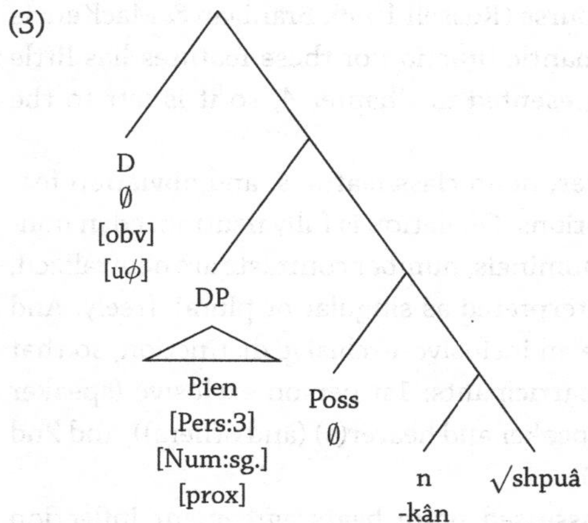

In such structures, D must be a phase head, which introduces unvalued ϕ features into the structure. The [uϕ] features of D find a value in the possessor, and these features must then be transferred to Poss with Feature Inheritance. The presence of Person features on Poss trigger the addition of a proclitic person marker—*u-* in (3b). And when the possessed noun raises to Poss, the agreement features in Poss are then expressed as suffixal inflection on the noun.

The requirement that a noun possessed by a proximate possessor be obviative is satisfied by an (interpretable) obviative feature in D, but the exponent of this feature is an *-a* suffix. But the obviative suffix in D does not bear a [uSTEM] feature—it is not a "strong" affix, so the noun does not raise to D. Instead, Innu-aimûn grammer employs affix-hopping to provide affixal D with a stem to which it can attach.

For structures like (4), a base structure for (2d), the combination of agreement processes, head-movement, and affix-hopping produce the double expression of obviation.

(4)

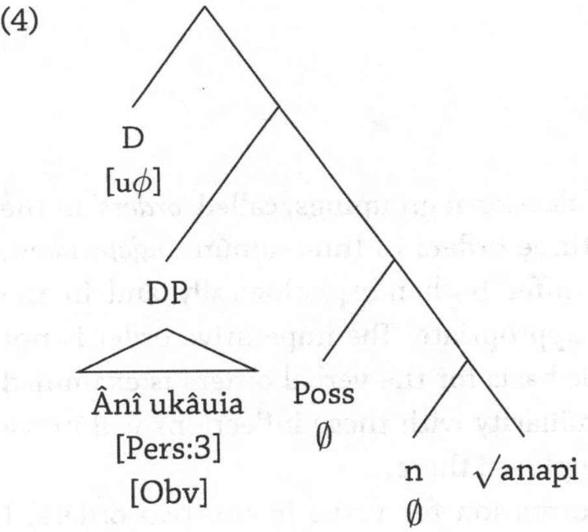

In this case, since the possessor is not proximate, the possessee need not be obviative. The [uϕ] features in the top D will find values in the obviative possessor *Ânî ukâuia*. When Feature Inheritance takes place, Poss will pick up the features [Pers:3, Obv], and these are realized as the *-nu* agreement suffix. But Feature Inheritance does not fully eliminate all ϕ features from D in Innu-aimûn. Just as in the clausal syntax of some Germanic languages, the phase head can preserve some features, even when they are transferred into its complement. In Innu-aimûn, D preserves a copy of the (uninterpretable) [Obv] feature, which is again realized as the affix *-a*. And just as in (4), affixal D must undergo affix-hopping, which produces the structure in which obvation agreement is expressed twice.

Plurality of possessed nouns is expressed by a plural suffix which follows the agreement inflection.

(5) a. ni-mushum-inân-at
1-grandfather-1p-p
'our grandfathers'

b. ni-shîpîm-inân-a
1-river-1p-p
'our rivers'

Again, this appears to reflect the properties of affixal D. The plural feature for possessed nominals is a feature of D, which is not displaced when Feature Inheritance transfers the agreement features to Poss. Instead, the exponent of interpretable number features is an affix which lacks a [uSTEM] feature, so again, the possessed noun does not raise, and affix-hopping must take place.

A.3.2 Verbal inflections

Verbs are inflected in two distinct inflectional groupings, called '*orders*' in the Algonquianist tradition. There are three orders in Innu-aimûn: *independent*, *conjunct*, and *imperative* and they differ both morphologically and in the syntactic contexts in which each is appropriate. The imperative order is not examined in this work. The syntactic basis for the verbal orders is examined in detail in Chapter 4, but some familiarity with these inflections will prove convenient in evaluating the data employed there.

In the presentation of gloss information for verbs in the two orders, I indicate suffixal agreement in the conjunct order tagged as such. Agreement suffixes in the independent order are provided with no tag, as the unmarked forms, but this is simply a matter of typographic convenience only. There is no implication that independent forms are in any way less articulated than conjunct forms.

Embedded *conjunct clauses* can serve a range of functions, as the (6) examples illustrate.

(6) a. *Ek^u nemenua ukâuia nekânî, tshissenimeu nienekâtshiâkannitî ukâuia.* (LITP)

ek^u nemenua u-kâui-a nekânî, tshissenim-e-u
then that.one 3-mother-OBV that.absent know-DIR-3

nienekâtshiâkan-nitî ukâuia.
suffer-CJ.3OBV 3-mother-OBV

'As for his mother, he knew she was abused.'

b. *Tshessenimât ekâ uâ nipâikut, enuet tshika pîtutetishâueu.* (LITP)
Tshessenim-ât ekâ uâ nipâiku-t, enuet tshika pîtutetishâu-e-u.
knew-CJ.3 NEG try kill-CJ.3 finally FUT invite-DIR-3
'When she knew he was not going to kill her, at least she invited him inside.'

c. *Anî uânitshissîtamûshapan shâsh kâtshi aimîshk.*
Anî uânitshissîtamûsha-pan shâsh kâtshi aimî-shk.
Annie forget-PRET already after call-CJ.3)1
'Annie forget that she already called you.'

d. *Pien aimîtâkue, nipâ uîtamuâpan eshpannitî ûkûmisha.*
Pien aimîtâkue, nipâ uîtamuâpan eshpan-nitî
Peter call-CJ.3.DUB1-would tell-1 how.go-OBV 3-uncle-OBV
û-kûmish-a.
'Had Peter called, I would have told him about his uncle.'

The use of conjunct clauses in embedded contexts is extended rather dramatically in narratives, where conjunct clauses are frequently found as root declarative clauses, as in the (7) examples.

(7) *Innu itâkanû papâmûteu. Ekue shâtshuâpâtâk nenu pâushtikunu, pâushtik[u] Piâssetshuânau.* (LITP)
Innu it-âkan-u papâmûteu. Ekue shâtshuâpâtâk nenu
person so-PASS-3 walk.around-3 then sees-CJ.3s that
pâushtikunu, pâushtik[u] Piâssetshuânau.
waterfall, waterfall Piâssetshuânau
'The story tells of an Innu person walking along. Then he sees that waterfall, the Piâssetshuânau falls.'

(8) *Mâniteu an, mâniteu Uâpush itâkanu. Pîtutshe anite, itâkanu. Ek[u] pâtutshet ne Uâpush mîtshuâpinu, innua nenua utîteu.* (LITP)
Mâniteu an, mâniteu Uâpush it-âkan-u. Pîtutshe anite, it-âkan-u.
visitor that visitor hare so-PASS-3 come-IMP there so-PASS-3
Ek[u] pâtutshet ne Uâpush mîtshuâpinu, innua nenua
then come-CJ.3s that hare house person that
utît-e-u.
meet-DIR-3
'The story tells of a visitor. The visitor is a Rabbit. Come in here, they (the Innu) say to him. Then the Rabbit enters the house and meets the Innu.'

For such cases, my working assumption is that the conjunct verb forms still serve as markers of subordination, even in these root clauses. But in narrative contexts, the subordinate marking serves a rhetorical function which is independent of the formal root/non-root distinction. In other words, I will assume that non-negative conjunct root declaratives can be treated as embedded clauses for a syntactic analysis. (An analysis of the rhetorical function of the choice of order in specific narrative contexts might certainly be revealing, but is beyond the scope of this work.)

Inflection in the verbal system is considerably more complex than in nominals, but is based on many of the same premises. The extra complexity reflects a number of factors. The first of these is the involvement of tense and evidentiality features, which I assume to be located in T. The second involves how the verbal inflection expresses agreement with both subjects and objects (or object-like agreement targets) at the same time. And the third involves the difference between the distinct inflectional orders: independent and conjunct. Much of the complexity of the last factor is covered in Chapter 4, where it is shown that the presence of an intervening Mood head blocks Feature Inheritance in the conjunct order. But the first and second factors are less central to the arguments for multiple head-movement developed in Chapter 4, so I provide some description of how they play out here.

Agreement, tense, and evidentiality in independent intransitive verbs

We can start with the relationship between tense and evidential features and agreement inflection in intransitive clauses, where there is only one agreement target to worry about. Within the verbal morphology, tense inflection distinguishes between a present/neuter tense and a past/preterite tense. Future tense is signified only with preverbs or adverbially. The relationship between tense inflection and time reference is not entirely clear. Neuter forms are fairly freely used to refer to events occuring in the past or present. Preterite forms are generally used for referring to events in the past, but in combination with specific modal preverbs, they may refer to events in the present or future as well.

Besides the tense distinctions, the verbal inflection distinguishes several types of evidentiality. For the independent order, Drapeau (2014) identifies dubitative, indirect, subjective, and conditional evidential modes. The subjective and conditional mode is discussed in Chapter 4. The indirect and dubitative are suffixal inflections which interact with tense, so they can be treated here.

In the independent order, the simplest structures are those where neuter tense is employed with no additional evidential features, as in (9).

(9) Inanimate intransitive (II) forms

a. *uishâuâu* "be yellow"

3s	uîshâuâ-u	3p	uîshâuâ-u-a
3s (obv.)	uîshâuâ-nu	3p (obv.)	uîshâuâ-nu-a

b. *âpatin* "be useful"

3s	âpatin	3p	âpatin-a
3s (obv.)	âpatin-nu	3p (obv.)	âpatin-nu-a

(10) Animate intransitive (AI) forms

a. *nipâu* "sleep"

1s	ni-nipâ-n	1pe	ni-napâ-n-ân
		1pi	tshi-napâ-n-ân
2s	tshi-nipâ-n	2p	tshi-nipâ-n-âu
3s	nipâ-u	3p	nipâ-u-at
3 (obv.)	nipâ-nu-a		

As these forms show, there are no 3rd person proclitics used in the verbal inflections, unlike possessed nominal forms. Singular non-3rd person agreement is zero in these forms, but the person features are fully expressed in the proclitics, adjoined to T. The plural agreement suffixes differ with animate (*-at*) and inanimate (*-a*) subjects.

Following Oxford (2019), I suppose that the ordering of the person features and the neuter tense suffix is indicative of a fission operation which operates on feature clusters in T, separating ϕ features off to the left. Oxford treats the suffix *-u* as a portmanteau expression of neuter tense and 3rd person combined. (Little turns on this, so I will continue to gloss *-u* simply as 3rd person.)

Like possessed nominals: verbs which agree with an obviative subject express the obviative feature twice. The obvious conclusion is that the same mechanism is responsible for double expression of obviative agreement. This can follow if the base structure for *nipânua*, for example, is (11).

(11)

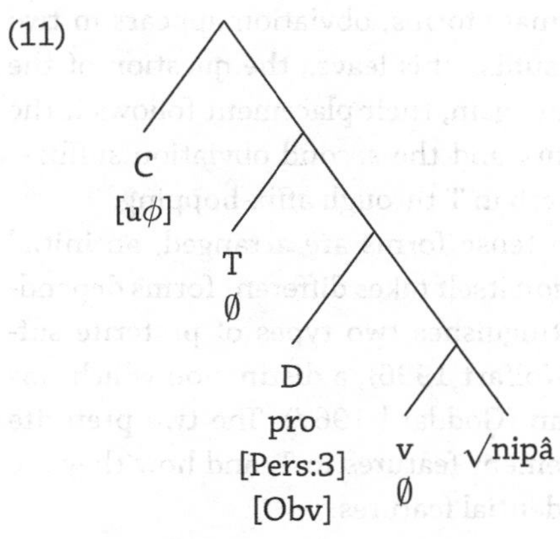

Valuation of [uϕ] in C will provide it with the 3rd person and obviative features of the subject, and Feature Inheritance will pass these along to T. But as with possessed nominals, C keeps a copy of the obviative feature to itself. The obviative feature in C is then realized as *-a*. And affix-hopping must then take place to attach *-a* to the end of the inflected verb raised to T.

Consideration of the 3rd person plural forms in (9)–(10) also reveals that the plural feature in 3rd person forms is also detached from the exponent of the person feature. This too can be captured by an affix-hopping analysis, if we suppose that C keeps a copy of the person ϕ feature complexes. Then the inanimate *-a* suffix and the animate *-at* suffix will also undergo affix-hopping from C to T.

Addition of dubitative and evidential inflection to the picture supports the affix-hopping analysis of 3rd person plural and obviative features.

(12) a. '*be yellow*' (dubitative)

3s	uîshâuâ-tshe	3p	uîshâuâ-tshen-î
3s (obv.)	uîshâuâ-nî-tshe	3p (obv.)	uîshâuâ-ni-tshen-î

b. '*sleep*' (indirect)

1s	ni-nipâ-n-atak	1pe	ni-nipâ-nân-atak
2s	tshi-nipâ-n-atak	1pi	tshi-nipâ-nan-atak
		2p	tshi-nipâ-nau-atak
3s	nipâ-tak	3p	nipâ-tak-at
3 (obv.)	nipâ-ni-tak-a		

One noteworthy characteristic of these evidential forms is that the order of non-3rd person features and the evidential features in T are the reverse of what we have seen. Evidently, the fission operation which breaks up T orders them differently, when T is evidential, rather than simply the neuter tense. In this case, the ϕ features are split off to the left. Another important pattern is that plurality is expressed in the 3rd person forms to the right of the evidential suffix, while it combines with person features *portemanteau* to the left in the non-3rd person forms. And in the animate forms, obviation appears in two positions, sandwiching the evidential suffix. This leaves the question of the agreement suffixes to the right of T, but again, their placement follows if the peripheral suffixes—3rd person plurality and the second obviation suffix—originate in C and are attached to the verb in T through affix-hopping.

Turning now to how past/preterite tense forms are arranged, an initial observation is that the preterite inflection itself takes different forms depending on the context. The literature distinguishes two types of preterite suffixes: P-preterites and HT-preterites (Wolfart 1996), a distinction which was apparently present in proto-Algonquian (Goddard 1967). The two preterite types differ in how they linearize agreement features in T, and how they are themselves ordered with respect to evidential features.

In Innu-aimûn, the P-preterite suffix is *-pan*, and it appears to be the default, *elsewhere* preterite form. In the simplest preterite forms, *-pan* is found in verbs which do not register agreement with any 1st or 2nd person participants, either as subjects or as objects. The HT-preterite is realized in several different ways on the surface. In verbs with plural 1st and 2nd person subjects, the preterite suffix is realized as /t/, and the initial consonant—/n/ or /u/—of the following agreement suffix is deleted. A complete paradigm which illustrates the overall output is in (13).

With II verbs, where the option of agreement with a non-3rd person is moot, only the P-preterite suffix is found. This is also the case for AI verbs with 3rd person subjects.

(13) *'be dry'*

3s	pâshte-pan	3p	pâshte-pan-î
3s (obv.)	pâshte-nî-pan	3p (obv.)	pâshte-nî-pan-î

(14) *'work'*

3s	atusse-pan	3p	atusse-pan-at
3 (obv.)	atusse-nî-pan-î		

These forms conform to the pattern seen with evidentials, where a fission operation appears to break tense and ϕ features in T into two parts, with ϕ features to the left and tense to the right. And the peripheral affixes again originate in C and affix-hopping then moves them to the end of the T-inflected verb.

When an AI preterite verb has a non-3rd person subject, the HT-preterite is used.

(15) *'work'*

1s	nit-atusse-ti	1pe	nit-atusse-t-ân
		1pi	tshit-atusse-t-ân
2s	tshit-atusse-ti	2p	tshit-atusse-t-âu

The HT-preterite functions like the neuter tense forms, with ϕ features fissioned off to the right of the tense morphology. In some dialects, the preterite *-t(i)* suffix takes a zero allomorph in singular forms (*nitatusse*, *tshitattuse*. In others, the allomorph used in singular forms is /-h/.[1]

What remains to consider are the intransitive verbs with agreement, preterite tense, and evidential morphology all combined, such as (16)–(17).

1. Clarke (1982) even observes individual variation in Sheshatshiu in the pronunciation of preterite endings in 1st and 2nd singular verbs; some speakers pronounce a final /h/ in this position.

(16) *'be small'* (indirect)

3s	apishâshi-sha-pan	3p	apishâshi-sha-pan-î
3s (obv.)	apishâshi-nî-sha-pan	3p (obv.)	apishâshi-ni-sha-pan-î

(17) *'sing'* (dubitative)

1s	ni-nikamu-tâ-ku-pan	1pe	ni-nikamu-tâ-na-ku-pan
		1pi	tshi-nikamu-tâ-na-ku-pan
2s	tshi=nikamu-tâ-ku-pan	2p	tshi-nikamu-tâ-ua-ku-pan
3s	nikamu-iku-pan	3p	nikamu-iku-pan-at
3 (obv)	nikamu-nî-ku-pan-î		

With the 3rd person forms in both inanimate and animate agreeing forms, the pattern simply extends what has already been seen. In this case, fission appears to split T into three components: ϕ features, an evidential affix, and preterite tense, in that order. The peripheral suffix which signifies 3rd person plurality or a second obviative exponent can be identified with an affix-hopping C. With the 1st and 2nd person forms, more is going on. The evidential feature and ϕ features are evidently still split off from T, but also *both* the HT-preterite *-tâ* and the P-preterite *-pan* appear in these forms: the former to the left of T's ϕ features and the latter to the right of the evidential suffix.

Inflections with transitive verbs

Transitive verbs in Innu-aimûn fall into two broad categories: verbs which agree with animate objects and verbs which do not. The latter may not agree because they select objects which are not animate, or they may simply not agree as a lexical property. The former are often called "transitive inanimate" (TI) verbs; the latter, "animate intransitive with object" (AI+O) verbs.

For the immediate purposes of this survey of inflectional patterns, the verbs which do not agree with objects can be assimilated to the class of intransitive verbs with animate subjects. For example, the conjugation of *tutam*ᵘ 'do it' in (18) shows the same inflectional patterns as have just been examined.

(18) *tûtam*ᵘ 'do it': preterite and neuter dubitative conjugations[2]

	preterite	*neuter dubitative*
1	ni-tûte	ni-tûte-n-âtshe
2	tshi-tûte	tshi-tûte-n-âtshe
1pe	ni-tûte-t-ân	nitûte-n-ân-âtshe
1pi	tshi-tûte-t-ân	tshi-tûte-n-ân-âtshe
2p	tshi-tûte-t-âu	tshi-tûte-n-âuâtshe
3	tûtam-û-pan	tûtam-û-tshe
3p	tûtam-û-pan-at	tûtam-û-tshen-at

2. The preterite forms given here reflect dialectal allomorphy in which preterite *-t(i)* is zero in singular forms, as also occurs in AI verbs.

Verbs which do agree with an animate object—TA verbs—raise other questions. For the most part, I adopt the analyses put forward by Goddard (1979), Brittain (2001), Oxford (2014), and others for these inflected forms. Let us examine some paradigms for the representative TA verb *uîtshieu* 'help'. The least complex possibilities are seen in (19).

(19) *uîtshieu* 'help': neuter non-evidential non-3rd person forms

1s	2s	tshi-uîtshi-ti-n	1pe	2s	tshi-uîtshi-ti-nân
	2p	tshi-uîtshi-ti-n-âu		2p	tshi-uîtshi-ti-nâu
2s	1s	tshi-uîtshi-n	2p	1s	tshi-uîtshi-n-âu
	1pe	tshi-uîtshi-n-ân		1pe	tshi-uîtshi-n-âu

There are two new properties of these forms. First, the proclitic adjoined to T is sometimes associated with the subject and sometimes, with the object. This implies that C must be able to agree twice in TA forms, at least when there are multiple non-3rd person arguments . And since subject and object are both speech act participants in (19), there are two potential sources for proclitics attached to the inflected verb, but only one actually appears, and that is always the 2nd person *tshi(t)*. It may be that Innu-aimûn proclitics are subject to *Condition on Clitic Hosts* (Arregi & Nevins 2012, Matthew Tyler 2018), which limits the number of clitics which may appear. In the TA verb forms, the repair strategy appears to be deletion of a 1st person clitic in the presence of a 2nd person clitic.

The second new property is the appearance of the '*directional*' suffixes. Here, the *-ti* suffix is used when the object is 2nd person; the *-n* affix, with 1st person objects. I take these to be reflect simple object agreement, which I assume occurs in the v phase head. It follows that the structure for *tshuîtshitinâu* following valuation of [uϕ] and Feature Inheritance is something like (20).

(20)

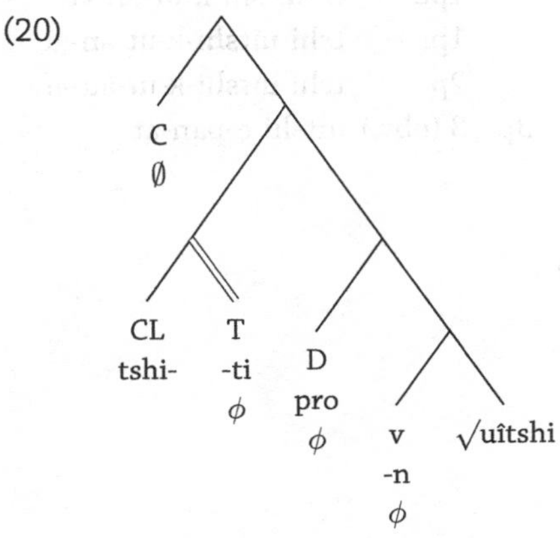

Feature Inheritance will transfer ϕ features from C to T in (20). Head-movement will then form the inflected X^0 form (21) in the position of T.

(21)

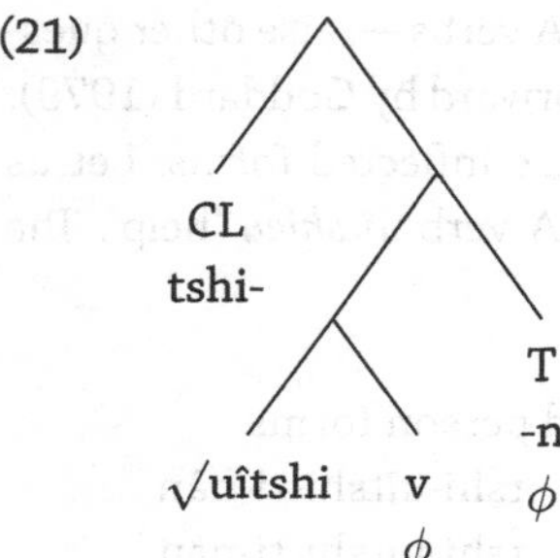

A subsequent fission operation will split the ϕ features in T off to the right of the neutral tense *-n*, after which the realization of ϕ features in v and T ensures the correct surface form.

When 3rd person arguments are included in the mix, the derivations become more complex. Consider the paradigm (22).

(22) *uîtshieu*: past non-evidential forms with 3rd persons[3]

1s	3s	ni-uîtshi-â-ti	1pe	3s	ni-uîtshi-â-t-ân
	3p	ni-uîtshi-â-ti-at		3p	ni-uîtshi-â-t-ân-at
	3 (obv.)	n-uîtshi-m-â-ti-a		3 (obv.)	n-uîtshi-m-â-t-ân-î
			1pi	3s	tsh-uîtshi-â-t-ân
				3p	tsh-uîtshi-â-t-ân-at
				3 (obv.)	tsh-uîtshi-m-â-t-ân-î
2s	3s	tshi-uîtshi-â-ti	2p	3s	tshi-uîtshi-â-t-âu
	3p	tshi-uîtshi-â-ti-at		3p	tshi-uîtshi-â-t-âu-at
	3 (obv.)	tshi-uîtshi-m-â-ti-a		3 (obv.)	tshi-uîtshi-m-â-t-âu-aua
3s	1s	ni-uîtshi-k-uti	3p	1s	ni-uîtshi-k-uti-at
	2s	tshi-uîtshi-k-uti		2s	tshi-uîtshi-k-uti-at
	1pe	ni-uîtshi-k-ut-ân		1pe	ni-uîtshi-k-ut-ân-at
	1pi	tshi-uîtshi-k-ut-ân		1pi	tshi-uîtshi-k-ut-ân-at
	2p	tshi-uîtshi-k-ut-âu		2p	tshi-uîtshi-k-ut-âu-at
	3 (obv.)	uîtshi-e-pan	3p	3 (obv.)	uîtshi-e-pan-at
3 (obv.)	1s	n-uîtshi-ku-n-î			
	1pe	n-uîtshi-ku-t-ân-î			
	1pi	tsh-uîtshi-ku-t-ân-î			
	2s	tsh-uîtshi-ku-n-î			
	2p	tsh-uîtshi-ku-t-âu-a			
	3s	uîtshi-k-upan			
	3p	uîtshi-k-upan-at			
	3 (obv.)	uîtshi-e-nî-pan-î			

3. Drapeau (2014) indicates these TA forms are characteristic of the Mamit dialect.

When the object is a 3rd person, the directional suffix is *-â*, unless the subject is also a 3rd person (proximate or obviative). When a 3rd person subject appears with an obviative 3rd person object, the *-a* suffix undergoes an ablaut rule which raises it to [e]. This same rule affects other /â/ vowels in the stem in some intransitive 3rd person forms (Goddard 1967), so this cannot reflect allomorphy in the directional suffix. When a 3rd person subject (proximate or obviative) appears with a non-3rd person object, the *inverse* directional affix *-kᵘ* appears. The inverse directional affix also appears when an obviative subject appears with a proximate 3rd person object.

Following Oxford (2015), I suppose that the inverse affix appears when the combination of subject features and object features are incompatible with each other. More precisely, since C can agree with both subject and object, v agrees with an object, and C transfers ϕ features to T, the situation sometimes arises in which both T and v will bear identical person features, and this violates a general ban on adjacent identical person features (Nevins 2011). Such a violation triggers a repair operation which deletes person features from v. The inverse *-kᵘ* affix is then the realization of an agreeing v from which person features have been deleted.

Besides the morphology provided by T and v, the forms in (22) also contain suffixes which are the result of affix-hopping from affixal C. These include 3rd person plural *-at*, which can realize features of either a subject or an object, because C can agree twice. They also include obviate subject agreement suffixes: *-î -(u)a*. When obviative subjects appear with obviative objects, then the familiar double expression of obviation results (*uîtshienîpanî*), because both T and C provide an obviative affix. The obviative agreement in T disappears in inverse contexts, however, leaving only the C obviative suffix.

When an obviative object is present, it is reflected in an extra *-m* suffix to the immediate left of the directional suffix, unless the subject is also obviative. The position of the obviative *-m* suffix can be attributed to a fission operation which splits obviative features off to the left of v. But when obviative agreement features are present in both T and v, then *-m* is not found. I suppose this is another effect of feature deletion on v which repairs a structure with two adjacent identical features. But in this case, the obviative feature on v deletes, and not the 3rd person features.

When evidential affixes are added into the TA verb forms, they appear to follow the same patterns as already seen with II and AI verbs.

(23) *uîtshieu*: assorted past evidential forms

a. tsh-uîtshi-tî-tâ-nâ-ku-pan-at.
2-help-2-PRET-1pe-DUB-PRET-p
'We (excl.) helped you (dubitative).'

b. n-uîtshi-â-ta-nâ-ku-pan.
1-help-3-PRET-1pe-DUB-PRET
'We (excl.) helped her (dubitative).'

c. uîtshi-e-ku-pan-at.
help-DIR-DUB-PRET-p
'They helped her (dubitative).'

d. uîtshi-ku-ni-pan-î.
help-INV-OBV-PRET-OBV
'S/he (obv.) helped her (dubitative).'

e. n-uîtshi-m-â-t-ân-âku-pan-î.
1-help-OBV-DIR-PRET-1pe-DUB-PRET-OBV
'I helped her (obv.) (dubitative).'

As the (23) examples show, both P-preterites and HT-preterites appear in dubitative verbs with non-3rd person arguments—(23a,b,e)—while P-preterites appear alone when there are only 3rd person arguments: (23c,d). Affix-hopping from C attaches 3rd person plural and subject obviative agreement affixes: (23a,c,d,e). This produces double subject obviative marking—(23d)—and double object obviative marking: (23e). Each of these patterns has been seen already, in non-evidential structures.

A.3.3 Verbal inflection in the conjunct order

In the conjunct order, the overall pattern is that the inflectional morphology uses different morphemes from the independent order although there is occasional similarity. Agreement morphology in both orders is appended to the verb, following the directional (v) suffix in TV verbs. A illustration of (incomplete) agreement patterns for both conjunct and independent forms of *minuateu* 'love' is provided in (24), where the hyphen separates the proclitics, stem, direction, and the rest of the inflections.

(24)

		Conjunct	Independent
1s	2s	minuât-it-an	tshi-minuât-iti-n
1s	2p	minuât-it-ikut	tshi-minuât-iti-nau
1e	2s	minuât-it-ât	tshi-minuât-iti-nân
1e	2p	minuât-it-ât	tshi-minuât-iti-nân
1s	3s	minuât-ak	ni-minuât-â-u
1s	3p	minuât-akau	ni-minuât-â-uat
1s	3OBV	minuât-im-akî	ni-minuât-imâ-ua
1e	3s	minuât-atshît	ni-minuât-â-nân
1e	3p	minuât-atshîht	ni-minuât-â-nânat
1e	3OBV	minuât-im-atshîtî	ni-minuât-imâ-nâna
1i	3s	minuât-âk[u]	tshi-minuât-â-nân
1i	3p	minuât-âkut	tshi-minuât-â-nânat
1i	3OBV	minuât-im-âkuî	tshi-minuât-imâ-nâna

2s	1s	minuâsh-in	tshi-minuâsh-in
2s	1e	minuâsh-iât	tshi-minuâsh-in-ân
2p	1s	minuâsh-iek^u	tshi-minuâsh-in-au
2p	1e	minuâsh-iât	tshi-minuâsh-in-ân
2s	3s	minuât-at	tshi-minuât-â-u
2s	3p	minuât-atau	tshi-minuât-â-uat
2s	3OBV	minuât-im-atî	tshi-minuât-imâ-uaua
2p	3s	minuât-ek^u	tshi-minuât-â-uau
2p	3p	minuât-ekut	tshi-minuât-â-uauat
2p	3OBV	minuât-im-ekuî	tshi-minuât-imâ-uauat
3s	3OBV	minuât-ât	minuât-e-u
3p	3OBV	minuât-âht	minuât-e-uat
3OBV	3s	minuât-iku-t	minuât-iku
3OBV	3p	minuât-iku-tau	minuât-iku-at

The first conclusion to draw from a comparison of the conjunct and independent forms in (24) is that the two share only limited inflectional similarities, if any. A second conclusion which seems viable is that the conjunct agreement inflections employ frequent portmanteau means to express subject and object agreement. The effects of a fission operation may be found in the 3rd plural and obviative agreement forms, where plural *-t* and obviative *-î* are apparently split off to the right. With the 3rd person plural forms in 1pe and proximate 3rd person subject forms, the fission operation produces an autosegmental affix which is realized as a low tone on the final syllable. This low town is indicated orthographically with the *h* written before final *t*. A third is that the form of the directional affix is contextually dependent. Particularly in the conjunct order, the directional affix has a visible form only when it expresses obviative or 2nd person agreement. For 1st person objects and proximate 3rd persons, the directional suffix is zero.

In conjunct verb forms which lack animate object agreement, such as the AI forms in (25), a different set of (portmanteau) agreement inflections are found.

(25) *atusseu* 'work': simple conjunct inflections

1s	atusse-iân
2s	atusse-in
3s	atusse-t
1pe	atusse-iât
1pi	atusse-iak^u
2p	atusse-iek^u
3p	atusse-ht
3OBV	atusse-niti

Here again, 3rd person plural agreement is expressed with low tone, resulting from a fission operation.

In the conjugation of TI forms like *petam*ᵘ 'hear (it)' in (26), the effect of the phonological rule which deletes nasals before obstruents can be seen.

(26) *petam*ᵘ conjunct order conjugation

1s	petam-ân
2s	petam-in
3s	petâ-k
1e	petam-ât
1i	petam-âkᵘ
2p	petam-ekᵘ
3p	petâ-hk
3OBV	petam-initî

The *-k* suffix in 3rd person forms triggers deletion of the stem-final /m/. In the 3rd person plural form, fission of the plural agreement feature also produces low tone on the final suffix in certain dialects.

In the conjunct order, past tense is expressed in a preverb, so there are no preterite conjunct inflections. But evidential distinctions are still available in the conjunct order.

(27) *pashteu* 'be dry' (dubitative)

3s	pashte-tshe	3p	pashte-tshen-î
3 (obv.)	pashte-ni-tshe	3p (obv.)	pashte-ni-tshen-î

(28) *atusseu* 'work' (indirect)

1s	atusse-uâne	1pe	atusse-uâtshe
		1pi	atusse-uâkue
2s	atusse-une	2p	attuse-uekue
3s	atusse-kue	3p	atusse-kuen-it
3 (obv.)	atusse-ni-kuen-î		

Here again, fission may be responsible for the presence of final plural and obviative agreement suffixes. Unfortunately, for these forms, there is little concrete evidence available to support further morphological analysis.

A.3.4 Initial change

In certain syntactic contexts, discussed in Chapter 4, the initial vowel in a verbal complex is altered by *initial change*, an ablaut process with the effects in (29).

(29) *Internal change effects*

a. /i/ → /e/
b. /a/ → /e/
c. /u/ → /ue/
d. /î/ → /â/ or /iâ/
e. /â/ → /iâ/
f. /û/ → /iû/

A.4 TRANSITIVE VERB PAIRS

As noted above, verbs which select a nominal complement—structurally transitive verbs—typically show morphological agreement with animate objects, but not with inanimate objects. Another way to say this is that only TA verbs—with animate objects—are formally transitive.

In many cases, TA verbs have a counterpart verb which takes an inanimate nominal complement. Some examples of such verbal pairs appear in (30)–(31). The (30) pairs show a TA verb paired with a TI verb. In (31), the TA verb is matched with an AI+O verb.

(30)

TA	TI	
mishkueu	mishkam^{u}	'find'
ausseueu	ausseim^{u}	'stir it using an object'
pakueueu	pakueim^{u}	'take a piece off it using an object'
amissueu	amisseim^{u}	'mix it using an object'
atatsheueu	atatsheim^{u}	'put a fence around it'
peshaueu	peshaim^{u}	'paint it'
kushapeueu	kushapeim^{u}	'submerge it using an object or projectile'
tatueueueu	tatueueim^{u}	'make noise hitting him/her'
tapitsheueu	tapitsheim^{u}	'comb or brush it/her'
apaneu	apanam^{u}	'warm it in one's hands'
nishaskuneu	nishuashkunam^{u}	'hold two of them (sticks) in one's hands'
shikuneu	shikunam^{u}	'crush it in one's hands'
tepinew	tepinam^{u}	'hold it completely in one's hands'
uetshineu	uetshinam^{u}	'hold tightly (hug) in one's arms'
uapikameu	uapikatam^{u}	'whiten it by putting it in one's mouth'
nishtumeu	nishtutam^{u}	'gather a bunch of it in one's mouth'
mashkumeu	mashkutam^{u}	'harden it in one's mouth'
apameu	apatam^{u}	'thaw, melt it in one's mouth'
utameu	utatam^{u}	'take it with one's teeth (or pliers), inhale it in'

putiputateu	putiputatam^{u}	'blow repeatedly on it/her'
aputameu	aputatam^{u}	'warm it by blowing on/in it'
pakuemeu	pakuetam^{u}	'bite a piece of it off
ashtueshkueu	ashtueshkam^{u}	'extinguish it with one's feet'
ashatshishkueue	ashatshishkam^{u}	'catch one's feet on it'
mushkauatshishkueu	mushkauatshishkam^{u}	'take it out of the sand with one's feet'
nemishueshkueu	nemishueshkam^{u}	'spread it everywhere with one's feet'
nishtushkueu	nishtushkam^{u}	'pile up with one's feet'
pakushkueu	pakushkam^{u}	'dry it by rubbing with one's feet'

(31)

TA	AI+O	
anakassipuneu	anakassiputâu	'saw it wide'
ashushimeu	ashushtâu	'lean against something'
atutaieu	atutatâu	'take it/her to another place'
kaneu	katâu	'hide'
kunuieu	kunutâu	'put snow on it/her'
kupuneu	kuputâu	'saw it down'
ishkuieu	ishkutâu	'make it a certain length'
ishipuneu	ishiputâu	'saw it in a certain way'
ishpanieu	ishpanitâu	'make her/it go in a certain direction
itashkatimeu	itashkatitâu	'let it/her freeze to a certain point'
itashtameu	itashtatâu	'put it/her in the wind in a certain way'
mashkuneu	mashkutâu	'harden it by hand'
nanuieu	nanutâu	'waste, let rot'
nauieu	nautâu	'spill'
nishupuneu	nishuputâu	'saw it in two, saw two at a time'
nishupuneu	nishtuputâu	'saw it in three, saw three at a time'
nukuieu	nukutâu	'make appear, reveal'
pakaieu	pakatâu	'boil it to cook it'
punieu	punitâu	'stop doing something to it/her'
tishuneu	tishutâu	'trap it/her'
uapieu	uapitâu	'whiten, lighten it'
unieu	unitâu	'lose, mislay'
utapuneu	utaputâu	'shrink it in the wash'

The only clear difference between the TI verbs and the AI+O verbs is the morpheme in stem-final position. In TI verbs, the final morpheme is *-(t)am*. This suffix is uniquely affected by local phonological adjustment rules which change /am/ to /e/ when followed immediately by a tense suffix: (32). This context is found in forms with non-3rd person agreement. (The silent HT-preterite found in singular 1st and 2nd persons in some dialects also triggers this change.) In conjunct forms, there is no suffixal tense inflection, so no such change occurs.

(32) Neuter independent conjugation *mishkam*ᵘ 'find it'

1s	ni-mishk-e-n	1pe	ni-mishk-e-n-ân
		1pi	tshi-mishk-e-n-ân
2s	tshimishk-e-n	2p	tshi-mishk-e-n-âu
3s	mishk-am-ᵘ	3p	mishk-am-u-at
3 (obv.)	mishk-am-inu-a		

I suppose, with Piggott (1989), that this morphological quirk does not mean that the *-(t)am* suffix is of a different category from other stem-final suffixes. In AI+O verbs, the most common final suffix is *-tâ*, which is invariant in form. In other words, the paired verbs for TA verbs usually end with either *-(t)am* or *-tâ* stem-final suffixes.

With that in mind, a general pattern characterizes almost all transitive verb pairs. The TA verb is typically equivalent to its counterpart, but with the stem-final suffix in the TI or AI+O verb replaced by animate object agreement morphology. In many cases, this pattern is transparent, but with both TI and AI+O verbs it is sometimes obscured by regular phonological alternations. For example, in the pair *kaneu; katâu* 'hide', the underlying form of the AI+O form will include a nasal consonant: *kan-tâ-u*. But in this context, /n/ is deleted before an obstruent. In the TA form, with no *-tâ* suffix, the original nasal consonant is preserved. The same is true of the TA/TI pair *apameu; apatam*ᵘ 'melt in one's mouth'.

In TI forms, the presence of *-tam*ᵘ triggers a phonological readjustment of preceding rounded velar obstruents, which become unrounded. The effect of this is seen in pairs like *mishkueu; mishkam*ᵘ 'find' or *ashtueshkueu; ashtueshkam*ᵘ 'extinguish with one's feed'.

Less obviously, in pairs like *ausseueu; ausseim*ᵘ 'stir using an object', the underlying form of the TI verb is derived from an original verb stem ending in /ah/, followed by *-am*. In such combinations, intervocalic /h/ is deleted, and then the sequence of two /a/ vowels is altered into an /ei/ diphthong. The same formation of /ei/ diphthongs is sometimes seen even between a preverb and a following verb (Clarke 1982), as in (33).

(33) Ni-ka=ashuâpamâu. → /nəgeišwabmaw/
1-FUT=await(TA)
'I will wait for him.'

Again, although the surface forms do not immediately make it clear, the relationship between the TA and TI forms appears to follow from the absence of *-(t)am* in the former.

At this point, the morphological difference between TA verbs and their counterparts can be derived from the syntactic derivation. Since animate object agreement appears in complementary distribution with the non-TA stem-final affix, we should analyses them as occupying the same initial morpho-syntactic position. It has already been established that direction markers are found in v; the same must then be true of final AM, TA, etc.

Suppose that the base structure of the verb phrase for both TA *mishkueu* 'find' and TI *mishkam*ᵘ is what (34) portrays.

(34)

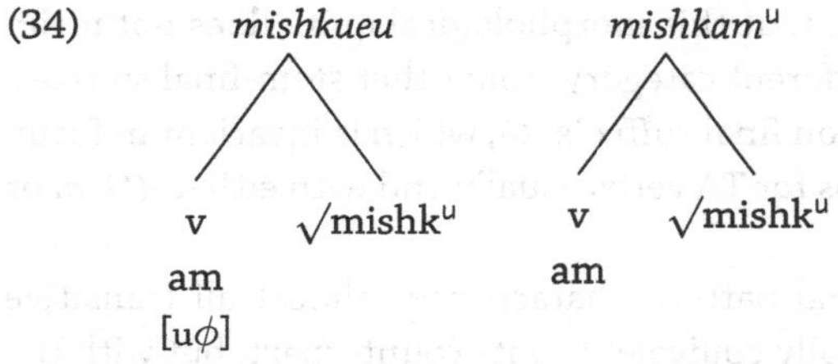

The only difference between the two structures is that the TA structure includes [uϕ] in v, which will take their value from the animate object. But valued phi features in v must have some morphological realization, and we have seen what that looks like above. But no exponence is possible if the final already provides its own phonetic content. The solution must be to delete either the original suffix or the ϕ features. And the answer chosen for Innu-aimûn grammer is to delete the original suffix, to preserve ϕ.

A.5 OTHER FINALS IN VERBAL MORPHOLOGY

Besides the stem-final morphemes found in transitive verbs, the Innu-aimûn lexicon includes a large number of other verbal "finals" which appear in intranstives. The recent generative literature on this topic tends towards a broad consensus, starting from the proposal by Brittain (2003) that at least some of these may also be identified with the syntactic *v* category, a hypothesis extended and supported by subsequent studies by Hirose (2004), Branigan, Brittain & Dyck (2005a), Branigan, Brittain & Dyck (2005b), Barrie & Mathieu (2016), and Ritter & Rosen (2005). If so, then the combination of a verb root with a single, simplex final can be accomplished through the usual head-movement operation which raises the root to *v*. For example with the verb *pâpû* 's/he laughs', with the final *-u*, the underlying syntactic structure of vP will be (35).

(35)

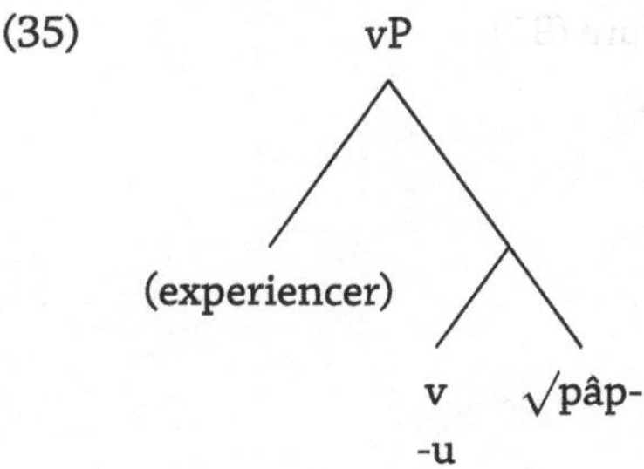

In both intransitive and transitive verbs, the stem-final morpheme appears to introduce meaningful lexical semantic content. For example, the initial syntactic structure for the intransitive verb *minuenimeu* [like] will be (36), with initial *minu-* and final *-enim*.

(36)

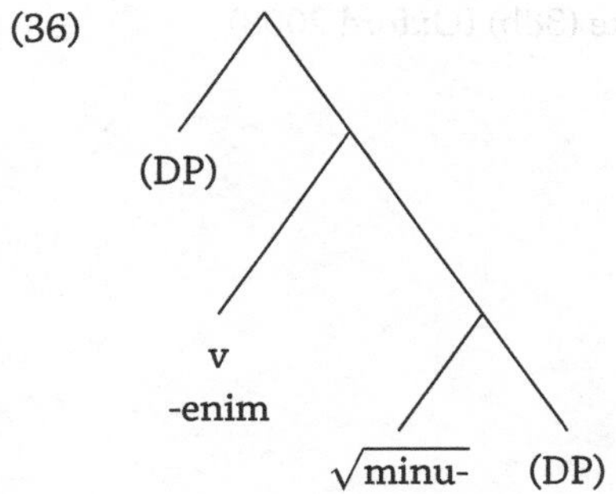

The same final appears frequently within verbs which signify a cognitive or emotional state, such as *aieshkuenimeu* 'worry about', *ishpitenimeu* 'respect', *kassenimeu* 'be troubled because of someone', *mûshtuenimeu* 'desire'.[4]

Finals which provide semantic content which is not contained in the meaning of the (initial) root may in fact be the norm. Here I consider a tiny sample, simply to illustrate some of the possibilities. The final *-âkuan* appears to provide sensory/evidential context, in forms like *nûtshimîumâkuan* 'smell like the bush', *pineumâkuan* 'smell of partridge', *shâshtemâkuan* 'smell rancid', *uâkâshinâkuan* 'be an eyesore'. Verbs which specify some 'sitting' activity will often use the *-ap* final, as in *ueuepapu* 'sway while sitting', *ueuetapu* 'sit down',

4. All verbs in which *-enim* appears in full are transitive, because the final is morphologically reduced in contexts in which an animate object is not agreed with. See section A.4.

askapu 'be tired from sitting', *kuessapu* 'change position while sitting, turn around'. Similarly, the final *-kuâm* appears within verbs where some activity takes place in a sleeping state, such as *aimûkuâmu* 'talk in one's sleep', *matuakuâmu* 'snore', *puetshitikuâmu* 'fart in one's sleep', *shamatîpîkuâmu* 'sleep sitting up'. Again, assuming Brittain's approach, a verb like *aimûkuâmu* 'talk in one's sleep' will originate with the structure (37).

(37)

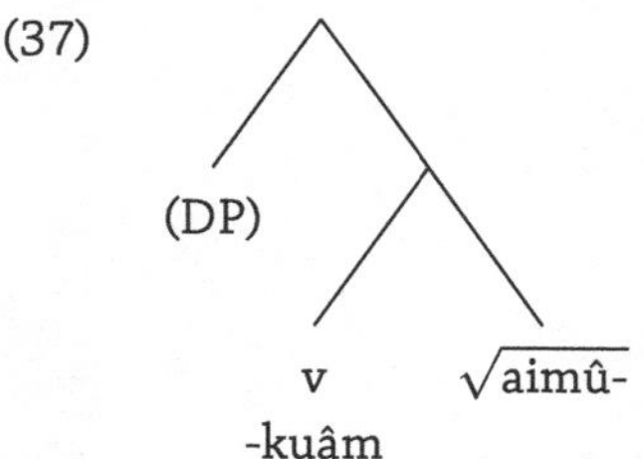

Similarly, some finals in other categories can best be characterized as functional heads which select an (acategorial) root and which supply a categorial identity (and some other meanings). So the noun *teueikan* 'drum' with final *-ikan* can be analysed as (38a), while the locative expression *mitshuâpit* 'at the house' with final *-ît* calls for a structure like (38b) (Oxford 2008).

(38) a.

b.

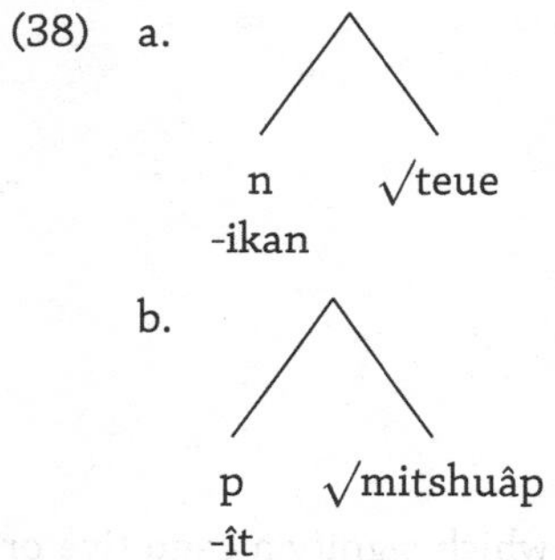

While many Innu-aimûn finals provide phonetic substance, some are silent (Bloomfield 1946), like their English v counterparts. Thus, *aimû* 'speak' shows no obvious "final" componenent. It will nevertheless appear in a bipartite syntactic structure, with the root *aimû* appearing as complement to a silent v. The categorizing function of the silent v final is evident from the use of the same root to form the noun *aimûn* 'speech', when combined with the nominalizing final *-n*. (Final *-n* can therefore be taken as head of an nP.)

Obviously, if Brittain's hypothesis is correct, then v in Innu-aimûn carries much more expressive content than v in a language like English. In English, v serves two purposes: it provides the grammatical category for an acategorial root (Marantz 1997), and it establishes the transitivity of the verb, by providing ϕ and Case features. In Innu-aimûn, the v final can carry out both of these tasks, but it also introduces additional semantic content. Not all the lexical semantic content in a verb phrase is provided by the verbal root.

There can be more than one "final" suffix within a single verb. Compare the endings in the (39) forms:

(39) a. *apuâ-tam*ᵘ 'roast it (on a stick)'
b. *apuâ-n* 'meat roasted (on a stick)'

In (39a), the final *-tam*ᵘ is a transitive v, replaced by its nominal counterpart *-n* in (39b). The same final also appears in verbs like *ishpitenitam*ᵘ [respect something] or *kassenitam*ᵘ [be sad], but in these verbs *-tam*ᵘ succeeds the *-enim* final used for verbs of cognitive or emotional states. (The final /m/ in *-enim* is deleted by regular phonological rule.) It follows that *-enim* cannot belong to the v category, because *-tam* is v in these verbs.

The implication is that some finals are v, and some are not. In any verb with multiple finals, only the final final can belong to the v category. And in fact, even the final final might not always be v, because the correct analysis for some verbs might require a silent v preceded by an audible non-v final.

Along these lines, we may model the structure of examples like Innu-aimûn *kass-eni-tam*ᵘ [be sad] as in (40).

(40)

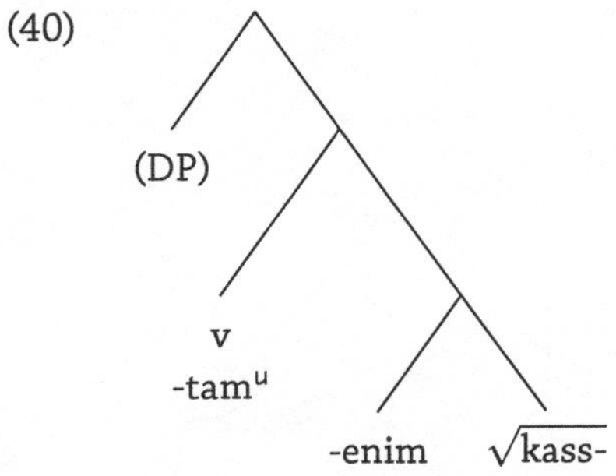

The categorial identity of the *-enim* in (40) remains unclear. The position it occupies, between v and the verbal root, is similar to that of a high applicative head, but *-enim* does not itself introduce an extra argument, so the two should probably not be equated. Happily for my purposes, a more precise characterization of such non-final finals is not necessary to understand the claims made in the main body of this work. All that matters is that non-final finals are distinct from the v final, and that there should be a mechanism for integrating them into a complex word. For the latter, it is sufficient to assume that normal, compliant head-movement displaces the verb root up to the non-final final position, and that a subsequent head-movement operation raises the result up to v, as in (41).

(41)

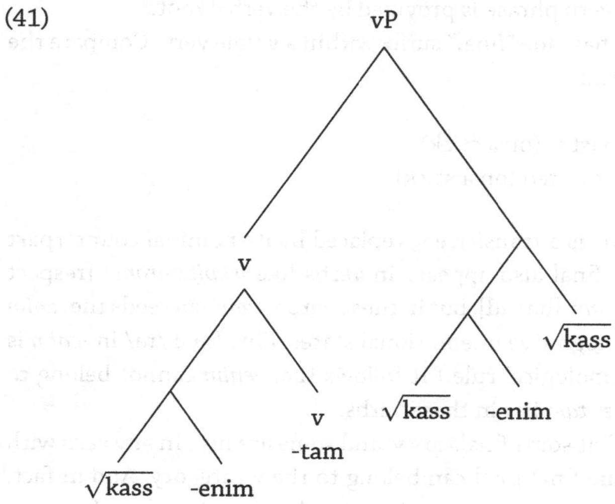

And even when there are multiple non-final finals, the same mechanism will be available for uniting the root with its full set of (final) suffixes.

(42) a. *Ânishkuâpîkâtam*ᵘ.
   ânishku-âpik-â-t-am-u.
   contiguous-cord-FNL-FNL-FNL-3
   'S/he ties it on to another.'

  b. *Kassenitamieu.*
   kass-enim-tam-i-e-u.
   sad-FNL-FNL-FNL-DIR-3
   'S/he makes him/her sad.'

For the most part, the presence of extra finals, i.e. recursive vP structures, will have no significant impact on the analyses of Algonquian morphosyntax develped here. But since final clusters are so common, they will be found in many of the data examined. To my mind, it would be distracting (and typographically expensive) to present all of the extra vP structure in any tree diagrams, so I adopt the practice of simply presenting final clusters as if they occupy a single v^0 head position. In other words, instead of the more accurate structure shown in (41), the reader can expect generally to see the more compressed version in (43).

(43)

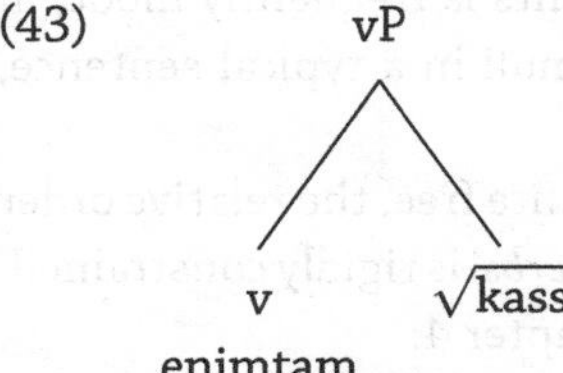

I depart from this convention only in section 4.4.1, where it is (briefly) important to the discussion to focus specifically on the role of distinct finals in the derivation.

A.6 WORD ORDER

Word order in Innu-aimûn is very free, as appears to be the case for any of the Algonquian languages. For a minimal transitive sentence, all possible permutations are typically acceptable, and evidently synonymous.

(44) *Pûn mûpishtuepan Mânîua.*
Pun mûpishtu-e-pan Mânî-ua.
Paul visit-DIR-PRET Marie-OBV
'Paul visited Marie.'

a. *Mûpishtuepan Pûn Mânîua.*
b. *Mûpishtuepan Mânîua Pûn.*
c. *Mânîua mûpishtuepan Pûn.*
d. *Mânîua Pûn mûpishtuepan.*
e. *Pûn Mânîua mûpishtuepan.*

This does not mean that all permutations are equivalent in all discourse contexts. There is reason to believe that they are not, and that word order changes affect the identity of clause topics, presuppositions, and foci of various types. But there is no exhaustive demonstration available of what is involved in these relationships, so it is difficult to use tests involving the order of core grammatical constituents to draw firm conclusions about sentence grammar.

Word order freedom is also limited in very specific ways. Wh-phrases must appear at the front of their clause, or when complex sentences are formed, at the front of the clause over which they have scope. Wh-phrases are often morphologically identical to indefinite nominal expressions, as seen in (45), and the indefinite counterpart to a wh-phrase is barred from clause-initial position.

The question of word order for nominal arguments is frequently moot, in naturalistic discourse. All core arguments may be null in a typical sentence, and often are.

While the order of predicates and arguments is quite free, the relative order of the verb and auxiliary morphemes and other *'preverbs'* is rigidly constrained, and this general pattern is the focus of much of Chapter 4.

REFERENCES

Abney, Steven Paul. 1987. *The English Noun Phrase in Its Sentential Aspect*. Massachusetts Institute of Technology dissertation.

Aboh, Enoch Oladé. 2009. Clause Structure and Verb Series. *Linguistic Inquiry* 40(1). 1–33.

Acquaviva, Paolo. 2009. Roots and Lexicality in Distributed Morphology. In *Fifth York-Essex Morphology Meeting (YEMM), 9th February and 10th February 2008, Department of Language and Linguistic Science, University of York*. University of York. Department of Language & Linguistic Science.

Aissen, Judith & David Perlmutter. 1976. Clause Reduction in Spanish. In *Proceedings of the Second Annual Meeting of the Berkeley Linguistics Society*, 1–30. Berkeley.

Aissen, Judith & David Perlmutter. 1983. Postscript to republication of "Clause Reduction in Spanish." In *Studies in Relational Grammar*, vol. I, 383–396. Chicago: University of Chicago Press.

Allen, Barbara J., Donna B. Gardiner & Donald G. Frantz. 1984. Noun Incorporation in Southern Tiwa. *International Journal of American Linguistics* 50(3). 292–311.

Arregi, Karlos & Andrew Nevins. 2012. *Morphotactics: Basque Auxiliaries and the Structure of Spellout* (Studies in Natural Language and Linguistic Theory 86). Dordrecht: Springer.

Atlamaz, Ümit & Mark Baker. 2017. On Partial Agreement and Oblique Case. *Syntax* 21(3). 195–237.

Babko-Malaya, Olga. 1999. *Zero Morphology: A Study of Aspect, Argument Structure and Case*. Rutgers University dissertation.

Bailyn, John Frederick. 1995. Underlying Phrase Structure and "Short" Verb Movement in Russian. *Journal of Slavic Linguistics* 3(1). 13–58.

Bailyn, John Frederick. 2011. *The Syntax of Russian*. Cambridge: Cambridge University Press.

Bailyn, John Frederick. 2017. Against a VP Ellipsis Account of Russian Verb-Stranding Constructions. In *Studies in Japanese and Korean Historical and Theoretical Linguistics and Beyond*, 93–109. Leiden: Brill.

Baker, Mark. 1988a. *Incorporation: A Theory of Grammatical Function Changing*. Chicago: University of Chicago Press.

Baker, Mark. 1988b. Theta Theory and the Syntax of Applicatives in Chichewa. *Natural Language and Linguistic Theory* 6(3). 353–389.

Bannister, Jane. 2005. *A Description of Preverb and Particle Usage in Innu-aimun Narrative*. St. John's, Newfoundland: Memorial University MA thesis.

Baraby, Anne-Marie. 2004. *Guide des conjugaisons en langue innue*. Sept-Iles, Quebec: Institut culturel et éducatif montagnais.

Baraby, Anne-Marie & Lynn Drapeau. 1998. *Grammaire Montagnaise*. Unpublished manuscript. Université de Québec à Montreal.

Barrie, Michael & Eric Mathieu. 2016. Noun Incorporation and Phrasal Movement. *Natural Language & Linguistic Theory* 34(1). 1–51.

Béjar, Susana & Milan Rezac. 2009. Cyclic Agree. *Linguistic Inquiry* 40(1). 35–73.

Benat Oyharcabal & Jono Ortiz de Urbina. 1993. Verb Agreement with Non Arguments: On Allocutive Agreement. In *Generative Studies in Basque Linguistics*, 89–114. Amsterdam: John Benjamins.

Bennis, Hans & Liliane Haegeman. 1984. On the Status of Agreement and Relative Clauses in West Flemish. In W. de Geest & Y. Putseys (eds.), *Sentential Complementation*, 33–53. Dordrecht: Foris.

Bermúdez-Otero, Ricardo. 2010. Cyclicity. In Marc van Oostendorp, Colin Ewen, Elizabeth Hume & Keren Rice (eds.), *The Blackwell Companion to Phonology*. Malden, Massachusetts: Wiley-Blackwell.

Berwick, Robert C. & Noam Chomsky. 2015. *Why Only Us: Language and Evolution*. Cambridge, MA: MIT Press.

Bhatt, Rajesh & Mark Walkow. 2013. Locating Agreement in Grammar: An Argument from Agreement in Conjunctions. *Natural Language & Linguistic Theory* 31. 951–1013.

Biberauer, Theresa, Anders Holmberg & Ian Roberts. 2014. A Syntactic Universal and Its Consequences. *Linguistic Inquiry* 45(2). 169–225.

Biberauer, Theresa, Anders Holmberg, Ian Roberts & Michelle Sheehan. 2013. Complexity in Comparative Syntax: The View from Modern Parametric Theory. Manuscript. Cambridge University.

Biberauer, Theresa, Anders Holmberg, Ian Roberts & Michelle Sheehan. 2017. Empirical Evidence for the Final-over-Final Condition. In Michelle Sheehan, Theresa Biberauer & Ian Roberts (eds.), *The Final-Over-Final Condition: A Syntactic Universal*, 11–25. Cambridge, MA: MIT Press.

Biberauer, Theresa & Ian Roberts. 2008. Subjects, Tense and Verb Movement in Germanic and Romance. *Cambridge Occasional Papers in Linguistics* 3. 24–43.

Bloomfield, Leonard. 1946. Algonquian. In Harry Hoijer (ed.), *Linguistic Structures of Native America*, 85–129. New York: Viking Fund Publications in Anthropology.

Bloomfield, Leonard. 1962. *The Menomini Language*. New Haven: Yale University Press.

Blumenfeld, Lev. 2012. Russian Yers and Prosodic Structure. In *Proceedings of the 29th West Coast Conference on Formal Linguistics*. Somerville, Mass. 20–28.

Bobaljik, Jonathan. 2003. Floating Quantifiers: Handle with Care. The *Second Glot International State-of-the-Article Book: The Latest in Linguistics*. 107–148.

Bobaljik, Jonathan & Phil Branigan. 2006. Eccentric Agreement and Multiple Casechecking. In Alana Johns, Diane Massam & Juvenal Ndirayagije (eds.), *Ergativity*, 47–77. Dordrecht: Springer.

Boeckx, Cedric. 2014. What Principles and Parameters Got Wrong. In Anne-Marie di Sciullo & Cedric Boeckx (eds.), *Linguistic Variation and the Minimalist Program*, 205–221. Oxford: Oxford University Press.

Borer, Hagit. 1984. *Parametric Syntax: Case Studies in Semitic and Romance Languages*. Dordrecht: Foris.

Borer, Hagit. 2014. The Category of Roots. In *The Roots of Syntax*. Oxford: Oxford University Press.

Borik, Olga. 2002. *Aspect and Reference Time*. Utrecht: Utrecht University dissertation.

Borsley, Robert D., Maria-Luisa Rivero & Janig Stephens. 1996. Long Head Movement in Breton. *The Syntax of the Celtic Languages: A Comparative Perspective*. 53.

Brandi, Luciana & Patrizia Cordin. 1989. Two Italian Dialects and the Null Subject Parameter. In *The Null Subject Parameter,* 111–142. New York: Springer.
Branigan, Phil. 2020. Multiple Feature Inheritance and the Phase Structure of the Left Periphery. In Sam Wolfe & Rebecca Woods (eds.), *Rethinking V2.* Oxford: Oxford University Press.
Branigan, Phil & Julie Brittain. 2018. Symmetry Breaking and Word Order in East Cree. St John's: Memorial University.
Branigan, Phil, Julie Brittain & Carrie Dyck. 2005a. Balancing Prosody and Syntax in the Algonquian Verb Complex. In *Proceedings of the 36th Algonquian Conference.*
Branigan, Phil, Julie Brittain & Carrie Dyck. 2005b. Prosody and Syntax in Algonquian Verbs. In *Proceedings of WSCLA 10.*
Branigan, Phil & Chris Collins. 1993. Verb Movement and the Quotative Construction in English. *MIT Working Papers in Linguistics* 18. 1–13.
Branigan, Phil & Marguerite MacKenzie. 1999. Binding Relations and the Nature of *pro* in Innu-aimun. *NELS* 29. 51–62.
Branigan, Phil & Marguerite MacKenzie. 2002. Altruism, Ā-Movement, and Object Agreement in Innu-aimûn. *Linguistic Inquiry* 33(3). 385–407.
Branigan, Phil & Douglas Wharram. 2016. Generating Low-Scope Indefinite Objects in Inuktitut. Unpublished manuscript. St John's: Memorial University.
Branigan, Phil & Douglas Wharram. 2019. A Syntax for Semantic Incorporation: Generating Low-Scope Indefinite Objects in Inuktitut. *Glossa.* 4(1). 1–33.
Brittain, Julie. 1997. The Conjunct Verb in Sheshatshit Montagnais. *Canadian Journal of Linguistics/Revue canadienne de linguistique* 42(3). 253–284.
Brittain, Julie. 2001. *The Morphosyntax of the Algonquian Conjunct Verb: A Minimalist Approach.* New York: Garland Publishing.
Brittain, Julie. 2003. A Distributed Morphology Account of the Syntax of the Algonquian Verb. In Stanca Somesfalean & Sophie Burrell (eds.), *Proceedings of the 2003 Annual Conference of the Canadian Linguistic Association,* 26–41. Département de linguistique et de didactique des langues: Université du Québec à Montréal.
Brody, Michael. 2000. Mirror Theory: Syntactic Representation in Perfect Syntax. *Linguistic Inquiry* 31(1). 29–56.
Bromberger, Sylvain & Morris Halle. 1989. Why Phonology Is Different. *Linguistic Inquiry* 20(1). 51–70.
Burgess, Janet. 2009. *Reduplication and Initial Change in Sheshatshiu Innu-Aimun.* Memorial University of Newfoundland MA thesis.
Caha, Pavel & Markéta Zikova. n.d. *Vowel Length as Evidence for a Distinction between Free and Bound Prefixes in Czech.* http://lingbuzz.auf.net/lingbuzz/002919.
Cardinaletti, Anna & Ur Shlonsky. 2004. Clitic Positions and Restructuring in Italian. *Linguistic Inquiry* 35(4). 519–557.
Čertkova, Marina Jur'evnja & Pei-Chi Chang. 1998. Evoljutsija dvuvidovyx glagolov v sovremennom russkom jazyke. *Russian Linguistics* 22(1). 13–34.
Cheng, Lisa L. & Rint Sybesma. 1999. Bare and Not-So-Bare Nouns and the Structure of NP. *Linguistic Inquiry* 30(4). 509–542.
Chomsky, Noam. 1957. *Syntactic Structures.* The Hague: Mouton.
Chomsky, Noam. 1965. *Aspects of the Theory of Syntax.* Cambridge, MA: MIT Press.
Chomsky, Noam. 1977. On Wh-Movement. In T. Wasow, P. Culicover & A. Akma-jian (eds.), *Formal Syntax.* New York: Academic Press.
Chomsky, Noam. 1994. Bare Phrase Structure. *MIT Occasional Papers in Linguistics* 5. Cambridge, MA: MIT Press.

Chomsky, Noam. 1995. *The Minimalist Program*. Cambridge, MA: MIT Press.
Chomsky, Noam. 2000. Minimalist Inquiries: The Framework. In Roger Martin, David Michaels & Juan Uriagareka (eds.), *Step by Step: Essays on Minimalist Syntax in Honor of Howard Lasnik*, 89–155. Cambridge, MA: MIT Press.
Chomsky, Noam. 2001. Derivation by Phase. In Michael Kenstowicz (ed.), *Ken Hale: A Life in Language*, 1–52. Cambridge, MA.: MIT Press.
Chomsky, Noam. 2004. Beyond Explanatory Accuracy. In Adrianna Belletti (ed.), *Structures and Beyond: The Cartography of Syntactic Structures, Volume 3*, 104–191. Oxford University Press.
Chomsky, Noam. 2005. Three Factors in Language Design. *Linguistic Inquiry* 36(1). 1–22.
Chomsky, Noam. 2007. Approaching UG from Below. In Uli Sauerland & Hans-Martin Gartner (eds.), *Interfaces + Recursion = Language?: Chomsky's Minimalism and the View from Syntax-Semantics*, 1–27. Berlin: Mouton de Gruyter.
Chomsky, Noam. 2008. On Phases. In Robert Freidin, Carlos P. Otero & Maria Luisa Zubizarreta (eds.), *Foundational Issues in Linguistic Theory: Essays in Honor of Jean-Roger Vergnaud*, 134–166. Cambridge, MA: MIT Press.
Chomsky, Noam. 2013. Problems of Projection. *Lingua* 130. 33–49.
Chomsky, Noam. 2015. Problems of Projection: Extensions. In Elisa Di Domenico, Cornelia Hamann & Simona Matteini (eds.), *Structures, Strategies and Beyond: Studies in Honour of Adriana Belletti*, 1–6. Amsterdam & Philadelphia: John Benjamins.
Cinque, Guglielmo. 1999. *Adverbs and Functional Heads: A Cross-Linguistics Perspective* (Oxford Studies in Comparative Syntax). Oxford: Oxford University Press.
Clark, Robin. 1988. On the Relationship between the Input Data and Parameter Setting. In Julie Carter & Rose-Marie Déchaine (eds.), *Proceedings of NELS 19*, 48–62. University of Massachusetts, GSLA.
Clarke, Sandra. 1982. *North-West River (Sheshātshīt) Montagnais: A Grammatical Sketch* (National Museum of Man Mercury Series). Ottawa: National Museum of Man.
Cole, Peter, Yurie Hara & Ngee Thai Yap. 2008. Auxiliary Fronting in Perenakan Javanese. *Journal of Linguistics* 44. 1–43.
Collins, Chris. 1996. *Local Economy*. Cambridge, MA: MIT Press.
Collins, Chris. 2002. Multiple Verb Movement in ǂHoan. *Linguistic Inquiry* 33(1). 1–29.
Collins, Chris. 2017. Merge(X,Y) = {X,Y}. In Leah S. Bauke & A. Blumel (eds.), *Labels and Roots*, 47–68. Berlin: De Gruyter.
Collins, Chris & Phil Branigan. 1997. Quotative Inversion. *Natural Language & Linguistic Theory* 15(1). 1–41.
Collins, Chris & Richard Kayne. 2020. Towards a Theory of Morphology as Syntax. Manuscript, New York University.
D'Alessandro, Roberta & Adam Ledgeway. 2010. At the C-T Boundary: Investigating Abruzzese Complementation. *Lingua* 120. 2040–2060.
Dahlstrom, Amy. 2000. Morphosyntactic Mismatches in Algonquian: Affixal Predicates and Discontinuous Verbs. In *Proceedings of 36th CLS Meeting*, Chicago Linguistic Society, University of Chicago. 63–87.
Déchaine, Rose-Marie & Natalie Weber. 2015a. Head-Merge, Adjunct-Merge, and the Syntax of Root Categorisation. In *Proceedings of the Poster Session of the 33rd West Coast Conference on Formal Linguistics, Simon Fraser University Working Papers in Linguistics*, vol. 5, 38–47.
Déchaine, Rose-Marie & Natalie Weber. 2015b. Root Syntax: Algonquian. In Monica Macaulay (ed.), *Papers of the Forty-Seventh Algonquian Conference*. Michgan State University Press.

Dékany, Éva. 2018. Approaches to Head Movement: A Critical Assessment. *Glossa: A Journal of General Linguistics* 3(1). 1–43.

Den Besten, Hans. 1983. On the Interaction of Root Transformations and Lexical Deletive Rules. In Werner Abraham (ed.), *On the Formal Syntax of the Westgermania*, 47–131. Amsterdam: John Benjamins.

Drapeau, Lynn. 2014. *Grammaire de la langue innue*. Québec: Presses de l'Université du Québec.

Dresher, Bezalel Elan. 1999. Charting the Learning Path: Cues to Parameter Setting. *Linguistic Inquiry* 30(1). 27–67.

Dresher, Bezalel Elan. 2016. Covert Representation, Contrast, and the Acquisition of Lexical Accent. In Jeffrey Heinz, Rob Goedemans & Harry van der Hulst (eds.), *Dimensions of Phonological Stress*, 231–62. Cambridge: Cambridge University Press.

Dresher, Bezalel Elan & Jonathan Kaye. 1990. A Computational Learning Model for Metrical Phonology. *Cognition* 34. 137–195.

Dunham, Joel & Mike Barrie. 2008. Noun Incorporation in Blackfoot. Paper presented at the 40th Algonquian Conference, University of Minnesota-Twin Cities in October 2008.

Ellis, Charles D. 1971. Cree Verb Paradigms. *International Journal of American Linguistics* 37(2). 76–95.

Embick, David & Rolf Noyer. 2001. Movement Operations after Syntax. *Linguistic Inquiry* 32(4). 555–595.

Emonds, Joseph. 1978. The Verbal Complex V'-V in French. *Linguistic Inquiry* 9. 151–175.

Flier, Michael S. 1984. Syntagmatic Constraints on the Russian Prefix Pere. In Michael S. Flier & R. Brecht (eds.), *Issues in Russian Morphosyntax*. Columbus, OH: Slavica Publishers.

Fodor, Janet Dean. 2001. 23 Setting Syntactic Parameters. *The Handbook of Contemporary Syntactic Theory*. Malden, Mass.: Blackwell Publishers. 730–767.

Ford, A. 1979. Une ambiguité structurale de surface en montagnais. In William Cowan (ed.), *Papers of the Tenth Algonquian Conference*, 218–226. Ottawa: Carleton University Press.

Forsyth, James. 1970. *A Grammar of Aspect: Usage and Meaning in the Russian Verb*. Cambridge: Cambridge University Press.

Fowler, George. 1994. Verbal Prefixes as Functional Heads. *Studies in Linguistic Sciences* 24. 171–185.

Georgala, Effi, Waltraud Paul & John Whitman. 2008. Expletive and Thematic Applicatives. *Proceedings of the 26th West Coast Conference on Formal Linguistics*. 181–189.

Gepner, Maria. 2016. The Semantics of Motion Verbs in Russian. *The Baltic International Yearbook of Cognition, Logic and Communication* 11. 1–31.

Gibson, E. & K. Wexler. 1994. Triggers. *Linguistic Inquiry* 25(3). 407–454.

Goddard, Ives. 1967. The Algonquian Independent Indicative. *National Museum of Canada Bulletin* 214. 66–106.

Goddard, Ives. 1974. Remarks on the Algonquian Independent Indicative. *International Journal of American Linguistics* 40(4). 317–327.

Goddard, Ives. 1979. *Delaware Verbal Morphology* (Outstanding Dissertations in Linguistics). New York: Garland.

Goddard, Ives. 1988. Post-transformational Stem Derivation in Fox. *Papers and Studies in Contrastive Linguistics* 22. 59–72.

Goddard, Ives. 1990. Primary and Secondary Stem Derivation in Algonquian. *International Journal of American Linguistics* 56. 449–483.
Goddard, Ives. 1994. The West-to-East Cline in Algonquian Dialectology. In William Cowan (ed.), *Actes du Vingt-Cinquième Congrès des Algonquinistes,* 187–211. Ottawa: Carleton University Press.
Goddard, Ives. 1996. The Classification of the Native Languages of North America. In Ives Goddard (ed.), *Languages,* vol. 17 (Handbook of North Amerian Indians), 290–323. Washington, D.C.: Smithsonian Institution.
Goddard, Ives. 2007. Reconstruction and History of the Independent Indicative. In H. C. Wolfart (ed.), *Proceedings of the Thirty-Eighth Algonquian Conference,* Winnepeg, Manitoba: University of Manitoba. 207–271.
Goeman, Ton. 1980. COMP-Agreement? In Wim Zonneveld & Fred Weerman (eds.), *Linguistics in the Netherlands 1977–1979,* 291–306. Dordrecht: Foris.
Gouskova, Maria. 2019. Phonological Words in the Syntax and in the Lexicon. *Journal of Slavic Linguistics* 27(2). 161–212.
Greenberg, Joseph. 1963. Some Universals of Grammar with Particular Reference to the Order of Meaningful Elements. In Joseph Greenberg (ed.), *Universals of Language,* 73–113. Cambridge, MA: MIT Press.
Gribanova, Vera. 2010. *Composition and Locality: The Morphosyntax and Phonology of the Russian Verbal Complex.* University of California, Santa Cruz dissertation.
Gribanova, Vera. 2013. Verb-Stranding Verb Phrase Ellipsis and the Structure of the Russian Verbal Complex. *Natural Language & Linguistic Theory* 31(1). 91–136.
Gribanova, Vera. 2017a. Head Movement and Ellipsis in the Expression of Russian Polarity Focus. *Natural Language & Linguistic Theory* 35(4). 1079–1121.
Gribanova, Vera. 2017b. Head Movement, Ellipsis, and Identity. Unpublished manuscript. Stanford University.
Gribanova, Vera & Boris Harizanov. 2017. Locality and Directionality in Inward-Sensitive Allomorphy: Russian and Bulgarian. In Vera Gribanova & Stephanie S. Shih (eds.), *The Morphosyntax-Phonology Connection,* 61–90. Oxford: Oxford University Press.
Gruber, J. S. 1965. *Studies in Lexical Relations.* Cambridge, MA: MIT dissertation.
Halle, Morris. 2007. *Russian Phonology: The Core.* Cambridge, MA: MIT Press.
Halle, Morris & Alec Marantz. 1993. Distributed Morphology and the Pieces of Inflection. In Ken Hale & Samuel Jay Keyser (eds.), *The View from Building 20: Essays in Honor of Sylvain Bromberger,* 111–176. Cambridge, MA: MIT Press.
Halle, Morris & Andrew Nevins. 2009. Rule Application in Phonology. In Eric Raimy, Charles Reiss, Andrea Calabrese, Bezalel Elan Dresher, Morris Halle, William J. Idsardi, Ellen M. Kaise & Thomas Purnell (eds.), *Contemporary Views on Architecture and Representations in Phonology.* Cambridge, MA: MIT Press.
Harizanov, Boris & Vera Gribanova. 2019. Whither Head Movement? *Natural Language and Linguistic Theory* 37. 461–522.
Harley, Heidi. 2014. On the Identity of Roots. *Theoretical Linguistics* 40(3–4). 225–276.
Haugen, Jason D. & Heidi Harley. 2013. Head-Marking Inflection and the Architecture of Grammatical Theory. *The Persistence of Language: Constructing and Confronting the Past and Present in the Voices of Jane H. Hill* 8. 133.
Hawkins, John A. 1983. *Word Order Universals.* New York: Academic Press.
Heine, Bernd. 1997. *Possession.* Cambridge: Cambridge University Press.
Henry, Alison. 1995. *Belfast English and Standard English.* Oxford: Oxford University Press.

Hiraiwa, Ken. 2005. *Dimensions of Symmetries in Syntax: Agreement and Clausal Architecture.* Cambridge, MA: MIT Press.

Hirose, Tomio. 2004. *Origins of Predicates: Evidence from Plains Cree.* New York: Routledge.

Holmberg, Anders. 1986. *Word Order and Syntactic Features.* Stockholm: University of Stockholm Press.

Holmberg, Anders. 2001. The Syntax of Yes and No in Finnish. *Studia Linguistica* 55(2). 141–175.

Holmberg, Anders & Christer Platzack. 2005. The Scandinavian Languages. In Guglielmo Cinque & Richard Kayne (eds.), *The Oxford Handbook of Comparative Syntax,* 420–458. Oxford: Oxford University Press.

Holmberg, Anders & Ian Roberts. 2014. Parameters and the Three Factors of Language Design. In M. Carme Picallo (ed.), *Linguistic Variation in the Minimalist Framework,* 61–81. Oxford: Oxford University Press.

Hornstein, Norbert. 2009. *A Theory of Syntax: Minimal Operations and Universal Grammar.* Cambridge: Cambridge University Press.

Idsardi, William & Eric Raimy. 2013. Three Types of Linearization and the Temporal Aspects of Speech. In Ian Roberts & Theresa Biberauer (eds.), *Challenges to Linearization,* 31–56. Berlin: De Gruyter.

Isacenko, Alexander. 1960. *Grammaticeskij stroj russkogo jazyka. Morfologija. ˇCastj vtoraja [Grammatical composition of Russian. Morphology. Part 2].* Bratislava: Vydavatelstvo Slovenskej Akadémie vied.

Jakobson, Roman. 1957–1984. Shifters, Verbal Categories and the Russian Verb. In L. R. Waugh & Morris Halle (eds.), *Russian and Slavic Grammar: Studies 1931–1981,* 41–58. Berlin: Mouton.

Janda, Laura A. 2007. Aspectual Clusters of Russian Verbs. *Studies in Language* 31(3). 607–648.

Johansson, Sara. 2011. Relative Clauses, or Clause-Sized Nominalization? A Consideration of Blackfoot. *Working Papers of the Linguistics Circle* 21(2), Calgary, Alberta. 1–15.

Johns, Alana. 2007. Restricting Noun Incorporation: Root Movement. *Natural Language and Linguistic Theory* 25. 535–576.

Jones, William. 1904. Some Principles of Algonquian Word-Formation. *American Anthropologist* 6. 369–411.

Kallen, Jeffrey L. 1990. The Hiberno-English Perfect: Grammaticalisation Revisited. *Irish University Review* 20(1). 120–136.

Karcevsky, S. 1927. *Systeme du verbe russe.* Prague: Essai de linguistique synchronique.

Kayne, Richard. 1975. *French Syntax: The Transformational Cycle.* Cambridge, MA: MIT Press.

Kayne, Richard. 1995. *The Antisymmetry of Syntax.* Cambridge, MA: MIT Press.

Kayne, Richard. 2000. *Parameters and Universals.* Oxford: Oxford University Press.

Kayne, Richard. 2013. Comparative Syntax. *Lingua* 130. 132–151.

King, Tracy Holloway. 1993. *Configuring Topic and Focus in Russian.* Stanford University dissertation.

King, Tracy Holloway. 1994. Focus in Russian Yes-No Questions. *Journal of Slavic Linguistics* 2(1). 92–120.

Kiparsky, Paul & Morris Halle. 1977. Towards a Reconstruction of the Indo-European Accent. *Studies in Stress and Accent* 209(238).

Kisseberth, Charles & Mohammad I. Abasheikh. 1974. A Case of Systematic Avoidance of Homonyms. *Studies in the Linguistic Sciences* 4. 107–124.

Koeneman, Olaf & Hedde Zeijlstra. 2012. One Law for the Rich and Another for the Poor: The Rich Agreement Hypothesis Rehabilitated. Manuscript, University of Amsterdam. Accessed in lingbuzz archive. http://ling.auf.net/lingbuzz/001462/current.pdf (February 6, 2014).

Krapova, I. & G. Cinque. 2008. On the Order of wh-Phrases in Bulgarian Multiple wh-Fronting. In G. Zybatow et al. (ed.), *Formal Description of Slavic Languages: The Fifth Conference. Leipzig 2003* (Linguistik International), 318–336. Frankfurt am Main: Peter Lang.

Landau, Idan. 2020. On the Nonexistence of Verb-Stranding VP-Ellipsis. *Linguistic Inquiry* 51(2). 341–365.

Larson, Richard K. 1985. Bare-NP Adverbs. *Linguistic Inquiry* 16(4). 595–621.

Lechner, Winfried. 2006. An Interpretive Effect of Head Movement. In Mara Frascarelli (ed.), *Phases of Interpretation*, vol. 847, 45–71. Berlin: Mouton de Gruyter.

Lema, José & Maria Luisa Rivero. 1989. Long Head Movement: ECP vs. HMC. *NELS* 20. 5–17.

Lemoine, S. 1901. *Dictionnaire francais-montagnais; grammaire montagnais.* Boston: Cabot & Cabot.

MacDonald, Jonathan E. 2008. *The Syntactic Nature of Inner Aspect: A Minimalist Perspective.* Vol. 133. Amsterdam: John Benjamins.

MacKenzie, Marguerite. 1980. *Towards a Dialectology of Cree-Montagnais-Naskapi.* Toronto: University of Toronto Press.

Makarova, Anastasia & Laura A. Janda. 2009. Do It Once: A Case Study of the Russian -nu- Semelfactives. *Scando-Slavica* 55(1). 78–99.

Marantz, Alec. 1991. Case and Licensing. In *Proceedings of ESCOL'91*, 234–253.

Marantz, Alec. 1997. No Escape from Syntax: Don't Try Morphological Analysis in the Privacy of Your Own Lexicon. *University of Pennsylvania Working Papers in Linguistics* 4(2). 201–25.

Marantz, Alec. 2000. Reconstructing the Lexical Domain with a Single Generative Engine. Cambridge, MA: MIT Press.

Markman, Vita G. 2008. On Slavic Semelfactives and Secondary Imperfectives: Implications for the Split 'AspP'. *University of Pennsylvania Working Papers in Linguistics* 14(1). 20.

Marusic, Franc, Andrew Nevins & Bill Badecker. 2015. The Grammars of Conjunction Agreement in Slovenian. *Syntax* 18(1). 39–77.

Matthew Tyler. 2018. Absolutive Promotion and the Condition on Clitic Hosts in Choctaw. *Natural Language and Linguistic Theory.* 1–59.

Matushansky, Ora. 2006. Head Movement in Linguistic Theory. *Linguistic Inquiry* 37(1). 69–109.

Matushansky, Ora. 2009. On the Featural Composition of the Russian Back yer. In *Studies in Formal Slavic Phonology, Morphology, Syntax, Semantics and Information Structure. Proceedings of FDSL 7, Leipzig 2007*, 397–410.

Matyiku, Sabina Maria. 2017. *Semantic Effects of Head Movement: Evidence from Negative Auxiliary Inversion.* Yale University dissertation.

May, Robert. 1977. *The Grammar of Quantification.* Cambridge, MA: MIT Press.

McCloskey, James. 1996. On the Scope of Verb Movement in Irish. *Natural Language and Linguistic Theory* 14(1).

McGinnis, Martha. 2001. Variation in the Phase Structure of Applicatives. *Linguistics Variation Yearbook* 1. 105–146.

Mellow, J. Dean. 1990. Asymmetries between Compounding and Noun Incorporation in Plains Cree. *Algonquian Papers-Archive* 21. 11.

Mezhevich, Ilana. 2008. A Feature-Theoretic Account of Tense and Aspect in Russian. *Natural Language & Linguistic Theory* 26(2). 359–401.

Michelson, Truman. 1917. Notes on Algonquian Languages. *International Journal of American Linguistics* 1(1). 50–57.

Mithun, Marianne. 1984. The Evolution of Noun Incorporation. *Language* 60. 847–895.

Miyagawa, Shigeru & Koji Arikawa. 2007. Locality in Syntax and Floating Numeral Quantifiers. *Linguistics Inquiry* 38(4). 645–670.

Moro, Andrea. 1997. *The Raising of Predicates, Predicative Nouns and the Theory of Clause Structure*. Cambridge: Cambridge University Press.

Muller, Gereon. 2009. Ergativity, Accusativity, and the Order of Merge and Agree. *Explorations of Phase Theory. Features and Arguments*. Mouton de Gruyter, Berlin. 269–308.

Nevins, Andrew. 2011. Multiple Agree with Clitics: Person Complementarity vs. Omnivorous Number. *Natural Language & Linguistic Theory* 29(4). 939–971.

Nevins, Andrew & Neil Myler. 2014. A Brown-Eyed Girl. UCLA Working Papers in Linguistics, Papers in Honor of Sarah van Wagenen. http://ling.auf.net/lingbuzz/002021/current.pdf?_s=PqndEa9SZLGVNrjd (February 19, 2014).

Newell, Heather. 2008. *Aspects of the Morphology and Phonology of Phases*. McGill University dissertation.

Newmeyer, Frederick. 2005. *Possible and Probable Languages: A Generative Perspective on Linguistic Typology*. Oxford: Oxford University Press.

Niyogi, Partha & Robert C. Berwick. 1996. A Language Learning Model for Finite Parameter Spaces. *Cognition. Compositional Language Acquisition* 61(1–2). 161–193.

Nobrega, Vitor. 2015. On Merge and Word Formation: The Case of Compounds. University of Sao Paulo (USP) handout. http://www.academia.edu/download/38383804/Nobrega_2015_On_Merge_and_Word_Formation_The_Case_of_Compounds.pdf (November 28, 2016).

Noyer, Rolf. 1992. *Features, Positions and Affixes in Autonomous Morphological Structure*. Cambridge, MA: MIT Press.

O'Meara, John. 1990. *Delaware Stem Morphology*. Montreal: McGill University.

Obata, Miki, Marlyse Baptista & Samuel Epstein. 2013. Parameters as Third Factor Timing Optionality. *LSA Annual Meeting Extended Abstracts* 4. 33. https://doi.org/10.3765/exabs.v0i0.805.

Oxford, Will. 2008. *A Grammatical Study of Innu-aimun Particles* (Memoir / Algonquian and Iroquoian Linguistics 20). Winnipeg, Manitoba.

Oxford, Will. 2011. The Syntax of Innu-aimun Locatives. In *UBC Working Papers in Linguistics, Vol. 31: The Proceedings of WSCLA 16*.

Oxford, Will. 2014. *Microparameters of Agreement: A Diachronic Perspective on Algonquian Verb Inflection*. Toronto: University of Toronto Press.

Oxford, Will. 2015. Variation in Multiple Agree: A Syntactic Connection between Portmanteau Agreement and Inverse Marking. http://home.cc.umanitoba.ca/~oxfordwr/papers/Oxford_portmanteau-inverse.pdf (May 13, 2016).

Oxford, Will. 2018. Inverse Marking and Multiple Agree in Algonquin. *Natural Language & Linguistic Theory* 37(3). 1–42.

Oxford, Will. 2019. Fission in Algonquian and the Status of Morphological Templates. In *Proceedings of WSCLA 23*, 15.

Oxford, Will. n.d. *The Algonquian Inverse* (Studies in Endangered Languages). Oxford: Oxford University Press.

Oxford, Will & Nicholas Welch. 2015. Inanimacy as Personlessness. Manuscript, University of Toronto.

Pesetsky, David. 1979. Russian Morphology and Lexical Phonology. Unpublished manuscript, MIT.

Pesetsky, David. 1985. Morphology and Logical Form. *Linguistic Inquiry* 16(2). 193–246.

Pesetsky, David. 1995. *Zero Syntax: Cascades and Experiencers*. Cambridge, MA: MIT Press.

Pesetsky, David & Esther Torrego. 2000. T-to-C Movement: Causes and Consequences. In Micheal Kenstowicz (ed.), *Ken Hale, A Life in Language*. Cambridge, MA: MIT Press.

Pesetsky, David & Esther Torrego. 2007. The Syntax of Valuation and the Inter- pretability of Features. In S. Karimi, V. Samiian & W. Wilkins (eds.), *Phrasal and Clausal Architecture: Syntactic Derivation and Interpretation*. Amsterdam: John Benjamins.

Piggott, Glyne L. 1989. Argument Structure and the Morphology of the Ojibwa Verb. In Donna Gerdts & Karin Michelson (eds.), *Theoretical Perspectives in Native American Languages*. Albany, NY: SUNY Press.

Polinsky, Maria S. 1990. Subject Incorporation: Evidence from Chukchee. In Katarzyna Dziwirek, Patrick Farrell & Errapel Mejias-Bikandi (eds.), *Grammatical Relations: A Cross-Theoretical Perpective*, 349–364. Stanford: Stanford Linguistics Association.

Pollock, Jean-Yves. 1989. Verb Movement, Universal Grammar and the Structure of IP. *Linguistic Inquiry* 20. 365–424.

Postal, Paul. 1969. Anaphoric Islands. In *Proceedings from the Annual Meeting of the Chicago Linguistic Society*, vol. 5, Number 1, 205–239. Chicago: Chicago Linguistic Society.

Preminger, Omer. 2017. What the PCC Tells Us about "Abstract" Agreement, Head Movement, and Locality. Manuscript, University of Maryland, URL https://ling.auf.net/lingbuzz/003221.

Preminger, Omer. 2018. How to Tell a Syntactic Phenomenon When You See It. Unpublished ms., University of Maryland.

Pylkkanen, Liina. 2002. *Introducing Arguments*. Cambridge, MA: MIT Press.

Reinholtz, Charlotte. 1999. On the Characterization of Discontinuous Constituents: Evidence from Swampy Cree. *International Journal of American Linguistics* 65(2). 201–227.

Rhodes, Richard Alan. 2006. *Clause Structure, Core Arguments, and the Algonquian Relative Root Construction*. Winnipeg, Manitoba: Voices of Rupert's Land.

Rice, Keren. 2006. *Morpheme Order and Semantic Scope: Word Formation in the Athapaskan Verb*. Vol. 90. Cambridge: Cambridge University Press.

Richard S. Kayne. 1989. Facets of Past Participle Agreement in Romance. In Paola Beninca (ed.), *Dialect Variation in the Theory of Grammar*. Dordrecht: Foris.

Richards, Marc D. 2007. On Feature Inheritance: An Argument from the Phase Impenetrability Condition. *Linguistic Inquiry* 38. 563–572.

Richards, Norvin. 1997. *What Moves Where in Which Language*. Cambridge, MA: MIT Press.

Richards, Norvin. 1998. The Principle of Minimal Compliance. *Linguistic Inquiry* 29. 599–629.

Richards, Norvin. 2004. The Syntax of the Conjunct and Independent Orders in Wampanoag. *International Journal of American Linguistics* 70(4). 327–368.

Ritter, E. & S. T. Rosen. 2005. Agreement without A-positions: Another Look at Algonquian. *Linguistic Inquiry* 36(4). 648–660.

Rivero, Maria-Luisa. 1993. Long Head Movement vs. V2, and Null Subjects in Old Romance. *Lingua* 89. 217–245.

Rizzi, Luigi. 1976. Ristrutturazione. *Rivista di grammatica generativa* 1. 1–54.

Rizzi, Luigi. 1978. *A Restructuring Rule in Italian Syntax. Recent Transformational Studies in European Languages.* Ed. by Samuel Jay Keyser, MIT Press. 113–158.

Rizzi, Luigi. 1982. *Issues in Italian Syntax.* Vol. 11. Berlin: De Gruyter.

Rizzi, Luigi. 1986. On Chain Formation. In Hagit Borer (ed.), *Syntax and Semantics, Volume 19: The Syntax of Pronominal Clitics,* 65–95. New York: Academic Press.

Rizzi, Luigi. 1990. *Relativized Minimality.* Cambridge, MA: MIT Press.

Rizzi, Luigi. 1997. The Fine Structure of the Left Periphery. In Liliane Haegeman (ed.), *Elements of Grammar.* Dordrecht: Kluwer.

Rizzi, Luigi. 2007. On Some Properties of Criterial Freezing. *Studies in Linguistics* 1. 145–158.

Rizzi, Luigi. 2017. Comparing Extractions from wh-Islands and Superiority Effects. *Festscrift fur Martin Prinzhorn (Wiener Linguistische Gazette (WLG))* 82. 253–261.

Rizzi, Luigi & Ian Roberts. 1989. Complex Inversion in French. *Probus* 1(1). 1–30.

Roberts, Ian. 2010. *Agreement and Head Movement: Clitics, Incorporation and Defective Goals* (Linguistic Inquiry Monographs). Cambridge, MA: MIT Press.

Roberts, Ian. 2020. *Parameter Hierarchies and Universal Grammar.* Oxford: Oxford University Press.

Romanova, Eugenia. 2005. Superlexical versus Lexical Prefixes. *Nordlyd* 32(2). 259–278.

Romanova, Eugenia. 2007. Constructing Perfectivity in Russian. http://munin.uit.no/handle/10037/904 (February 20, 2014).

Russell, Kevin. 1992. Palatalization and Epenthesis in Plains Cree. In *Proceedings of the 1992 Annual Conference of the Canadian Linguistic Association.*

Russell, Kevin. 1996. Does Obviation Mark Point of View? In John D. Nichols & Arden C. Ogg (eds.), *Nikotwasik iskwahtem, paskihtepayih!: Studies in Honour of H. C. Wolfart,* 367–383. Winnipeg, Manitoba.

Russell, Kevin. 1999. The "Word" in Two Polysynthetic Languages. In T. Alan Hall & Ursula Kleinheinz (eds.), *Studies on the Phonological Word,* vol. 174 (Current Issues in Linguistic Theory), 203–221. Amsterdam & Philadelphia: John Benjamins.

Sakas, William Gregory & Janet Dean Fodor. 2012. Disambiguating Syntactic Triggers. *Language Acquisition* 19(2). 83–143.

Shlonsky, Ur. 1988. Complementiser-Cliticization in Hebrew and the Empty Category Principle. *Natural Language and Linguistic Theory* 23. 443–468.

Simpson, Andrew. 2021. *In Defense of Verb-Stranding VP-Ellipsis.* https://ling.auf.net/lingbuzz/005907/current.pdf?_s=ia5DJVnqwHq77Tsg.

Smith, Carlota S. 2013. *The Parameter of Aspect.* Vol. 43. Berlin: Springer Science & Business Media.

Spencer, Andrew & Marina Zaretskaya. 1998. Verb Prefixation in Russian as Lexical Subordination. *Linguistics* 36(1). 1–40.

Starke, Michal. 2001. *Move Dissolves into Merge.* University of Geneva dissertation.

Suner, Margarita. 1992. Subject Clitics in the Northern Italian Vernaculars and the Matching Hypothesis. *Natural Language & Linguistic Theory* 10(4). 641–672.

Svenonius, Peter. 2005a. Slavic Prefixes and Morphology: An Introduction to the Nordlyd Volume. *Nordlyd* 32(2). 177–204.

Svenonius, Peter. 2005b. Slavic Prefixes inside and outside VP. *Nordlyd* 32(2). 205–253.

Svenonius, Peter. 2012. Spanning. CASTL, University of Troms0. http://ling.auf.net/lingbuzz/001501/current.pdf (June 24, 2016).

Takehisa, Tomokazu. 2017. Remarks on Denominal -ed Adjectives. In *Proceedings of the 31st Pacific Asia Conference on Language, Information and Computation*, The National University (Phillippines). 196–205.

Taraldsen, Knut Tarald. 1978. On the NIC, Vacuous Application, and the That-trace Filter. Distributed by the Indiana University Linguistics Club, Bloomington, IN.

Tatevosov, Sergei. 2008. Intermediate Prefixes in Russian. In *Annual Workshop on Formal Approaches to Slavic Linguistics*, 423–445. http://otipl.philol.msu.ru/staff/people/tatevosov/intermediate.pdf (October 21, 2013).

Tatevosov, Sergei. 2011. Severing Perfectivity from the Verb. *Scando-Slavica* 57(2). 216–244.

Tatevosov, Sergei. 2015. Severing_imperfectivity_from_the_verb.pdf. In *Proceedings of FDSL10, Leipzig 2013*, 465–494. Frankfurt am Main: Peter Lang.

Tatevosov, Sergei. 2014. Notes on the Hierarchical Structure of Russian Verb. http://otipl.philol.msu.ru/staff/people/tatevosov/verb_stem.pdf (July 18, 2014).

Toops, Gary H. 1998. The Scope of "Secondary" Imperfectivisation in Bulgarian, Russian, and Upper Sorbian. In *American Contributions to the Twelfth International Congress of Slavists, Cracow*. 515–529. Bloomington, IN: Slavica.

Townsend, Charles E. 1967. Voice and Verbs in -sja. *The Slavic and East European Journal* 11(2). 196.

Travis, Lisa. 1984. *Parameters and Effects of Word Order Variation*. MIT dissertation.

Valentine, J. Randolph. 2001. *Nishnaabemwin Reference Grammar*. Toronto: University of Toronto Press.

Valois, Daniel. 1991. *The Internal Syntax of DP*. UCLA dissertation.

Weber, Natalie. 2020. *Syntax, Prosody, and Metrical Structure in Blackfoot*. University of British Columbia dissertation.

Westergaard, Marit. 2009. *The Acquisition of Word Order: Micro-cues, Information Structure, and Economy*. Vol. 145. Amsterdam: John Benjamins Publishing.

Wolfart, Hans Christoph. 1971. Plains Cree Internal Syntax and the Problem of Noun Incorporation. In *Proceedings of the Thirty-Eighth International Congress of Americanists*, vol. 3, 511–518.

Wolfart, Hans Christoph. 1973. *Plains Cree: A Grammatical Study. Transactions of the American Philosophical Society, New Series 63, Part 5*. American Philosophical Society.

Wolfart, Hans Christoph. 1996. Sketch of Cree, an Algonquian Language. *Handbook of North American Indians* 17. 390–439.

Yang, Charles. 2002. *Knowledge and Learning in Natural Language*. Oxford: Oxford University Press.

Yang, Charles. 2016. *The Price of Linguistic Productivity: How Children Learn to Break the Rules of Language*. Cambridge, MA: MIT Press.

Zalizniak, Anna A. 2017. Russian Prefixed Verbs of Motion Revisited. *Zeitschriftftir Slawistik* 62(1). 1–22.

Zinova, Yulia & Hana Filip. 2013. Predicting the Grammatical Aspect Category in Russian. In *Workshop on Aspect*. http://www.illc.uva.nl/Tbilisi/Tbilisi2013/uploaded_files/inlineitem/zinova.pdf (May 29, 2015).

Zwart, C. Jan Wouter. 1993. Verb Agreement and Complementizer Agreement. *MIT Working Papers in Linguistics* 18. 297–340.

Zwart, C. Jan-Wouter. 1997. *Morphosyntax of Verb Movement: A Minimalist Approach to the Syntax of Dutch*. Dordrecht: Kluwer.

INDEX